Are We There Yet?

THE ULTIMATE ROAD TRIP:
ADOPTING & RAISING 22 KIDS!

"Nellie
It has been
a privilege to
get to know
you — thanks
for your
commitment and
dedication —
Sue
Badeau

HECTOR and SUE BADEAU

4/ 2014

Carpenter's Son Publishing

Are We There Yet? The Ultimate Road Trip: Adopting & Raising 22 Kids!

© 2013 by Hector and Sue Badeau

Scripture taken from the NEW AMERICAN STANDARD BIBLE®, Copyright © 1960,1962,1963,1968,1971,1972,1973,1975,1977,1995 by The Lockman Foundation. Used by permission.

Published by Carpenter's Son Publishing, Franklin, Tennessee

Published in association with Larry Carpenter of Christian Book Services, LLC
www.christianbookservices.com

Cover and Interior Layout Design by Suzanne Lawing

Edited by Robert Irvin

Cover photograph by Laurie Beck Peterson

Printed in the United States of America

978-0-9885931-7-6

Praise for *Are We There Yet?*

This family's journey is an inspiration and a perfect example of Divine intervention. Would that we all had the patience, the unconditional love, the tenacity, and the good humor to do for humanity what Hector and Sue Badeau have done. It's got to be read to be believed.

—*Lucie Arnaz (daughter of Lucille Ball) and Laurence Luckinbill, award-winning actors of stage and screen*

As a friend of mine once said, we can all debate what a family looks like, but everyone knows what a family feels like. Sue and Hector Badeau opened their hearts and home through adoption, introducing 20 children from all walks of life to the incomparable and irreplaceable feeling of familial love and devotion. The Badeaus' story is a beautiful testament to the miracle of adoption and family love.

—*U.S. Senator Mary L. Landrieu, Cochairwoman, Congressional Coalition on Adoption Institute*

I laughed, I cried. I felt at first that this book is a reading must for every adoptive parent. And then I thought: No, this is a book for every parent—the ups, the downs, the pregnancies, the graduations, the jobs, the low incomes, the deaths, but under it all the absolute, enduring, unquenchable love and faith and hope that sustains all.

The Badeaus do not mince words: there were headaches, doubts, sickness, and questions about whether to go on. But why they went on, to me, is the story: not how wonderful they were to "rescue" these kids, but how much they received, how love begets love: they weren't adopting kids, they were multiplying love. Journeying, as Abraham, a consistent theme in

this book, is not really about obedience, but about trust, about love, that the journey will result in and propagate love.
—*John A. "Jack" Calhoun, author of* Hope Matters: The Untold Story of How Faith Works in America

The Badeaus are heroes to children. Having spent almost ten years in foster care, I know what it is like to be waiting for a forever family, and there are so few who will take on children of any age, color, or need. The Badeaus have not only raised 22 children, they have worked to change the laws that help thousands of children.
—*Ashley Rhodes-Courter, author, NY Times bestseller,* Three Little Words

In the adoption community, people often talk about the joys and challenges of raising children who have special needs. *Are We There Yet?* brings those joys and challenges to light as it allows us to join the amazing Badeau family on their adoption odyssey. This inspirational book reminds us that all children deserve a permanent, loving family, and all families raising children who have experienced trauma need their own community of support. NACAC is proud to have been part of the Badeaus' support network over the years.
—*Joe Kroll, Executive Director, North American Council on Adoptable Children*

Are We There Yet? is the inspiring biography of a family grounded in faith and driven by the belief that all children deserve unconditional love, care, and opportunity. The story of the Badeau family is honest about both the challenges and rewards of building a family that is not limited by color, age, or disability. The family teaches us lessons about love, growth, miracles, and loss; the importance of knowing who we are, what we want, and the willingness to risk to achieve it. This is a must read!

—*Carol Wilson Spigner, DSW, Professor Emeritus, University of Pennsylvania*

Are We There Yet? depicts a beautiful picture of a heavenly family. The Badeaus' dinner table is a reflection of the diversity we will witness at the wedding supper of the Lamb. It is written by a couple who are not only true experts in the field of child welfare and fighters for justice for the oppressed, but rooted in a deep Christian faith.

—*Scott Hasenbalg, Executive Director, Show Hope, Inc., and Kerry Hasenbalg, Founding Director, Congressional Coalition on Adoption Institute*

What a wonderful story of love! Not all of us are called to parent 22 children as Sue and Hector Badeau were, but their story can inspire all of us to open our hearts wider and to be more open to the journey of love—a costly journey at times. As an adoptive mom myself, I love Sue and Hector's realistic picture of adoption.

—*Nancie Carmichael, author of* Selah *and* Surviving One Bad Year

Are We There Yet? is the question every parent hears along the journeys they take with their children. But imagine hearing this regularly from more than six children! Or more than ten, or a dozen! Imagine these words echoing between van windows from the sweet voices of 22 children. Sue and Hector

Badeau's journey is filled with the happiest—and saddest—of moments. You don't want to miss this.

—*Eva Marie Everson, author of* The Cedar Key Series

There are few people as limitlessly generous, determined, and bullheadedly optimistic as Sue and Hector Badeau. They decided not once, not twice, but twenty times to adopt into their family a child who was, as they put it, "most in need of a home and least likely to get one." The story of their family is the story of humans doing an astonishing thing that seems impossible—until somebody does it.

—*Larissa MacFarquhar,* The New Yorker

Welcome to Sue and Hector Badeau's glorious journey. A profound and thrilling chronicle of what it truly means to be fearless in the mission of aiding America's most vulnerable children on the journey from darkness into the light. And the unexpected bounty of love, hope, and healing that a mother and father receive as the result. On the pages of this book you will find the manifestation of true and unconditional love, something we all instinctively long for and all too rarely find in the world. A simply beautiful story.

—*Janiva Magness, Blues and Soul singer, and spokesperson for National Foster Care Month/Save a Lifetime Campaign*

Are We There Yet? is a beautiful and passionate family story. Sue and Hector Badeau share an inspiring message of unconditional love for children that needed a home and a heart to connect to. Their selflessness has saved lives and paved the way for the next generation to know what love and joy are. The

Badeaus are wonderful examples of never giving up and truly believing that each child is a gift from God.

—*Derek Clark, speaker, author, ambassador, Foster Care Alumni of America*

With 22 kids, 20 through adoption and many with special needs, Hector and Sue Badeau put a whole new meaning to the words blended family. *Are We There Yet?* takes you on a transparent journey through the joys and sorrows, the highs and lows of living, and loving the patchwork life. Love is truly the universal, color-blind language in this family. Their family picture is a rainbow of faces and toothy smiles of African-American, Latino, Chinese, Indian, and Caucasian children. Wheelchairs and braces dot the landscape. This is one book you'll never forget.

—*Vonda Skelton, author, founder of Christian Communicators Conference*

Are We There Yet? is a giant roadmap of a book. To read Hector and Sue Badeau's story is to climb into their family van and join them on the adventure of raising 22 children, 20 of them adopted. You'll crisscross the United States with them as they take summer camping trips, attend adoption conferences, drive thousands of miles to welcome sibling groups into their family, meet the president of the United States, and advocate for changes in federal foster care and adoption laws. So fasten your seatbelt and hang on for a wild ride full of laughter, tears, and unconditional love.

—*Jolene Philo, author of* The Different Dream Parenting Series

Superheroes aren't just for the fantasy world of comic books and action movies. I now know super heroes are real, and they are the Badeaus. Not everyone can be foster or adoptive parents, but the one thing this book showed me is that whatever we do to help, we can always do more.

—*Ida Hawkins, Casey Family Programs*

Almost anyone who has had the honor of meeting Hector and Sue is immediately inspired by their amazing devotion to one another, to their family, and to God's plan. *Are We There Yet?* is the beautiful story of how 20 children found their way home.

—*Kathleen Strottman, Executive Director, Congressional Coalition on Adoption Institute*

Are We There Yet? is a fascinating and uplifting journey through the world of adoption and raising a large, multicultural family. Just when you think the Badeaus cannot accommodate another lost soul, they stretch and find room in their home and hearts. They display an unshakeable faith through tragedy and triumphs.

—*Gay Courter, author,* I Speak for This Child: True Stories of a Child Advocate

You may not have 22 children, but you can come alongside the Badeaus to experience their journey in times of calm and chaos. Be encouraged by God's presence in both. I couldn't put down this book!

—*Lynda T. Young, author,* the You Are Not Alone Book Series

A remarkable and compelling story of how relentless faith, prayer, and determination have given the most vulnerable children a lifetime of love.

—*Gloria Hochman, NY Times bestselling author*

Are We There Yet? provides a glimpse of a family that opened their hearts to children in need. From across the ocean to across a few states, the Badeaus have brought some of the neediest children into their loving arms to help them heal from physical and mental anguish. And in that process, the Badeaus have felt some of the deepest joys in watching their children blossom and some of the most difficult sorrows as their children have struggled with teenage pregnancies, drug and alcohol abuse, incarceration, and death. The book opens a greater understanding that people don't have to be perfect to love a child in need.

—*Kim Phagan-Hansel, Editor of* Adoption Today *and* Fostering Families Today *magazines, and* The Foster Parenting Toolbox

Are We There Yet? is the powerful story of the journey of a uniquely special family. You will laugh, cry, celebrate, and contemplate while reading this poignant book. Most of all, you will be inspired to open your heart to greater love, compassion, and to a decision to say yes when God invites you in to the adventure of a lifetime.

—*Carol Kent, speaker and author,* When I Lay My Isaac Down

I personally know Sue and have worked with her over the years. The unconventional family she and Hector have stitched together reminds me of a quilt—many sizes, shapes, shades and textures—each uniquely beautiful and strong on its own, but so much more so when woven together with the thread of love. It is that beauty, and the warmth it provides, that characterizes family. . . . The Badeaus have shown, in a way few others have, what it means to live an abundantly fulfilled life. *Are We There Yet?* is a journey of immense faith, immense joy, immense love, immense capacity. It's the journey of one couple opening their arms, their hearts, their home, and their lives to "the child most in need of a home and least likely to get one." . . . Just as the waves and the pressure of the ocean could not destroy the resilience and strength of the broken seashells, the Badeaus' story teaches us that there are no challenges that our children will face in their lifetimes that they cannot overcome through a life fortified by unconditional family love and unfailing hope.

> —*Dr. William C. Bell, President and CEO, Casey Family Programs*

Hector and Sue Badeau love big and love well! *Are We There Yet?* chronicles the Badeaus' journey of caring for orphaned and vulnerable children – a journey that hasn't always been easy. However, the Badeaus' decision to love has forever impacted the lives of their children and their story will inspire you and leave you asking, 'How might I, too, love bigger and love better?

> —*Mary Beth Chapman, Cofounder and President of Show Hope, Author of New York Time's bestseller* Choosing to SEE

Dedication

"Then the Lord said to me,
'Arise, proceed on your journey . . .'"
Deuteronomy 10:11

If any man among you thinks that he is wise in this age, he must become foolish, so that he may become wise." I Corinthians 3:18

As I write this dedication, a ray of sunshine catches my mother's ring and its many tiny gems are shimmering in the light. This ring, filled with bits of diamonds, rubies, sapphires, and more gold-encircled birthstones, is the perfect symbol of our family.

These gems and the gold itself are considered precious and of great value throughout the world. And yet, none of them are easy to obtain—they do not hang easily from tree branches like apples, nor do they grow plump and fat on vines like watermelon. To obtain these precious metals, many have lost their lives, digging in mines, fording rivers, and braving all manner of weather conditions. The gems themselves are often covered with mud, encrusted with coal, or otherwise not immediately recognizable as valuable. People who sought these gems were often called fools, crazy, or both.

Likewise, we had to overcome many barriers and clear many hurdles to bring our children home. We were often called crazy, or fools, in the process. Yet, like the pioneers seeking gold, we believed the mother lode was just around the next bend—and we were right!

Our children, each more valuable than all the diamonds and gold in the world, were not always recognized for their unique qualities and priceless beauty. Many of them had received labels like "special needs" or "hard to place" or the phrase used often in this book: "most in need of a home; least likely to get one." We know that none of our children like these labels, and we don't blame them. Who wants to be labeled?

We are so thankful that, to us, these labels meant nothing more than that they were precious gems, waiting to be brought together as a family, ready to catch the light of the sun, and to shine. Therefore, this book is dedicated to each of our children, our grandchildren, and our future generations. This is your inheritance, the story of our family, the legacy that proves you each have value greater than rubies, that you shine more brightly than sapphires. *So . . . shine on.*

Acknowledgments

"In everything, give thanks . . . "

We are grateful to all the friends and colleagues in our adoption, foster care, juvenile justice, and trauma networks for continually pushing us to tell our stories, especially Joe and Becky, Maris and Stu, Pat, Lisa and John, Brenda, Grace, Debbie, Patty and Gary, and my always-encouraging online sister-friends Judy, Chelle, Della, Karen, Deanna, Marguerite, Tisha, and Julia.

Family members and close friends were cheerleaders who helped us nail down accurate details. Our sisters—Nancy, Stephanie, and Irene—Aunt Deanna, brother David, and their spouses and children were all part of the team. We also thank our friends from the Mill River House Church and Summit Presbyterian Church for believing in this project with us.

In the craft of writing, fellow authors in the Advanced Writers and Speakers Association and the Christian Communicators Conference nudged us forward. Memoirist Susan Gregory Thomas taught us how to create the arc of our own story. Special thanks to author Lynda Tinnin Young for introducing us to her publisher, and now ours, Larry Carpenter. Larry and his team—editor Bob Irvin, designer Suzanne Lawing, and our cover photographer Laurie Beck Tarver—thank you ALL!

Finally, we thank our children and grandchildren for enriching our lives and giving us the stories contained in this book, and God, for giving us the grace, strength, and sense of humor needed to write it all down. It's been a wild ride and we're still moving forward!

Contents

Part III: Rivers to Cross

Epilogue: "Miles to Go"

Afterword

Foreword

We have 22 children, 20 through adoption. Some say that makes us crazy, while others say it makes us saints. To us, it simply makes us sojourners along the path God has set before us, albeit in a somewhat larger caravan than most.

It has been a scary, challenging, thrilling, joyous, confusing, frustrating, and rewarding journey from the day we joined our lives together with vows to travel as a team for the rest of our lives, until today. It has been a journey that we would definitely repeat if we had the opportunity to live our lives over again (with a few course corrections we can now see clearly in hindsight)! So we have written this book, both as a "travelogue" of our personal journey and a bit of a road map for you to consider as you take your own journey—whether your journey includes adoption, parenting, or other adventures.

Hector and I have worked on this book together. It is our story, shared through our eyes and our memories. Through it, we also share many of our children's stories—at least the parts of their stories that are intertwined with our own. We recognize, honor, and value the fact that the fullness of each of their stories belongs only to them, so we have tried to strike a balance between sharing our stories and respecting their privacy.

We decided to write the book in present tense in hopes that as you read, you will feel as though you are traveling alongside us. We wanted you to experience our stories as they unfolded with both freshness and in anticipation of what will happen next. To accomplish this, most of the book is written in Sue's voice. Yet we wanted to incorporate Hector's voice in a meaningful way, and so we have chosen to include his personal introduction and three standalone chapters—"From a Father's Heart"—throughout the book.

After the introductions, the story begins on our wedding day in 1979 and follows our travels through early 2013. If you wish to know a little more about our own backgrounds, how our childhood experiences shaped our faith and our life vision, and how we met and dated as teenagers, we have included a section in the Afterword on our early years.

Thank you for deciding to take this journey with us. It is our hope that as you read, you can pretend you are sitting in a travel agent's office, and we are your customer service representatives, eager to inspire and tempt you as you plan your own unforgettable trip to all of the magical destinations God has in store for you.

Hector: From a Father's Heart

"So let it be written, so let it be done." These words made famous by the movie *The Ten Commandments*, starring Charlton Heston, became my marching orders to my kids whenever I gave them instructions. Nowadays, they joke about it. However, little did I know that somehow these words would apply to me as well.

Have you ever made an off-the-cuff remark that changes the direction of your life? Looking back, I nailed down one comment that changed mine, and the future of many others. It was a warm September day in 1973 as I was watching the Spaulding High School girls' field hockey team practice in Barre, Vermont. I asked my friend Pete, "Who's the cute girl with the nice butt?" He answered, "That's Sue Hoag. I think I know her." A few months later I spotted her in the gym watching a wrestling match. I said to Pete, "I'm going to ask her out."

I believe the good Lord used those words on me: "So let it be written, so let it be done." I did ask Sue out in February of 1974 and the rest is history, as they say. Twenty-two kids, 35 grandkids, and six great-grandchildren later, we've taken the road less traveled—and would do it again.

We dated for over six years before our wedding day, growing as a couple toward the calling God had for us. No, we did not know at the time it entailed having 22 children, 20 by adoption and two by birth. However, from the very beginning, He did put in our hearts a desire to serve "the least of these."

THE JOURNEY BEGINS

"Are we there yet?" has probably been said over a billion times over the course of history, by every man, woman, and child who has ever traveled farther than a mile from home. The question has probably driven every adult who has ever traveled with children crazy—especially when it is asked every four or five miles. Imagine traveling, as I have done, over a thousand miles with 15 kids in a van in one stretch!

It's a natural question for kids to ask. After all, they want to get to the destination. The question, "Are we there yet?" can also be used for other aspects of our lives—as we focus on our marriages, careers, spiritual journeys, or even the size of our families. Looking back over the years that Sue and I have been married, I've come to realize that we've mostly been traveling in the same direction, usually on the same road, and often in the same car.

Depending on which aspects of our lives we focus on, we may be going in the same direction, but in different cars. In our journey, there were the times when we were traveling not only in very different cars, but on totally different roads, in completely opposite directions. At these times, when one of us was going the wrong way, the other would slow down and stop, waiting until the other was ready to turn around and get back on the right track. These represent some of the rocky patches in our relationship. The same can be said about our spiritual journey and all the choices and decisions we made over the years.

In traveling to a particular destination, you know when you've arrived because nowadays the GPS tells you, "You have arrived!" However, in other aspects of life, we may never really "get there," because no matter how long we work at it, there is always room for growth and improvement.

All of life's roads—spiritual, physical, emotional—have played into our journey together and greatly affected our relationship and how we raised our children together. All aspects of our lives are a part of this journey, and so often it is too easy to become so focused on the destination that we miss the joy and pleasure to be had along the way. Looking back over the years, there were many times when I should have "pulled over" at a rest area to stop and smell the roses, but I didn't. Whether it related to my relationship with Sue or one of the kids, my own physical health, or spiritual growth, often I was too intent on "getting there" to stop and take in the joys of the moment.

Granted, there were dozens of roses I did stop to smell along the way, and did they smell great! From the birth of our first child, Chelsea, to the day that Geeta, the last child we adopted, came home, there were priceless moments to be savored. The joy of bringing a sibling group of six teenagers back together for the first time after years of separation in foster care is one big bouquet of roses I will never forget. And as the Poison song reminds us, "Every rose has its thorn." We've experienced both the roses and the thorns—the good Lord has given us quite the bouquet. Adopting three terminally ill children and releasing each of them into the arms of God as they took their final earthly breaths—these are among the roses I never would have chosen to ask for, but I am so thankful for every one of them.

> Granted, there were dozens of roses I did stop to smell along the way, and did they smell great! From the birth of our first child, Chelsea, to the day that Geeta, the last child we adopted, came home, there were priceless moments to be savored.

Our bouquet is filled with roses of many colors and hues, which seems fitting since the song that Sue and I chose as "our song" while dating in high school was "Colour My World" by Chicago. It was the song for the first dance at our wedding and it has continued to turn up on the radio, often in the middle of the night while we were driving on our many family summer road trips. Each time I hear it, I marvel at all the ways God has colored our world since we started our journey. Of course, the most obvious is when you look at a family picture and see all the diverse skin tones of our children, who are African-American, Latino, Indian, Chinese, and Caucasian.

God has given us both the blessing and challenge of bringing all of these children together to create one family. Sue often took the lead, making sure that we honored and integrated each child's heritage into our daily lives. From holiday customs to learning how to care for our black children's hair (for years, a significant line item in our family budget!) to learning and educating others about institutional racism, it has all become a part of our family life.

The Brady Bunch we were not, nor were we like any of the large families with their own reality shows in recent times. We have many wonderful experiences to highlight from our summer road trips, to going to Disney with 15 children, to Christmas, Thanksgiving, graduations, and weddings with all the family and many, many more.

In addition, there are realities, not acted out for television, but lived through in the valleys with heart-wrenching pain as we sought to meet the individual needs of each of our children and the collective needs of the family all at the same time. This entailed seeing to their physical, emotional, educational, and spiritual needs, a very big assignment. On top of all that, we had to maintain our own personal health, well-being, and marital relationship, which proved to be challenging at times.

We all bring baggage into a marriage and every adopted child brings their own baggage into the new family they join. Needless to say, in our house that meant there were a lot of bags that needed to be opened and unpacked. Let me tell you, some of those bags had some stinky socks in the corners!

Like a road trip, all parenting, especially becoming parents through adoption or parenting children with special needs, takes planning, preparation, and anticipation. When God called us to begin a family, we knew that we were taking the first steps in what would become our lifelong journey—yet we had no idea how the many detours, delays, side trips, dangerous mountain terrain, and treacherous valleys would both thrill and terrify us while shaping our lives in ways we never would have predicted.

On our summer trips, detours and delays were often headaches to endure, but we found that they also became opportunities to explore, to spend time together, to make new friends, see new sites, or learn something unexpected. Some of our favorite travel memories are from the times we detoured off our planned route, or when our van broke down (which it often did!). We had a chance to take pony rides against a spectacular Idaho mountain backdrop, share fresh sweet corn with farmers in Illinois, and enjoy a glittering display of fireworks while eating Domino's pizza in a parking lot in Salt Lake City—all of these moments were unexpected and unplanned, but very memorable.

Your life journey, too, will be filled with delays and detours. You may not smoothly glide from one destination to the next. But we hope you will find, as we have, that the detours can become interesting experiences and "teachable moments," not simply hassles and heartbreaks to be endured.

Many people who hear parts of our story often ask, "How did you do it?" Perhaps you are thinking the same thing. For us, it was the grace and wisdom of God, friends who helped, giving and receiving forgiveness, nurturing self-acceptance for each of our kids, hard work, and lots of prayers. We'll take you through some of the deepest ruts and rocky patches we traversed and we hope you will rejoice with us each time we experienced a mountaintop moment. We will describe some of the valuable tools God has given us to fill our toolbox, and most importantly, the incredible Triple AAA plan he has provided through His Word and His people.

It is our hope and prayer that we will entertain, inspire, and challenge each of our readers to be bold and brave as you begin or continue the road trip God has in store for you. Whether you are reading this as you are just starting out on your own life journey, or refueling at a stop along the way, we hope that you will have a rewarding trip. We hope you will take time to smell the roses, enjoy the view, and cherish the lessons that come even when you feel stranded or lost.

Jump in our van and come along for the ride!

Part I: "We're on Our Way!"

*"Whoever receives one such child
in my name, receives me . . . "*

Matthew 18:5

Preface: Wayne

I feel a little shaky as I walk toward the car, cradling Wayne gently in my arms. As Hector steps ahead of me to open the passenger door, I am struck by a sudden urge to strap Wayne securely into a seatbelt in the backseat. I don't say this out loud; instead, I slip into the front seat, holding Wayne snuggly on my lap for the short ride home.

"He sure did love road trips," Hector says in a voice choked with emotion. "I guess this will be the last one we take with him."

In my head I know that the ashes in this dark blue urn are not really Wayne, but they are all we have left of him, and I can't bear to let him go. As I walk into the house, I just want to sit, holding the urn in my arms, holding on to all the memories of Wayne bringing joy and laughter to my life. The very thought that I will never hear that distinct little chortle again overpowers me and the sobbing starts once more.

Several of the kids are here and, within the next few hours, they will all gather in our living room. Hector and Todd have carried the photo boxes down from the third floor and, in what has now become an all-too-familiar ritual, we begin sorting through hundreds of photographs, selecting the ones we want for Wayne's good-bye video which Chelsea will make in the days ahead.

"Oh! Look what I found!" exclaims Renee, holding up a photo of Wayne sitting on the edge of a picnic table on one of our family camping trips. "Remember that time he went right over to the campsite next to ours and started eating the food off their table?" Although there have been many tears today, and I know there are more to come, it feels so good to hear the sound of laughter. Renee's find has kicked off a round of storytelling, reminiscing, and laughing as we all recall one after another of the funny moments over the 20 years that Wayne was part of our family.

"He loved snatching food off other people's plates—I remember once he took a piece of chicken right off my plate when I walked by!"

"And remember how he lined up all the shoes?"

"Oh, what about the time he escaped during the night and the milkman brought him home at four in the morning?"

By now, laughter and tears are mingling together as we relive these moments and many more.

Stuck in a pile of photos from the early 1990s and totally out of sequence, I see a photo of our first silver Toyota Corolla, with a canoe strapped to the top, ready for the first camping road trip Hector and I took together, to Maidstone Lake for our honeymoon in 1979. While the kids continue to pull out photos of Wayne, I show the Toyota photo to Hector.

"Who would of thought?" he says, shaking his head. "I know I never could have imagined on that day that a day like today would ever be in our future. A day when we would be planning a funeral for a child—we never dreamed of all the miles we would travel together from that trip to today."

"I know, if we had truly known the full meaning of the 'for better or worse, in sickness and in health' part of the vows we took in 1979 . . . " I smile, lost in the memories.

"I remember you taking a nap in the car on the way to Maidstone, and when you woke up, asking if we were almost there— we were so excited—just like little kids! Little did we know what was ahead . . . . So, now, what do you think, Sue? Are we there yet?"

1

Chelsea

Fog rolls in across Lake Morey as I stand on the dock in my bathing suit at 6 AM. After six years of dating, the day has finally arrived to marry my high school sweetheart, and it looks like rain. "Please, God!" I beg. "Keep the rain away." My heart is set on an outdoor wedding.

It's been a busy spring. In May, both Hector and I graduated from college. In June, we bought Logos, the Christian bookstore I worked at while at Smith College. And now, July 14, Bastille Day, is our wedding day! I slip into the water for my early morning swim, hoping and praying that the fog will burn off.

A few hours later, guests are starting to arrive and the sun is shining. It's time to get dressed. Everything is exactly the way I dreamed and I want to savor every moment. The rolling hills around beautiful Lake Morey form the perfect backdrop for the pictures. The guests are already enjoying the beautiful singing of my college friends Monica, Donna, and Kharmia. My cousins, Ingrid and Jill, are handing out the packets of wedding wheat (not rice!) and handmade programs. No turning back now; the fairy tale is about to unfold.

"Just a few more miles and we'll be there," Hector says as he nudges me awake. I can't believe how fast the last 24 hours have flown by. After years of dreaming and months of planning, our wedding is over and we are nearly at our destination, Maidstone Lake, for our camping honeymoon.

"Well, Mr. Badeau, thank you for getting us here safely, and letting me have a little nap," I say.

"You are most welcome, Mrs. Badeau," he replies, and we both chuckle, enjoying our first day of married life. Maidstone is such a special spot. A picturesque lake in the pristine Northeast Kingdom of Vermont, my family camped here every summer, and I am so excited for a honeymoon week here in the Larch lean-to. (Larch is the name of an area tree, so the lean-to carried that name.) We plan to swim, canoe, plan our future, and . . . well, enjoy all the romantic things you do on a honeymoon!

Seven days later, we are back in our little silver Toyota, recapping the highlights of our week and summarizing the plans we made. Soon after pulling into the driveway at my parents' home, where we'll stay a few days organizing our wedding gifts and writing thank you notes before we move, we share our decisions with them.

"We've decided that we're going to have four children!" I excitedly let them know.

"That's right," Hector adds. "We plan to have two and adopt two."

"That's pretty specific," my father says. "How did you come up with that plan?"

I remind my parents of all the times I begged them to adopt a child after I read the book *The Family Nobody Wanted*, by Helen Doss, when I was twelve. "I've always wanted to adopt, and now I have a husband who shares that dream with me."

"That's pretty specific," my father says. "How did you come up with that plan?"

"That's your dream too, Hector?" Dad asks.

"Well, being the great guy—and husband—that I am," he laughs, "I want to make Sue happy and this sounds like a good plan to me."

Years later, Hector told me he often wondered who—or what—caused him to be so agreeable, but he believes now that the Spirit was already working in our lives, setting plans in motion far beyond what we could see or imagine.

"But don't worry," he says to my dad in a more serious tone. "We know it'll take five years to pay off our college loans and the loan for the bookstore. So we don't plan to start having kids until then."

We are sitting on the couch in our first apartment enjoying a quiet Saturday evening after getting home from a day at the bookstore when Hector bursts out laughing. "What's so funny?" I ask.

"I am just picturing your mom trying to help us move this couch into the apartment," he chuckles. "I thought her head was going to get wedged between the couch and the stairwell." Soon we are both laughing and retelling more of the funny moments from our moving-in day just a month earlier, while we wait for our two favorite Saturday night shows, *Fantasy Island* and *The Love Boat*, to begin.

"Do you ever feel like we are just playing house?" he asks. "Our life seems so perfect—working together at the bookstore every day, coming home to our little apartment . . . it's hard to believe this is real life."

"Yeah, it's like we have our own little Love Boat and Fantasy Island right here in Massachusetts!"

Life in Northampton during the summer is pretty quiet. The college students are mostly gone, and we're slowly getting to know the local people who come into our store. We work together six days a week, and then we rest. We even found a church that meets Sunday evenings so we can stay in bed half the day every Sunday.

I joined Mill River House Church as a college student, and this small, somewhat countercultural community was exactly what I wanted. It's Bible-centered, the members really try to live out their faith in everyday life, and it's fun! Besides worship, we share potluck dinners, softball games, and good times.

And then there's "Baby Beth" and "Little Daniel." So far, these are the only children in our church, and they are just so cute. Every Sunday we come home talking about their antics, and Hector says to me, "Sue, we need to get one of those." It's a running joke now, but I am beginning to wonder—will we really hold out five years before we have a child?

A few weeks later, I have my answer. Our church is going to Southern Vermont for a retreat weekend and I've just learned that I am pregnant with our first child. We can't wait to tell our friends the news. So much for our five-year plan!

"The mind of man plans his way, But the Lord directs his steps" (Proverbs 16:9).

Little did we know at that time how soon our dream of having "one of our own" would explode into the family we have today. God is surely planting many seeds in us, and it will be years before we see the full harvest.

I'm shelving books in the children's corner when I hear the

phone ring, but can't get to it in time. Hopefully, Hector can answer it. Now that I am seven months pregnant, I don't move about the store quite as fast as I did in the fall. After the last Jane Yolen book is settled on the shelf, I walk toward the front of the store.

"Who was on that on . . . ?" I start to ask, but I see that Hector's face is ashen. "What is it?"

Slowly, he tells me about the phone call. His father has had another heart attack. The family is all gathering in Vermont, and it doesn't look good. I look at the clock behind the cash register, mentally calculating what time we could get to Vermont if we leave right now. "You go gas up the car, I'll lock up the store. I'll call Betsy and see if she can work tomorrow, and well, maybe for a few days."

Hector doesn't move.

"I can't," he says. "We won't make it in time, and I need to just be alone with my thoughts and my memories. We'll go in the morning."

I know how complex Hector's relationship with his dad has been, so I don't push the issue. Silently, I pray that God will give him wisdom, comfort, and peace. I pray, too, for Hector's long-suffering mother, that she will get through the next few days alright. I feel helpless, knowing there is nothing I can do for either of them. It's not a comfortable feeling. *Lord, show me how I can be a comfort. Help me know what to say and what to do.*

The trip to Vermont is difficult. Winter weather makes it challenging physically, but, of course, the greater challenge is the emotional one. Hector had never really made peace with his father during his life. All the years of alcohol-induced violence and verbal abuse had taken their toll. And yet, now, the grief is real. The positive memories are swirling together with the bitter ones and the forever-lost opportunities for reconciliation.

There are only a few miles left before we arrive back at our Easthampton apartment when Hector reaches out and places his hand on my very pregnant belly. "I hope and pray," he says quietly. "I hope and pray that I can be a better father than the one I just buried, but I am scared. Scared that I will repeat the past."

I know this man will be a terrific father. I am confident in that, but it seems trite to say the words aloud at this moment. So I hold his hand in silence as tears roll down both of our faces.

As we open the store after three days away, Mr. Skibiski is our first customer. "Hi Skibi, what can I help you with today?" Hector calls out to one of our favorite regulars.

"I need a birthday card for a doctor," he replies, adding, "What do you prescribe?" This cracks Hector up, and it is such a joy to see him laughing that I want to run over and give Skibi a big bear hug.

Skibi is one of many men, and a few women, who were dramatically impacted by legal actions during my senior year at Smith College. These legislative actions resulted in the deinstitutionalization of both the state hospital and the veteran's hospital in Northampton. While many were able to live with relatives and others were resettled into community programs, many became homeless. Getting to know Karl, Gene, Skibi, Ethel, and others has already been one of the greatest joys and biggest challenges while managing Logos.

Just a few days before our Vermont trip, Gene told us he had nowhere to stay, so he stayed on our couch for a few nights. After he went to sleep, I talked to both Hector and God, asking, "How can this be? This is America. These men have served our country and now they are on the streets—it just isn't right." We prayed that God would show us how to help. This is one prayer God has answered both quickly and continuously throughout our life together.

As we arrive at church, our friend Ellen introduces us to some guests joining us for tonight's service. College students, they had spent the summer working with Mother Teresa in India, painting, cleaning, and repairing the areas where many of the orphaned children she cared for were living.

"Wow, that was powerful," Hector says later as we start driving home. "Seeing those slides, and listening to them talk about the people in India who are homeless and don't have enough food from one day to the next really makes me appreciate our little apartment even more."

"Yes, and it makes me think about our prayer for men like Karl and Skibi and Gene. I think helping starts with the children. If every child can grow up in a safe home with a family that loves them, maybe fewer will be homeless when they are adults."

"Remember our dream of adopting two children? I think God is showing us he wants us to start with a baby from India."

"Speaking of babies, this one is starting to move around a lot more!" I say, rubbing my expanding belly. "I don't know if they will let us adopt while I am still pregnant, but we can at least start learning more about it."

"I made the appointment, Hec," I say while we eat our lunch over the Logos jewelry counter. "We go in two weeks and meet with a social worker named Mary Diamond."

"Why do you want to adopt? Seeing how you appear to be expecting a baby any day now . . . " Ms. Diamond says as she peers curiously at us across her desk.

"We strongly feel God is calling us to do this," I say, and two hours later we are walking out the door with a giant stack of paperwork to complete and another appointment scheduled for after the baby is born.

"Ugh. Paperwork. I hate paperwork," Hector groans.

"It's not as bad as diapers," I jokingly reply.

"To me it is!"

"OK, then," I say. "I'll make you a deal—I'll do all the paper-work and you do all the diapers."

"Sure, you've got a deal," he quickly agrees, as if he got a bar-gain, although I'm quite sure I got the better end of this one!

Each day lately, our customers ask me how much longer I'm going to keep working before the baby is born. Each day I say the same thing: "As long as I feel good enough, why would I want to stay home?" But tonight, I'm thinking that maybe to-morrow I will stay home. I'm feeling a little queasy—maybe from the spaghetti we had for dinner, and we have all those cute new baby clothes from the shower our friends gave us that need to be washed, folded, and put away. My mom calls to check in and I tell her, "I think I'll stay home, take a day off tomorrow." She's been urging me to do this for a couple of weeks now, so she's relieved.

All night I toss and turn, can't get comfortable. I'm so rest-less, Hector finally heads out to the couch just to get a little sleep. These "cramps"—are they really just from the spaghetti, or could labor be starting? I look at the clock again—it's 5 AM and I decide it is fair enough to wake Hector up and get his opinion.

"Do you think I am in labor?" I ask. He sits with me, timing my "cramps," and we are both pretty sure that something im-portant is happening. "Let's call the doctor," he says.

"You look nervous," I say to Hector as he pulls the car up to the hospital entrance. "We learned everything in Lamaze class. It will be fine."

"Well, I know how to play hockey too, but I was still nervous when it was the state championship game," he deadpans.

I've decided I want a natural childbirth, but it's not long before I am screaming at Hector: "GET ME SOME DRUGS!"

"Breathe in. Breathe out," he replies. "It's too late now for the drugs. You can do this."

"Shut up and get me drugs!" I plead.

"You shut up and breathe," the nurse says. Wow. That shocks me into a moment of calm. Who does she think she is telling me to shut up?

It's Wednesday, May 21, 1980. The ashes from the Mt. St Helen's volcano are making their way across Massachusetts, and I am a mom. Wow! Chelsea Lynne came into the world with a perfectly round little head, bright, alert little eyes, and a strong personality. I'm instantly smitten—head over heels in love with this perfect little person. I can't take my eyes off of her, the powerful emotions are nearly overwhelming. I know my life will never be the same; I just don't yet understand how thoroughly my life will change. I think of the passage about Mary "pondering all of these things in her heart" and I know that every mother throughout history has had this moment of pondering and tucking away the powerful thoughts and feelings of becoming a mom into the deepest, safest corner of her heart.

A few days later, my parents, sisters, and baby brother arrive to meet Chelsea. "What day is it?" I jokingly ask. "The days all seem to be running together."

"It's Sunday. The day for sleeping in," Hector laughs.

"Ahhhh, no more sleeping in for you two," my dad teases. At the time I didn't realize he meant: No. More. Sleeping. In. Ever. Again.

"I'm getting the hang of hand-to-hand diaper combat," Hector brags to my sisters, and I point out that he is also eating on Chelsea's schedule—making himself a peanut butter and jelly sandwich every two hours during the night while I nurse her.

For a week I stay "cocooned" with Chelsea in our little apartment while our friends Carol and Betsy help Hector to hold down the fort at the store. My mom helps me settle into a comfortable routine of nursing Chelsea, washing diapers, and writing thank you notes for the many gifts we have received. The day after she leaves to go back to Vermont, I am once again overcome with emotion. I have just finished nursing the baby and she has drifted off to sleep, still clutching my pinky finger. She looks so peaceful, so content, so trusting. Suddenly, I have a vivid image of myself as a teenager, arguing with my parents, storming off to my room, slamming the door, and screaming, "I hate you!"

I look at Chelsea and tears begin to roll down my face. I want to tell my parents I'm so sorry for all the times I hurt them. I want to thank them for all the love they wrapped around me my whole life. I never want Chelsea to scream "I hate you!" at me. "But I suppose you will, one day, won't you?" I whisper to her as I nuzzle the soft top of her head.

Soon, I know the time has come to go back to work. I have heard the African proverb "It takes a village to raise a child," and I am so thankful every day for this wonderful village we have at our bookstore. Every customer is praying for our baby, and they all have lots of tips about parenting. We've read all the books, of course, from *What to Expect When You Are Expecting* to Dr. Spock's wisdom, before she was born, but as Hector keeps reminding me, "There is nothing like on-the-job training."

Chelsea is such a social baby. She's already made friends with many of our regular customers, several of whom stop by almost daily to see her—especially Karl and Miss Ethel, who has christened her "Roll-ey Poly."

"*Dallas* is on tonight," I remind Hector as he clears our dinner dishes. "It's a rerun; there won't be any new ones until the fall when they reveal 'Who Shot JR.' Kind of fun that we will be in Dallas while they are filming that top secret episode."

"Really? How do you know that?"

"I read about it—they are actually going to be doing some of the filming on the SMU campus while we are there. Wonder if we'll get to see any of it?"

We're heading to Dallas, just days after Chelsea turns six weeks old, for the annual Logos association meeting and the Christian Booksellers Convention. I'm so thankful my little sister Stephanie has agreed to come with us and help with the baby while we are busy with bookstore meetings.

We step off the plane near midnight and I can hardly breathe. The air is so hot I feel as though I've walked into a furnace. Dallas is in the throes of a record-setting heat wave: 42 consecutive days of 100 degrees or higher. I want to get back on the plane and go home.

By the end of the next day, I'm glad I stuck around. We've already heard Amy Grant live in concert and we're going to hear BJ Thomas later this week. It's a joy meeting all the other Logos Bookstore owners and my head is spinning with ideas to try at our store when we get home. As I walk through the Convention Hall, I am a bit overwhelmed by all the stuff for sale. I love all the books, but the chocolate bars with labels saying, "Taste and See that the Lord is Good" seem a little ridiculous, maybe even sacrilegious, to me.

All at once, I hear some thunder. The hall goes instantly silent, and then we hear it again—it is definitely thunder. As soon as the rain starts pounding its rhythmic beat on the cavernous convention center ceilings, a cheer rises from the floor. Everyone is so excited—clapping, singing, cheering, and giving thanks. Dallas needed this rain in the worst way. What a thrill to be here when the skies opened up! All too soon, the trip is over and it's time to go home.

Summer is drawing to a close, and I am enjoying the relatively cool evening air, nursing Chelsea, and watching our team, "El Equipo," play softball. Hector is up to bat and socks a good one. As he turns the corner at second base, I realize it may be a home run. I jump to my feet, cheering him on when he suddenly leaps over the catcher and lands safely on home plate—the craziest home run I have ever seen. I'm quite sure Dan and Pam will be telling the rest of our friends about this one next Sunday at church!

Walking into the apartment after the game, I see the light on the answering machine flashing. "Can you check that message while I put the baby to bed?" I call out.

"It was Mary Diamond," Hector says. "She wanted to remind us of our appointment next week to continue our adoption application."

"Yikes! I guess I better get busy finishing up that paperwork. Did you write your part of the autobiography yet?"

I work a little each day for the next several days, and finally get it done. Just one question left: "This paper is asking us what type of child we want to adopt—how can I answer that? How do we know what child God has planned for us?"

"Just write: The child most in need of a home and least likely to get one," Hector says, and it sounds just right. From that moment forward this becomes our family-building motto, although we had no inkling at the time that it would one day include terminally ill children and teenagers. We just thought we were adopting a baby needing a family.

Driving to Vermont to celebrate Chelsea's first Christmas with the grandparents gives us time to reflect on all the changes we've experienced in the past year, and those on the horizon in 1981. Business is going well at Logos, we love our friends and our church family, Chelsea has learned to sit up, and we just completed the home study for our adoption. We laugh as we acknowledge that God has placed us on a fast track—we are way ahead of schedule on our five-year plan, but it's all good and we are feeling richly blessed.

We've only been home a few weeks when we get our first taste of the twists and turns our adoption journey will take. Mary Diamond calls to tell us that India has temporarily put a "hold" on all adoptions to the U.S., but in the same breath lets us know that she has learned there is an urgent need for families for children from El Salvador.

"Will we consider El Salvador?" is the question she asks me to discuss with Hector, pointing out that the children needing families are not babies, but older children—as old as two or three years old.

This is a big surprise; we had never considered adopting an older child, and what would it mean for Chelsea to go from being the first child to having an older brother or sister? It's a lot to think about.

So we talk and pray before calling her back, saying, "Of course we'll take a child from El Salvador! That must be the child most needing a home and least likely to get one."

The next day, sitting in Mary's office, she gives us directions to an address on Cape Cod. This is where we have to go to meet with Ronnie, the liaison and lawyer who coordinates the El Salvadoran adoptions. Over the next few weeks, we drive back and forth to the Cape (three to four hours from our home) several times, with Chelsea strapped safely in the back seat. Crossing the "big bridge" onto the Cape becomes one of her highlights—she claps her hands and points each time we go over the "big bridge." She has no way of realizing just how big of a bridge we are really crossing as we enter this territory of international adoption.

We've completed all of the paperwork, and we've been accepted to adopt a child from El Salvador—now all we need to do is write a check. Ronnie tells us to come back the next time with $3,000, which will cover the legal fees and the child's plane ticket, along with an escort, to the U.S. Our annual income from Logos is under $10,000. Coming up with $3,000 seems both overwhelming and impossible.

Reminding me that with God all things are possible, Hector urges me to call the president of our hometown bank back in Vermont. He knew me as a little girl, and saw me grow up. Surely if anyone will loan us $3,000 on good faith alone, he will do it.

I am stunned as I hang up the phone. I sit for a few moments in silence.

"Well?" Hector asks. When I don't respond, his face drops, "He said 'No,' didn't he?"

"He said YES!" I scream. "It's really happening! We're on our way to adopting!"

We cross the big bridge and ease into Ronnie's driveway. We have the $3,000 check and a small duffle bag filled with the items we were told to bring—some toddler-sized clothing, lotion, soaps, powder, and other child-care items. The last thing we put into the bag was a handmade baby blanket quilted by Hector's mother, Mamere, matching the one she had made just a few months ago for Chelsea.

The meeting is incredibly short. We hand over the check and the duffle bag, Ronnie gives us a few last pieces of paperwork, and she tells us to go home and wait for a phone call about our child. "Expect it to take anywhere from a few weeks to a few months," the lawyer says as we head out the door to get back on the road toward home. In the years since that day we have often said, "If we knew then what we know now, we'd have asked a lot more questions."

But we didn't, so we drive home feeling a little uneasy about the whole situation. "We'll call Mary in the morning," we agree. "She'll know if it is all on the up and up."

And sure thing, the next morning, Mary reassures us that she has worked with these folks before and everything is legitimate. "Before you know it, you will have a child in your arms," she says.

We've created a nursery in the back room at Logos, and I've just put Chelsea down for a nap when I see Hector standing next to the phone with tears streaming down his face. *Oh no*, I think to myself. *Now who died?*

He takes one look at me, and his face lights up in a smile. "Congratulations," he says. "We have a son!"

A few days later, the photo and documents about our soon-to-be son, two-year-old Douglas, arrive in the mail. We quickly fall in love with the dear little boy in the photograph and Hector immediately puts it in his wallet. Our customers and Mill River House church friends are delighted with the news and quickly plan a shower for us.

The next few weeks fly by as we set up a second crib in Chelsea's room and complete other preparations for our son's arrival. Suddenly, the excitement comes to a dramatic halt as we once again receive a life-changing phone call while we are at work at Logos.

It's Ronnie, calling from the Cape to tell us that Douglas has relatives in El Salvador who have come to the orphanage to claim him. While we are happy for Douglas, our hearts are broken. And then, Ronnie says, "Wait, I have more to tell you." There are two other children in immediate need of a family, and one can be our child. But we have to decide right away. Which one will we take? The woman will give us a couple of hours, but we have to call back today. One is a two-year-old boy named Jose and the other is a three-year-old girl named Elsie.

We lock the front door, walk to the back of the store, and pray. How can we choose? Why can't we take both? How can we "get over" Douglas so fast? Slowly, the answer fills our hearts and our minds—we know which child is ours and, as Hector unlocks the door of the store, I pick up the phone to call Ronnie with our decision.

2

Jose

Logan Airport in Boston is eerily quiet tonight. Just yesterday, a small bomb killed a man at Kennedy Airport in New York. As a result, today no one is allowed to walk down to the gates to meet the arriving passengers. "We're meeting a child, a baby," we say to the security guard, pulling our paperwork out of my purse as proof. After being shuttled around from one security person to another, we are finally allowed to walk to the gate and await the arrival of our son. It's 11 PM and we're the only ones here.

"Boss, da plane, da plane," Hector jokes—mimicking the famous line from the show *Fantasy Island*—as a large plane approaches the gate. Just then a cleaning lady comes along. Just as the first passengers began to emerge from the plane, she plugs in her vacuum cleaner and the quiet is broken as it roars to life. Dozens of passengers file off the plane and hurry away toward baggage claim. At last, a weary-looking woman steps off; she is carrying a small boy in her arms. She approaches us and begins to speak in Spanish. I hold out my paperwork as she thrusts a passport into my hands, hands the child to Hector, and walks away.

With the roar of the industrial vacuum cleaner as our soundtrack, we meet our son for the first time.

The child goes immediately to Hector. I look at the passport, confused. It has a picture of the child in front of us, but the name on it says "Douglas," the child we were told we were not getting. I whisper to Hector, speaking softly. He turns to the little boy and says, "Douglas?" No response. I try: "Douglas, Me da gusta verte!" He looks at me quizzically, clinging to Hector's arm a little tighter, but still no response. And then we hear "Jose." And again, "Jose. Me llamo Jose." "Jose!" we both say, laughing and covering him with kisses! Yes! This is our son, the child we've been waiting for. The child who became our son that day in the back room of Logos as we talked and prayed about whether God meant for "Jose" or "Elsie" to join our little family.

Zipping him into the small blue spring jacket we've brought, we head out of the airport. Jose is saying something sounding like "Papa" over and over. "How cute," I smile at Hector. "He's already calling you his daddy." It's pouring rain and takes us more than an hour to drive to Aunt Deanna and Uncle Freddy's house in Rhode Island, where we're spending the night. Throughout the ride, we talk excitedly, pinching ourselves that this is real. We really have our little boy after the months of phone calls, drives to the Cape, and paperwork. He is here, in the backseat, softly saying "Papa" over and over in a sweet singsong voice.

It's nearly 1 AM when we roll into the driveway; Aunt Deanna and Uncle Freddy meet us at the door. Freddy speaks to Jose in

Spanish. He turns to us, asking, "Does he have a diaper on?"

"I'm not sure. We didn't check."

"Well, this child needs the bathroom—quickly!" Freddy explains that the cute word Jose was repeating was not "Papa" at all—it was *popó*. He was telling us he needed to go to the potty! Poor little guy! It's been more than two hours since he got off the plane. As soon as we sit him on the toilet, it's very clear— Uncle Freddy was right. And as we put him into pajamas, we notice for the first time the scarring on his back and buttocks. Sadly, we wonder if he'd been beaten in the past for not making it to the potty on time?

Back home in Northampton, we immediately call Mary Diamond and tell her about the problem with the passport. "He is Jose," I explain. "He clearly responds to that name and he was clutching a small Polaroid photo of himself. Written on the bottom, it says Jose Rogel Carlos Lopez. He doesn't respond at all to the name Douglas, but that is what his passport says." She suggests we call our El Salvador liaison on the Cape and see what more we can learn.

"Oh this sort of thing happens all the time," Ronnie tells us. "It is no big deal. But you'll have to petition the court to change his name when you finalize your adoption, that's all."

"His birth date seems wrong too. He has Douglas' birth date on the paperwork, but we think Jose is a little older."

"That's not uncommon, either. Just take him to your dentist and pediatrician and they'll help you figure out his age. Then you can petition the court to change his birth date as well." This seems very odd to us, but we don't question it. After all, we are new at this adoption stuff.

The next day, Chelsea's one-year doctor's appointment is scheduled, giving Dr. Kenney the opportunity to meet Jose for the first time. We show him the "medical records" we had received about Jose—typed on a single sheet of paper is: "Healthy two-year-old male child."

"He's at least two and a half," Dr. Kenney says. "And although he seems basically healthy, he does have a few parasites we're going to have to treat immediately."

After filling the three prescriptions, we head over to Dr. Parisian's office. "His teeth are in great shape," Dr. Parisian says. He concurs with Dr. Kenney's pronouncement that Jose is at least 30 months old.

As we prepare for Chelsea's first birthday party, just a few days away, we realize we need to "make up" a birthday for Jose. Since he arrived on May 17, and his birthday is approximately half a year away, we decide on November 17. It wasn't until my first trip to El Salvador many years later that I fully understood the implication of Jose's "missing" birthday information.

As we settle into our new routine with two children, we face a few challenges. First, it's the battle of the "horse pills," as we call the medications we have to give Jose to clear up the parasites. He doesn't want anything to do with these giant pills—and frankly, I don't blame him. We try everything, crushing them into milk, juice, applesauce, pudding. He kicks, flails, cries, and spits. Ultimately, we have to hold him down and "force-feed" him the nasty pills. It sure doesn't feel like a very nurturing way to bond with our new son. I'm so relieved when we manage to get him to swallow the last of these pills.

Jose has a few fears that give us only the smallest glimpse into the terrors he must have lived through while war was raging in El Salvador. Whenever we drive over a bridge, he screams, "No *chuchos*, no *chuchos!*" Although I'm pretty fluent in Spanish, this word means nothing to me, so I have no idea what he's so afraid of. One day, we're out walking and a man is walking a dog on the other side of the street. Jose freezes in fear, points to the dog, and screams, "NO! No *chucho*, no *chucho!*"

"It must mean 'dog,'" Hector says.

"No, the word for 'dog' is *perro*, I reply, smugly.

Weeks later, a UMass student from El Salvador comes into Logos and we strike up a conversation about life in Salvador. "Oh—and the most important question: Can you tell us what *chucho* means? I can't figure it out."

"*Chucho* is the word for dog," he says.

"*Chucho*, not *perro*?" I ask.

"That's right, *chucho* is dog in Salvador."

I describe to him how Jose becomes rigid with fear when we cross a bridge and screams "No *chucho*!" "That makes sense," he tells us. "In Salvador, many times the gang members and militia hide under bridges with their guns and guard dogs, and many people have been ambushed this way." I hug my boy a little tighter that night and wonder what horrors he had seen or heard near a bridge thousands of miles away. "Dear God," I pray, "please help him to know that he is safe here, and take away his fear of bridges and dogs."

Jose wants nothing to do with the Spanish language. Most of my extended family, many of our Mill River House Church friends, and even some of our Logos customers are so excited to speak Spanish to our new son, and we've been looking forward to raising a bilingual child. We believe that by speaking with him in both Spanish and English, he'll not only learn English while retaining his Spanish, but Chelsea will become bilingual as well. Yet every time anyone speaks to him in Spanish, he freezes, or runs away. I know just enough about trauma to understand that the Spanish words are a trigger for him, making him feel unsafe or even causing him to relive some of his painful past experiences.

With Richard Scarry as his tutor, Jose learns English very

quickly. Thanks to *The Best Word Book Ever!*, he tackles the names of body parts, items of clothing, food, and animals. He especially loves horses and one of the few times he'll use his Spanish is whenever he sees a picture of a horse. He'll call out excitedly, "Mira, Papa, Papa, mira! *Caballo! Caballo*, Papa, mira, mira!!!"

Jose also loves to eat and before even finishing the serving on his plate, he wants to know if there will be more. *Quiero mas* is another Spanish phrase he hangs on to for a long time, but it sounds more like "Cello-ma." With his plate still loaded with food, he'll look up and say, "Cello-ma," to which Hector replies, "*Soolaimon*," and bursts out singing the Neil Diamond song by that name. It's just a quirky family thing that became a sort of tradition, but we all enjoyed it. Before long, we are all singing and laughing gleefully.

Not long after Jose's arrival, we celebrate Chelsea's first birthday with a big party at the bookstore. We invited our friend Val, who's also a professional clown, to provide the entertainment. Somehow this Smith-educated early childhood development major had forgotten that a room filled with two dozen children under the age of two would not be happy to see a clown! Yikes! It's a wild and crazy disaster with most of the kids crying for their mommies, but Jose thinks it's great fun playing with the red clown nose, and soon, Val and her husband Ken become his special buddies.

Jose and Chelsea, who he calls by the endearing name of "Chuffy," quickly become the inseparable duo—and thanks to gifts from my mom they are even dressed in matching OshKosh outfits on many days. They spend a lot of their time with us at the bookstore, charming our customers, playing with blocks, and, mostly, reading lots and lots of books. We don't have a car, but we do have an antique baby carriage big enough for both of them as we take walks back and forth to the bookstore, playground, Bart's Ice Cream, and the "train store"—all favorite spots. They're becoming well known around town.

At home, Jose and Chelsea play with cars, read more books, and love "helping" me to make bread or cook dinner. Soon, we discover that Jose is really good at putting together puzzles, and as we give him progressively harder ones to try, he completes each one like a champ, getting only a little frustrated when Chelsea comes along and messes up his progress. His fears seem to be receding into the background, emerging only at night, when he still wakes up with night terrors. As we rush to his bedside, we find his PJs in a heap on the floor and a frightened little boy crying in his sleep. He doesn't like to be put to bed in the room he shares with Chelsea; he wants to be in with us. In fact, he never wants us to be out of his sight.

Not wanting to further traumatize him, we keep him by our side every minute of every day, but his agitation when we walk out of the room—even to go to the bathroom—becomes worse, not better, with the passing days. None of what I learned while getting a college degree in early childhood development seems to be helping, so we decide to discuss this at our next appointment with Dr. Kenney, hoping he will have some suggestions.

"He needs to see you leave him and then come back," Dr. Kenney tells me. "The more time goes by when you never leave his side, the greater his fear that one day you will leave and never come back. We don't know the circumstances of his abandonment in El Salvador, but clearly, his experience was of a mommy and daddy that were there one day, and then one day they were gone, never to come back. Although it will be hard to leave him with a babysitter, you need to do it several times, each time coming back so that he will begin to understand that he is safe with you and can trust you."

Back at Logos after the appointment, I explain Dr Kenney's advice to Hector. While we agree that it makes sense, we cannot imagine leaving him with a sitter and listening to him shriek and cry as we walk away. We decide that Ken and Val will be the best babysitters for our first trial run at leaving him. We call and arrange for them to come spend a few hours at our apartment with Jose and Chelsea the next evening.

Jose and Chelsea chortle with delight when Ken and Val arrive, and soon they are sitting on the floor working on puzzles together. We quietly get ready to leave, and just as we ease the door open to step out, Jose starts to whimper. By the time we reach the porch, we hear him sobbing loudly.

"I can't do this," I say to Hector as we step out into the yard, the cries from our second-floor apartment reaching a fevered pitch. We had plans to go to a movie, but we cannot tear ourselves away from the yard. We take a short walk about the block and decide it's time to go back inside. The sobs have diminished a little, but the fear in his eyes is still blazing. We feel like the worst parents ever to put him through this torture.

"It really wasn't so bad," Val says. "Let's try again in a few days." We are not convinced. Is this really the right thing to do? Will he forgive us? Will he trust us? This is just the first of the many times we will question our parenting abilities.

Several mornings later, I go into the kid's room to get them ready for the day and am alarmed to find Chelsea is not in her crib. "Hec!" I shriek. "Come here! How did this happen?" Chelsea and Jose are quietly playing with blocks in the corner of the room. "Did Jose somehow get Chelsea out of her crib?"

"She must have climbed out."

"No, she is way too young to be able to climb out of her crib!"

"I am pretty sure Jose can't lift her. She must have climbed out."

Three days in a row, she's out of her crib each morning. We tell our friends about this at church on Sunday and they laugh, telling us that it's time to take down the crib and put the kids in beds. Kirk offers to make a set of bunk beds for us, and we agree; it's time to redecorate the room, getting rid of the "nursery" feel and making it into a toddler room. Maybe with a theme of trains or horses.

The day arrives for Kirk to bring the bunk beds over and the kids are jumping, clapping, and dancing with excitement. As he and Hector assemble the bunk beds, Kirk asks, "What shall we do with the cribs?" We quickly take one apart and stack the pieces on the porch, but as Hector begins to tackle the second crib, I stop him. I'm not sure why, but for some inexplicable reason, I cannot bear for him to take the second crib apart. "Let's just keep it in the room a little longer," I suggest. "Just until we know that Chelsea will adjust OK to the new bed."

Later that evening, the fresh paint still drying on the bunk beds, we decide to have a slumber party and we pile both kids into bed with us, making a tent with the blankets, sharing snacks, reading stories, and exchanging tickles until the giggles lead to singing, and eventually, everyone except for me is asleep.

The kids are going to adjust just fine, I realize. So what is my problem; why can't I let go of the crib? Ending my day with a prayer, I thank God for our good friends, Ken and Val, and Betsy and Kirk, and for the fun day we had. I end by asking, "Lord, what do you have in store for us next? And what does the crib have to do with it?"

3

Isaac

"There it is! Turn left—see the sign?" Throughout the summer, we took many long bike rides on Sunday afternoons, with Jose on the back of Hector's bike and Chelsea on mine. But now that fall has arrived, and we have a vehicle again, we've started taking Sunday afternoon car rides instead. The rolling hill towns around Northampton are beautiful this time of year, and although we love our little Bright Street apartment just blocks from the bookstore, we keep dreaming of owning a home of our own, perhaps out in one of these towns like Sunderland, Deerfield, or Conway.

There are two particular types of homes that we dream about—the first are old barns converted into family homes, and the second are stone houses. Every week when we take a drive we aim for a barn or old stone house for sale so we can drive by, look, and dream. As we turn toward a barn that we saw advertised, another sign catches my eye: "4-acre wooded lots, $500 per acre."

"Let's check it out!" We follow the sign and wind our way up the steep, wooded hillside, finally reaching a spot where it is safe to park. Unbuckling the kids, we begin to walk around the lot, drinking in the fresh air and beautiful setting.

The lot is littered with stones and rocks of all sizes and shapes. Jose and Chelsea begin picking up small stones and tossing them down the hill, watching them roll faster and faster, snagging twigs, leaves, and small wildflowers along the way. But I can see that Hector's eyes are on the larger stones. "We could build a house here," he says. "I could build it. A stone house. After all the stone walls I built for your dad and the neighbors, I'm sure I could do it."

"And we can afford it. Just think: we could have four acres for only two thousand dollars! We can come here every weekend and start clearing the area—collecting the stones for the house and moving others out of the way!"

We're so excited we can hardly contain ourselves—the dream of our own home seems within reach for the first time. Jose and Chelsea are having great fun; they've caught our enthusiasm. We walk the property from corner to corner and hardly notice the time until we realize the sun is dropping in the sky.

Taking down the phone number for the Realtor, we strap the kids back into their car seats and begin driving toward Dan and Pam's house for church, hoping we won't be late. We can't stop talking about "our land," and by the time we pull into their driveway 20 minutes later, we have nearly built our house—in our minds at least!

Monday morning, I call Vermont's Garden Way publishers and order a book, *Build Your Own Stone House*, and we close the store for an hour at lunchtime to walk up to the bank and apply for a $2,000 loan. The ball is rolling!

On the fourth Sunday visiting "our land," we bring a picnic lunch. We have such a wonderful afternoon together, reading, sketching ideas, moving stones around, playing ball with the kids, and even napping, that we hate to leave, driving back to town for church. It feels so perfect that I shock myself when the words tumble out: "We can't do this."

We are in the car, driving back to town, and I say it again: "We can't do this."

"I know," Hector says. "I don't know what came over us, but who are we trying to kid? We have two babies and a bookstore. How the heck am I going to build a house?"

While having dinner with our friends at church, I tell Pam and Betsy that we've decided not to buy the land. "Oh, I'm so relieved," Pam says. "Dan and I have been praying about it ever since you came up with that crazy idea, and we just knew it wouldn't work, but you were so excited, we didn't know how to tell you not to do it."

Well, it wouldn't be the first or last time we have been called crazy—the challenge is always to discern which crazy idea is really God-sent, and which is just truly crazy.

Well, it wouldn't be the first or last time we have been called crazy—the challenge is always to discern which crazy idea is really God-sent, and which is just truly crazy. This one was in the latter group, and I'm thankful we figured that out before we got too much further down the wrong road.

Ginger, a regular customer we haven't seen in a few weeks, bursts through the door and hurries toward the jewelry counter. "She's here!" she exclaims, unbundling her new baby, just two weeks old, and plunking her one-year-old Ruby down on the floor next to Chelsea. The store has been quiet this morning, so Hector and I both have time to ooh and ahh over the new baby, a robust little girl named Ivy. Soon Ginger is pulling out photos from her home-birth experience and spreading them out across the jewelry counter. I've seen plenty of birth photos before, especially during our Lamaze classes, but for some reason, I suddenly start to feel a little queasy. I'm so thankful when Carole comes in to help me plan for the talk I'll be giving for the Smith College Inter-Varsity group next week. We walk toward the back room where Jose is playing with a small train set and chat about the theme for my talk. The queasiness doesn't leave me, and soon I have to excuse myself, heading for the bathroom.

"That was odd," I say later to Hector. "Pictures have never made me feel nauseous before."

"Well, thanks for leaving me there alone to go through those pictures. It was a little awkward," he says, recounting how he tried to be tactful while not actually looking at the photos. "I just can't look at another woman's . . . well, you know . . . even though it is all natural and everything—that was really too much for me!"

We are still laughing as I poke my head into the kids' room and make sure they have fallen asleep. Once again, they are both snuggled together on the bottom bunk bed surrounded by a crowd of farm animals, toy cars, and books. I love watching them sleep, with their tussled hair and footie pajamas. You would never know that one's adopted and the other is not. How did I get to be so blessed?

"Sick again?" Hector asks as I come up from the bathroom, a little green around the gills. This is the third morning in a row that I can't make it past 10 AM without throwing up. "I don't think it's still Ginger's pictures that are making you sick," he jokes. "I think it's time to make that doctor's appointment."

I hate to admit that he is right, but I know he is, so I head for the phone. "They can get me in next Tuesday. That's the same day I speak at Smith. You'll have the kids and the store all to yourself that day."

"I'll manage, but I hope Carole can drive you, so the van will be here for me to take the kids home while you're at Smith." Our family vehicle is a very old, white Volkswagen van with stickers from nearly all 50 states plastered all over it. We jokingly call it our "hippie van" and hope we can keep it long enough to visit all those states ourselves! We dream of taking the kids on a cross-country road trip someday when we can afford to hire an assistant to run the bookstore. For now, our longest road trips are to Vermont and back, so Jose and Chelsea can spend time with their grandparents, aunts, and uncles. We are so thankful for the van, sold to us for a dollar by a couple of our favorite customers, the Lundgrens. They have also promised to teach Jose to play the violin, because he loves having dinner at their house and listening to Don and his kids play their instruments and tell stories about their many mission trips around the world.

Late Tuesday afternoon, Carole picks me up from my doctor's appointment to take me to the Smith Inter-Varsity meeting. We plan to stop for a quick dinner. As soon as I get into her car, I burst into tears.

"What's wrong?" she asks.

"I'm pregnant!" I blurt out, crying even louder. I can't believe I'm saying this to her. I haven't even told Hector yet.

Carole looks perplexed. She knows how much we love children, and she has heard many times about our "life plan" to have two children and adopt two. She has no idea why I'm so distraught.

"I'm not ready. I can't do this," I tell her. "I just know there's no way I can handle three children. God's design for everything is in twos," I babble. "Adam and Eve. Noah's Ark. Naomi and

Ruth. Everything is two by two for a reason. We each have two hands, two eyes, two ears. Seriously, Carole, everything is in twos. How on earth does God expect me to manage three children? I don't want three children. I don't want four children. Forget our plans. I am happy with two children. Life is good right now. I don't want another baby. Not now. Not ever. I just can't do it. I can't. I'll lose my mind!"

Carole, still a college student herself, has no idea what to say or do. She roots around in her purse and pulls out a Hershey bar, handing it to me. "It'll work out," she says. "God has a purpose in this."

With tears still staining my face, I tear open the Hershey bar and burst out laughing. "You've learned a lot from Anne and Sandra," I say to Carole, thinking of our friend Anne, who introduced the Sandra Boynton cards to our store—and remembering her favorite card: "Things Are Getting Worse" it says on the front, and, inside, "Send Chocolate."

Later, in bed, Hector asks me how the Smith talk went, and I decide it is time to tell him our news. "Remember the day you and Kirk put up the bunk beds?" I begin. "And how I refused to let you take down the crib? Well, now I know why."

"Good morning, good morning, good morning! It's time to rise and shine!" I cheerfully sing to Jose and Chelsea, opening the blinds in their room. Turning to Jose, I say, "It's a special day today—we get to go see the judge and he will tell us we can be your mama and papa forever and ever and ever!"

We're a little nervous, sitting in the waiting room with Mary Diamond, hoping nothing will go wrong today. "Do you think he's going to wonder whey we're changing Jose's name from one that sounds more Americanized to one that sounds more Spanish?" I wonder aloud. We have heard that it is more common for families adopting children from other countries to change their names to simple, easy-to-pronounce names that don't sound "foreign," but we want Jose to have the name that belongs to him—it's the only thing left from his country that he still has to keep.

"No, the name issue will be fine. I can't imagine him questioning that. I'm a little more concerned about how he will address the changing of the birth date. I've never actually tried to do that before," Mary reminds us. "But all the papers are in order, so it should go smoothly."

Enjoying ice cream sundaes a little later, I marvel at how smoothly and quickly it did go. It seemed almost anticlimactic. I'm not sure what I expected—maybe just a little more pomp and circumstance! The judge didn't even wear a robe!

In the months since Jose's adoption, we have come to know several local adoptive families, all part of a group called The Open Door Society, and we're looking forward to attending our very first adoption conference. Marylou, an adoptive mom, stops by Logos and brings us the registration brochure and a few extras we can hand out to customers who might be interested.

"I can't wait to go to the conference, Marylou! We're so happy with our adoption, it will be such fun to meet other families who have adopted kids. Just look at that little boy—he has already given us so much joy." I point to Jose and Chelsea sitting on the floor, reading books together.

"Never forget, Sue, your joy as a mom to Jose is built on the ashes of another mother's grief."

Marylou looks at Jose, and then looks at me, smiling. Her face becomes more intense as the next words out of her mouth burn into my heart, where they have stayed to this day: "Never forget, Sue, your joy as a mom to Jose is built on the ashes of another mother's grief."

I've never really thought about it this way before. Oh, I have thought about Jose's birth mother and even thanked her in my heart for the gift of her son, but I've never let my mind or emotions go to that place where I could imagine her grief at losing her precious little boy. This is another "ponder in my heart" moment of mothering, and it forever changes my thinking about adoption. My mind goes immediately to Isaiah 61, and I begin to pray for his birth mother: "Lord, please give her beauty and comfort from the ashes of her grief and please show us how to honor his birth mother and all birth mothers as we continue on this adoption journey."

With the conference brochures on our counter, more customers strike up conversations about adoption, and we are surprised to learn how many have some kind of adoption connection in their own family. I don't recognize the woman reading over the brochure right now, but I am guessing she is about to tell me her own adoption story.

"Hi," she says. "I am with the *Daily Hampshire Gazette* and National Adoption Day is coming up. We'd like to do an interview with you and your husband to run on that day. Would you be willing to do that?" She slides me her business card.

"Oh no," I groan, reading the paper. "Hec, our article is in the paper today. You've gotta read it."

"The picture looks great," he says. "Why are you groaning?" As he reads, he understands. "Ooops. I guess we should have known if we told that reporter we were expecting, she would put it in the article. Guess we better tell your parents."

Now the whole world knows about our plan to have two and adopt two. Little did we know how many times that article would give us a laugh in the years ahead.

We step back into our apartment and notice the answering machine light is blinking. The kids' cheeks are bright red after our outing with the sled, Jose's first time seeing snow. Hector begins to unbundle the snowsuits and I listen to the message.

"It's Mary Diamond. She has two questions. She wants to know if we want to keep our India adoption application active, and she also wants to know if we're willing to be emergency foster parents to a teenage girl. We need to call her back."

"Go ahead, call her," Hector replies. "Say yes to both."

We know nothing about teenagers or foster care, and Fiona spends only a few nights with us before the agency settled her into her own rented room; they call it "transitional housing." She seems so alone in the world; it is hard to imagine a 17-year-old girl with no parents to guide her. I know I fought a lot with my parents when I was 17, but underneath it all, I was still thankful to have them. And now, as I stumble along trying my best to be a good parent, what would I do if I didn't have my own mom, and Hector's mom, to call for advice? "I think we need to learn more about foster care," I say to Hector. "It's bad enough when we see older guys like Gene with no home, but the idea of a teenager on her own is really upsetting."

"We'll need a bigger place to live," he points out. "Our couch was fine for an emergency, but I think we'd need an extra bedroom if we were going to do this again."

"I know, you're right, and we'll be needing a bigger place after the baby is born anyway, so we should probably start looking."

The baby's June 25 due date has come and gone and the sweltering heat in our second-floor apartment is nearly unbearable. Hector has a men's Bible study at Dan and Pam's house, and I can't imagine being cooped up here with Jose and Chelsea so I ask him to drop me off at Look Park so we can play and breathe a bit.

"Mama, mama, take us to the swings!" Jose pleads gleefully as he and Chelsea run ahead of me, away from the duck pond. Our bag of bread crusts is empty, the ducks' bellies are full, it's time for a new activity.

"Stop. Wait," I call out. I can hardly breathe as a searing pain tears me from the inside. Right there, my water breaks. Oh Dear God—what can I do? This part of the park is virtually empty, my two toddlers are obliviously romping and playing a few hundred yards ahead of me, Hector isn't due back to pick me up for more than an hour, and the park's only pay phone is impossibly far away in a different direction.

Isaac Stephen is perfectly round and bald. As uncertain as I was in the beginning of this pregnancy, I am instantly in love again.

I feel as though I have climbed a mountain by the time I collect Jose and Chelsea, and we dial Pam's number from the pay phone. "Hurry," I say, anxiously. "I don't want to have the baby in the park!"

Two weeks before our third anniversary, we are parents for the third time. Isaac Stephen is perfectly round and bald. As uncertain as I was in the beginning of this pregnancy, I am instantly in love again as I drink in the sweet smell and nuzzle the softness of the top of his head. I can't wait for Jose and Chelsea to meet their new brother.

July Fourth: we are on our way home from the hospital, and the air is as thick as pea soup. How will we cope with this heat? "Let's go to the movies!" I suggest, and Hector looks at me as if I have lost my mind. "Air conditioning" is all I can say.

"How about a ride on the alligator today?" I ask Jose and Chelsea, and they begin cheering. Throughout July, one-dollar movie matinees and the "alligator"—escalator—at the mall have become our favorite places of refuge from the heat. After Isaac was born, we quickly realized that we could not bring all three children into the bookstore every day, so Hector and I have been taking turns staying home with the kids or going in to operate the bookstore.

Before we can head out to the mall, Isaac is hungry again. This little bugger wants to eat every two hours—and he gets so intense. "Look at your face all red," I say to him, trying to calm him down while I get positioned to nurse him. "You're acting like you've never eaten before and might never eat again." I chuckle.

He calms down and latches on for his feeding and I close my eyes for a moment. *I know, I know, Lord, you're right,* I think to myself. The picture of Isaac getting so worked up before I feed him makes me think of how I am before God. Screaming, crying, acting frantic, and praying desperately when faced with challenges, as if God has never fed me before nor will again. *I get the picture, Lord, I need to be more trusting and patient. You will always be there for me, just like I'll always be there to feed this hungry munchkin.*

I can hear Chelsea and Jose chattering even before the alarm goes off. I stumble out of bed to quiet them down before they wake the baby. He's only been asleep for an hour. Hector has to leave for work soon. Isaac has had his days and nights mixed up for five weeks now. It's not just that he doesn't sleep *through* the night, he doesn't sleep during the night *at all.* We've tried everything we can think of, from late night baths to lots of stimulation during the day; nothing is working. I am completely stumped and more than a little bit terrified, uncertain how much longer I will be able to cope.

"This is it!" Our search for a bigger apartment has led us to start taking Sunday afternoon car rides again and we have finally found a big old house in Conway that feels perfect. It's a bit of a "fixer-upper," so we can afford the rent and it has plenty of room not only for the kids we have now but for moving ahead with our plans to become foster parents. And our child from India, whenever that door opens for us. We've added a puppy, Homer, to the family, and the landlord is OK with that too. Amazingly, our Mill River House Church friends agree to help us move—again. This is the fourth move in less than four years. We are blessed to have such great friends!

I'm still peeling old wallpaper in the room we intend to make into a playroom when, at midnight, Hector finally swings the van into the driveway. Since I haven't been working at the store as much, we've had to hire our friend Bob to manage it. Things are really tight financially, and Hector is moonlighting as a short-order cook at the famous "Miss Flo's Diner" at night and working a shift on the line at a factory early in the morning.

"I saved you some dinner," I say, offering him a bowl of lentil and carrot soup. I sit with him and we begin to talk about our day. I took the kids to the library for story hour, a long walk up a steep hill with two toddlers and a baby carriage. It's my weekly workout. On the way back I stopped in to see Syd, the postman, and pick up our mail. "We got the official foster care license today, and a letter from Downey Side—that agency Mary Diamond told us about. They're having a movie night next week and they want us to come so we can meet some of the kids and learn more about their program. I'm excited that this is moving forward. We'll have to hurry and get that extra bedroom ready." We talk a bit more about our foster care plans and then Hector tells me about his day, then asks about the morning.

"I have to be in Holyoke by 8, so I need to leave pretty early— I'd say no later than 7." To supplement our income, I've taken a job on Saturdays, teaching in a special program for the children of migrant workers. It also helps me to keep up my teaching certification.

Tessa, our 15-year-old first "non-emergency" foster daughter, my friend Jayne, and I are carrying boxes of clothes down from the attic. We're looking at my high school prom dresses, hoping something will be a perfect fit for Tessa to wear next weekend when we go to Vermont for my sister's wedding. Tessa has been in our home for a month and our hearts break as we imagine all the pain she's been through in her short life, but today she is excited about going to her first wedding. She holds up one of my favorites, a peach and cream colored Laura Ashley, and starts dancing around the room. Yes—this one looks like it will work!

"It's pretty exciting," Jayne says to me, "and scary at the same time." After Tessa leaves the room, we're drinking lemonade and talking about adoption. Jayne and Rob are the first of our close circle of friends to decide to adopt. I'm so excited that we will have this bond to share. They are just completing the process and are expecting a baby to be in their home soon. "We're not using our cradle right now, and it'll be awhile before our baby from India comes, so I think you should use it," I say, giving Jayne a quick hug.

"I don't really think you are going to stop with just adopting two," Jayne says to me. "I just have a feeling God has a bigger plan for you and Hector. Have you heard about this family called the DeBolts? They made a movie about them—they have 19 kids, I think. You and Hector really remind me of them."

I laugh along with Jayne, when I really want to say, "Get behind me Satan! Don't you know it's only been a few months since I overcame my fear of having three kids! How dare you even mention something as crazy as 19 kids!" Yet something stirs in my heart, and I begin to wonder if God is using Jayne to tell me something about our road ahead.

Sunday at church, we once again ask for prayers for the bookstore. Sales are not good, and we are struggling to keep it afloat. Meanwhile, we're feeling more and more pulled in the direction of foster care and not sure we can juggle everything anymore. Kirk and Dan approach us and ask if they can come over Monday night. "We have some ideas about the bookstore," they say. The same day, we buy the Boston Globe and start looking at help wanted ads, thinking maybe we can combine our love for children with a career option if we could get hired as a couple to run a group home.

Our van is packed; we're ready to go. Three kids, a dog, and all our earthly possessions are in the van as we roll on to Interstate 91 toward Vermont. I haven't said a word for over 20 miles.

Hector reaches for my hand. "You know it's the right decision," he says. "We have prayed about it, listened to the advice of people we trust, and Mark and Betty were crazy enough to offer us this job. All the pieces are coming together. God has directed us to this road; everything will work out."

"I know," I say. "I'm just so sad that Tessa had to move again, and I know the bookstore is going to thrive again, but right now, knowing that Bob doesn't have a job—it's all just pretty overwhelming."

For weeks since that meeting with Dan and Kirk, we've agonized over the decisions God laid before us. Hector had many sleepless nights, torn apart about the way some of these decisions would hurt people we care about, and yet now, I can see he's at peace. I need to trust him, and God, and find that peace myself.

Have we made the right decisions? Uprooting our little family, selling the bookstore, moving away from our church home? My head is spinning. I turn to look at the kids in the back: Jose is looking at a book while Chelsea and Isaac are both asleep, so I close my eyes too.

4

Raj

"Those two weeks of training sure flew by," I say to Hector as we pull out of my parents' driveway and head for our first official day on the job living and working in a group home as "teaching parents" to six teenage boys. "Do you feel like we're ready?"

"I was born ready!" Hector replies, using one of his well-worn lines.

Twenty minutes later we're in for a surprise as we pull into the driveway of the group home. All six of the boys are on the roof. "I don't think there was anything in the manual about how to handle this situation," I joke. "Do we really have to start right out by giving them all negative points?"

"Sue's home. Come help with the groceries!" I hear Hector call out to the boys, and Tom and Ned soon appear next to the Suburban. They begin bringing in bags of food as I unbuckle Isaac from his car seat. In the kitchen, we quickly unpack the bags and repack them for the week—one bag per day of breakfast, lunch, and snack items marked "Monday," "Tuesday," and so on.

As soon as the bags are lined up in the pantry, the boys return to their activities and I head out to check on the progress of the swing set and jungle gym Hector is building in the backyard. Jose and Chelsea are "helping" and Homer is running around in the woods chasing squirrels.

"It'll be finished just in time for Isaac's birthday party," Hector announces. We're so pleased that we have found a good church and made new friends, many with young children the same ages as Jose, Chelsea, and Isaac. Next week, many of them will come to the group home for the first time as we host Isaac's party. Just then I notice that Jose is no longer in sight.

"Jose!" I yell. "Where did you go?"

"He's probably in the driveway with the older boys—he likes to hang out with them when they shoot hoops."

"I'll go check."

"I found Jose," I say when I return with him to the backyard ten minutes later. "You'll never guess where."

"He wasn't with the boys?"

"Oh, you could say he was with them," I reply. "He was inside a trash can, with the lid on top, and Ricky was sitting on the lid."

"Oh no! Is he OK?"

"He was a bit scared, but he's OK now. No one would fess up, so they all had to get docked points. I decided to take 60,000 points from each of them—what do you think?"

"Sounds about right." We are not sure we will ever get the hang of this point system. To tell the truth, our focus is more on building relationships with the boys. We really want everyone to feel like this is their home, and family. But with our first evaluation coming up in just under a month, we have to sharpen our use of the Teaching Family Model, including the point system.

These boys sure do eat a lot! I think to myself as I pull into the driveway, shaking my head. "I can hardly believe it's already grocery day again."

I can see that Hector is by the door, but instead of calling everyone to come help, he's just standing there. As I get closer, I realize he's smoking a cigar—how odd! He runs to get the door for me and says, "Congratulations, you have a new son!"

"What?!" I am guessing that we have received a new teen for the group home to take the place of Mike, who recently moved back home with his parents. But why the cigar?

"I got a phone call from India while you were gone!" he explains. "They are starting up their adoption program again and they selected us for a baby boy—a very tiny baby boy. He's premature and only weighs 3 pounds!"

For the next hour we forget about the groceries as I excitedly pepper Hector with questions about our new baby. I learn he may have cerebral palsy and that his "crib name" (the name given to him by the nuns caring for him in the orphanage) is Isaac. Of all the names they could have picked, they chose Isaac! But when we completed our paperwork for the Indian adoption, we have selected Raj Ashish—which means "the king's blessing"—as the name for our baby if he were a boy, and so as soon as we accept this referral, they'll begin calling him Raj.

"Oh no!" I groan, hanging up the phone. I've just called

Mary Diamond to tell her the good news that we're finally going to be able to get our child from India. She's happy for us, but breaks the bad news to us: she can't help us with the final stages of the adoption since we have moved out of state. It had never occurred to us that our move to Vermont would make our Massachusetts home study useless.

"We have to find a Vermont agency to work with us and get a whole new home study done," I tell Hector when he comes in after driving the older boys to school. "Fingerprints, physicals, the whole works—we have to do it all over again. And that special package of immigration papers that took forever . . . we have to do that over again too."

"Will India wait while we do all that? I am already attached to Raj. I don't want to lose him just because of paperwork delays," Hector says.

Mary has referred us to an agency in Vermont that handles inter-country adoptions and she has promised to call and smooth the way for us. In spite of her efforts, we know that the new process could take months, so all we can do is hope and pray that the orphanage in India will be understanding while we work our way through the hoops and hurdles.

I can see that Hector is beginning to steam, although trying to stay calm. Our new social worker has just told us that she is not sure she'll approve our new home study because of Raj's cerebral palsy. She's not sure we know what we are getting into.

"Did you read the notes from Mary Diamond?" Hector asks. "The part where we said we wanted the child 'most in need of a home and least likely to get one?'" We knew that meant we could get a child with a disability. We understand that and we may not know everything we need to know, but we'll learn as we go along."

"I believe you are dedicated and idealistic. I'm just not sure you're realistic," the woman says. "I want you to go to make an appointment with the Vermont Special Children's Early Intervention specialist"—she hands us a business card—"and learn more about the realities of raising a child with cerebral palsy. After you do that, come back and we'll talk about it and then we can decide if you should proceed with this adoption."

This is just another delay, on top of the FBI losing our fingerprint cards and the immigration office in St. Albans requiring us to come up for an "in person" interview before they approve the "I-600" form which will allow us to bring Raj into the U.S. Dropping into bed, exhausted, at the end of the day, we pray, "Lord, we believe you have chosen us to be Raj's parents. Please, help us bust through all these hurdles so we can bring him home."

With all the paperwork submitted and the last of the hurdles seemingly cleared, all we can do now is wait for the news from India that Raj's flight is scheduled. Meanwhile, the day-to-day routines with three small children and six teenagers, as well as preparing for our second evaluation as teaching parents, is keeping us plenty busy.

"Seriously? He's been adjudicated as a delinquent for stealing a package of bologna from the Grand Union?" Hector and I look at each other in disbelief as we sit across the living room from Betty. She's going over the paperwork with us on the newest teen scheduled to move into the group home in a few days. "There has to be more to his story than that," I say, just as the phone rings. I excuse myself for the phone.

When I return to the living room, Betty is gone. "It's all set. We will be getting Porter on Monday and we have an appointment for his physical on Tuesday, so hopefully it won't be too many days before we can get him into school," Hector says. There's always a lot of jockeying for position every time a new boy joins the home. We are hopeful that it will go smoothly this time. "So, who was on the phone?"

"It was the orphanage in India. They have the escort and the date for sending Raj here. He will be coming to Logan Airport in Boston in two weeks! Finally! They are so glad he is ready to travel; they said he is too big to stay with them any longer. He weighs 7 pounds now and they think he is sooooo big." I laugh. I'm really happy that he has gained weight, more than doubling his 3-pound birth weight in the four months he has been in the orphanage. I can hardly wait to hold him in my arms!

It took longer than expected to get Porter into school, due to a glitch with his immunizations, but one day before our trip to Boston, we're able to get him enrolled. Sharon, our substitute, has arrived, and I'm going over each of the boys' point status and chore assignments when Hector returns from giving Ned a driving lesson in our family Subaru.

Jose runs in ahead of Hector, yelling, "Ned hit a tree! Ned hit a tree!"

"What?"

"No big deal. Everyone is OK and only a small dent on the right fender," Hector says. Ned looks a little shaky. "Good thing both Chelsea and Jose were buckled into their seats!" he laughs.

"Cover your ears!" I say to Sharon as I scoop up Chelsea and check to be sure she is really all right. I don't want Sharon to hear that we have been giving the boys unauthorized driving lessons in our family car. But I'm quite sure she won't be reporting us. She shares our goal of trying to do as much as we can to make life as "normal" for these teen boys as possible—even though they live in a group home and function on a point system.

I'm glad my dad has volunteered to drive us. I'm strangely nervous as we await the arrival of our newest son. The airport is bustling with activity and feels much different than that eerily quiet night with only the cleaning lady as a witness when Jose joined our family two years earlier. Jose and Isaac are enjoying some time with my mom, "Mamie," and Chelsea has come to Boston with us. Suddenly, there is some commotion, and people begin streaming out of the door by the gate. After what seems like an eternity, two women emerge, each carrying a basket.

"This can't be good," I think, knowing there are four families here waiting for babies from India. We've had time to get acquainted while waiting . . . and waiting . . . and waiting here at the airport. The flight has been delayed twice, and now it appears that only two escorts with babies are deplaning.

The escorts walk over to where we are waiting with the other families and begin to call out names. As they get closer, we can see that there are two babies bundled securely in each basket. "Will you look at that?" my dad exclaims. "Two babies in a basket barely bigger than a shoebox." We all chuckle softly, having no idea how many times we'll hear that story repeated in the years ahead!

I take this tiny little person into my arms, cradling his face in my hands, and marveling over his long, thin fingers. Once again, I'm instantly smitten, and I feel like I'm in my own little world. All the noise and activity of the airport fades away as I look into the beautiful brown eyes of my new son. "Welcome home," I whisper, brushing his forehead with a gentle kiss and uttering a silent prayer that God will grant me the wisdom and grace to be a "good enough" mother to this precious little boy. "I can only imagine how scary this is for you," I say to him. "Your whole world has turned upside down, but I hope you'll soon trust how much we love you and how long we have hoped and prayed and waited for you to be our son."

Remembering the words of my friend Marylou about the grief of birth mothers, I also raise a silent prayer for his birth mother, that she will receive comfort and peace and know that her son is being treasured and cared for.

My reverie is broken as my dad urges me to look up and

smile for a picture. He's been snapping away for several minutes, as well as chatting up the escorts and learning about their travels escorting babies from India and Korea to their new families in America. As a result of his friendliness, our escort has offered to give Chelsea the special basket the babies came in to use for her dolls.

Hector is dozing off in an armchair at Aunt Ruth's house minutes after finishing Thanksgiving dinner. "Didn't take him long!" Uncle Bill laughs. "I'm usually the first one to fall asleep!"

"Well, every night this week he's been up with the new baby," I explain. "He couldn't help with the nighttime feedings for Chelsea or Isaac since I was nursing, so he has decided that the middle of the night is his special bonding time with Raj. He gets up to feed him a bottle and together they watch reruns of *Star Trek*. I'm sure he needs a little extra sleep."

I am walking into the house with the mail in my hands. Chip is walking around the living room holding Isaac in his arms and they are sharing the headphones, be-bopping and listening to Aerosmith's "Come Together." The boys in the group home are all attached to our kids, and even though they are sometimes a little rough with Jose, I think it's good for them to have small children to relate to. Chip, in particular, is totally attached to Isaac; this scene is not at all unusual.

Betty and Mark, our bosses, have wondered if we could really manage it all—they say that no couple with four small children has ever been certified as Teaching Parents within the entire Teaching Family system. Now I'm holding the letter in my hands that will tell me if we made it or not.

"I feel like it's college acceptance time all over again," I joke to Hector, handing him the envelope. "Go ahead—you open it."

"Well, Mrs. Badeau, we have passed with flying colors!" he exclaims and begins to twirl me around the living room. We grab Chip and Isaac and urge them to dance with us. Ned walks in to see what the commotion is and looks amused. Porter and Ricky come in from the kitchen and start laughing. It takes a moment for me to realize that Raj is crying; he must have just awakened from his nap.

The new *OURS* magazine for adoptive families is sitting on the nightstand next to my bed; it's been there for three days and I haven't had a minute to read it. Finally, everyone is asleep and I still have enough energy to read for a few minutes, so I pick it up. After reading a few of the stories, my eyes fix upon the advertisement for a conference for adoptive families coming up in the summer. Called NACAC, this conference will be held in Chicago, and something inside is telling me we have to attend.

I've been doing the calculations, and I'm ready to sell it to Hector. "I think we can afford the hotel rooms and the conference registration as long as we drive and bring a cooler with our own food."

"I agree. Let's do it!" he says immediately. Well, that didn't take much. I love it when we are on the same page. "We'll drive through Canada," he says. "We can take the kids to Niagara Falls and have some fun along the way." This will be our first road trip with the kids, and we can hardly wait to get started.

"I was also thinking we could contact that family we read about in the church magazine. The family with 12 adopted kids? Remember? They live just outside of Chicago, so maybe we can visit them too. Who knows, maybe while we are at NACAC we will meet that DeBolt family that Jayne compared us to when we first adopted Jose!"

With more than 15 hours of driving ahead of us and four sleepy kids drifting off to dreamland in the back seat, we have plenty of time to talk and recap all of the exciting moments of the past week. The conference was so eye-opening; there is so much more to learn about adoption. Hearing the DeBolts speak was a highlight, but an even bigger one was driving up to Janesville, Wisconsin and spending an evening with a family who adopted 12 children, including two sets of siblings. The warmth and love and sense of security in that home was palpable. We were spellbound most of the evening, and something stirred in us as we left their home. "I think God is using this group home experience to prepare us for something else," I say to Hector. "Something involving sibling adoptions. I just can't get that out of my mind."

"I know. I feel like this job is a stepping-stone on the way to our next adventure. There are so many kids out there that need families . . . . we've got to do more to make a difference," he says. "But for now, can you check the map and let me know how much farther before we can hit a rest area? All this coffee is starting to get to me."

"Well, one thing I am sure of: children need families that are theirs forever, not group homes or institutions. No matter how hard we try to make a normal life for the boys at the group home, it's not normal and we'll never really be their parents." While saying all this, I'm wrestling with a map. Then, I go on. "I'm really glad you agreed that we can drive all night so we can make it back to Montpelier for that meeting of the new group forming to advocate for children. I really feel a need to be a part of it from the beginning. Who knows where this will lead?"

As I wait my turn to testify before the Vermont legislature, an advocate for the state agricultural budget speaks before me.

He has several poster boards with fancy charts and graphs providing the legislators with all kinds of data as he urges them to increase the budget for critical needs within the farming community.

I haven't brought any charts or graphs. I'm prepared to share stories about the boys we have been working with in the group home, and stories from the other group homes around the state, as I advocate for funding for children's services. Suddenly, I get an idea and begin scribbling some notes on the back of the agenda.

"Thank you for this opportunity to testify on behalf of children who frequently have no voice in places like this," I begin, my voice quavering a little from nerves. Ever since I helped create the newly formed Vermont Children's Forum, I've had more and more opportunities to speak up on behalf of children in our state, but this is the first time at the legislature. "As I was listening to the testimony just before me, about the agricultural budget, I started thinking about the boys who've lived in the group home where I work with my husband."

I am warming up to my subject and the nervousness is gone. "In just under two years, 23 teenage boys have lived there. They are all part of the Vermont foster care system and many have also been in trouble with the law. These 23 boys have spent an average of eleven years in foster care. While some have just entered the system, others have spent their entire lives in foster care! And they've moved an average of nine times each. Nine moves. Think about that in contrast to what we just heard about our state's farming industry.

"Can you imagine any farmer taking a healthy plant and transplanting it nine times and expecting it to live? . . . Even if you transplanted it into the best soil and provided the best care and sun and water for it, we all know that nine moves would probably kill the plant. And if it did survive, it probably would not thrive or produce much fruit."

I pause for a moment to see if they are with me, and then finish my testimony. "Yet this is what we are doing to Vermont's must vulnerable children. We take them from their homes. We move them seven, eight, nine times. We don't always give them the best environments or care. And somehow we expect them not only to survive but to thrive.

"This makes no sense. I urge you to appropriate sufficient funds to the budget so that we can stop this cycle of moving children again and again and again in foster care. Every child needs a home where they can take root and become stable. The budget needs to be adequate to support that goal."

I can't stay to talk with the advocates or reporters who are milling around. I have to hurry to my car and dash off to pick Jose up from kindergarten at the Community Christian School in Montpelier. I can't wait to get back to the group home and tell Hector about this. I have a feeling this is a day I will remember for a long time. A million ideas are buzzing like flies in my head. I know this is the beginning of something new in our lives. I can't quite see around the bend, but I'm dying to know where this road is going to take us.

5

Joelle

"I can't believe this is really our house!" I say as we turn into the U-shaped dirt driveway at 127 West Hill Pond Road in Cabot. "If this is a dream, I don't want to wake up!"

"Oh, you're definitely not dreaming, but don't get any ideas about me carrying you over the threshold," Hector jokes as he lets the kids out of the van. One by one, Chelsea, Jose, and Isaac hop down, followed by Ricky, Tom, and Derek from the far backseat. Finally, he hands Raj over to me as he goes around to the back of the van to grab his toolbox.

We've been eager to get over here since we finalized the "lease-to-buy" paperwork on Thursday. It's a beautiful fall Saturday, a perfect day to explore our new house and yard—five acres of yard! We have three weeks to finish up at the group home, and then we will move in here and the next leg of our journey begins.

"This is awesome, dude," Ricky says. "I still can't believe you talked my social worker into letting me move in with you guys instead of staying at the group home! How did you do it, anyway?" he asks.

"When we gave our notice at the group home, we suggested the idea that the five of you guys that are at the group home now come with us as foster care placements so that the new teaching parents can start fresh with all new boys. We thought it would be an easier adjustment for everyone. We remember how hard it was for us when we first moved in to inherit a house full of boys. Surprisingly, the group home board of directors *and* social services all agreed."

"Dude, you should have seen how Sue convinced them!" Hector laughed. "We walked into the office of the state foster care director with a whole plan mapped out, about the transition for the group home, about you guys, and also about the new organization we plan to start. When Sue finished talking, the director took off his tie and handed her a watering can."

"I don't get it. What's with the tie and watering can?" Derek asks.

"Well, he told Sue that it sounded like we were on our way to taking over his job, so I could have his tie, and all he asked was for us to please water his plants!"

"No way!" Tom says as he saunters over to join the conversation.

"Yes way," I say. "That's really how it went! Of course, we told him we didn't want his job, but we thanked him for his confidence in us."

"Speaking of water," Hector says, changing the subject, "we're here to get some work done, so are you all ready to help with the cleaning? Take these buckets inside and fill them with hot water so we can get started."

The little kids are buzzing around the big empty rooms inside the house. I step in just in time to stop Jose from sliding down the bannister on the center stairway. The whole house feels like a playground to them.

I set up the boom box we have brought with us and pop in a cassette tape. Soon, the chipper voices of Nathaniel, Tails, Rounder, and the other "Grublets" are providing a cheerful soundtrack as we set to work sweeping and cleaning our new house.

Over the next three weeks, I come out to the house as often as I can, working at a makeshift desk we set up in front of the giant picture windows in the kitchen. I laugh as I think of the ways God takes the sometimes foolish dreams of our youth and polishes them up and gives them back to us in ways we never would have imagined. This house was never a barn, nor an old stone house, but it's shaped like a barn with soaring ceilings and rugged beams throughout, and it's built on a sturdy foundation of old field stones. The centerpiece of the house is the magnificent stone fireplace, a special one called a "Russian furnace" that is not only beautiful but will provide our heat as well. Much better than what we might have created if we had mistakenly bought that piece of land in Western Massachusetts a few years back.

By the time moving day has come, I've finished my project—creating the articles of incorporation and bylaws for the new organization Hector and I have decided to create, called Rootwings Ministries. While still serving as licensed foster parents, it's our dream to build an organization, supported by churches, that will help reduce the need for foster care. The testimony I gave to the Vermont legislature just poured out of me on the spot that day, but ever since then we have been doing research and are convinced that what children need most is a family where they can put down roots forever—and then they will have the stability to thrive and eventually sprout the wings they need to become successful adults.

When we adopted Raj, one of the gifts we received was a handmade cross-stitch with the quote, *"There are only two lasting bequests we can hope to give our children. One of these is roots; the other, wings."* We knew we had found the slogan and name for our new ministry. At first we weren't sure who said these words, but when we learned they were attributed to Hodding Carter Jr., we thought it was cool, not only because of the work he had done fighting racism and promoting nonviolence, but because I had personally met his son, Hodding Carter III, when I rode on a press bus during the 1980 Presidential Campaign as a representative of my college newspaper. Further digging led us to the nugget that Carter himself had originally borrowed the quote from the Reverend Henry Ward Beecher, a famous Christian social reformer and brother of famous abolitionist Harriet Beecher Stowe. It gave us chills to trace God's hand in leading us to this quote, with its rich history, to start our work on behalf of children needing families.

It gave us chills to trace God's hand in leading us to this quote, with its rich history, to start our work on behalf of children needing families.

"What do you think? Do I look grubby enough to be a Father Grublet?" Hector asks, coming in from his first day taking down old barns.

As he closes in to hug me, I playfully back away, saying, "Oh, you sir are exceedingly grubby. Get thee to a shower before you even think about hugging me!"

While we work to build a board of directors and raise funds to start Rootwings, we still have to feed our brood, which now includes four small children and five teenage foster sons. So Hector has started a small business taking down barns and silos and selling the wood, beams, doors, and other materials to a local salvage company. We have named his business Father Grublet's after the character in one of the kids' favorite music tapes.

"Mommy," Chelsea says, appearing in the kitchen while I am stirring the spaghetti sauce. "When I am getting a sister?"

"A sister? I don't know. Why do you ask?" I reply.

"This whole house is full of boys, boys, boys," she says in response. "Big boys and little boys and baby boys and daddy is a boy."

"Well, I'm a girl," I point out. "And so are Lisa and Fanny and Butterscotch."

"Mom," she says with all the indignation that a four-year old can muster. "Really? The pets don't count as kids. I want a sister."

"I promise to talk to Daddy about it," I say, also reminding her that if there's something really important she wants, she can talk to Jesus about it during prayer time.

"That girl, the things she comes up with," Hector says a week later as he comes down the stairs after putting the kids to bed.

"What did she say this time?" I ask.

"This is the sixth or seventh night in a row that she ends her bedtime prayer by saying, 'And Dear Jesus, don't forget to bring me a sister soon.' Where did she come up with that?"

"Ooops. I forgot to tell you about my conversation with her about a week ago," I reply, retelling the story.

"You know, that's funny," Hector comments, "because I've been thinking it's probably time to update our home study. I mean, you know, just to be ready, just in case."

"Ready for what?" I ask. "We've completed our dream family

already—we had two and we adopted two. That's what we have been telling everyone was our master plan for years now. Now we focus on helping kids in other ways. That's why we started Rootwings, right?"

"Well, yes. Yes and no, I guess. Yes, it's why we started Rootwings, but I'm not sure our master plan was really God's master plan for us. Remember our conversations after we came home from NACAC? We knew that our time in the group home was just God's way of showing us we not only can handle a big family, but we love it. I think he has more kids planned for us. Maybe one will be the sister Chelsea is praying for."

"It can't hurt to update the home study," I slowly agree. "It's always best to be prepared."

"Sue, Hector." A friend named Peggy calls us. "There is a call for you on the office phone." It's a Wednesday night during Lent and we are at a church potluck dinner and service with Chelsea, Jose, and the older boys. Isaac and Raj are spending the night with my parents, a few miles away.

"Who would call us here?" I wonder as Hector heads for the phone while I continue dishing soup out to the kids.

He steps out of the office and his face is completely pale. "What is it?" I ask.

"Derek, help Chelsea, Jose to get their coats on," he says. "Earl, Tony, go find Ricky and Nick—we need to leave now." Derek and Ricky are still with us, but some of the other boys from the group home have moved back to their parents' homes and we have recently added some new foster sons to the family.

"Hector, what is it?" He still hasn't told me about the phone call.

"It was your dad. The dog, Coco, bit Isaac in the face. They're at the hospital. I'll drop you off there and take everyone else home," he says, his voice beginning to break.

"What? How? . . . . " I gasp. I'm at a loss for words. Coco has never bitten anyone; he has been part of the family for years. I hear the words but don't understand what he's saying. I must be missing something. This can't be right.

"Ah, look at the tough little man with two black eyes—how does the other guy look?" Derek jokes as we bring Isaac into the house three days later. Thankfully, and miraculously, the dog bite narrowly missed Isaac's eyes, sinking in just above and below them, creating a patchwork pattern of black-and-blues, hot red scabs, and stark rows of stitches zig-zagging across much of his face.

Happy to be out of the hospital, Isaac heads for his Big Wheel, ready to go play with Jose in the driveway. "Hold up." Hector snatches him up and steers him toward the playroom off the kitchen. "I think playing with your cars and trucks inside is a better idea right now." Raj is already over there, lining up his matchbox cars along the windowsill.

"Mommy, mommy." My sleep has been interrupted by a tiny whimper. Isaac is standing in his footie pajamas next to my bed.

"Oh sweetie, what's wrong?"

"My head hurts," he says. He has been home from the hospital for a week and nearly all the swelling is gone. He seemed fine all day, so this is a little surprising. I touch his forehead and he's definitely running a fever. Suddenly, without warning, he lurches forward and begins to throw up.

"Hec, Hec, wake up. I need a hand here," I say. We work together to get Isaac cleaned up, changed, and give him some children's Tylenol. We snuggle him in bed between us and try to go back to sleep. Hopefully it is just a little bug. *The joys of winter in Vermont*, I think to myself as I doze off.

"Do you think we should call Dr. DiNicola?" I ask Hector three days later, not noticing that he's already on the phone;

Isaac seems no better. "I have never seen him this lethargic and he whimpers whenever he moves his head. It's definitely more than a 24-hour bug."

Hanging up the phone, Hector insists that we take Isaac to our doctor right away. It's a 40-minute trek to Randolph, where his office is located, so I've been hoping it wouldn't be necessary; it's a bit of a treacherous ride on winter roads. "That was my mother I was just talking to," he says. "When I told her what was going on with Isaac, she became very upset. She said it reminded her of what happened to her first baby, Irene. She says we shouldn't wait another minute before we take Isaac to the doctor."

"Do you think we should call Dr. DiNicola?" I ask Hector three days later, not noticing that he's already on the phone; Isaac seems no better.

"OK, I'll leave now, and hopefully we can be home by the time the boys get out of school," I say. I know this mention of Mamere's first baby, Irene, has shaken Hector. The baby, a sister he never knew, died after a head injury a few years before he was born, and just the thought of that possibility is enough to prompt quick action.

"Don't worry, I have things at home covered. Just take care of my little man." Hector bundles Isaac into his car seat with a worried look on his face. "Even with the Tylenol, he's still burning up."

Yesterday, when I brought Isaac to the doctor, he thought he was dehydrated, and suggested an overnight in the hospital on IV fluids. I'd been expecting to head home this morning, but although Isaac is now well hydrated, he's clearly still in a lot of pain, especially when he moves his head. The doctors have suggested several more tests, including a spinal tap. Waiting in his room, pacing, I worry about the possible outcomes and call Hector to give him an update.

Suddenly, there's a bit of commotion in the hall as several doctors, interns, and nurses approach me. "It appears Isaac may have spinal meningitis," they say. "We don't feel our hospital is best equipped for that. We want to transfer him to Burlington as soon as possible. We have some papers you need to sign to get the process started. Do you have any questions?"

The next few minutes are a blurry mix of hugging and dressing Isaac, signing papers, and asking questions. In the middle of all that, I try to call Hector, but am surprised when Derek answers the phone. "Hector left," he says. "He was so worried when you told him about the spinal tap, he decided to go to the hospital to be with you. I'm watching Jose and Chelsea and Raj until Mamere gets here. Your dad is driving her over now."

It's time to leave. I want to ride in the ambulance with Isaac, but I'm told it is against protocol and I have to take my own car. I don't understand; people always are riding in the back of ambulances on TV shows! Hector hasn't arrived, so I leave word at the front desk, asking them to tell him to immediately come up to Burlington.

"What's the update?" Hector says, out of breath, as he finally catches up with me at the Medical Center in Burlington.

"The doctors say it's touch and go right now—he might not make it through the night." I can barely breathe as I eke out these words. "It's Good Friday. Oh dear God, I know this is the day you lost your son, but I beg you, please don't take our baby today!" I cry out suddenly. Hector gathers me up into a bear hug and we both break down, sobbing.

Nurses are bustling around us, setting up the IV, taking his pulse and blood pressure, and undoing his diaper to get an anal temperature check. Isaac has been listless on the bed, barely reacting to any of the commotion, when it sounds like he's trying to talk.

"What, Isaac? What is it? Mommy and Daddy are right here with you, sweetheart," I say, gently touching his blond curls, matted with sweat from his fever. I lean in closer and now I can hear him. I turn to the nurse. "He says he needs to go to the bathroom." Isaac has been potty-trained for less than a month.

"Oh, Isaac, it's OK. You have a diaper on, I'll tape it back up and you can go ahead and go," the nurse taking his temperature says.

Suddenly, in a clear voice we all can hear, Isaac says, "I want to use the potty. If I can't use the potty, I will poop on your hand."

We all burst out laughing! "Well, I guess that was our sign from God," Hector deadpans. "Isaac is a fighter and he's definitely going to make it!"

"Let us take you out to dinner, Susan," my mom says. "You need a break." I have been sitting at Isaac's bedside day and night for a week. He's definitely out of the woods, but due to a few complications needs to stay in the hospital a little longer. "Stephanie will stay with Isaac," she continues. My sister Stephanie is a nursing student at UVM and has been visiting as often as possible.

When I get back to Isaac's room after a pleasant dinner with my parents, Stephanie says, "Hector called. He said you should try to call him back tonight if you can. But he also said not to worry, there is no problem at home."

"You'll never guess who called me today," he says, after getting an update on Isaac's status.

"OK, you are right, I'll never guess. Tell me."

"Oh, you're no fun," he says, "Well, OK, it was Ann Clark. She says our home study has been approved by the agency in

Florida and they have two babies needing immediate homes. She said we can choose—one is a boy named Sidney and the other is a girl named, well . . . she didn't really know the girl's actual name. She said the foster parents call her Raisin." Ann is our new social worker, and we have really clicked. She seems to understand our family and our dreams as well as Mary Diamond did back in Massachusetts.

"This is a joke, right?"

"No joke, this is for real. The boy is four months old and he was born full-term and everything seems to be normal. The girl is eight months old and she was born prematurely. She weighed under two pounds when she was born. The doctors aren't sure how that will effect her development—they say she will probably have delays, but she is out of the hospital now and doing well with a foster family. Both babies are black."

We've been praying about our next adoption, and Chelsea, especially, has been praying for a sister.

"It doesn't make any sense," I say. "Why would God even think about sending us a baby with Isaac still in the hospital? And why do we have to choose again between two babies? It doesn't make sense."

But the timing is crazy. "It doesn't make any sense," I say. "Why would God even think about sending us a baby with Isaac still in the hospital? And why do we have to choose again between two babies? It doesn't make sense."

"Well, I guess this is where that verse you always quote when you are out doing your church presentations for Rootwings comes in," Hector chuckles, reminding me of I Corinthians 1:25: *Because the foolishness of God is wiser than men, and the weakness of God is stronger than men.*

"How long before we have to answer?" I ask.

"Ann says we can have a day, but they need an answer because they also have to contact other families to make sure both babies have a home as soon as possible."

"Well, we need to sleep on it, and pray on it, for sure. I just don't know what to think. I want to say, 'Yes, let's take the girl' and Chelsea will get her sister, but the timing couldn't be worse. Let's talk some more tomorrow. And don't say a word to Chelsea in the meantime." Exhausted, I fall into a restless sleep next to Isaac's bed and start to have some crazy dreams about little dolls wearing pink dresses.

The next morning Isaac is scheduled for arthroscopic surgery to drain some of the fluids that have blown his knees up the size of softballs, a rare and strange side effect of his meningitis. After they wheel him away, I have some quiet time to myself, and I spend it praying about the two babies and our next adoption. I start dozing off when the phone startles me awake.

"I know it sounds crazy because of the timing," Hector says. "But I'm totally convinced that this little girl is meant to join our family."

"Oh good! I'm so glad we're on the same page," I say. "I thought it was crazy too, but this is exactly what I'm feeling. Do you want to call Ann back and give her our decision? And find out what the next steps are."

"The phone is for you, Ms. Badeau," the Governor's assistant says, pointing me to the phone on the desk across the room.

"For me? Who in the world would be calling me on the Governor's line?" Fellow members of the Vermont Children's Forum and I are meeting with Governor Madeleine Kunin on a series of critical policy issues related to the needs of children in Vermont.

"Are you serious?" I say, incredulous. "We have to appeal that decision. Let me think about what we can do and we'll talk when I get home."

I return to the meeting, saying, "That was my husband. We're in the process of adopting a premature baby from Florida. Everything has been approved in both states, but now we are told that the person in charge of the Interstate Compact on the Placement of Children here in Vermont is denying the placement—on racial grounds."

"What?" three stunned members of our team ask in unison.

"She says she doesn't want to approve a black baby coming into a white family in a white state like Vermont," I say, shaking my head.

"Sue, your family isn't white, exactly, is it?" the Governor asks, rhetorically. She has met my children during the signing of the National Adoption Day proclamation.

"Sue, your family isn't white, exactly, is it?" the Governor asks, rhetorically.

"No, we are not a white family. We are a very mixed family. I understand her concerns, but this baby was born drug-addicted and weighing less than 2 pounds. She may have developmental delays. I can't believe anyone would want to deny her the chance to have a stable, loving family. We aren't perfect, but . . . " I am shaking as I try to articulate my jumbled thoughts and feelings.

"Perhaps the Interstate office just needs some more information," one of my colleagues suggests.

"Perhaps," I hesitantly agree, as we turn back to the discussion at hand.

The next day, we receive approval to bring our baby home. I never heard any more about what transpired in the intervening hours; some things it's best just not to know. All I know is that our ICPC problem vanished, although it did create a learning opportunity and began a lifelong interest of ours in the intersection of race, culture, identity, and family, which has continued to influence our values, work, and efforts to this day. This interaction, and our experiences raising all of our children of color, set me on a path, as an advocate and person of faith, of learning about and speaking up on issues of racial equity, institutional racism, and justice.

What a whirlwind these last few weeks have been, I think to myself as I sit across the desk from the social worker at the Children's Home Society in Daytona, Florida.

"Just a few more papers to wrap up and you can meet your baby," she says. "What name have you decided to give her?"

"Joelle Christina," I say. "Unless you can tell us her birth name. We believe in keeping children's birth names. It's the only thing they have from their birth family, so we hate to take it away from them."

> It's breathtaking, this miracle of adoption. I'll never cease to be amazed at the depth of love I've felt for each of my children—in the span of one heartbeat they go from being a photo and a name to my child . . . my child that I would do anything for. Smitten. Again!

"Those are sweet sentiments," she says, "but the confidentiality rules here in Florida are strict. I can't give you any information from her original birth certificate." I shake my head, dismayed. "OK, then Joelle Christina it is. I hope she will grow to like it."

"It's a beautiful name—for a beautiful child. Wait until you see her!" She picks up her phone, pushes a couple of buttons, and asks for the baby to be brought in.

"Oh, oh, oh," is all I can say. This precious baby has taken my breath away. She's smiling at me from a face softly framed in a froth of silky dark curls. She begins to coo, and she has me hook, line, and sinker. It's breathtaking, this miracle of adoption. I'll never cease to be amazed at the depth of love I've felt for each of my children—in the span of one heartbeat they go from being a photo and a name to my child . . . my child that I would do anything for. Smitten. Again!

Sitting in the crowded Newark airport waiting to hear when our delayed flight for Vermont will finally depart, I begin to worry that I will run out of formula. For a baby that was born so small, this girl likes to eat! I hope I can make it home on the supply I have left. The cancellations and delays have postponed our trip home for more than 24 hours. Hector and the kids have already driven from Cabot to Burlington, only to have to go home and, now, head back again today.

"I wonder what all the kids will think about their new baby sister," I say to Joelle, and suddenly I burst out laughing as I realize what day today is. "Oh Lord, this is a good one. As if we needed a confirmation!" The delayed flights mean that instead of arriving home on May 20, we will arrive on May 21, Chelsea's fifth birthday. "The little girl who has been praying for a sister for nine months gets a sister on her birthday! How perfect is that?"

Our first son, Jose, arrived within days of Chelsea's first birthday. Now, her much anticipated baby sister arrives on her fifth birthday. *I don't dare to even imagine what she will ask for on her next birthday!* I think to myself, just as the loudspeaker announces that our flight is finally ready to board.

6

Foster Care

"Camping now! Hooray!" Jose sings out loudly from the back of our Toyota van. Soon, all of the kids are joining the merriment, singing and clapping along with Psalty the Singing Songbook's spirited Camping Adventures.

Ahead of us, Hector is driving our new (used, very used) green pickup truck, the first purchase we have made to concretize our plans to travel across the country this summer—a trip that will last five weeks. Next stop, a farmhouse about six miles from our house, where we will buy our new (used, very used) camper to sit atop the truck.

"Boy that Father Grublet business has sure turned you into a real Vermon'ah, ah'yup," I chide Hector. "But I'm so glad you were able to bond with Mr. Whitcomb so we could buy this he'yah camp'ah at a reasonable price." By now I'm spitting my lemonade and barely holding back from launching into a laughing fit.

"Ain't nuttin' wrong wi' shootin' the breeze on a fine summer afternoon," Hector replies.

"Well, it got the job done, so now we're really ready to go! But it took a lot longer than expected, so I'll have to throw dinner together fast if we want the kids to be fed, bathed, and in bed at a reasonable time."

"You go ahead, I'm going to drag out the hose and wash this baby down, and I'm sure the kids will have fun helping. And that will kill two birds—they won't need a bath after that!"

Jose, Chelsea, and Isaac leap at the chance to help Hector wash the truck and camper, along with Earl and Tony. Ricky heads up to his room, and Raj heads over to his stash of matchbox cars. I put Joelle in her walker on the porch so she can watch the activity in the yard, and head toward the kitchen to begin dinner when I notice it already smells good in here.

"I saw you all weren't home when you thought you'd be, so I hope you don't mind, I decided to make some goulash for dinner. I've been wanting to try this recipe for awhile now." Derek turns toward me, wearing an apron and wielding a spatula.

"Great, smells wonderful. I've got a few things I can do while you finish up. Thanks for taking initiative." I start to head for my desk, and then turn back, saying, "Oh, and give yourself 20,000 points for that!" Then I duck quickly before I catch a sponge, potato, or whatever he decides to throw at me. Of all our group home boys, Derek hated the point system the most, so it is a running joke now that he lives with us full time. He graduates from high school in less than a week, and he is heading off to live in Arizona with his sister. We'll miss Derek for sure.

It's been a month since Joelle joined the family, and aside

from getting used to the distinctive aroma of her special formula, we're all adjusting well. Isaac's last follow-up appointment revealed that he's in tip-top shape, and two of our foster sons have been reunited with their birth parents. When Derek leaves, we'll be down to three foster sons—Ricky, Earl, and Tony—and our five little ones. Perfect timing to take a five-week trip around the country.

Although we've wanted to take such a road trip for years, it was the announcement that the NACAC conference would be held in Albuquerque, New Mexico that spurred us to begin making firm plans. Since we're still in the fundraising stage at Rootwings, we have the flexibility to leave home without the usual job constraints. We started planning the trip before Isaac's dog bite, and before Joelle joined the family, but neither of these events seem to be good enough reason to delay our long-dreamed-of road trip.

Financing the trip is our biggest challenge. We run on a shoestring budget. A very thin shoestring at that. So we made a deal with ourselves. If we could figure out how to travel for five weeks without spending any more money than we'd spend at home during that same period of time—for food, transportation, utilities, and miscellaneous expenses—we'd do it. We're confident it's possible, especially if we eat a lot of P, B & J along the way.

"Are you coming to bed?" Hector calls out to me. He's already sprawled out across our futon, and at the moment all the little people are in their own beds.

"Ten more minutes," I reply. This morning, Joelle and Raj had appointments at Special Kids clinic to check on their development, and I used the opportunity to stop by the AAA office in Montpelier and pick up the AAA Tour Books for 48 states. Sadly, I know we don't have a chance to go to Alaska or Hawaii on this trip, but I'm now plotting a route that will take us through as many of the lower 48 as possible. Typing away on my trusty Smith Corona, I'm in the groove and want to finish making the itinerary for our trip. Niagara Falls, Yellowstone Park, Yosemite, Malibu Beach, Grand Canyon, the Great Salt Lake Desert, Cherokee Trail of Tears—and of course we have to be sure to stop in Omaha to visit the original Boys Town campus, since our group home was a Boys Town affiliate. I've found state and national parks we can stay at for as little as $2 per night, so I am confident we can stay in our budget. Nifty, neat-o, groovy, cool! We can do this.

"This one, this one!" Jose yells, running toward the biggest train on the grounds at the Illinois Railway Museum. He's always loved trains, ever since our weekly visits to the "train store" in Northampton when he was just two years old. Now, he's the leader of the pack, with Chelsea and Isaac trailing behind him. Ricky has Raj and Earl has Joelle as everyone climbs aboard for a picture-taking session. This jewel was not on our itinerary, but we were so excited to find it just when we needed a break from driving. As we leave the museum, we pick up some fresh corn on the cob at a little roadside farmstand for our dinner. It proves to be a godsend for Joelle, who is teething fiercely this week. She can gnaw on the corncobs to her heart's content!

A few days later, we roll into Cheyenne, Wyoming, planning to pass through and keep moving toward Yellowstone, when the banners proclaiming "The Big Daddy of 'em All" capture our attention. "That would be you," I joke to Hector. "We need to get you one of those T-shirts." This quickly becomes another unplanned stop, lasting two days, as we can't get enough of the carnival rides, rodeo, citywide pancake breakfast (pancake batter churned up in a cement mixer!), and the opportunity to hear Lee Greenwood in concert!

"Well, now I can legitimately use that saying," Hector says as we roll up our sleeping bags and prepare to roll out of town and head for Yellowstone.

"What saying is that?"

"It's not my first rodeo," he chuckles.

Jose has been begging to ride a horse all summer, so today he, Hector, and the bigger boys are taking a horseback ride on a trail at Yellowstone, and I'm waiting with Raj, Joelle, Isaac, and Chelsea at the base. There's a pay phone here so I use the opportunity to check in with my parents at home. In a short time, I'm excited to report back to Hector.

"I talked to my dad and he told me to call Dave Otterman, the attorney handling the lawsuit for Isaac's injuries. I got ahold of him and he said the settlement with the insurance is all finalized. So, Isaac's medical bills will all be paid and he'll have some money for college once he turns 18. They didn't go for the 'pain and suffering' clause, though, so there's no extra money for us. Good thing we didn't have our hearts set on it!"

"I'm just so thankful the hospital bills will be taken care of."

"Yeah, me too."

By the time we arrive in Nevada, Earl and Tony's constant bickering is about to make us all crazy. "I've had it with you two!" Hector declares while we regroup at a gas station. "You see where we are? This is the desert. We're going to find a nice open space and you two can just duke it out and be done with it."

A few miles down the road, he sees the ideal spot and pulls the truck over. I follow with the van. "OK," he says. "Have at it!" Tony and Earl circle each other a few times in a boxing stance, each taking quick looks over their shoulders to see if we're serious. "Go ahead. What are you waiting for?" Hector asks. "You've been threatening each other all summer, so now's your chance. We don't have all day, we still have some miles to go before we hit our campground, so let's do this." They continue to bounce on their sneakers, jabbing the air, not sure what to make of the situation.

"I don't really want to beat him up, Hec," Tony finally says.

"Me neither," Earl adds.

"OK, that settles it. You had your chance, and you chose not to fight, so let's call this a truce. No more arguing and one-upping each other for the rest of the trip—is that a deal?"

"Deal," they both say, with relief audible in their voices.

A few minutes later, we roll into Carson City and decide to stop for ice cream to celebrate. All our little guys line up on a bench eating ice cream cones, and one by one they all get up and walk away to explore the fascinating Old West town. Finally, Raj is left alone still eating his ice cream. It's a precious Kodak moment and a great way to cap off the day.

"I'll go see if we can check in," I say after we park our two vehicles, delighted that we have made it to Albuquerque. I doubt they'll let us check in this early, but after four weeks of fairly primitive camping, I'm so looking forward to three nights in a hotel for the NACAC conference, so it's worth a try. This is the big splurge of the trip, and we are all very excited.

"I don't feel like such a rookie this time," Hector says as we hit the sack at the end of the first full day of the conference. "I'm actually seeing some people I remember from last year, and I understand at least half of what the presenters are talking about this time!"

"I'm so happy that the kids are loving their program. It's such a great chance for them to be with other kids who are also adopted or have mixed-race families."

"It's a good thing none of those social workers were witnesses to our stop at the Grand Canyon," Hector teases, chiding me for a moment I'll never live down. "If they saw how you perched

Raj on that ledge just to get a photo, I don't think we could ever pass a home study again."

"Ha ha, very funny. And what makes you think we need to pass a home study again?"

"Oh, you know when we came to NACAC last time, we had this feeling that adopting a sibling group was somewhere in our future?"

"Yes, after our visit with that family in Wisconsin."

"Well, after meeting the Forderer family here, I am more convinced than ever that God is leading us toward siblings as the next step on our adoption journey."

"We'll call Ann Clarke when we get home—she won't be surprised at all," I reply, sleepily. "But for now, let's get some shut-eye. It'll be another intense day tomorrow."

"Fanny! Butterscotch!" Jose is calling for our dogs the minute he tumbles out of the van when we arrive back home in Cabot. As much fun as we had on the road, it's true—there is still "no place like home." The dogs, who've been well cared for by our neighbors in our absence, come running when they hear their names, and Chelsea goes off in search of Lisa, the cat. Joelle fell asleep in the car, so I gently carry her inside and lie her down in her crib. We have less than a week left of summer to get all the laundry done and everyone ready for school.

"Looks like it might rain," Hector observes. "Ricky, Earl, come help me get a few things in from the truck before it starts. Tony, go help Sue put the food away."

"Who wants to play whiffle ball?" my brother-in-law Bobby asks, and soon he has gathered enough takers for a game in the field. It's a picture-perfect late summer evening, the final weekend before school starts, and we've gathered my parents, sisters, brother, and nephews for a cookout.

We haven't told Tony yet, but this will be his last gathering with our family. His social worker called earlier in the day and said that she was moving him to a foster home where he'll be closer to his birth mother. I hope that's a good thing. He's moved the most times of any of our foster sons, and it's been hard on him. Inside his rough and sometimes annoying exterior is a scared and sometimes sad little boy. I'll let him enjoy the evening and we'll talk with him later. Moments like this convince me more than ever that we are doing the right thing to focus on adoption not only in our personal life, but also at Rootwings.

"What's the news on the agency?" my dad asks while the kids are busy with the whiffle ball game.

"I have three speaking engagements with churches lined up in September," I tell him. "Hopefully, that will generate interest and spur our fundraising efforts. It's our goal to raise fifty thousand dollars by Christmas so we can open an office and hire a director. We'll hire someone with fundraising expertise, so it should get easier after that, and I can focus on the educational part of the program."

"Would you like me to see if there might be an opportunity for Hector to come talk about Rootwings at the Rotary club? We're always needing speakers."

"Oh, Dad, that would be great!" I give him a big hug. I know my parents have been concerned about some of our choices, both in our careers and building our family, so it means so much when they throw their support behind our work. Even so, I wasn't quite ready to tell them that we were in the process of updating our home study so we could adopt again—siblings this time!

"I think it is going to take longer to get Rootwings off the ground than we hoped," I say to Hector over coffee before he heads out to be Father Grublet for the day. "So I've been thinking that I probably should get a part-time job. We really need a little more cash flow coming in. I was thinking that I could be a greeting card rep, like the ones we used to work with at Logos. If I represented a few lines, I could make a little money but still work on Rootwings and be home enough for you to keep up with your Father Grublet commitments. I don't want any of the kids in daycare, so we'd have to be good at juggling our schedules. What do you think?"

"I'm not sure," he replies slowly. "I'll be working out at an abandoned barn site all day by myself. Plenty of time to pray on it. Let's talk tonight when I get back."

"Sounds good."

Pawprints, Oatmeal, Renaissance, Suzy Zoo, and my favorite, Marcel Shurman. Seems like a pretty good collection of greeting card lines to represent. They all sold well at Logos, and I hope they'll be popular at gift and book shops around Vermont. I only have the southern half of the state, so two days a week on the road should do it; the other days I can be home with the kids and continue working on getting Rootwings off the ground. The drive home from Manchester is long, and it's late when I pull into the driveway after my first day on the job.

The house is quiet; all the kids are asleep. I am a little sad that I missed bedtime. Snuggling on our futon and reading stories is one of my favorite parts of the day.

"Hey," Ricky says.

"Hey, yourself. How did your day go?"

"Terrible. Pops will tell you. I got in trouble at school."

"You never get in trouble at school, Rick. What happened?"

"I got into a fight. I socked a kid. I got suspended."

"Oh boy. That's not good. I imagine you and Hector have had a talk about consequences."

"Yeah, and he had to call my caseworker too. She's coming over tomorrow." He looks worried.

"I'm sure it'll work out," I tell him. "Where is Hector anyway?"

"I think he fell asleep reading with the kids again. I haven't seen him since he went up to put them to bed."

"OK, well, speaking of bed, it's getting late. I know you don't have school tomorrow if you are suspended, but it's not vacation. It's time for you to be getting to bed."

"Yeah, I was already in my room. I just came to get something to drink."

"OK, good night."

"Good night."

The meeting with Ricky's caseworker is a little contentious. She wants to move him to another group home. We strongly advocate keeping him here. She calls her supervisor. They agree to let him stay with us, but with a warning that "next time" he is in trouble, he will have to move to a more restrictive setting.

"I'm not in favor of fighting," I say to Hector after she leaves, "but . . ." He cuts me off.

"Don't I know it!"

"But," I start again, "seriously. An occasional fight in the schoolyard is normal kid stuff. If Ricky wasn't in foster care this wouldn't be a blip on anyone's radar. Here, they want to make a federal case of it. How will kids learn to solve problems if they're just moved every time there is a problem? All they learn from that is to run from problems. It's not right."

"I agree. I would have been in a dozen foster homes myself if I got moved every time I had a little fisticuffs when I was a kid. . . . Did you hear that? Sounds like someone pulling into the driveway—are we expecting someone?"

"What day is it?"

"Tuesday."

"No, what date is it?"

"Um, October 29th, I think."

"OK, then, yup, we are expecting Ann Clarke. For some

reason, I thought it was tomorrow. She is coming to finish our home study update and talk about some siblings she knows about, in Florida, I think."

"Good thing she is not a white glove kind of social worker," Hector says, glancing around the living room.

"Yeah, that would never work with us," I say as I walk toward the door.

Just as Ann is leaving, our mailman arrives. "Bye Ann! Drive safely! Keep us posted about those four boys in Florida," I say as I walk toward the mailman, with Joelle on my hip and Isaac tagging along. "Say bye-bye, Joelle?" I prod, and she lifts her hand to wave to Ann.

7

Abel, SueAnn, George, and Florinda

Our home study is complete and we are approved to adopt a sibling group. When sending our post-adoption reports to Joelle's Florida social worker, Ann has learned of four small brothers ages four to eight in need of a home. After going over the information she brought us, we have encouraged her to send our newly minted home study to the worker.

"It's in God's hands now," I think to myself as I start to sift through the mail. The new "Los Ninos," an adoption newsletter from New Mexico with pictures of children waiting for adoption, has arrived. I immediately notice two sets of siblings here whose faces and stories pull on my heart. The first is a group of six teenagers. Our work in the group home and as foster parents to teens has impressed upon us the fact that even though teens have one foot on the stairway to adulthood, they still need the stability and guidance of parents.

The second was a group of two brothers and two sisters, ages four to nine. I flip through the rest of the pages but keep coming back to their page. Inside the house, I check on Raj, put Joelle down in a circle of toys, and hand the "Los Ninos" to Hector without a word.

"Ooops. Ann Clarke left too soon. We'll have to call her in the morning," he says. "There is just something about these kids . . ." Hector is pointing to the same pictures I've been looking at. "I think they're meant to be ours."

We had no way of knowing how deeply our lives would be touched by all three of the sets of siblings whose pictures we prayed over that day.

"Look, Mommy, this tree sparkles!"

"Oh my, it surely does!" I exclaim. We're all working around our large dinner table, making mini-Christmas trees out of the giant sugar pine cones we brought home from our stop at Lake Tahoe on our summer trip. Chelsea has just poured almost an entire container of glitter on the tree she is making. The extra glitter that didn't stick to the pinecone has landed in Joelle's hair as she sits in her walker next to Chelsea.

"I'm keeping mine. It's mad cool," Earl proclaims.

"You can make one to keep, Earl," Hector says, "after you make one to give away. Remember, these are for gifts."

"Dad, Jose won't let me have the scissors!" Isaac yells. Meanwhile, Raj hasn't made a peep but has organized all the remaining pinecones in a perfect line.

"Who are they for, again?" Ricky asks.

"Grandpa and Mamie," Jose says. "And Aunt Ruth and Mamere."

"And my teacher!" Chelsea adds.

"After we finish, we're going to talk into the tape recorder to send a message to our new brothers and sisters, OK?" I remind them. "And then we'll have some eggnog before bed."

After being approved for two of the three sets of siblings whose pictures we looked at in late October, we were once again faced with the dilemma of making a choice. After much thought and prayer we decided to accept the four children from New Mexico, which meant we reluctantly had to say no to the four boys from Florida.

Although we didn't fit the profile—at all—of the type of home the psychologist, Dr. Adams, said he recommended for the children, we knew in our heart and soul that they were meant for our family. He suggested a "well-to-do" family with "no other children" yet "extensive parenting experience." We didn't quite understand how anyone would fit that description. But in his own words, Abel, the oldest of the four, said, "I want a dad who will introduce me as his son. I want to go camping. I want to be the oldest in the family." And SueAnn said, "I want all four of us to stay together."

> "I want a dad who will introduce me as his son. I want to go camping. I want to be the oldest in the family."

We knew we fit the children's description, and it was a match. Tonight, we're making a cassette tape to send to them, along with a photo album we've put together to introduce them to our family.

"Do you think we'll ever get all that glitter out of Joelle's hair?" Hector laughs as we finally sit quietly on our couch after all the children are in bed.

"Hard to say, but it's OK for a little girl to have some fairy dust in her hair!" I reply. "It was a great project, and it made carting that huge bag of pine cones all the way back from Nevada worth it."

"You know," I say, changing the subject, "I'm totally at peace about our decision to adopt these four children and not the four from Florida, but I really don't understand why God keeps putting us in this position where we have to choose. We had to choose between Elsie and Jose, and then Sidney and Joelle, and now we have to choose again. It's such a wrenching decision each time, and even though we think it through, talk it through, and pray it through, I just wish we didn't have to keep going through that. Why do you suppose this keeps happening?"

"I don't know," Hector replies. "But I have a feeling it has to do with our commitment to starting Rootwings. I think God is continually showing us that we can't take every child that needs a home, and that for every child we do take, there are more still waiting, so we have to do more. That's where Rootwings comes in."

"Wow—that was deep," I say with a smile, leaning over to give him a kiss.

"Yeah, once in a while, God grants me a little wisdom. Serenity, not so much," he jokes as he kisses me back. "Ummm, your lips are sweet. Everyone is asleep—quick, let's go to bed before someone wakes up!"

"We'll always love you, Earl," I say, choking back tears. Chelsea is inside the house refusing to come out; she's very sad. Jose and Isaac are fiddling around in the yard, Raj and Joelle are watching from the porch. We've hugged, we've cried, we've taken pictures, we've checked and double-checked the house for stray clothes or other items. It's hard to believe the moment has really come to say good-bye to Earl, the last of our foster sons.

After Tony left in September, we decided not to add more foster children while pursuing the adoption of siblings. But we believed Ricky and Earl would be with us for a long time to come. Then came the barn incident. A barn in lower Cabot burned to the ground on Halloween, and weeks later, the police knocked at our door, identifying Ricky and Earl as the culprits. Earl had been accused of setting a fire years earlier, before coming to our home. With much advocacy, we managed to stop the efforts to lock them up, but we could not convince social services that they should stay with us past Christmas. Ricky was moved to a group home last week, and today Earl leaves for a placement out of state.

"When we get our new brothers and sisters, I'm not even going to look at them," Chelsea blurts out during dinner.

"Why would you say that, Chels? You've been so excited about getting the new kids —especially two more sisters."

"But if they just have to leave again like Ricky and Earl, then I don't want to look at them," she says firmly.

"Oh, sweetie, I know it's hard to understand, but Ricky and Earl and the other big boys were only here for a little while. They had to move. Its sort of like we were their special teachers, or like when Isaac was in the hospital—he stayed for a while, but then he moved out of the hospital and came back home." I try to explain: "When Abel, SueAnn, George, and Flory come, they are going to be our very own children, and they are never going to leave. I promise."

"What if they want to get married?" she asks.

"Well, OK, they can leave when they are all grown up, but they will never leave before that, OK?"

"Looks like everyone is finished eating. Jose, can you say our prayer?" Hector says.

"Dear Jesus, thank you for the food. And help us have a good day in school tomorrow. And please take care of Ricky and Earl. Amen."

This would be the first of many nights for years to come when our evening prayers would end with the plea, "Please take care of Ricky and Earl."

"Bienvenidos!" We are greeted warmly at the door with big hugs as we meet our children's foster parents, Rita and Eddie, for the first time. Within moments, Rita is showing me how to make homemade sopapaillas and making me promise I will make them for the children once they are settled in Vermont.

The next three days fly by in a whirlwind of activity. Abel, SueAnn, George, and Florinda ("Flory," or "Popper") stayed with us at the hotel in downtown Albuquerque. We've been swimming in the hotel pool (where SueAnn threw up) and later Hector went for a Gondola ride to Sandia Peak with three of the kids. I stayed at the base with SueAnn, whose tummy was still a little upset. It provided the first of several endearing bonding moments with our newest children. We had a chance to visit their school and meet with their psychologist, who asked us very earnestly if we knew what we were getting into by adopting a child, George, who "most likely will never graduate from high school."

Now, on the morning of our last day in New Mexico, we are sitting together having breakfast and Abel asks us if his name will change once we adopt him.

"Your first name won't change at all," I promise. "We'd like you to have our last name. What would you think about that?"

"I'd like that," he says, "because that means people will know I'm your son."

"But what about a middle name?" SueAnn asks.

"You don't have a middle name now," I say. "So you can pick any middle name you want."

"Any middle name, really? Anything we want?" SueAnn asks incredulously.

"Yes, really," Hector says, "Do you have one in mind?"

"Well, I'd like it to be Kim so I can always remember my best friend," Sue Ann says.

"I want Christopher," George pipes up. "That's my best friend's name!"

"Really? You sure you don't want it to be Limberger?" Abel jokes. George recently played Limberger in a church production of Charity Churchmouse and the Singsational Servants.

"That's not funny, Abel!"

"It's OK. You can have Christopher for your middle name, George."

Hector turns to Abel. "And what about you?"

"Rocky," he says definitively.

"Popper, what about you? Do you want your middle name to be Popper?"

Flory shakes her head back and forth and very quietly says, "I want Kim too."

"Hey little dude," Abel says to Isaac upon arriving at the Burlington airport. "Can I have some of that gum?"

Chelsea is so excited to have two more sisters, including one "exactly the age of me!" that she runs up to greet Flory with a squeal and a hug. Flory is a little overwhelmed and grabs Rita's hand a little tighter.

"Jackie?" SueAnn softly whispers to her caseworker. "Does this really mean we never have to move again?"

After loading all the bags into our van, we head for home, and there is not a single pause in the chatter for the entire hour-plus drive. We enter Cabot and turn off the paved road onto our dirt road for the final three miles. Just short of our house, Hector pulls the van into an abandoned house we all call "the haunted house."

"Here we are, kids! This is home!"

The van instantly becomes quiet, until Jose breaks the ice by bursting out laughing. "Dad, you're so mean!"

Soon everyone is laughing, and Hector pulls back out and a

moment later turns into our driveway, much to the relief of the children's social worker and foster mother.

It's the last day before Rita and Jackie fly back to New Mexico, and there is still one important task remaining. In spite of multiple attempts to learn, I haven't mastered the art of French braiding the girls' hair. "OK, you almost have it," Rita says, checking my latest effort. "Just pull a little tighter, like this."

"Owie, owie, owie! That hurts!" Flory calls out.

"Oh hush, Popper, now you look *muy bonita* for church!"

Indeed, the entire family is looking very handsome for church today, and I see Abel beaming from ear to ear as I hear Hector introducing him to our pastor, saying, "I'd like you to meet my son Abel."

I squeeze SueAnn's hand as we ease into our seats before the service begins, feeling lucky to have a daughter who will share my name. I look around at my nine children and chuckle to myself. *So nine it is, hmmm, Lord? I once felt sure my family was complete after two children, certain I could not handle any more. Then You brought me Isaac. Then I knew it was complete after we accomplished our "master plan" of having two and adopting two when Raj came home. But You smiled and listened to a little girl's prayer for a sister and brought us Joelle. Surely that meant our family was complete. But then, You filled our heart with a desire to adopt siblings, and Lord, you gave us these four beautiful children. To top it off, it makes our total number of children nine—Hector's "lucky" number, the number he always wore on his hockey uniform. Surely our family is complete now, right Lord?*

Finishing my prayer, I stand up for the opening hymn.

8

Todd

"Guess who just called, Hec," I say, walking into the kitchen.

"Let me guess. The President?" he replies.

"Not this time," I joke.

"It was Maggie Maurice from the *Burlington Free Press*. They want to do an article about our family and Rootwings. She's going to come over on Wednesday to interview us and take pictures."

"Wow, that's great," he says, looking around. I know he's calculating how much work we need to do around the house to make it presentable for pictures. We did an interview in February for the local paper, but this is statewide, so it will get a lot more attention. "As long as it promotes adoption and kids find homes out of it, I'm game," he says.

"We'll need to prep the kids, and I think a few of them might need haircuts."

"So, tell me Mr. Badeau, what inspired you to start Rootwings? You already have nine kids . . . doesn't that keep you busy enough?"

"Well, Ms. Maurice," he begins. "We've had a dream since high school. I always talked about opening a YMCA in the Barre area, but then a friend who spent a summer in India opened our eyes to kids all over the world that need families. Things took off from there. We never expected we'd have nine kids, and we know we can't adopt all kids who need families, so that's why we decided to start Rootwings. Our aim is to provide advocacy and support to more kids than we'll ever be able to adopt ourselves."

"So, do you plan to adopt more?"

"Well," Hector chuckles. "If I've learned one thing, it's never to say never. But at this point, we feel like our family is complete, and we're focused on getting Rootwings off the ground."

"Fabulous title: 'A House Full of Love: Badeaus Have Filled Their Home; Now They Want to Fill Others.' And it's above the fold, first page of the *Living* section; we couldn't ask for better than that," I say the day the paper comes out, a week after the interview. "It's not a bad family picture. Everyone is looking except for Raj."

"Pretty decent article too," Hector replies, looking up from the paper. "That woman didn't do a bad job. I've only found a few small mistakes."

"The best thing is, I've already gotten three calls today from people who saw the article and are interested in learning more about Rootwings or adopting."

"Wonderful, that's just what we were hoping for!"

"I know, it's pretty exciting. On another note, don't forget: today is the day we have that meeting about the summer exchange students from Guatemala. It's in Plainfield, at the co-op."

"You go and get the information. I'll stay home with the kids," Hector offers.

"OK, sounds like a plan."

"Mom, Mom! The clown is here!" George comes running into the house, skidding to a stop inches from the refrigerator.

A few weeks ago, we met a clown named Chelsey at a fair in Danville. We signed him up on the spot to come and entertain the children at a double birthday party for Chelsea and Flory. Outside, nineteen children—seven of ours, and twelve guests—are playing "Red Rover" with Hector and a few of the other parents. I'm in the kitchen with Raj and Joelle finishing up frosting the cake.

"That's great, George! Chelsea and Flory will be excited to see him. Let's go out and introduce him to the birthday girls."

Soon, Chelsey the Clown is making balloon animals for each child and they're having a great time. Moments after we serve the cake and ice cream, Joelle is covered in frosting, so I get a washcloth to clean her up, when Hector taps me on the shoulder. "Sue, Claudia is here."

I turn and see our friends Pete and Eileen, with a beautiful and shy-looking young lady at their side. "Hola, bienvenidos. Me llamo Sue," I say, nervous about my limited Spanish fluency.

"Hola. Me llamo Claudia." We get as much information as we can from Pete and Eileen, inviting them to stay for the rest of the party, and introducing Claudia to Abel and SueAnn, since they are closest in age. At thirteen, she's older than all of our kids, but not much taller than SueAnn. I'm relieved to know that Claudia is fairly fluent in English.

"Mommy, Mommy! Look at the big truck!" Isaac is excitedly pointing out the window. George comes racing down the stairs and soon seven of the kids are outside in the driveway.

"Hec! The books are here!" I yell toward the back of the house, where Hector is sorting some barn boards into salvage and firewood. Since beginning our adoption journey, I've been collecting and reading as many adoption books as I can get my hands on. Often I have to special order the books from the back of OURS magazine because they are hard to find anywhere else. This gave me a great idea: to help generate income for our family while we start Rootwings, we've decided to go back to selling books. This time, instead of operating a store, like Logos, we're going to try being the booksellers at conferences. We have a few small conferences lined up and then NACAC, later in the summer, will be our big opportunity.

"We have to get these boxes organized and put away tonight, because we can't have them lying around the kitchen tomorrow when people arrive for Isaac's party," I remind Hector, calling Abel and Jose to give us a hand. With nine kids, it seems like it's always somebody's birthday, and tomorrow, Isaac turns three.

The party has been in full swing with kids racing around chasing balls and balloons outside for about an hour, so we decide to head inside for the cake and ice cream when the phone rings. "Start dishing up ice cream, Hec. I'll get the phone."

"Guess who just called?"

"Not again? It's only been a month since the last newspaper article."

"No, not another newspaper," I say. "It was this woman, Margaret Betts. She's an adoption facilitator for open adoptions and she's working with a woman who just had a baby. She wants to place her baby with us."

"What? I don't understand? What are open adoptions?" Hector asks.

"It's when the birth parents and the adoptive parents get to know each other and stay in touch," I explain. "And then the child can grow up knowing their birth parents. One of my friends has been reading a book called *Dear Birthmother, Thank You For Our Baby*, and it is pretty eye-opening. I ordered some copies for our book table and I'm going to read it myself. We've always wished we could have known the birth parents of our kids—it makes total sense to me."

"Well, anyway, it's a baby and you know what I said about babies. Just to be clear. No. More. Babies. I'm already buried in diapers."

"I told her . . . . " I start, but Hector interrupts me.

"Wait a minute. How does this woman know anything about us? Out of the blue she wants us for her baby? Now this really doesn't make sense! All the kids are eating cake and ice cream. Can we go out on the porch for a minute and you can fill me in a little more about this conversation?"

"She saw our picture in the *Free Press* article," I say on reaching the porch. "She noticed that our family is racially mixed and her baby is a mixed baby. She doesn't want him to grow up in an all-white family. But you are right. We agreed: no more babies. So I told Ms. Betts that we are not adding any more babies to the family, but we have been getting a lot of calls from families who want to adopt after that article came out, and maybe we can help find a family for this baby."

"Good answer," Hector says. "It's a wild story, but good answer. Let's go back inside and check on the party."

We get inside just in time to catch Isaac and his little friend Mark throwing clumps of cake across the table at Chelsea and Flory. "Whoa, cake is for eating, not for throwing!"

Hector pours a few beverages for the other parents, and then whispers to me, "I think you should call this Betts woman back. We should ask a few more questions."

"Questions? Like what?" I whisper back.

"Come outside again for a minute," he says.

By the time Isaac's party is over, we've been in and out four or five more times, going back and forth on what to do about this baby in Bennington. We talk, we ask questions, we pray, we call Ms. Betts back, and finally we end up talking directly to the birth mother, Darlene. All in the space of this one afternoon.

"I know it's crazy," Hector says as the last of our party guests pulls out of the driveway. "But I believe this baby is meant to be ours."

"Bu . . . bu . . . but you are the one who was so firm about 'No. More. Babies,'" I remind him.

"Yes, I know, but I believe God used that newspaper article to plant the seed of the idea in Darlene's heart to choose our family for this baby, and I just believe in my heart he's meant to be ours. Let's find out when we can pick him up."

> "Yes, I know, but I believe God used that newspaper article to plant the seed of the idea in Darlene's heart to choose our family for this baby, and I just believe in my heart he's meant to be ours.

We spend a quiet July 4 swimming and picnicking at Caspian Lake, staying for the fireworks and then settling everyone down as quickly as possible; we have a three-hour drive to Bennington first thing in the morning. Everyone except for SueAnn will make the trip. She's away at Camp Aloha for two weeks; she won a scholarship at a fundraiser we attended in the spring. As I drift off to sleep, I'm thinking of SueAnn and wondering how she'll feel coming home from camp next week to a new baby brother.

"That was one of the most interesting events I've ever been a part of," Hector says as he guides our van onto Route 7 North. Our newest son, six-day-old Todd, is asleep in his car seat, watched over carefully by Flory and Chelsea on either side of him.

"It sure was." On the drive down to Bennington, the kids had peppered us with questions. We gave them as much information as we could, including the fact that Todd was mixed. When they asked what that meant, we said, "He is half white and half black."

We'd planned an outdoor picnic in a park near Darlene's home, but it was pouring rain, so we moved the picnic inside. "Considering how crowded it was with all our kids and her two boys, everyone was incredibly well-behaved and really seemed to hit it off," I reflected.

"He sure is a cutie," Hector said. "It sure must have been hard for Darlene to hand him over to us when it was time to leave."

"I know. She is so brave and strong. I wonder if I could have been so selfless if I had been in her shoes. I really admire her," I say, and suddenly, tears are spilling from my eyes.

Hector reaches over and squeezes my hand, adding, "I know, my heart aches for her. I'm really glad she'll be able to see Todd once a year. I hope he'll understand when he's older why she decided to place him for adoption while raising his two brothers."

"We'll cross that bridge when we come to it," I say, checking on the back rows of our van. Everyone except for Jose is fast asleep. "I guess between last night's fireworks and today's festivities, we wore them out. Wore me out too—do you mind if I doze a little while you drive?"

"Doze away," Hector replies. "You can have night duty with the baby."

I am awaken in a start as we turn on to the dirt road leading to our house. "Wait," I say to Hector. "Go back to the general store."

"Why?"

"Let's rent a movie for the kids to watch. They're going to be up for awhile since they slept on the ride, but I want an easy, quiet activity for them. I just want to sit in the rocking chair with Todd, and cuddle him, and, you know, sounds corny, but I just want some quiet bonding time."

"OK," Hector says, turning the van around. We have an old TV, but no cable, so it only gets one channel and is rarely watched. For an occasional treat, we rent a VCR and movie for the kids to watch, typically on a rainy day.

Once the kids are settled in for the movie, I slip upstairs with Todd, rocking him, touching his soft curly hair and drinking in his newborn scent. "How did we end up with a newborn baby?" I whisper aloud. "I never thought there would be another newborn in our house. You are an unexpected blessing, sweet boy." I nuzzle his neck, realizing that the miracle has happened again— I am head-over-heels in love with this little person. I continue rocking until I notice he feels a little wet. "I'm really going to surprise your daddy—I am going to change your diaper! But don't get used to it—it's not in my contract!" I laugh.

I've just stripped Todd down naked when George walks in. "Is the movie over, bud?"

"No," he says, staring at Todd. "Mommy? I thought you said he was half black and half white."

"That's right, George. His first mommy is white and his first daddy is black."

George continued to study him for a moment, then says, "I don't see any white or black on him," and runs off to rejoin the movie. I'm left wondering what he was expecting Todd to look like, chuckling as I consider that he imagined a tiny zebra was hiding under the baby clothes.

"We have a lot of driving to do today—did you remember to check the oil?" I ask Hector a few days later. Our dashboard lights and gauges don't always work in our van, so I want to be sure all systems are go before we head out to pick SueAnn up from Camp Aloha, and then drive Jose and Abel to their adventure camp in Vershire.

"Sure did, all systems are go," he reports.

"I packed a cooler with plenty of drinks and mixed up a quart of Nutramigen for Joelle."

"OK, so let's pack up the babies . . . . "

"Got it!"

These camp scholarships have been a godsend, helping us address some of the stickier adoption issues that come up in families adopting older children. SueAnn was so used to being the "mom" for her siblings (or the "parentified adult," as they call it in the books), she needed time and space to just enjoy being a kid. And now with the new baby in the family, she will still be able to use her nurturing side when she gets home.

For the first few months after the four siblings joined our family, Abel and Jose have struggled to find their place. Each was used to being the oldest. On top of that, Jose and George, just a month apart in age, often get into scuffles, and Abel always takes George's side, no matter what, creating some tense family dynamics at times. Abel and Jose actually have a lot of interests and abilities in common, so we decided to send them to two weeks of camp together, hoping that they'll find their own common ground and forge the beginnings of a brother-to-brother relationship. George will go to a local day camp with Chelsea and Flory when we return from NACAC later in the summer.

"Guess who just called, Hec," I say the next morning while he's giving Todd a bottle.

"Well, it better not be anything about another baby," he replies. "I'm already in love with this one, but three in diapers is more than enough."

"Haha, not this time. It was my dad. My parents want to

come out here, to Cabot, and babysit all the kids so we can go out to dinner for our anniversary. And they're giving us a gift certificate to The Creamery Restaurant in Danville."

"Really? Wow. That's amazing. They've never watched all the kids together before; they usually take them one or two at a time. And always at their house, never here. This will be an adventure for them."

"Yeah, especially since they don't know about Todd. Or Claudia."

"Did you tell them?"

"I was too stunned by the call. I told my dad I'd talk to you about the dinner plans and call them back. We have to tell them about Todd, and also, they don't even know we have Claudia, our summer exchange student here from Guatemala. So we'll have to tell them about her too."

"Happy anniversary, Mrs. Badeau," Hector says, lifting his wine glass to clink with mine.

"Happy anniversary, Mr. Badeau," I reply, leaning in for a kiss. We entwine our wine glasses, just as we did on our wedding day, and take a sip.

"I was just remembering: last year we spent our anniversary at a campground near the Grand Canyon."

"And we only had five kids—now we have 10. What a difference a year makes."

"So, Sue," Hector looks at me earnestly. "Do you think we will ever have an anniversary where we've been married more years than the number of kids we have?"

"Only God knows the answer to that one," I laugh. "I wonder how my parents are making out with all the kids."

"Me too—I'm just glad they recovered from the shock after we sprung a new baby, and a Guatemalan exchange student, on them. I have to hand it to them, they didn't back out of the offer to babysit. This is such a nice treat. I am so thankful to them. We needed a little time for the two of us. As you said, it's been quite a year."

9

David, Trish, Renee

"Sue, you awake?" I can't sleep. Hector whispers to me on our third night back home in our own bed after traveling to Florida for this year's NACAC conference. It was our second year as the official booksellers and we're still worn out from the trip.

"I'm awake, but barely. What's up? It's after 11 and I have to be in the office early in the morning, remember? I'm meeting with the Kirpans about the siblings they're hoping to adopt from Texas."

"I'm glad they are moving forward with that," he says, then continues. "Those six siblings from New Mexico—I just can't get them out of my mind, and I can't sleep. Ever since that social worker told us that they are scattered all over in different homes,

I just keep thinking that maybe we can pull them back together as a family."

"I'll call their worker tomorrow and see if I can learn more about what's going on with them," I promise. "But for now, please, let's go to sleep."

"All right. All right."

After Todd's adoption last summer, we traveled to NACAC in Toronto with all ten kids, plus our exchange student, Claudia, and ran the official book table for the conference. Following that, the next twelve months flew by in a blur; everything seemed to happen at once. We met the Debolts in person and they invited Rootwings to join their AASK (Adopt A Special Kid) America Network. They came to Vermont and did a fundraiser for us and we raised enough money to hire a director and open an office. I wrote a curriculum called "The Adoption Roadmap" to prepare prospective parents, and we placed our first several children into adoptive homes. It's been a heady, exhilarating time, knowing that we are really helping kids get the one thing they need more than anything—a permanent, loving home.

On weekends Hector and I took turns traveling around our region of the country—as far south as Virginia or as far west as Illinois—in our big van, toting boxes of books to sell at conferences and spending one-on-one time with each of the children in turn. We get so busy with the book sales, we hire our friend Doug Farnham to help. Our van breaks down more times than we can count, but other than that, life is good.

When it is time to attend this year's NACAC conference in Orlando, Florida, we travel in a caravan, with several other Rootwings families, including the Kirpans from Moretown. As soon as they got involved with Rootwings, Patty and Gary became our closest friends and strongest supporters. Like us, they have a particular heart for sibling groups; they've already adopted four children and are now considering three more.

While at NACAC in Orlando, a social worker from New Mexico stopped by our table to buy some books and recognized us, asking if we were the family that had adopted Abel, SueAnn, George, and Flory. As we continued talking, we asked her if a family had ever been found for the six teens who had been on our hearts for nearly two years. Sadly, we learned that not only were they still waiting for a family, but that they were scattered in different homes across the state of New Mexico.

"Look what came in the mail today," Hector says, a week later. "The new *Los Ninos* from New Mexico. But look at this: instead of picturing all six of the kids, they left out the two oldest boys—this time they only have pictures of Lilly, Renee, Trish, and David. I can't believe that. Have you heard anything at all back from the social worker?"

"As a matter of fact, I got a call from her today," I reply. "She told me that they decided to stop looking for a family for JD and Fisher due to their ages, and actually, even though they pictured Lilly in *Los Ninos*, they've decided that they're really only going to focus on the three youngest ones. After two years of looking, they've decided that there just aren't any families for six teenagers."

"That breaks my heart," Hector says. "I know it's hard to find families for all six, but the thought of splitting them up is terrible. Sometimes when things are tough in your family, your siblings are the only people you can trust."

I know Hector knows this, in part, from his own family experience with an alcoholic father. If it weren't for his brother Bernie and his sister Irene, his life might have been very different.

"Two years ago, they weren't interested in our family—we were too young, too white, and lived too far away for them to even look at our home study. What will they say now?" Hector wonders aloud.

"I asked her to send us the updated information and she said she would. She also asked us to send our most recent home study over to her so she can review it with her supervisor."

"Sounds like a plan for now. In the meantime, let's pray about it. Who knows? We handled six teenage boys at a time at the group home; maybe that was meant to be our training ground. Meanwhile, maybe we should try learning a little sign language," Hector adds, remembering that the youngest of the six siblings, David, is deaf.

School begins and, after a few adjustments, we've found our rhythm with ten kids. Hector gets up at five to have his quiet time before the craziness begins. By 7:30 five kids are on the bus to Cabot Elementary School, and George is on his way to school in Barre. Isaac, Raj, Joelle, and Todd keep Hector busy at home. His days are filled with mountains of laundry, some house cleaning, and lots of time reading stories—all of our kids love story time! Most days, I head in to Rootwings and work alongside Peter, our executive director, or travel around the state teaching classes to prospective adoptive families.

Occasionally, there is a day like today, when Hector has a Father Grublet project and I stay home with the four little ones. We've just finished snack time and are waiting for the school buses to come up the hill with the big kids when the phone rings.

"Head lice!" I recoil in shock. "I don't understand. How did this happen?" The school nurse in Barre just called to tell me that there's been an outbreak of head lice in George's second-grade classroom and, unfortunately, George is one of those afflicted. I'm mortified. When I was a child growing up, we only heard about one or two cases of head lice, and it was very clear that it was something that never happened in "good" families.

I listen numbly as the nurse tells me what I have to do. I'm shaking as I hang up the phone and dial Dr. DiNicola's office, asking them to please call in a prescription shampoo to the pharmacy in Barre. As soon as all of the kids are home, I pile them into our van and we head in to town to pick it up.

"I'm going to die!" I yell as Hector comes into the kitchen. The sight in front of him must be shocking, I think, and suddenly I burst into tears. I'm standing at the sink in my bra and panties scrubbing Joelle's head under a spray of hot water. The rest of the kids are shivering around the table, stripped down to their underwear.

"What in the world? . . . . " he asks.

"Lice!" I scream.

"Calm down and tell me what's going on and what you need me to do," he says.

I explain the instructions I received from the nurse. Every person in the house has to be shampooed with Quell, for a full three minutes, in hot water. Every item of clothing in the house has to be washed and dried on the hottest cycle. All of the towels and bedding have to be washed, and all the stuffed animals and pillows put into plastic bags and not taken out for three weeks. The furniture has to be sprayed. And then we have to comb everyone out with this special little metal comb.

"You've got to be kidding me," Hector says in disbelief.

"Do I look like I'm kidding?" I shriek. "I'm going insane here. Joelle's shampoo is last—I've been scrubbing heads for an hour under scalding water. My hands are numb. I haven't even started the laundry. That's why the kids have no clothes on. I can't handle this."

"I'll work on the laundry," he offers. "I'll get at least one load done quickly with PJs for everyone so they can get something on."

"Thanks. But you have to strip down and shampoo yourself first," I tell him. I'll get the PJs going while you do that. Then you can help with the combing out—I haven't even started that part yet. We have to figure out some dinner, too."

"I'm glad we're done with that project, Sue," Hector says when we finally fall into bed—on our sheetless mattress, with no blankets—at three in the morning. "If another kid ever comes home with head lice again, I'm going to shave all their heads, even the girls."

"Yeah, they'll love that," I say. "We'll be known as the 'Baldie' family instead of the Badeau family.

Head lice plagued us repeatedly for months after that. We never did shave heads, although Hector's mother did cut SueAnn, Chelsea, and Flory's hair quite short one day when she was helping us after another lice outbreak. At the time, it was the most stressful event of my life. Little could I imagine that the day would come when I'd laugh about it.

I walk into the kitchen with the mail in my hands. "You must have been busy today. You left the mail in the mailbox," I say to Hector.

"Yeah, a lot of laundry today," he says. "Why, anything special in the mail?"

"As a matter of fact, there is. Look at this."

"Vermonter of the Year?" he says. "How did that happen?"

"Read the rest of the letter. One of our volunteers at Rootwings wrote a letter nominating us and we were selected. It's based on our work with Rootwings and the kids we have adopted. I'm pretty overwhelmed."

"Wow, that is really something. It's pretty funny," Hector muses. "It seems that some people think we are completely crazy and others think we are saints. No one seems to believe we are just a normal family trying to live out our faith one day at a time."

"Well, it says here that they will do an article on us in the *Vermont Sunday* magazine. Maybe we can convince them we are normal," I laugh. "And if not, at least maybe the article will inspire a few other people to adopt some kids too."

"Yeah, as long as it helps kids, it's worth it. But when will the interview be? We leave for New Mexico in four days," he reminds me.

After going back and forth with the social workers all fall, they have decided to approve our family to adopt the youngest of the six teen siblings. We'll travel to New Mexico next week to meet David, who's deaf, and bring him home with us to Vermont. We're hoping while we're there to at least meet the other five. We know the older kids have more say on whether or not they want to be adopted, but maybe once they meet us they will be interested in our family.

"Now boarding. US Air flight to Burlington, Vermont."

"Let's go, Renee and Trish," Hector says, "That's our flight." He motions for David to join us and slings a backpack across his shoulders.

As we board the plane, we notice Vermont Governor Kunin seated in first class. We greet her, and she agrees to take a photo of us with our newest family members once we land in Vermont.

"We did it, Hec," I say. "We convinced the muckety-mucks that Renee and Trish still need a family."

"Not bad," he replies, "We're batting .500 on this trip. I'm glad we got to meet all of the kids. It's too bad Lilly missed the going-away party for David at the School for the Deaf, but I'm glad we got to meet her when we visited Hobbs."

"Yeah, thankfully we survived our ride on the crazy little plane. What were there—ten seats on it? That was worse than a roller-coaster ride," I say. He knows how much I hate amusement park rides.

"Well, at least we got their worker to agree to bring Fisher, Lilly, and JD to Vermont for a visit next month. This way at least they will have a chance to see where their siblings are and get to know our family a little better. Who knows what will happen after that?"

"I'm looking forward to that. In the meantime, I have all the arrangements made with the Austine School for the Deaf to get David started, but since we didn't know Trish and Renee were coming, I'm starting from square one with Spaulding."

"You'll get some interesting looks and comments when you register Trish and Renee. There are quite a few teachers, and the assistant principal, still there from when we were students. They might have a hard time figuring out how we managed to have teenagers so soon—and black teenagers at that!"

"Coach Poirier is still coaching hockey at Spaulding too. He'll be excited to hear there are some new Badeaus in the high school—I wonder if JD or Fisher are interested in hockey? I have a feeling this newest leg of our journey will be filled with interesting experiences," I say.

We arrive at home and eight of the kids come tumbling out the porch door, nearly knocking us down in their excitement. Mamere, who was babysitting, is waiting in the living room with Raj and Joelle. The kids are especially eager to try out their sign language skills on David. We've been taking lessons from a couple, Dennis and Jean, who are fluent signers and also recently adopted an older child through Rootwings. As each child tries to out-do each other with their signing skills, they eventually get around to taking David upstairs to show him his new room. When Hector, Trish, Renee, and I catch up with his entourage, David is standing in the middle of his room, looking at all of his new siblings and making the sign for family over and over. I catch Hector's eyes and notice that his, like mine, are brimming with tears.

This is our first glimpse of David's contagious smile, optimistic spirit, and hard-working readiness to jump in to new experiences with both feet. It's no wonder that we'll soon be calling him our "family ambassador."

10

JD, Fisher, and Lilly

"Can you believe this snow?" I say to Hector. "Of all days, a real nor'easter has to hit the day they're coming. But I just got off the phone with US Air and they say the flight is still coming in, so I guess I better start heading up to Burlington."

"Just drive slowly. You'll be all right," he says, "Trish! Renee! If you still plan to go to the airport with Mom, come on. It's time to go!"

We've had more than a few cups of hot chocolate at the small Burlington airport, but sure enough, their flight is landing. I see them walking toward us before they see me, and I can tell that they are all shocked to see a whirlwind of whiteness just outside the window. All three of them, and Nancy, their worker, are wearing very "hip" and decidedly un-wintery clothes. After our initial greetings, they wait for their luggage while I go to a pay phone to call Hector and let him know they finally landed.

"You should get a room in a hotel there in Burlington and drive home tomorrow, Sue," he says.

"No, it wasn't that bad on the way up—as long as I went slow. We'll be fine," I say.

"Well, it's still snowing like crazy here," he adds. "We've got at least 16 inches of fresh snow since you left and more on the way."

"We'll be fine."

Driving slowly, following the plow as often as I can, I'm confident we'll make it home. Nancy is sitting in the front, looking a little shell-shocked about the situation. JD, Fisher, and Lilly are in the back peppering Renee and Trish with questions about life in Vermont. "Are there any other black kids at your high school?" Lilly asks.

"Yeah, a few," Renee says.

"No, not really," says Trish. "You know there are a few that look black, but they don't act black."

Finally, I'm making the turn from Lower Cabot onto the hill that leads to our house—just three miles to go. Less than a mile from the bottom, I can see that we're not going to make it, so I turn around and decide to go the longer way. It's a more gently sloping hill and I'm hopeful I'll get more traction. We're doing well until, about a mile from our house, a car is stuck crossways on the road and we can't go any further. We have to walk. I tell the kids they can leave their stuff in the van; it'll be locked and safe. But Fisher won't leave without his boom box.

"I'm freezing!" Lilly yells as she lurches into the house ahead of the others, waking up Hector, who's dozed on the couch.

"Quiet down, you knucklehead," JD says. "You want to wake

up the dead?"

Nancy shakes snow from her clothes, and Fisher brushes snow off his boom box. Everyone huddles around the warmth of the Russian furnace.

"We had to start walking about a mile from here," I explain, "but then Rusty came along in his truck and picked us up, so we're OK. We'll have to walk back in the morning to get the luggage."

"Well, I'm glad you all made it. I'll show you to your rooms so we can all get some sleep, and we can talk more in the morning," Hector says, whispering to me as we lead the way. "I told you to get a room!"

When we finally fall into bed, Hector gives me a quick kiss and says, "Well, this is off to a great start. I'm pretty sure they're *never* going to want to come back here again."

"Who knows?" I say, sleepily. "You never know what God has up his sleeve."

"Hey, JD," I hear Hector say while I'm making coffee the day before they're scheduled to head back to New Mexico. "I need to split up some wood outside, do you want to give me a hand?"

"Sure, Mr. Hector," he says, and both he and Fisher head out the door.

Several minutes later, the three of them come inside, and Hector says that they would like to talk to Nancy and I. "We've been thinking," JD begins.

"About your offer to include all of us in your family," Fisher adds. "JD and I would like that. We'd like to move up here. We were just talking to Mr. Hector about it. We want to be a family again with David and our sisters."

"The snow adventure didn't discourage you?" I say, somewhat in shock.

Nancy turns to Fisher, adding, "I know JD is out of school, but this is the last semester of your senior year. Are you sure you want to move three thousand miles across the country at this stage of your life?"

"To be reunited with my siblings, it's worth it," he says.

"What about Lilly?"

"She's not sure yet," JD says. "But we're ready."

"What time is it?" Hector says as we plop into bed.

"It's midnight."

"What a day. Can't believe JD and Fisher decided they want to join the family. What Fisher said about it being worth it to move three thousand miles even in his senior year of high school—that really touched me. Although I have to admit, I am a little scared. Do we really know what we are getting into? Those guys are both over six feet—they tower over me!"

"Don't worry, Hec. They're good kids. It'll be a great adventure. And our batting average just went up a few hundred points—five out of six of them are being reunited. What a blessing!"

"Let's get some sleep—love you."

"Love you too—good night."

Fisher has a car. So the plans are made for me to fly to New Mexico to meet up with him, pick up JD, and drive back. We'll have to drive straight through because I have an important licensing meeting for Rootwings that I can't miss. After saying good-bye to Lilly, we hit the road—JD, Fisher, and I each taking four-hour driving shifts with about 2,500 miles to cover.

As we cross from New Mexico into Texas, Fisher says to me, "I smoke, you know." And a few minutes later, "I sometimes drink a beer." I expected to be tested when parenting teens— the group home gave us plenty of practice—and this seems mild so far.

"Hector and I will work with you on that," I say. "We've been around the block with teenage boys. Nothing you do is going to surprise us or make us change our minds about welcoming you into our family. "

On the ride, I learn that Fisher feels he needs more time to complete high school, so we agree to enroll him as a junior instead of a senior. Since JD is out of school, I talk to him about working in our family book and packaging business and helping with the conference book sales. We have a big conference coming up in the Catskills, and I can really use his help. It's a new group called Families of Tomorrow. They met us at NACAC and asked us to be their official bookseller. They promise a couple of thousand attendees at their conference—this could really help our business grow!

When March rolls around, JD and I head for New York. We have a great time at the conference. He gets to meet a lot of my adoption friends, and we take a drive into the Big Apple one evening with our friends Brus and Diane and their daughter. While walking on 42nd Street we are surprised to see Bernadette Peters exit the stage door of one of the theatres. What a treat.

The conference, however, is a bust. We'd ordered a huge inventory of books and sold very few. The promised thousands of participants didn't materialize, and we're left holding the bag, along with all the other vendors who had been lured to the conference. As we pull into our driveway back in Cabot, I am worried about how we'll pay for all these books when the bills come due in thirty days. *Lord, I'm trusting you to provide a way—you just gave us five more mouths to feed. Please help us with the finances.*

That worry quickly evaporates as Hector comes to the door and says, "Batting a thousand!"

"What are you talking about?" I ask.

"Lilly called. She talked for a while with Trish, and then

asked for you, but since you weren't here, she settled for me," he jokes. "She says she wants to come join her family after all. I told her you will call Nancy tomorrow and make the travel arrangements. She heard we enrolled Fisher as a junior and she wants to do that too. She'd like one more year of high school."

"Wow, what brought that about?"

"She didn't really say, but basketball season is over and she wants to make the move before track season begins."

"Interesting. God sure does work in mysterious ways. After all these years apart, they will now be together . . . That's so awesome!"

"I have some cool news, Hec."

"What's that?"

"Well, I just got off the phone with Nancy in New Mexico. I fly out there on Thursday, sign all the papers, and fly home with Lilly on Friday. And it seems that the only seats left on the flight she is arranging for Lilly and I are in first class. I've never flown first class before. I'm psyched!"

"How can I know that we can really trust you? What makes you different than all the other families who made promises to us and then let us down?"

"How can I know that we can really trust you? What makes you different than all the other families who made promises to us and then let us down?" Lilly is questioning me just as soon we are settled into our comfy, first class seats.

"We've made a commitment to you: you're part of our family now. That commitment is just as serious to us as the marriage vows Hector and I said to each other nine years ago when we got married—'for better and for worse.' We feel the same way about adoption. We're making a commitment not only to you but also to God, and with his help we intend to keep it. It doesn't matter what you do—get pregnant, go to jail, get hooked on drugs, drop out of school—no matter what happens, you are our family, we are your parents, and we'll all be in this together."

Little did I know that every single thing on my list of 'worst-case scenarios' would come true within the next 10 years. But I did know that God would walk this path with us every step of the way.

"Great job, Fisher and Lilly," Hector says as we walk towards the parking lot at Spaulding. "I'm not an expert on track, but you left everyone else in the dust—that was amazing."

"Thanks. There was a lot more competition in New Mexico," Lilly says. "I think we'll do OK here in Vermont, but that wasn't my best time."

"Looked great to me," Hector says. "And Fisher, your long jump was incredible. You really took it to them."

As we approach the vehicles, Fisher and Lilly head for Fisher's car. Hector and I, along with our crew of little kids, walk toward the van. "Can we ride home with Fisher?" Renee asks.

"If it's OK with him," I say.

"Don't forget, mud season has hit—watch yourself on our hill, Fish," Hector cautions.

We arrive home before the kids and our answering machine light is flashing. As I retrieve the messages, one is from Marialisa Calta from the *New York Times*. They saw the Vermonter of the Year article on our family, and they want to do an article on us.

"Hec, listen to this message—the *New York Times*! Can you believe that?"

"Wow—all this publicity. It is a little much. Not sure how to react," he says.

"This will bring national attention to kids who need homes," I say.

"As long as we remember our purpose and calling. It's to help kids find homes and give the glory to God—not to us."

"I know, we have to be careful not to let it go to our heads, but be thankful for the opportunity."

Just then, Renee comes storming into the house with Trish close behind her. "What's going on?" I ask.

"Fisher got his car stuck in the mud," Renee answers. "Him and JD are trying to get it out, but it's only getting worse. We decided to walk home, but Lilly didn't want to ruin her shoes so she's sitting in the car,".

"How far down the hill?" Hector asks.

"Down by the flat part before the steep part," Trish says.

"Oh, half a mile or so. OK, I'll go give them a hand."

"You should have seen the mess they were in," Hector says after he steps out of the shower. "When I was walking toward the car, they were cussing a blue streak, but as soon as they saw me, it stopped. I guess they have a little respect and discretion. Anyway, it took a lot of pushing, and we all were covered in mud, but we made it. What a mess—now Fisher is outside washing his car."

"Hmmmph," I say. "That's a losing battle during mud season!"

"Another stack of mail came today," Hector tells me as I come in from Barre; he has a pile of envelopes in his hand. I ride to and from Rootwings with Fisher and Lilly now, and my schedule revolves around their school and track schedule. Every day since the *New York Times* article appeared, we have received phone calls and mail. Most are from people interested in adopting, or some who want to donate to Rootwings. The phone at the office has been ringing off the hook, too.

"It's so exciting to see the response—exactly what we prayed for. So many children are going to get families," I say, just as the phone rings.

"You can't begin to imagine who that was," I say when I get off the phone. "It was Lucie Arnaz—you know, the daughter of Lucille Ball and Desi Arnaz? She is in the hospital recuperating from something and she read the article about our family. She and her husband want to come to Vermont and meet us."

"Yeah, right. And she wants to sell us a bridge in Brooklyn too, right?" Hector says, not quite believing me.

"No, really. It was *her*."

"Well, you'll have to tell me all about it when I get back. I have to leave with Jose, Abel, and SueAnn for Little League practice. I cooked up some burgers—the little kids ate already. You and Fisher and Lilly can have what's left. Oh, and Flory has a homework assignment she needs a little help with—in math. I saved it for you."

Lucie Arnaz and her husband, Larry Luckinbill (an actor in his own right), decided to come visit on a day when Lilly has a basketball game. They agree to join us at the game and then we go out to dinner at a local diner in Barre before we head back home to Cabot and they leave for the airport in Burlington. Earlier, they spent the day meeting all of our other kids at our house. They've invited us to visit them in California next time we take a summer trip, and they promise to explore other ways to support our family efforts to find homes for waiting children.

"You just never know what is around the next curve in the road," Hector says.

The phone is ringing as we enter the house. It's JD. He has been detained by the police in Barre. "What? Are you kidding? Let me talk to the officer—what's his name? Oh brother, I know him," Hector says, taking the phone.

"Yes, he's our son, and yes, he has friends in that neighborhood. What did he do that caused you to detain him?"

"What's going on?" I ask.

"I guess racism is alive and well in Barre," Hector says, shaking his head. "One of the policemen in Barre who has arrested my brother a few times when he got into fights after drinking has detained JD for no good reason. The officer says JD's car was parked in a neighborhood where it 'looked like he didn't belong.' I'd like to wring his scrawny neck." Needless to say, Hector is steaming.

"That probably won't help. I knew our kids would face some racism, but I didn't expect it in the town where we grew up and everyone knows us." I'm shaking my head. "Who knows what other issues we will encounter?"

The kitchen is a disaster. Hector and I have been outside enjoying the warm spring evening and chatting with our neighbor when we hear a crash in the kitchen. A trail of spilled juice leads from the kitchen to the playroom. Peanut butter is smeared on the counter and shards from a couple of broken plates are strewn on the floor. We hear Raj crying in the playroom.

"Everyone get in the kitchen, right now!" Hector yells. The kids come running in, doing their best to look innocent. "What happened here?" No one comes forward.

I go to Raj and pick him up, comforting him, as he says, "He hit me, kicked me, pulled my hair."

"Who?" I ask. Raj doesn't reply.

"I will give you one minute to step up and tell me what happened, or else it will be early bed for everyone," Hector says. After waiting a minute, he begins to count down: "Ten, nine, eight, seven . . . "

"I made the mess," Jose says. "I was making the juice and I spilled it, then I dropped the plates. And then I went in the playroom and started bugging Raj."

No one else says a word. "Is that right?" Hector asks, looking into each child's face. "That's the whole story? OK, Jose, you stay in here and clean up and then you have half an hour early bed."

"Jose didn't do all that by himself, you know," I say to Hector as we walk out of the room to get Joelle and Todd ready for bed.

"I know that. He always wants to take the consequences when no one else steps forward. We have to figure out a way to break that pattern."

Now it's my turn to be furious. Barre City School district has sent us a certified letter billing us for thousands of dollars of tuition, and saying that we can't send Fisher, Lilly, Renee, or Trish to Spaulding next year since we live in Cabot. We had advocated for them to attend Spaulding when they first arrived, feeling that they would adjust better in the larger high school with more academic and sports options than in Cabot's small school. Although everyone was agreeable for the rest of this school year, they have now reversed course.

"We can fight this, Sue. But to tell you the truth, I've been thinking that we should consider moving into Barre. It's not just the teenagers, but also our doctors, our grocery store, the Root-wings office. . . . It's just a lot to have to drive back and forth all the time, especially when the roads are bad."

"I hate to give up this house and land," I say. "And all the younger kids are doing so well here, I hate to uproot them."

"I know there are lots of great memories here. Like going out into the back woods with the kids to get our Christmas tree every year. Chelsea's first day of kindergarten. Or running races with JD and Fisher and Doug, our friend from church, when he visited. JD always scrambling to make an excuse when Fisher beat him. And then the *Woman's Day* article and how they made that funny family photo, sticking Fisher and Lilly in the window when they weren't really here at the time."

"All the birthday parties and cookouts," I add. "And the kids decorating their bikes for the Fourth of July parade. Making so-papaillas for Flory's class. Raj and Joelle and Todd all learned to walk here. The clubhouse in the back, and the year you made the playroom as the special Christmas gift—an indoor sandbox, jungle gym, ballet barre—we'll never replace that. All the kids putting on plays, Abel and George making tree forts, picking rhubarb and making pie, skiing out the back door . . ."

"Yeah, and the time Jose was skiing with Earl and Ricky and they skied over the top of his head!"

"That was a great memory?" I ask.

"Well, it's a memory, maybe not so great, but funny now. Or the time Isaac jumped out the window of his second-floor bedroom trying to be Superman—how many stitches did he need? And the day you were so mad you started breaking plates."

"Lilly breaking the window on the van . . . SueAnn getting hit in the head with a baseball bat at Abel's game, or the day we got called because JD had driven his car into the river . . . "

By now, tears are rolling down our cheeks we are laughing so hard. "I'll miss this place. But you're right, I think we do need to move to Barre. At least we have a friend from church who is a Realtor; she won't swindle us, and we can trust her. I'll call her in the morning," I say.

"When we bought this house, I thought I would grow old and die here," Hector says. "And be buried in the backyard. But I can see now that this was just a stepping-stone on the road God has for us. Not sure what the next phase will look like, but like Doug always says in Bible study, 'When you take it to the Lord in prayer, be prepared to be surprised by His answer.'"

11

Alysia

"That was a great game tonight. Spaulding really kicked some butt," Hector says to me. "Lilly really showed them how the game is played."

I nod, adding, "I love the way they play that song, 'Basketball Jones,' when she's warming up. Tomorrow we get to do it again. Fisher has a game."

"Flory, Chelsea, George . . . let's go." As Hector buckles Todd and Joelle into their car seats, he says, "I'm so glad we're in Barre now. That constant back and forth from Cabot was killing me. I still wish we had gotten the house on French Street; it was so perfect."

"I know. Short Street isn't ideal, but it will do for now. And thank goodness for all our church friends stepping up and helping us turn every inch of extra space into another bedroom! Who knew you could turn a three-bedroom house into a nine-bedroom house in less than a month!"

"And don't forget the support from the Luckinbills. That was a godsend. . . . I never imagined we'd end up around the corner from the old Bugbee Avenue house I lived in as a kid," Hector chuckles.

"I was on my way back to the Rootwings office from visiting an adoptive family out in Orange, so I thought I'd stop in and grab those files I was reviewing last night," I say as I breeze into the kitchen at lunchtime. "Whoa, what's Isaac doing here? Didn't he go to school today?" Isaac is sitting at the dining room table with his arms crossed and an uneaten sandwich in front of him.

"I got a call from Brook Street School and they said they were sending him home for lunch—not just today but for at least two weeks. He's not allowed to have school lunch anymore—at least for now."

"What? How can they do that?"

"Well, apparently, he lost his temper at some kid and tipped his desk over during lunch and then chased him outside until the other kid was cornered against the fence."

"Isaac did that? What's the rest of the story?"

"Well, turns out he was defending another kid who was being picked on. The teacher said that the kid he attacked is constantly bullying this other kid, and Isaac is always coming to his rescue. So today, I guess he snapped. The teacher was actually kind of proud of Isaac for stepping up, because both the bully and the kid he was hassling are two years older and a lot bigger than Isaac. But she says she can't have kids throwing desks around and beating each other up during the lunch break."

I try to hold back the big smile that is creeping across my

face. "Well she's right, of course. He can't go around beating people up, but I have to agree, I'm super proud of him for defending a child that was being bullied. Only five and he's already a little knight!"

"And he has the Badeau temper," Hector adds. "We'll have to keep our eye on that."

"Hey Mom, Dad," Trish says at dinner. "I'm going to try out for the flag team. Renee and Lilly and Fisher are all on the track team. I'm not good at track, but I want to do something after school."

"Good for you, Trish," I say. I'm proud of her for trying again after getting cut from the cheerleading squad in the fall. I don't want to encourage the kids to see racism everywhere, but it was hard not to in that instance. Trish has great gymnastic talent, I watched several of the try-outs, and she was able to jump higher, do cleaner splits and cartwheels, and was just generally better than several of the girls who made the team. But she wasn't blonde like the rest of them.

Hector says: "Keep me posted on the schedule. I'll pick you up when I can, but some nights you'll have to walk home because I'll be in the middle of making dinner."

"Mom, is it my special day this week?" Flory asks.

"Yes, that's right, on Thursday. Have you thought about what you want to do?"

People sometimes ask us how we have enough one-on-one time for each child when we have so many. We use a lot of strategies, both planned and spontaneous, but one of my favorites is having "special days" with each child. Once a week, one child has a day with me. They can come to work with me, we go out to lunch together, and they get to pick out one activity they want me to do with them. With sixteen kids, it takes a few months to get to everyone, so no one misses too much school. We all look forward to it. Hector takes one child a week out to breakfast at the diner on the weekend, and I also take a few different kids grocery shopping with me each week.

"I want to go visit the Stuwes and see the horses," Flory replies.

"Oh that would be fun. I'll call Ruth later tonight and see if we can make that work." Changing the subject, I turn to Hector and say, "Did you tell the kids the news?"

"What news is that, Dad?" Trish asks.

"Mom got a funny call today at Rootwings. They told her we won an award called the Kleenex Says Bless You Award." Abel and Jose start sneezing and "blessing" each other and everyone starts giggling.

"I know, I know, it sounds silly," I say. "But it turns out it's real. They're going to give two thousand dollars to Rootwings and Dad and I get to go to Washington, DC to get the award. We'll get to meet Paul Newman while we're there."

"When do we go?" SueAnn asks.

"Well, it's not the whole family. Just mom and I go," Hector explains.

"That's no fair," George complains.

"Who's going to watch us when you're gone?" Flory asks.

"Those are all details we'll figure out. Don't worry. Now let's finish dinner so we can have a little play time before bed."

"That was great," Hector says as we buckle our seatbelts for the flight home. "Two whole days of just me and you in a hotel. When will that happen again?"

"Who knows? It was heavenly. And that whole basket full of snacks and goodies they left in the hotel room—the kids will be thrilled with those treats."

"Willard Scott was hilarious—we were so lucky we got to sit at his table. And I was really humbled by the other award winners. Those people are doing great things— helping children who are dying from cancer, feeding thousands of homeless people every day. I can't believe we were in the same room with all of them."

"Well, it was a little over the top, but now we're back to reality," I say as our plane begins to descend toward Burlington. "Just a few weeks to finish up all the plans for JD's wedding. Who knew we'd be planning a wedding so soon?"

"Who knew I'd be a grandfather at 33?" Hector says.

"Well, I read that Loretta Lynn was a grandmother by the time she was 29, so we have her beat a little. Maybe someday that will be the title of my autobiography: Me and Loretta Lynn," I joke.

"JD has given us some good laughs," Hector adds with a smirk on his face.

"I know. I can't stop laughing every time I think about the time he took that girl to the Spaulding Prom. He was getting ready to go and said he was a little nervous about pinning the 'croissant' on her dress. I'll never look at a corsage the same way again." We're both laughing loudly as we walk off the plane.

"It's a good thing God gave us a sense of humor, or else I don't know how we'd cope some days. When JD told us Melissa was pregnant, I felt like I had been sucker-punched. We try so hard to teach our kids the right values and to wait and work toward God's plan for their lives . . . " He trails off.

"I know. We were both devastated. Not to mention embarrassed to tell our parents, or friends at church. It makes me feel a little like a fraud, or a failure as a parent, when we win awards like this, but then things at home run off track." I sigh. "We have to rely on God now to give us the grace and wisdom to make sure our response shows love and compassion and acceptance without encouraging any of the other kids to follow the same path."

"That will be tricky."

We pull into the driveway and see several faces in the bedroom windows on the second and third floors. "Looks like not everyone is asleep. Big surprise," I say as we head into the house.

"What an awesome day," I say, leaning back into Hector's arms as we collapse on the couch moments after the last of the guests leave. "After the tense meetings between us and Melissa's parents in the last two months, I'm so thankful we worked everything out. They seemed happy, and I think JD was really happy with his day."

"Yeah, we were crowded. I can't believe we pulled off both a ceremony and reception in this tiny house," Hector adds. "Considering the tight space, everyone was well-behaved. The service was really sweet and meaningful. Although our kitchen is definitely too small as a dance floor."

"Oh, come on, I know you can dance anywhere. I even heard you once danced on a table in college, although I am glad I didn't witness that!"

"Hey, where'd you hear that?" he asks with a most innocent-looking expression.

"Oh, I have my eyes and ears everywhere! Anyway, the only down moment was when Uncle Philip had to leave. I sure pray things get better for him soon."

"Yeah, me too. Speaking of prayer, I pray that everything will work out for JD and Melissa—it's got to be tough starting a marriage with a baby on the way."

"At least they have strong support from both her family and ours. And they have good heads on their shoulders. Changing the subject here: do you mind if we finish cleanup tomorrow? It's after 1 AM already and I'm dead tired."

"Good idea. Let's go to bed."

"Ummmmm, smells good," I say as I step into the kitchen, home a little early from work a week after the wedding.

"Fisher volunteered to cook. The kids love it when he cooks instead of me," Hector says as I take a peek under the lid of the simmering pot of sweet rice, next to a pan of crackling fried fish.

"They love your cooking too, Hec. You're just too predictable . . . if it's Wednesday it must be shepherd's pie . . . . they want a little variety. I really need to get a little more organized about making that family menu plan I've been talking about. But for tonight, I'll just enjoy!"

"So, how was your day? Any progress on finding families for those five babies from Texas?"

"Yes, it's great—we've found families for four of them. Just one left."

"Oh, so did your cousin Victor and his wife decide to adopt one of those babies?" he asks.

"Yes, I'm so excited. This is the third member of our extended family to adopt since we started Rootwings—your brother Edgar, the Langevins, and now the Garcias. I love that! Anyway, I brought home the photo of the one baby that we still need to find a family for. Her name is Alysia. I thought if I put her photo on our fridge, we can all remember to pray for her until a family is found."

But I have still more to share. "Oh, I got another call at the office I have to tell you about," I say as the kids start piling into our tiny dining room from all corners of the house. "It's embarrassing."

"Embarrassing? What? Did one of my brothers do something crazy again?" he asks.

"No, nothing like that. It was the hotel where we stayed when we were in DC. They told me we owed them over three hundred dollars."

"What? I thought the Kimberly Clark Foundation paid for everything on that trip."

"Well, yes, but this was different. You know that basket of

goodies in the room? The one I took home for all the kids? Well, that wasn't a gift from the foundation. That was part of what they call the 'in-room mini-bar'—I never heard of such a thing, but apparently we were supposed to pay for all those treats."

"Oh no! That is embarrassing. How in the world will we pay for that?"

"Fortunately, I got them to drop it to fifty dollars. That will still hurt, but at least I've learned my lesson. I'll never touch a snack in a hotel room again!"

"Renee, can you go get that picture of a baby off the fridge and bring it in here?" Hector says at the end of the meal. "Kids, when we pray tonight, we're going to pray for this little girl. She's in Texas and she needs a family. She has something called cerebral palsy . . . "

"Isn't that what Raj has?" Jose asks.

"Yes, but this baby has it much more severely than Raj. Her doctors say she'll never walk or talk or feed herself. But she still needs a family. So we're going to pray for her."

"Oh, she's so cute!" SueAnn squeals. "What's her name?"

"It's Alysia," I say. "And she is a doll baby, isn't she?"

"Why don't we adopt her?" Trish asks. "Her crib can go in my room."

"Yeah, we need another girl. There are too many boys in the family!" Chelsea adds. Flory is nodding vigorously beside her.

"Whoa, whoa, whoa," Hector says. "We can't adopt every child that needs a family. That's why we started Rootwings. Now let's pray. SueAnn, why don't you start."

"Good morning, Sue," Hector says cheerily as he hands me my coffee three days later. "I've been thinking about this baby." He waves Alysia's picture at me.

"Good morning, Sue," Hector says cheerily as he hands me my coffee three days later. "I've been thinking about this baby." He waves Alysia's picture at me.

"Uh oh," I say, as I see a familiar look on his face, "Do I need to remind you of our 'No. More. Babies.' Policy? Getting out from under diapers is in sight. Joelle is really starting to show some interest in using the potty."

"I know all that," he says. "But every time I pray about her, two words come into my head: She's ours. I can't believe I'm saying this myself, but, there you have it."

"Well," I say, hoping a reality check will slow this train down a bit. "Let's review everything we have going on this year. Fisher and Lilly both graduate from Spaulding in June and we're trying to help them both get into college. JD has a new wife and new baby on the way. We're battling with the school over Renee's IEP so she can go to the human service program at U-32. Trish and Flory have dance recitals coming up, six or seven of the kids will start baseball in a few weeks. And that doesn't count the everyday chores of running the household or managing Rootwings."

"I know. It makes me tired just to hear you list it all," he says. "Good thing we have that color-coded chart or I wouldn't know which day to do what!" He laughs. "But seriously, I believe in my heart she's meant to be ours, so what do we have to do next?"

"You know it will be whole new territory for us, right? Nearly all of our kids had some kind of special needs label before we adopted them, but this is the first child who really has a significant physical disability."

"I know, and I think we need to pray more, talk to Pastor David, get more information, read up on it, and talk to people who understand what it means to raise a child with more severe cerebral palsy than Raj, but at least we have good connections there at the Special Children's Clinic. So, let's get the ball rolling."

"Well, the first step will be getting our home study updated, so I will call Ann Clarke. We can't do it ourselves at Rootwings," I laugh.

"Sounds like a plan, but first things first. I detect a diaper that needs changing. Joelle, is that you?" he asks, finishing the sentence in French, laughingly imitating his mother's approach to diaper-duties.

"What?" I ask a week later, knowing immediately from the look on Hector's face that something's not quite right.

"Ann Clarke called today. She just heard back from Texas about our home study. They have concerns about our family." He starts ticking them off on his fingers: "We have too many kids, we live too far away, we're too young, too white, we don't make enough money—and get this: our house is not wheel-chair-accessible. She is not even one yet, and we don't know for sure if she will need a wheelchair, or what house we will live in when that time comes, and that is their excuse for holding her back from a permanent home. Unbelievable!"

"We'll have to make an appointment with Ann and figure out a strategy for addressing those issues. We can't change being white, but I think we can adequately answer everything else on that list. And although she will have white parents, she will also have eight black siblings. That should count for something."

"Done. I already made an appointment. Ann is coming next Tuesday—can you get off work a little early? She will be here at 4."

"I'll make it work. Oh, just to let you know, I finished the paperwork for the baseball signups today. Jose, Chelsea, SueAnn, Abel, George, and Isaac are all signed up."

"Great, maybe Jose and George will be on my brother Bernie's team; that's the age he coaches. What about the paperwork for Fisher and Lilly's financial aid? There will be no college if they don't get some money."

"I've finished the VSAC and the FAFSA. Now we have to try to find some private scholarships. I showed Fisher an application for a scholarship for kids who grew up in foster care, but in the application it says something about 'abused, neglected and orphaned' and he got really mad. Says they were never abused or neglected and they are not orphans. It really hit a sore spot. I guess he is not ready to talk about some of those issues. Anyway, I'm going to see if they qualify for any track and field scholarships. That's the best hope, I think—they are both such stars in that area."

"Hey Dad," Chelsea says, coming into the room. "Can we go tag-sale shopping this Saturday to find stuff for our summer trip?"

"Yeah, let's!" SueAnn chimes in. "When do we leave anyway?"

"First week in July, but first Dad and I are going to Texas to get your new baby sister. Then, when we get back, we have to plan the party for Fisher and Lilly's graduation. Do you girls want to help with that?"

A week later, we are sitting across the desk from Carolyn Chamberlain at Marywood Children and Family Services in Austin, Texas. "Mr. and Mrs. Badeau, we are so happy you've decided to adopt Alysia. She's a delightful baby, and we truly believe that if she is going to thrive, it will be in a family like yours with so many kids to stimulate her and give her all the attention she needs and deserves."

Hector squeezes my hand. We've not only overcome their objections to our family, but turned them around so they see them as strengths. It's something I strive to do with all the families we serve at Rootwings, so it's nice to see our approach worked when it came to advocating for our own family! I am getting a little teary-eyed, so I'm glad when Hector begins to talk.

"Thanks, Ms. Chamberlain. She's so beautiful. Our whole

family is so excited about her. And we have lined up a physical therapist to meet with as soon as we get home. By the grace of God, we plan to have this girl walking, even though the experts don't think she will."

"I love your optimism. And your faith. That gives us a great opportunity to walk on over to the chapel for the commitment ceremony. Sister Margaret will bring Alysia in for the ceremony."

I am instantly spellbound by this beautiful child. She has such life in her eyes and such a spirit of strength and energy. "What roads will you take us on, sweet baby?" I whisper in her ear just before the prayer begins.

For the next several weeks, Alysia goes everywhere: mostly to Little League games and track and field events—on our backs. It's the same backpack Chelsea, Isaac, Raj, Joelle, and Todd have used. Fisher and Lilly's friends are especially attracted to the cute little baby. Even my parents, who were a little concerned at first, have been won over by her charming personality.

We told all the kids what Alysia's prognosis is, and they said, "Oh yeah?" They are so determined to teach her to walk. Night after night, they stand her on the dining room table after dinner and "walk" her around the table from one kid to the other, using a yardstick as a railing. They encourage her struggle to climb up the stairs. They dance with her. At first, we were disappointed to learn that our medical insurance will only cover eight sessions a year of physical therapy, but we decide to bring the whole family to those eight sessions so everyone can learn the exercises and then we can continue doing them at home. We're confident she'll walk one day and the wheelchair question will be a moot point.

"Boy, is it hot today," Hector says as he loads the kids into the van.

"Well, better heat than rain. Remember how miserable your graduation was—it had to be inside due to the rain? I am so glad this one is outside. The kids can run around in the field."

"True," Hector says, and then he bursts out laughing.

"What?"

"I was just thinking that Fisher and Lilly will be easy to spot in the line of graduates. I am pretty sure they are the only black kids in the class."

I playfully punch him in the arm, and add, "Well, for sure we must be the youngest parents of any of the graduates. I doubt anyone has us beat on that."

I head down toward the field as the Senior chorus lines up for their class song, "Lean on Me." As I position myself to take a few pictures, I look into Fisher's eyes as he sings the song we often sang on our car rides from Barre to Cabot. My eyes fill with tears. We have surely done a lot of leaning on one another, and God, in the past few years. Although I believed adopting teenagers could work, I never really knew until we did it how deeply and completely I could love kids that were already taller than me by the time they joined the family.

After the ceremony is over, my dad corrals everyone for the group photos. Hector throws his arms around Fisher and Lilly, hugging them both, saying, "I'm so proud of you both. You had a hard road, but you both made it. " His eyes, too, are filled with tears.

"OK, Jim, take the picture," my mom says. "We are all ready to start the party."

"OK, everything's loaded up. Let me have the maps," Hector says early in the morning, the day he leaves for the summer trip.

"Yeah! Let's go!" George and Jose say almost simultaneously.

"We got all that great stuff at the tag sales!" Chelsea brags. "Two new tents and all those flashlights!"

"OK, so Lilly and I will follow you in Lilly's car as far as New York. We'll all go to the Statute of Liberty together, but then I will take Lilly to JFK airport for her trip, and drive home—and you guys are on your own after that. Fisher is your second driver until you hit New Mexico. Lilly and I will meet up with you out there after she gets back from Scandanavia."

We're so proud that Lilly was selected to represent the United States for an international track competition. We even learned she'll meet famed Olympian Carl Lewis while she's there. I'm so pleased we were able to raise enough funds from family and friends so she can go.

"OK, and you're sure all the campground reservations are set, right?"

"Everything is set. Just call me every third day at 7:30 like we agreed, and we'll go over the next few days' plans."

"Got it, OK. Dosey-doe and away we go!" Hector slams the van door shut, and Lilly and I get into her car. Trish and Renee are riding with us for this portion of the trip.

"Just follow the yellow brick road . . . " I say, laughing. "He has plenty of maps and Triple A books—they will be fine," I say to the girls as we pull out.

"He's pretty brave, Mom, to drive six thousand miles as the only adult, with fourteen kids," Lilly says.

"He has Fisher."

Lilly, Trish, and Renee bust out laughing, all at the same time.

"How are things in Barre?" Hector asks when I pick up the phone for our planned call.

"Great. We've had two placements at Rootwings since you left."

I don't tell him about the three checks that bounced.

"How was Disney?"

"Things are going great. Although this time, more than other years, the 'Are we there yet?' and 'How many more miles?' chorus is driving me a little batty. But let me tell you about the Disney adventure . . . What? . . . . Yes, we left, I am at a rest area now on our way across Alabama. Anyways, before you interrupted me, I started to say, Fisher lost his car keys at Disney. We searched for what seemed like hours, and finally had to have a new key made. They have a locksmith in a van roving around the Disney parking lot. I guess we are not the only ones who have done that. It set me back a hundred bucks. That was a big dent in our budget. More P, B & J ahead," he laughs.

I take two weeks of vacation from Rootwings so I can join the family in New Mexico and travel with them to visit our kids' relatives and former foster families, then on to the NACAC conference, and visiting more friends in California, including the Luckinbills. It was an amazing trip, but we are all happy to see our house when we roll into the driveway in mid-August.

"I can't wait to use my own shower and toilet!" Abel exclaims. "Some of those outhouses at the campgrounds were really nasty."

Shoes, stray socks, cups, pillows, books, and other assorted items tumble out of the van as the kids scramble to get into the house. "This will be a lot of work to clean up," I say to Hector.

"Yes, but so worth it," he replies. "I can't wait until you develop all the pictures. Especially the ones at the Grand Canyon when everyone lined up by height. Lord, thank you for getting us home safely."

It's September 1, and we are packing the van again. No vacation this time—tomorrow we leave to drive Fisher to the University of Lowell. Hector will drive the van with Fisher's suitcases and boxes. I'll ride with Fisher in his car and then ride home with Hector.

On the way home, I really have to come clean, I think to myself. I have to tell Hector about the problems I've been having managing the money at Rootwings and at home, and the checks I've bounced. He needs to know. *Lord, please help me with this.*

After we finish unloading Fisher's things—and carrying them up sixteen flights of stairs because the elevator isn't working—we're exhausted. But still, we have to make the three-hour drive home. Before we leave, we decide to call home and check in on the other kids.

"What? When? Really? Oh my goodness. I hope we make it home in time!"

"What was that about, Sue?" Hector asks.

"I just talked to Trish. JD called to say he and Melissa are on their way to the hospital. She's in labor. I hope we can get home before the baby is born!"

"Wow, let's get on the road, then." Hector extends his arm to shake Fisher's hand. Fisher looks at him, confused. "I'm just kidding. Come here, let me give you one last hug." Hector pulls Fisher in close. "I'm proud of you. Study hard and don't party too much."

I, too, give Fisher a big hug and, before I know it, we're back on Interstate 93 North heading home. It has been such an emotional day already, and with the news about Melissa being in labor, I just can't bring myself to talk to Hector about the financial issues. I convince myself that it can wait until tomorrow.

"She's so beautiful. I just can't believe it, Dad," JD says. "I want to give her everything I never had when I was growing up. I want to be the kind of dad you are. I have learned so much from you and Mom."

"So, how does it feel to be a dad, JD?" Hector asks.

"She's so beautiful. I just can't believe it, Dad," JD says. "I want to give her everything I never had when I was growing up. I want to be the kind of dad you are. I have learned so much from you and Mom."

"We know you'll make great parents, JD—you and Melissa both. Hey, you haven't even told me what you named her."

"Kirsten," he says. "Kirsten Lillian Jones."

"A beautiful name for our first grandchild," I say. "It's going to take some getting used to—being called Nanna and Poppa."

"You can say that again," Hector adds. "Our first grandchild. First of how many, I wonder?"

12

Dylan

"Uncle Philip looked great today. I'm so glad he was able to come for Thanksgiving," I say to Hector as we start putting away the clean dishes after the kids are all in bed.

"Yes, he did. I was happy about that too. Kirsten was the big hit of the day. She got passed around so much, I didn't get enough time to hold her myself," Hector says.

"You're such a sucker for the new babies! And I've never seen a baby that doesn't love you—it's amazing the way she calmed down when she was crying and then you held her."

"I know, I have the touch," he laughs. "I was wondering . . . "

"What, did you forget your train of thought?"

"No, it's silly, but holding Kirsten made me wonder what our next baby would have looked like if we had another one after

Isaac and Chelsea were born."

I look at him cross-eyed. "Are you kidding me? Well, I'm sure that any baby we had would have been beautiful, but it's never going to happen again, so don't get any ideas."

"Oh, I know. I'm perfectly happy with our family, and we definitely are enforcing the 'No. More. Babies.' Policy. We'll get our baby fix from grandchildren from now on." He suddenly scoops me up in a bear hug, adding, "But we can still practice . . . " as he runs his hands up and down my back and pats me on the bottom.

"Hec! We are in the middle of the kitchen!"

"Everyone's in bed," he says. "And we are married . . . I think it's OK if I seduce my wife in my own house," he says flirtatiously.

"Well, let's forget the rest of the dishes and go to bed, then," I say, happy for an excuse to get off my feet.

"I can't get out of bed today," I say to Hector, looking at the clock. It's 5:30 AM on the last Saturday before Christmas, but my throat, head, and entire body are aching and I can't move. "There's so much to do, but I just can't do it."

"It's OK, it'll be fine. Just help me review what's on tap today and we'll get it covered."

"Well, Isaac's hockey practice is first—at 6, then Abel, George, and Jose at 7:30. SueAnn and Renee's figure skating is at 9:30. Trish is going over to JD's to babysit Kirsten so JD and Melissa can go up to Burlington to do some Christmas shopping. Flory and Joelle's dancing lessons are at 10, up on Trow Hill. David has that tap class at 10:15, but the teacher is coming here to pick him up. Chelsea and Raj have art class at 11. Then I promised all the kids they could go buy presents for their Secret Santa this afternoon, so you will have to take them down to Harry's. I would offer to let you leave Todd and Alysia with me, but I don't want them to catch what I have, so I think they should just ride with you when you take everyone to their activities." I'm barely audible by the end of that and reach for the glass of water next to the bed.

"I can manage. And I promised Isaac he didn't have to continue with hockey. He really doesn't want to do it, and I don't want to force it."

I doze off amidst the noisy bustle of everyone having breakfast and getting ready for their activities. Suddenly I realize that the loud pounding I hear is not just part of my dream, but someone is at the door and no one else is home. I jump out of bed and throw some sweat pants on, feeling woozy and disheveled. *"Who can it be?"* I wonder.

It's Ruth Clark, our friend and real estate agent who helped us find our house. She's at the door with two other people I don't recognize and a huge box of wrapped Christmas gifts. "Come in, come in," I say hoarsely.

"We wanted to 'adopt' your family this year," she explains. "We have gifts here for all of your children. And a little something for you and Hector too," she adds, tucking an envelope into my hand.

I'm overwhelmed. With all the money problems I've been having, I had no idea how I was going to manage Christmas gifts for the kids. Christmas is only a week away, and I hadn't figured it out yet. and then God sends this angel to my doorstep. I start to cry. "Thank you," is all I can manage to say.

A few weeks after Christmas, Fisher calls from college. "What's up with Fisher?" Hector asks when I get off the phone.

"He's in trouble. He was at a party and there was a fight. The police showed up. Not everyone was arrested, but he and two other guys were. He needs help."

"What can we do?"

"I told him we would go down to Lowell for the hearing. I'll ask Dave Otterman if he knows any lawyers down that way, although I have no idea how we would pay for a lawyer."

We manage to scrape up enough funds for a lawyer, and Fisher's charges are reduced. He's able to get back to college, but something definitely seems different. So I'm not surprised when, two weeks later, he calls again.

"He's dropping out of school, Hec," I say, filled with disappointment. "He feels he's over his head academically, and he's failing everything. I should've seen this coming."

"You had no way to know. We wanted to give him the chance to try college, and we did," Hector says.

"I know, but I wish I had been more on top of his academics in high school. I was all over it for Renee and Trish, but Fisher and Lilly just came across so confident. I never realized they might've needed extra help too. I have a degree in education. I should've been more aware," I say, kicking myself.

"It's true, maybe we could have been more aware, but also none of the teachers ever told us there were any issues. You can't beat yourself up. What are Fisher's plans now?"

"He wants to find a job in Burlington. A lot of his friends from high school at are UVM, and he hopes to get a job and apartment up there."

"OK, sounds like he has thought it through, so that's good," Hector replies.

Neither of us realize this is just the beginning of a path that will only spiral downward for Fisher. The possibility that he's using drugs and that this is part of the problem does not even occur to us at this time.

"I ran into a social worker I know while I was at a meeting

today," I tell Hector while the kids are doing their homework at the dining room table. It's early March and the worst of winter seems to be behind us.

"Were you walking with your head down?" he asks.

"Haha, very funny. No, that's not what I meant. Do you remember the worker who adopted a baby from India not long after we adopted Raj? We see her sometimes at those India Adoptive Family gatherings? Her name is Judith."

"Yes, I remember her. Did you have a nice chat?"

"Well, yes, but there is more to it. A few days ago, she sent a referral over to Rootwings. The child is a four-year-old boy who was born 'normal,' and, at around six months of age, he was shaken and suffered severe brain damage. It's called Shaken Baby Syndrome. He has severe cerebral palsy, he's blind, he'll probably never progress developmentally past the four-to-six-month-old stage.

"Wow. Poor little guy," Hector says. "That makes me think of some of the children we see when we go to NACAC. I always admire the families that adopt kids like that, but I know I could never do it."

"Exactly, I know. Even though we started out on this journey with the motto that we would adopt the child 'most in need of a home and least likely to get one,' we've always known our strengths and limitations. Older kids, kids who have deep emotional wounds. We always knew that was the type of child we do best with. It was a stretch to take a child with the kinds of physical disabilities Alysia has, but she's amazing."

Just last week, Alysia began not only to walk, but also to dance. We took a videotape of her walking, dancing, and eating with a spoon to send to the workers in Texas who thought that would never happen.

"So I know with God all things are possible, but I agree, medically fragile and 'total care' children are way outside of our capabilities. That's why I never even told you about this referral.

I've just been working with Judy and Fran at the office to try to find a family for him. He's been in what they call a medical foster home, but this single mom can't keep him any more and he's about to be placed in an institution."

"That's pretty sad. I really hope Rootwings can find a family for him. So what did the worker say when she saw you today?"

"Well, that's the odd thing. She said, 'Sue, I feel a little funny saying this, but I'd like to ask you and Hector to personally consider adopting the little boy we discussed. I just feel in my gut that he's a Badeau.'"

"That took a lot of nerve! What did you tell her?"

"I told her we really weren't adopting any more kids, but I would talk to you anyway."

"Well that was a wishy-washy answer," he chuckles. "Is she one of those people who thinks just because we have a lot of kids it means we can't say no? Did you tell her that even though we have 17 kids, we've actually said no at least a dozen times over the years? Because we think, learn, talk, and pray, we don't just go on autopilot and say yes?"

"I didn't get into all that with her. She just asked me to please consider it."

"Yeah, it has been, what? Ten months since Alysia joined the family? It must be time for another kid, right?"

"Oh stop, Hec. Let's just be open-minded. She did slip me his picture."

"I don't want to see it," he says—too late—as I am holding it in front of him.

"Oh my goodness, what a cherub-faced little munchkin he is."

We get busy with our routines for more than a week before we circle back to discuss this child. But all the while we are helping kids with homework, doing PT with Alysia, settling Fisher into his new apartment, traveling to Massachusetts to watch

Lilly play college volleyball, and attending hockey and figure skating events, this little guy is on our minds and in our hearts. The Spirit is up to something.

"Let's at least go meet him," Hector says to me over coffee after the kids leave for school. I'm not going in to Rootwings today because we have appointments at the Special Kids clinic in Burlington for Raj, Joelle, and Alysia. It'll probably be the last for Raj. They've told us he is doing so well, he doesn't need their support any longer.

"Meet who?" I say. Hector has this habit of starting up a conversation in the middle, and sometimes it takes me a few minutes to catch on to the topic.

"The little boy, the 'shaken baby,'" he says. We haven't been told the child's name for confidentiality reasons.

"Seriously?"

"Yes, really. I feel we need to meet him before we know what to do."

"OK, I'll call Judith and set it up."

Driving back to Short Street from the foster home, I ask, "So, Hec, what do you think?"

"He sure is beautiful. And I can't believe he's really blind. I swear his eyes were following me."

"I know, I felt the same way. But that's what the medical records say."

"I just loved his laugh. When his foster mother did the Velcro on his shoes, he started cracking up. You could never be gloomy around that laugh."

We ride in silence for a moment and then Hector surprises me by saying, "I'm sure I can care for him, Sue. I think learning to feed him will be the trickiest part, but I'm sure I can learn.

"I just loved his laugh. When his foster mother did the Velcro on his shoes, he started cracking up. You could never be gloomy around that laugh."

The foster mother says you have to get the consistency of his food just right when you blend it up. And of course he would be the first child we have needing regular medications. But how hard can that be?"

"You're serious, aren't you?"

"Why wouldn't I be? It just feels right. I think he'll fit right in to the family. And I think he'll go farther than the doctors are predicting once he gets around our crew. I mean, look at what they did for Alysia."

"But speaking of our crew, the foster mother says he bites. She really doesn't think he should be in a family with other children."

"Well, it's a good thing she's not the one making the decision, I guess. I think the best plan is to ask Judith if she can arrange a visit for him to come to our house and we can see for ourselves how he does with the other kids. Then we can make a final decision."

"That sounds like a good idea. Oh, one other thought—how do you think he'll do on the summer camping trip?"

"I think he'll do great. His foster mother says he loves car rides and he laughs whenever she hits a bump—sounds like he'll be laughing all summer!"

A week later, the kids are swarming around him, oohing and aahing over how cute he is. "Can you teach me to feed him, Dad?" Flory asks. Hector gently shows her how to prop him just the right way so he can take his food without gagging. None of us could imagine at the time how many meals Flory would feed him in the years to come before he would need a feeding tube.

"Let me hold him, Dad," Isaac says. "He's so cute."

"Oh, Dad. Do you think he's a little scared?" Trish asks. "He is making a Popeye face with a big lip."

"He likes noises, but maybe all the noises here are just a little too much," I suggest. Just then, Jose starts playing one of his video games. I see the Popeye face relax and he starts laughing. "He must like the beeps and bings of your game," I say to Jose. But Jose is to into his game to hear me.

"What's this?" George asks, holding a cassette tape in his hands.

"That's his favorite music. It's the Smurfs."

"Oh, can we play it?"

"Sure, put it on."

He instantly lights up when he hears the familiar music. Alysia starts dancing too. Raj and George are laughing at the silly lyrics.

"Call Judith," Hector says. "Tell her she was right. This child's name is meant to be Badeau. He's ours. Number 18."

"Call Judith," Hector says. "Tell her she was right. This child's name is meant to be Badeau. He's ours. Number 18."

For legal reasons, we are asked, as part of the adoption, to change his name. This is a little hard for us; we have always felt so strongly about keeping our children's birth names, but we comply. We decide to name him Dylan, and immediately it suits him.

"It's amazing," I say to Hector as I sit on the blue recliner in the living room, holding Dylan on my lap.

"What's that?"

"You just never know the capacity of your heart until it is stretched. I never knew how deeply I would fall in love with a baby until Chelsea was born. But then Jose showed me that I could have an equally deep connection to a child not born to me. Each time we add a child, no matter how confident I am that it's the right thing to do, I always wonder: What about this time? Will it be the same? Do I have enough love left? And each time, I am just blown away by how intense my feelings are for each child. Even those big, tall teenagers. And now, we have a four-year-old boy who can't talk, can't walk, can't even see us, and yet, I look into his eyes and I just love him so much. It's like he has always been a part of me."

"I know what you mean, Sue. It hits me at different times with each kid, and I always get filled with tears."

"I know—you cry at the drop of a hat," I laugh.

"Yeah, just don't tell my brothers that, or they will disown me. . . . But, seriously, with Jose, it was right at the airport in Boston. With Raj, it was the first time I fed him while watching *Star Trek*. With Chelsea, it was the moment she was born. With Isaac, it was after we were home and I was walking around with him in the middle of the night. With each kid, the moment is different when it hits me how much I love them and would do anything for them. With Lilly, it was the first time I saw her run track. I felt my eyes fill up with tears and I thought, *I really love this 'ice cube girl*,'" he says, referring to Lilly's nickname.

A few days later, I am at my desk at Rootwings and Melissa calls. "Sue, I need to talk to you. I don't know what to do."

"What is it?"

"I think I might be pregnant again."

"So soon?"

"I know. I didn't think it was possible, but I have all the symptoms. I'm so scared."

"Well, first let's find out if it's true. Let's just take one step at a time. Have you made an appointment with a doctor?"

"No, I'm too scared. I guess I'm in denial a little bit."

"It's OK. I can understand that feeling," I say. "Make an appointment and I'll go with you."

"Well, you knew your body. You're right," I say as we walk back to the car.

"What will I do now? I can't imagine taking care of two babies. The due date for this one is before Kirsten even turns one."

"I know it seems overwhelming now, but it will all work out.

Just think how close they will be—almost like twins. Look at Chelsea and Flory, or Isaac and Raj. It's nice to have kids that are close in age. They become each other's best friends." I go on to tell her how terrified I was when I first learned I was pregnant with Isaac.

"I hope you're right," she says, still a little shaky.

I lean over to give Melissa a hug as I drop her back off at her Graniteville apartment. "You'll see. It'll all be fine. It'll be rough for awhile, but it'll be fine. Put your faith in God and ask for the strength you need, one day at a time."

"Mom, Mom, guess what?" Chelsea bursts in the door ahead of the other kids as they return from an evening with Hector at Wedgewood. When we learned that a family membership costs less than one time out at the movies, we jumped at it, and the kids all love to swim.

"David went swimming!" SueAnn exclaims. "He didn't just sit on the side and dangle his feet—he went all the way in!"

This really is a miracle, and I am quickly catching their enthusiasm. Isaac, Raj, and George hurry in, shivering because they are still wet. "Why didn't you three dry off before you came home?" I ask.

"Dad was rushing us," Isaac answers.

"Hmmm, I'm sure." David walks in beaming from ear to ear. "He really went in?" I ask Hector, who is last in.

"Yes, he really did, and he looked so proud of himself."

"I can see that," I say, as I quickly sign "I'm proud of you" to David. He gives me a high five and heads off to his room.

David was terrified of water when he joined our family. We never really understood why; he wasn't able to say. But clearly, there was something traumatic in his memory related to swimming pools. Every time we go to a pool, he sits on the side and dangles his feet in the water, watching the other kids play. We've been gently encouraging, but never pushing, and so this break-through tonight is wonderful. "He must finally be feeling really safe here," I reflect.

"I know. It gave me chills," Hector says. "Speaking of chills, there's no school tomorrow, so I promised the kids ice cream tonight, as soon as they're changed into their PJs."

The words are barely out of his mouth when at least eight of the kids are back in the kitchen clamoring for ice cream. "OK, OK, I'll scoop it out. Just line up," Hector says.

George and Isaac get into a bit of a pushing match as they both try to be first in line. The others all try to get as close to the front as they can. Raj doesn't join in the pushing, so he ends up at the back. Jose is off to the side of the line.

"Raj, come here. I'll serve you first," Hector says.

"What! I was first!" Isaac calls out.

"No fair, I was first," says George.

"Don't you guys know the drill by now?" Jose says, laughing. "The first shall be last and the last shall be first."

"That's right, Jose: Matthew 20:16. Just for that you get to be second after Raj." All the other kids groan. Hector serves Joelle, Todd, Flory, Chelsea, David, Abel, SueAnn, and Alysia before finally serving George and Isaac. Renee wanders down from the second floor and asks what all the excitement is about, and she decides to have some too, and takes one upstairs for Trish.

"Can Dylan have ice cream, Dad?" Flory asks.

"Well, you can put a little on your finger and put it on his tongue and see how he reacts to the cold. Just be careful he doesn't bite you."

"He's smiling," she says a few minutes later. "I think he really likes it. I'm going to give him more."

"It's OK if you give him a little more. Just not too much. He's not used to cold food, so we don't want his tummy to get upset," I say.

"Time to eat!" Hector yells out the door. It's the first warm day of spring and everyone is outside. Trish and Renee are sitting on the porch doing their homework, and the other kids are riding bikes or playing in the yard. Pretty soon they're all scampering in and sitting at the table.

"Listen up. I have some things to go over while Mom is dishing up the food," Hector says. Abel and Jose continue talking.

"What did I say?" Hector glares at the two of them.

"SueAnn, can you remind these two knuckleheads of the rules?" Hector never used the term *knuckleheads* until JD came along. Now it's part of his standard vocabulary.

"OK, Dad. It goes like this, Abel, Jose. If Dad says 'jump,' we say 'how high?' And if he says 'poop,' we say, 'what color?'"

This has everybody cracking up. I even hear Dylan's contagious laugh starting to bubble up.

"Good job, SueAnn. Now seriously, if I can have your attention. Your mother and I have to decide if we're going to take another summer trip this year and we want your opinions."

Soon everyone is talking at once, and the consensus is that a summer trip definitely has to happen. "Well, it's great we all agree," Hector says as he tries to bring some order back to the table. "We've always been very thrifty on these trips. Your mother and I agreed years ago: we couldn't spend more money while we are gone than we would at home, and we've stuck to that, mostly. But gas costs more now, and even the campgrounds are starting to cost more. So we need to figure out how to afford the trip. If we really want to go, we have to think of some things we can cut now, so we can do it."

"I'll contribute my paper route money," Chelsea offers, and this kicks off a round of brainstorming that lasts for some time after dinner is over.

"Looks like we have a plan," Hector says later. "Now it's time to get on with homework and bedtime. So everyone can be excused, and Abel: don't forget you have after-dinner cleanup."

"Can I do it later?" he asks.

"Dad, what color did you say he should poop?" SueAnn asks, and everyone is laughing again.

"That was a lot of fun at dinner," I say as we get into bed. "You sure know how to get everyone involved."

"It was fun, especially SueAnn with her description of the rules." He laughs. "When everyone gets going, we do have some good times. It's always fun to hear their perspective on things. Like when Fisher tells the story about the trip I took to the Cape with just the boys. I never really understood laughing so hard you pee your pants until I heard him tell that story."

"Oh I know. Just the way he says, 'I was sleeping and then I thought it was raining, until I looked up and saw David standing over me half asleep, peeing inside the tent.' Oh my goodness. Hilarious!"

"There will be a lot more memories to come," I say. "Oh, tomorrow, there are some things about Rootwings I really have to fill you in on, Hec. I know you've been busy with the kids, but I have to update you on some stuff before the board meeting rolls around."

"OK, sounds good," he yawns. Almost instantly, he is asleep.

"What's going on in here?" Hector charges into the kitchen as chairs go flying.

"You're not my mother and you can't tell me what to do!" Renee yells at me—and suddenly she slaps me across the face and tackles me to the floor.

Hector jumps in and pulls her away from me, holding her tightly as she struggles to wrestle out of his grasp. "Get off me," she says.

"Not until you calm down," he says. "This is not acceptable."

After several more moments of struggle, she heaves a huge sigh and stops fighting.

"I don't know what that was about, but in this house, hitting your mother is absolutely not acceptable. This is my wife, your mother, and you will show respect."

After we all sit in a tense silence on the floor for several minutes, Hector suggests we go to the living room to talk. An hour later, after many tears, Renee has apologized. "I'm so sorry. I didn't mean to hit you," she says to me. "I miss my mom and dad so much. Why did all those bad things have to happen to us?"

Three hours later, we've had a really good conversation, more tears, prayers, and hugs. We're all thoroughly exhausted, and Renee heads up to bed.

"That was intense," Hector says. "Are you sure you are OK?"

"I'm fine, but I'm so glad you were there. You have a much better rapport with her when she gets upset," I say.

"I'm glad she agreed to counseling, and I think Jim and Jaya will be the right match for her. Can you call them tomorrow to make an appointment?"

"Definitely. It will be important to get a few sessions in before you leave in July for the summer trip."

"I'm a little worried that you're doing the trip with only one driver this time," I say to Hector as he finishes packing the van.

"It will be fine. I'll take it easy. I'll stop whenever I need to. I'm actually looking forward to a few weeks on the road with all the kids, but no phones, TV, or even their friends. Just the family. It'll be good for all of us."

"I wish I could go for the whole trip, but I can't leave Rootwings that long now that we've moved into our new location. There's a lot to manage here. Plus JD and Melissa will be having their baby soon, and I want to be here for that and to help with Kirsten. I wish I could be in two places at once!"

Inside, I am getting more and more stressed about the conversation I keep putting off regarding the finances. I know I should've come clean sooner, and probably quashed the summer trip plans. But I justified it by reminding myself that we never spend more on the trip than we spend at home during the same period of time. My stomach is in knots and I feel a migraine coming on.

"I know." Hector leans over and gives me a kiss. "I'll miss you, but we'll all be together for NACAC in Anaheim. Take care of things at home, and don't get stressed. We'll talk every few days. Now get some sleep. It's getting late," he says as he kisses me once more, then rolls over.

13

Wayne

"I'm lucky I survived the day to make this phone call," Hector says, calling from a pay phone at his campground.

"What? Did something happen? Is everyone OK?"

"Oh calm down. I'm just joking, but let me tell you what Isaac did to me today. He begged me to go on the roller coaster and even got Trish in on it—she volunteered to watch Dylan and Alysia so I could go with Isaac. Now you know I love roller coasters, but this one was really big, so even I was a little nervous. But anyway, we get in line, and Isaac keeps moving to the right, letting people pass us. I'm not sure what he's doing, but I stay next to him. Finally, it's our turn to get on, and all of a sudden I realize he was calculating the entire time, and he has positioned us to have the very front seats in the roller coaster."

"Oh, I think I would have passed out," I say.

Hector laughs. "Yup, the little bugger tricked me. As we're getting off, he says, 'Wasn't that fun, Dad?' Meanwhile, I'm doing a Fred Sanford imitation, clutching my heart. I really thought it was going to give out. I like roller coasters, but I'll never again sit in the front seat.

"So, how are things at home?"

"Big news here. JD and Melissa had their baby yesterday. I wanted to call you right away, but of course, had no way to reach you, so I couldn't wait for you to call me tonight. It's another girl, and they named her Whitney Mae. She is stunning. Beautiful. Precious." I know I am sounding corny, but this baby just stole my heart.

"Wow, that's great. Is Melissa doing all right?"

"Yes, she's fine. Kirsten's here with me for a couple of days, and I'm working on some family photo albums in the evening hours. Or at least I was until the baby was born. Wait till you see the cool photo collages I'm making for each of the kids. I feel bad I taught classes about life books and yet was never very good at keeping up with them for our own kids. But these collages will be pretty special for each kid."

"That all sounds great. We're having a wonderful trip, but I really do miss you, Sue. I'm glad we're heading east again soon. It won't be long 'til I see you again."

"How is Dylan handling the trip?"

"Oh, just as we predicted—he loves it. And everyone has been really helpful with him, especially Flory. And Trish is great with Alysia, so as long as I don't lose Todd again, I think we're all set."

"Again? You lost Todd once?"

"Ooops. I forgot I hadn't told you about that. It's all good—we found him," Hector laughs. "Anyway, I'm running out of quarters for the pay phone, so let's say good night."

"OK, good night, Ralph."

"Good night, Alice," we joke. "You'll always be my favorite Honeymooner."

Unbeknownst to me, a week later, after hundreds of Pop Tarts, P, B & Js, hot dogs, hamburgers, and Tang . . . and dozens of sunrises, sunsets, meeting new friends, mosquito bites, salt water, animal sightings and campfires, Hector and the kids decide to surprise me by heading home a week early. They agree that they've had an awesome five weeks, but they also agree that they're exhausted and there've been one too many problems with the van. So they pack up and leave from the Gulf Coast in Alabama and drive 27 hours straight home, with only a three-hour rest stop for Hector to catch a little sleep along the way. They pull into the driveway at 1:30 in the morning, and I'm asleep.

I'm startled awake by loud shouting coming from the kitchen. "What in the world is going on here?" It sounds like Hector's voice, but how can that be? He's in Alabama, isn't he? I shake myself awake and head downstairs.

"It looks like a tornado came through here!" Now I know it is Hector's voice. *What is he doing here?* I wonder.

I step into the kitchen, which is littered with beer and soda cans, pizza boxes, and dirty dishes. "Uh, hi," I say tentatively. "Welcome home. Is everything OK? I wasn't expecting to see you for a week when we meet at NACAC."

"Everything was peachy until I walked in to this pigpen." He glares at me, daring me to make an excuse.

"I'm sorry. I really wasn't expecting you back. I told Lilly she could have a few friends over. One of her friends from college is here. They had a little party and Lilly promised to clean up."

Hector picks up a dirty cereal bowl, saying, "This mess isn't just from one party. There's a lot of cleaning to do here." Without waiting for me to respond, he marches up to Lilly's room and throws the door open.

Lilly is in her room with her boyfriend, John. They are sitting on the floor, talking, and Hector is fuming. "You. Leave. Now," he says to John. "You and I will talk in the morning," he says to Lilly.

He storms back downstairs as sleepy children start to wake up and straggle in from the car. "What happened to the house?" Abel asks.

"Never mind. Just go to bed," Hector says.

"Mommy!" SueAnn runs over to give me a big hug.

Trish walks in with Alysia and heads straight for the third floor. David and Jose quickly head down to their room. The others are still asleep in the van.

"What were you thinking, letting Lilly have a boy in her room?" Hector is seething.

"I didn't know he was here," I say. "I went to bed. I had another migraine."

"You need to know what's going on in your own house," he says through clenched teeth. "I have to go bring Dylan in. We'll finish this conversation tomorrow."

I feel like my whole world is falling apart. It's only been two days since I broke down and told Hector the whole story about the check bouncing and the lying I'd been doing to cover up. I feel depressed, nauseous, dirty. Now today comes the news that Lilly is pregnant and planning to quit college. I never would have suspected she would go that route. She was so motivated to do well in college, and she has goals for her life. And of all the older kids, she seemed most grounded in her faith. How did we fail as parents? As role models? As Christians? What will it take to turn this ship around? I don't even have the energy to pray.

It's the third straight day that I've refused to get out of bed, go to work, or do anything with the children. Hector comes into our room with a bowl of soup.

"I'm not sick, you know," I say. "Not like that, anyway."

"I know. I just don't know what else to do. I just got back from your parents' house. I told them everything that is going on."

"You *what?* Oh no, now I can never face them again. They must hate me."

"No one hates you, Sue, but you need to get yourself together. Mentally. Physically. Emotionally. Spiritually. We can't go on like this. The kids need you. I need you. The money part we can work out. We have Judy to run Rootwings. You and I can get jobs and work around the kids' schedules, just like we did when we lived in Cabot. It's not the end of the world. But I can't do it alone. I need my partner."

"I let everyone down," I sniff, trying to hold back tears. "I let God down. I really believed every step of the way we were doing what God wanted us to do. So then how did we go so wrong? How did I end up lying and bouncing checks, and how did we end up with another unplanned pregnancy in the family? Are we being punished for my sins?"

"You know better than that," Hector says. "And we were doing what God wanted us to do—we still are. We just aren't perfect. We're human. We make mistakes, we fall. But we have to get up. God doesn't want you to stay stuck in this muddy rut—it's not mud season in Cabot. This is real."

"I hear your words, but I just don't know what to do."

"When I was talking to your parents, we agreed that you needed to get away, spend some time with someone we trust, someone that will help you get your head—and your heart, and your spirit—back on track. So I called Dan and Pam, and I talked to Betsy too. And they got together and called me back and said the Johansens have a spare room where you can stay for as long as you need to. You can be with our best Mill River House Church friends. When someone is physically wounded, they need to be nursed back to health. Our friends will nurse you emotionally and spiritually back to health. And then when you come back, we will figure out together how to fix the other problems."

I'm stunned, ashamed, humiliated, overwhelmed. Yet a small voice inside tells me he's right and, if there's anywhere I can go to get back on track, it's to Northampton, to my closest friends and spiritual mentors.

A week of sleep, long walks, fresh air, Bible study, prayer, tea, baths, friendship, and reading completely renews and restores my spirit. I return home ready to face the changes that need to be made and to re-embrace my husband, children, and other responsibilities. It's hard to say good-bye to Joan, Anne, Betsy, Pam, and Carole, but I also can't wait to see Hector and hug every one of my babies.

"Mom, can we talk?"

"Sure Lilly, what's on your mind?"

"John and I have been talking about getting married, now that I'm pregnant. But I'm confused. I don't know if I'm ready."

"It's a big step and a big commitment."

"I was talking to Elaine and she offered for me to come spend some time with them in New Mexico until I figure out what I should do," Lilly says, referring to her former foster mother.

"Is that what you want to do?"

"I was talking to Dad about it while you were in Massachusetts, and he thinks it's a good idea. He says getting a fresh perspective might be helpful. But I wanted to know what you think."

"Well, I'm glad you value my opinion," I say cautiously. "I know it's been a little rocky around here the last few weeks. We all need to get back to our basic faith and values. I think spending some time with your New Mexico family might be smart. And we'll talk on the phone and write letters. We'll still be connected."

"If you want to dance, you have to pay the fiddler" is one of Hector's favorite truisms. Just yesterday, he said it to one of the kids. Today, I am realizing that it applies to me. When Root-wings wasn't bringing in enough money to stay afloat, I tried to secretly keep it going by shifting money from our personal account to cover the Rootwings expenses. That well went dry quickly, and that's when I began bouncing some checks. Coming clean about all of this was so freeing; I was so thankful not to be carrying the secrecy around anymore. But it also meant we had to face the facts that Rootwings wasn't bringing in enough money to continue to operate as a fully licensed agency.

Our board decided to separate from the national AASK America organization and let go of our child-placing license. We agreed to continue as an education, advocacy, and support ministry—all services we could provide on a much smaller budget with less staff. One result of this shift was some hard feelings and loss of trust among some of the staff that had to be let go. People I care about and consider friends. It's been a hard loss to accept. I'm so thankful for Judy, Patty, and Gary and a few other steadfast friends who continue to ride through this storm with us.

"That was Patty on the phone," Hector says, snapping me out of my reverie.

"Funny, I was just thinking about them," I say.

"They have a job idea for me. Washington Country Mental Health is looking for someone to work as a job coach and mentor for a mentally disabled man. It could be perfect for me—the hours are flexible, and with my background as a foster parent, I can probably get the job. Mostly, I could work when the kids are in school. What do you think?"

"I think it sounds perfect; you should definitely look into it. Do you want me to help with a resume? I have to put mine together anyway for that job I saw advertised in the *Washington World*, the one we talked about yesterday, the overnight position at the group home for adults with mental illness in Plainfield."

"If we get these jobs, it'll be a real blessing. They use our background and experience and the schedules work with our kids' schedules. God really provides exactly what we need."

"I know. A month ago, I felt hopeless and depressed. Now, I feel hopeful again."

"And look around at our family," Hector says, pointing to the photos on the wall behind us. "Alysia is walking and dancing. Dylan is happy and gaining weight. Raj has 'graduated' from the Special Kids network and is doing great. George is back in a regular classroom at the same school with the other kids. Isaac, Jose, Abel, SueAnn, Flory, Chelsea, Joelle, Todd—they are all getting great reports in school, they have friends, they're happy. David is swimming like a fish, Trish and Renee are both on the honor roll and singing in the chorus. JD and Melissa are happy and doing a great job with their two babies, and Lilly is sorting things out with her former foster family, but she'll be back in the spring before her baby is born.

"The only one I'm really worried about right now is Fisher. He seems different ever since he moved to Burlington. I hope I'm wrong, but I'm beginning to think drugs might be involved. But do you see what I see when I look at all these pictures? I see a normal family. We've weathered some storms. There will be more to come. But we are strong and we are together. And that was our vision, right? To create a family. It's not a fairy tale, but it's still pretty awesome."

"Well, it may not be a fairy tale, but I still feel like you're my knight," I say, giving him a big hug.

"Oh, I forgot to show you this," he says, going to the kitchen and taking an envelope from the top of the refrigerator. "This couple from Long Island that saw us in the *New York Times* wants to come visit us. Actually, they'll be coming for dinner tomorrow."

"OK, why?"

"They just want to learn more about adopting older kids. They said they'll treat us to pizza. They just want to meet us and talk. I hope you don't mind. I said it was fine."

"Of course it is fine. It's what we do."

The kids have been entertaining our new friends, Lorraine and Marty, for two hours. When they arrived they were interested in possibly adopting one child. As they get ready to leave, they are already talking about sibling groups. It reminds me of the family we visited in Wisconsin after we read about them in our church magazine. It feels like we have come full circle. I'm so thankful for this affirmation that we are still on the right track.

"That was a fun evening," Hector says after they leave.

"I'm pretty sure we'll be seeing them again. I really like them. How many kids do you think they'll end up adopting?"

"Good question. I could tell they were ready to go as soon as Joelle started telling them about our summer trip. It was so cute when she called it a field trip."

"Yeah, double-check and make sure she's really in her bed. I think they might've taken her home if we'd let them," I laugh.

"Hi Vince. How are you today?" I ask when Hector brings his client by the house for lunch a few days later.

"I did my paper route. Two dogs barked at me," he says. "One hundred twenty-seven days until my birthday."

"Ahhh, that's good to know, Vince. Your birthday is sooner than mine." Turning to Hector, I add, "Guess who called this morning? Maris Blechner."

He looks at me blankly for a moment. "The social worker from New York—she and her husband started their agency around the same time we started Rootwings," I say. "She came here and helped trained our staff when we were first getting licensed."

"Oh yeah, yeah, yeah. I remember now. Sorry. It's been a couple of years."

"Well, we see her every year at NACAC."

"OK, so she called. What about?"

"Take a deep breath," I say. "She wanted to tell me about a little three-year-old boy. His name is Wayne. He's Chinese."

"And . . . " Hector says.

"And she thinks he would fit perfectly into our family."

"What? Why?"

"Well, he has a terminal illness, a disease called Sanfilippo Syndrome . . . "

"Stop right there, Sue," Hector interrupts me. "First of all, you know we agreed we aren't adopting any more kids. And secondly, I just know I can't handle adopting a child that's going to die. My heart couldn't take that."

"I know. That's what I told her. It hasn't even been a year yet since we adopted Dylan, and it's been a really rough year. But we could learn about the syndrome, so maybe we can help find a family for him. And pray for him."

"Yes, we can do that. Tell me more."

"Well, this syndrome is a degenerative disease." I say. "Babies who have it seem to be completely normal when they are born, but then they start losing some of their functioning. Already, Wayne has lost his hearing."

"Is that why Maris thought he fit our family? Because he's deaf and we have David already?"

"Well, that might be part of it. There's more. Eventually, he will lose his gross motor skills and his fine motor skills. Children with this disease also become very hyperactive and don't sleep a lot."

"Ah, now I see. It's the not-sleeping-a-lot thing that made her think of us."

"Ha ha."

"Where is he now?"

"He was adopted as a baby by a couple in New York. Maris says they love him beyond words, but feel they are not equipped to continue to meet his needs as the disease progresses. That must be such a painful decision for them."

"Yes, I can't imagine. Well, God sometimes uses people we don't expect as his messengers, so I won't say no immediately without giving it some thought and prayer and taking time to learn a little more about this San—what was it?—disease."

"Sanfilippo."

Within a few weeks, we know the answer: Wayne is our son. He is in some very real, very mystical, preordained way, already our son, so now all we have to do is bring him home.

Another home study . . .

More letters of reference . . .

Physicals for *every* member of the family . . .

Lots of learning, getting the house ready, getting the kids ready. Lots of conversations about what it will be like to love a child who will die in a few years.

While we are getting everything in place on our end, we get an unexpected phone call from Maris.

"Are you serious? I've never heard of that. OK, I'll make arrangements to come down—do we both need to come? That'll be really difficult. OK, let me know. Thanks."

"The judge in New York doesn't understand why our family would want to adopt a child who's going to die. He's holding things up by not approving the termination of the parents' rights until he hears from us. Maris needs us to go to New York to testify at the hearing."

I further explain to Hector: "It's so unusual. I never heard of anything like this. She's finding out if I can go alone or if the judge will require both of us to be present."

A week later, Maundy Thursday, we are in the car driving to New York. "I'm glad that judge listened to you," Hector remarks. "I know. It was nerve-wracking. But all I did was talk about our family and how we were looking forward to bringing Wayne home. I told him our original motto and he had to agree that if any child fit that description, Wayne does. So, he agreed, and here we are—another road trip! I wonder how many miles we've logged together since we took our first trip to Maidstone for our honeymoon just twelve years ago?"

"The real question is, how many miles do we still have ahead of us?" Hector chuckles. "It's really nice of Maris and her husband to let us stay at their house tonight, especially since they're preparing for Passover."

"I agree. It'll be fun. She and Stu are definitely our kind of people!"

"Hello, Mr. and Mrs. Chan. This is Hector and Sue Badeau. May we come in?" Maris introduces us to the Chans on the steps of their lovely home in Queens. The moment we walk in, we see this enchanting little boy playing with a drum set on the floor. "And this is Wayne," Maris adds.

Hector and I look at each other and I can see it in his eyes—instant love. Wayne has a melt-your-heart smile, dimples, and cheeks you can't resist squeezing. The Chans are so kind and clearly love Wayne to pieces.

"He loves fresh squeezed orange juice for breakfast," Mrs. Chan says.

"And when *Wheel of Fortune* comes on TV. He loves to watch that!" Mr. Chan laughs.

After visiting for an hour, Maris tells the Chans she needs to take us out for coffee to do some paperwork, and then we'll come back to get Wayne and drive home to Vermont with him this afternoon.

"What do you think?" Maris asks.

"I love him already," Hector replies. "I can't believe the way he came right over to me and sat on my lap."

"After he took our shoes and lined them up!" I laugh. "That was so cute."

"I just feel so sad for the Chans," Hector says. "It has to be so hard for them. It's obvious how they love Wayne and they've given him such good care. What a blessing."

"Yes, that's very evident," Maris replies. "If you two are ready to go forward, I'll let the Interstate Compact office know. Just spend another hour or so with the Chans, and I'll call their house when you can leave for Vermont."

"Sounds good. I think it'll be harder for them if we linger, so we'll head out as soon as you give the word," Hector says.

"Yes, and hopefully that means we'll make it home in time for our family Good Friday activities," I add.

Two hours pass at the Chans' home and we haven't received the call. I ask to use their phone and call Maris; she tells me that the ICPC approval has not come through yet. "It's getting a little awkward here," I tell her in a whisper. "I think the Chans need some time and space to grieve. Is it OK if Hector and I leave and just drive slowly toward Vermont? We won't cross out of New York State without checking in with you. We'll call in from pay phones every half hour."

I come back into the room and let Hector and the Chans know that it's time for us to go. Mr. Chan and Hector are loading everything into our car. Wayne sure has a lot of stuff! It's amazing we fit it all in. Then it's time for the good-byes. We are all crying when we finally pull away from their home.

"That was intense," Hector says. "This is the second time we have gone into someone's home and left with their child. I didn't really look at it that way at the time when we got Todd, maybe because it was so hectic with all the other kids around. But this time, all I could think about was how painful this must be for the Chans. My heart is breaking for them."

"I know," I say. "When we agreed to follow God on this journey, we had no idea what we were getting into. I just can't imagine how they feel now that their home and their arms are empty. It must almost feel like a death to them."

"I was thinking the same thing, Sue, and it's odd, because even though we don't know how they feel today, the day will come when we will. One day Wayne will come to the end of his journey, and we'll know, like them, the feelings of losing a son."

We're both crying now—while Wayne is in the back seat singing away. "It gives me chills that this is happening on Good Friday—and Passover. If anyone can relate to losing a son, it's God."

We drive, stop, phone Maris.

Drive, stop, phone Maris.

Drive, stop, phone Maris.

The approval still hasn't come, and we're at the last rest area before we cross the state line. We stop, buy some snacks, and wait.

Finally, the approval comes through. At last, we're ready to drive home and let the rest of the kids meet their newest brother.

It will be a joyous Easter indeed.

14

More Babies

"I've been asked to help out on a complicated adoption case in another state," I explain to the kids over dinner. "I'll be gone about a week, and it's going to be very difficult, so please pray for me while I'm gone."

"Why is it difficult, Mommy?" SueAnn asks.

"Well, it involves a family that looks kind of like ours on the outside—they've adopted a lot of kids from many different backgrounds. But some people are saying that inside their house, the kids are not being treated right, so my friend and I have to go and try to help them. It might mean some of their kids have to move. I think it will be hard and sad."

"You mean the parents aren't fair?" George asks.

"No, George. It's OK if parents aren't fair once in a while,"

Hector laughs. "This is different—the parents aren't taking care of the kids, and maybe even hurting them."

"Parents should never hurt their kids," Renee says. "They don't understand what that does to them deep down in their heart. When their heart is hurt, it hurts for a long time."

"Yeah, and kids who are adopted should never have to move again, right Mommy?"

"That's right, Joelle. That's what makes this so hard. And Renee, you are right too: no one should ever hurt a child, especially a parent. Hurts in the heart are the hardest ones to heal."

"You know our family has had its ups and downs," Hector begins.

"Like a roller coaster," Isaac says, mimicking the movement with his arms.

"You'd know about that," Hector smiles, continuing. "But we never have and never will hurt any of you, and none of you will ever have to move again. You belong to us forever, like it or not! Now let's eat up and we'll pray for this family and for mom before we start on homework time."

Later, I fill Hector in further on the plans for my trip. "This is a new opportunity, Sue. People around the country respect your knowledge about adoption. God might be using this to open a new door."

"It's possible," I say. "It's a little scary, too. Am I really an expert? I am not sure I feel like one."

"Don't deny your gifts—God gave them to you. Go forth and use them," he says before he starts tickling me, and we both fall into bed laughing.

The trip out west is far more intense than I could have imagined, and Michelle, the social worker from Philadelphia who coordinated it, and I quickly bond over this shared experience. She and her husband started an adoption agency and they focus on placing the so-called "harder to place" children. A week after we are home, Michelle calls me.

"I'll have to talk it over with Renee and Trish, but it sounds like a great opportunity for a summer job," I tell Hector. Michelle has offered to hire the girls to work in the on-site day care center she started at her agency.

"We could drive them down there on the first leg of our summer trip," Hector suggests. "We've never included a tour of Philadelphia on any of our other summer trips."

"That would work—and then Lilly and I will be driving out to New Mexico with the baby to join you near the end of the trip, and we can pick them up on the way home."

"Sounds like a plan."

"And there's one more thing. Michelle says they are going to be ready to hire an adoption director by next January. She's asked me to consider taking the job."

"In Philadelphia? Wow, that would be a big change for the family. I don't know how I'd feel about living in a city like that," Hector replies, stunned.

"I know. It's a big decision. Fortunately, we have plenty of time to think it over, pray about it, and get all the information we need to decide. We've talked before about moving someplace with more diversity, and the timing for a transition could be good as far as where all the kids are in school."

"Well, it's way more than we can talk about right now. I have to get to work," Hector says, checking the time. "Oh boy. I'm going to be late picking up Vince. He really doesn't like that, so I better get rolling. Do you work overnight tonight? I forget your schedule this week."

"No, not tonight, but I do work all weekend. Tonight is the night I'm going up to my mom's to help with addressing Stephanie's wedding invitations. Nancy's coming too; it will be a girls' night."

"That should be fun. I gotta run. We'll pray about this and

talk more after we get through Stephanie's wedding," he says, giving me a quick peck on the cheek as he heads out the door.

I'm looking at our family calendar when the phone rings. We sure have a lot going on in the next few weeks. Lilly's baby shower. Stephanie's wedding. Renee's prom and graduation. Packing for the summer trip. Whew!

"Hello," I say, expecting it to be my mom reminding me about tonight. Instead, it is Jose's teacher at Spaulding Graded School.

"OK, I'll be sure to talk to him," I say, a little dazed. *This is so unlike Jose*, I think to myself.

"Look at this, Mom. What do you think of this design?" Jose is showing me a drawing of a sneaker he created. "I don't think the Air Jordans they sell are designed right. I think if they did it like this, basketball players could jump higher and run faster."

"Wow, Jose, that's really cool. Maybe we should send it to Nike and see what they think? You might be able to make some money for college," I say, only half in jest. (Little do I realize that Nike will come out with its Air Jordan III in less than two years and it will look exactly like Jose's design! I wonder how his life might have changed if we'd really mailed his artwork to Nike back in 1991!)

"How can I interview my birth mother, when no one knows who she is? I don't even know my real birthday or anything about my life as a baby. I didn't know what to write, so I just wrote up the story of Hansel and Gretel and turned it in."

"While I have your attention, Jose, I need to talk to you about a call I got from the school today. Your social studies teacher said you never completed an assignment that's worth more than half your grade for this report card. Can you tell me what happened?"

"She said to write an autobiography starting with the day we were born. We were supposed to interview our parents to get the information. How can I interview my birth mother, when no one knows who she is? I don't even know my real birthday or anything about my life as a baby. I didn't know what to write, so I just wrote up the story of Hansel and Gretel and turned it in. She thought I was being smart, so she gave it back and told me to do the real assignment or I'd get an F."

"Wow, she wasn't very understanding, was she?" I say, collecting my thoughts and holding back tears.

"Can you tell me why you chose Hansel and Gretel as the story you wanted to turn in?"

"Well, I doubt my birth mom didn't care about me. I know there was a war and the situation was bad, but I always felt like Hansel."

"Tell me more."

"Like I had laid breadcrumbs so I could find her again, but then when I tried to follow the trail the bread crumbs were gone, and I was alone. I was angry at myself. I thought I should be invincible."

"Sweetheart, you were two years old," I say. "It must be really hard to wish you could be invincible in such a tough situation."

We sit quietly for a few moments, then Jose adds: "It's nothing against you and Dad. I'm happy here. I just hope she finds peace, and if she's still alive I hope she's not angry with me for getting lost. Anyway, I pray for that."

"Thanks for sharing that with me, Jose. I think you're pretty invincible in a lot of ways. But it's OK just to be a kid too, all right? I'm going to ask your teacher to accept your Hansel and Gretel paper for the assignment this time. Next time, if you get a tough assignment like that, will you promise to talk to me or Dad first so we can figure out how to help you deal with it?"

"Yeah, I guess so."

I tousle his hair, which he hates, and he squirms away from

me. "Speaking of homework, I guess I better go do mine."

"I sure hope Lilly has this baby before Stephanie's wedding," I say to my friend Patty. She's come to Burlington with me to help me find clothes for the kids to wear to the wedding. It's fun to spend a day with Patty. Plus, she is the best bargain-hunter I know.

"Well, if Lilly goes into labor the same day as the wedding, I'll go and wait at the hospital with her until you can get there," Patty offers.

"Thanks, that eases my mind a little. OK, so what do you think of these two dresses for Chelsea and Flory? They have to match the colors of the wedding party because they'll be circulating the guest book."

"Mom, Mom, I can't take this." I am wiping Lilly's forehead with a cool washcloth as we wait for the anesthesiologist to come in. "When is that doctor coming to give me the epidural?"

"He'll be here soon. Let's just try to breathe through it together," I say, and then I burst out laughing.

"You think this is funny?"

"No, I am remembering when I was in labor for Chelsea and the nurse told me to 'Shut up and breathe!'"

"If a nurse talks to me like that, I'll pop her—*owwwwwww-www!*"

"Breathe, breathe, breathe," I say, grateful that I can be with her while she gives birth. I was at the hospital, but in the waiting room, when Kirsten and Whitney were born, so this will be the first time being in the delivery room since Isaac was born nine years ago.

"You have another niece. Her name is Ashley Victoria," I hear Hector tell the kids in the background as soon as I give him the news on the phone. To me, he adds, "Give Lilly a hug for me. I'll stop up to visit tonight. Does she need anything from home?"

"Just me," I say. "She's asking me to stay for the night, so can you bring me some sweats to change into?"

"Thank goodness you're here. I was getting stressed," I say to Fisher.

"I told you I'd be here. What's the big deal?"

"The wedding starts in 10 minutes, and you're singing at the beginning of the service. You shouldn't have cut it so close."

"Just chill, it's cool. I got it covered."

Fisher sings beautifully during the service, but I'm not appeased. I think Hector is right; I'm starting to see signs of drug use. We have dealt with this before, with Uncle Philip, and thankfully he is doing great now in his recovery. I'm not ready to walk that path with Fisher. Maybe Philip can reach out to him. I'll talk to him after the wedding.

"I got accepted! I am going to college!" Renee is running up the driveway to share her good news. With graduation less than two weeks away, she's been feeling let down; so many of her friends have college acceptance letters or else know what they are doing next year. Now she knows too. We were so thrilled to find the Threshold Program at Leslie College for students with developmental disabilities. Renee had her heart set on college, but academically we couldn't imagine a college she could get into—until we found Threshold. Now as long as we can get the financial aid, her dream will come true.

It's a rare moment when Hector and I are both home in the middle of a weekday, while all the kids, except Alysia, are in school.

"I think I'll walk over to the Grand Union and pick up something easy to make for dinner," I say, opening the door to head out. I'm startled to see a car pulling in with Trish and a woman I don't recognize.

One look at Trish and I know something's wrong. "Are you OK? Are you sick?" I ask, stepping back into the house and making room for the two of them to come in.

"I'm Ms. Snelling, a nurse at the health clinic near Spaulding. Do you and your husband have a few minutes to talk with us?" I guide the nurse to a seat in the living room.

Time stands still. Ms. Snelling is pulling out of our driveway. Lilly is screaming and sobbing. Trish is ashen and silent. I can't breathe; the air has been sucked completely out of the room.

"I still don't understand why you didn't think you could talk to us, Trish. We've always been available to talk about anything." Hector says softly.

"I don't know, I was just scared," she says finally, "After JD and then Lilly, I just didn't want to let you down."

We have just learned that Trish is not only pregnant, but due in September. How could we have missed the signs?

Lilly is beside herself. "Not you too? Noooooooo . . . . . . " she cries.

"But this is different. You were raped," I say to Trish, having trouble even saying the word out loud. "I wish I could have helped you after that. Oh, sweetheart." I suddenly can't control the tears and wrap her in a big hug. Here's the backstory: our oldest kids have some friends in Burlington, and they sometimes go there and spend the weekend so they can go out dancing at a teen club. It always seemed safe . . . but not for Trish, at least not that one time.

"Oh Lord, why didn't you protect my girl!!!" I cry out, angry, sad, confused.

"Eeeewwwwww!" Trish screams. "There are bugs in the

bathtub."

"Nasty!" Lilly says. "I'm not taking my baby in there."

"Thankfully, we are only here for a few hours. Try to catch a little sleep and we'll be back on the road in no time," I say. Two days after Renee's graduation, Hector left Vermont, bringing Renee and Trish to Philadelphia and continuing westward for the summer trip. Lilly, baby Ashley, Trish, and I are on our way to meet up with them in New Mexico. Renee stayed on in Philadelphia to continue working at the daycare. After driving more than twenty hours since leaving Philadelphia, we've pulled over into a 'no name' hotel in Tulsa to get a few hours of sleep before continuing our travels.

None of us sleep much, so we are back on the road before the sun comes up. Nine hours later, we pull into the campground in Hobbs, New Mexico, where Hector and the family arrived last night. Ashley has proven to be a good little traveler. I smother her cheeks with a few extra kisses before she goes off with Lilly to stay with her former foster family instead of roughing it at the campground.

The next day, as we are pulling up stakes and ready to move on to our next destination, Lilly comes back to the campground. "Do you think Trish can stay with me at Elaine's house?" she asks. "We can take a bus back to Barre in a few weeks."

"A bus?" Hector says, surprised. "You really want to travel all that way on a bus with a new baby? And you, Trish? Won't that be pretty uncomfortable?"

"Sure. Ashley likes riding, it'll be fine. And the bus stops often enough, Trish'll be all right."

"And it's OK with Elaine and the rest of her family?"

"They suggested it," Lilly says. "They even offered to help pay for the bus tickets."

"OK, I guess that settles it. Just make sure you get back before school starts."

"Oh we'll be back by August 10," Lilly says, "We already

checked the bus schedules."

"Ms. Sue, the phone is for you." A resident at the group home where I work in Plainfield is calling to me. It's nearly midnight and I'm working a crossword puzzle on the dining room table. "Who would be calling me at work at this hour?" I wonder aloud.

It's Hector: "Can you get someone to cover for you? Trish is in labor and she needs you here."

"What? She is not due for another month. This can't be good. Are you sure it's really labor?"

"I've been through this a few times now," Hector reminds me. "It's definitely labor. How soon can you get home?"

"I'll do my best to get coverage. It will be tough at this time of night."

Phillip James, although a month early, is a perfectly formed little peanut. "He reminds me of Raj," I say to Trish. "He's too cute for words." At just 3 pounds, they have whisked him off to the NICU to be thoroughly checked; we had only a moment with him after the delivery. "He's tiny now, but he has a big name to live up to!" I joke. His first name is in honor of Hector's middle name, and James is after both JD and my dad. I think I might just call him PJ, although "Peanut" is what I find myself whispering to him through the glass in the NICU.

"Dear Lord, I'm sorry I was so angry when I learned Trish was pregnant. Please protect this little peanut, and give Trish the wisdom she needs to be a good mom. Help her to manage both school and being a mom so she can graduate. Amen."

"Ms. Sue, the phone is for you." I haven't had a personal call at the group home since the night Trish went into labor four months ago. I know no one is pregnant. I wonder what it is this time.

It's Hector. "I have some sad news," he starts. I can hear in his voice that he has been crying. "I really hate to tell you on the phone, but I know you'd want to know right away."

I sit down, shaking. "Tell me."

"Your dad just called. Aunt Ruth passed away today."

I can't speak.

"Sue? Are you still there?"

"I, I . . . I don't know what to say. I know she was getting older, but I never thought the day would come when we wouldn't have her anymore. Have you told the kids?"

"I'm waiting for you to get home. Your dad says the funeral is in a couple of days."

It'll be the first funeral for most of our kids, and the first close family member's funeral for Hector and I since his dad died when I was pregnant with Chelsea.

"I'm glad we know she is in Heaven," I tell Hector and the kids. We've called a family meeting to give them a chance to process their feelings. "But it's still hard to say good-bye to someone we love very much. And she loved all of you so much too."

Aunt Ruth was a pillar of my faith foundation, and as a single career woman, teacher, and guidance counselor, she fueled my passion for reading and writing and nurtured my dreams for education and professional opportunities. I majored in education largely due to her influence. With no children of her own, my siblings, cousins, and I became her children, and she adored our children. She relished her title of "Great Grand Aunt" bestowed on her when Chelsea was born.

Oh, how I will miss her. At her house after the service, I look through her bookshelves and my eyes light upon *The Family Nobody Wanted* by Helen Doss. Wow, I read that book when I was just a kid, and dreamed about having a big adoptive family one day. *I haven't thought about this book in years*, I say to myself as I tuck it in my purse. *Maybe I need to read it again.*

"What's so special about this day?" Joelle asks as we get the house ready for guests. I chuckle as I realize she is using the same question we taught them for our Passover celebration in the spring.

"It's a holiday called Kwanzaa. It's a special time after Christmas to celebrate the heritage of everyone who has ancestors from Africa."

"Like me?"

"Yes, like you and lots of our family. I just learned about Kwanzaa from my friend Marek—he also has adopted black children. So we decided to celebrate together. He's bringing some real African drums. Won't it be fun?"

"Yeah. JD told me there will be lots more black people when we move to Philadelphia. I won't be the only one in my class anymore. Is that true?"

"That's true, sweetie. That's one reason we decided to move, so you and your brothers and sisters will have a chance to meet more people of all different races."

"Are you sure this is the right thing to do?" Hector asks, the day before I leave to start my new job working for my friend Michelle's adoption agency. "This move is going to be a big adjustment for the kids."

"Are you sure this is the right thing to do?" Hector asks, the day before I leave to start my new job working for my friend Michelle's adoption agency. "This move is going to be a big adjustment for the kids."

"The kids will be fine, but are *you* sure it's the right thing to do? You told me you felt a peace about it before I accepted the job and gave my notice at the group home."

"I know, and I'm sure there will be so many more opportunities, more options for school, arts, doctors, therapists, everything we need. I guess I'm the one who's getting a little nervous," he says. "I never pictured myself as a big-city person."

"I know, but if the kids can adjust, I'm sure we can. I'm most nervous about finding my way around. My job will require me to visit pregnant women in their homes and at hospitals all over the city. That's what scares me!"

"Well, I just hope you can find us a house in a good neighborhood, near good schools and a good church. After that, everything else will fall into place."

Hector had no way of knowing what God was preparing him for while he was growing up in a large family. Back Row, Victor, Madeleine, Cecile, Germaine, Rejeanne, Richard; Middle Row Bernard, Leonard, Edgar, Irene, Front Row, Gaspor, Philorum, Edward, Gerard, Hector, Delvina (known as Mamere) and Theodore, 1961

Sue's family, the Hoags, camping at Maidstone State Park in VT, Summer, 1976 – where Hector and Sue would later spend their honeymoon and 25th anniversary.
L to R Nancy, David, Marie, Sue, Jim, Stephanie

High School Sweethearts,
Prom 1974

Newlyweds starting a life
journey, July 14, 1979

We soon became a family of 4 – L to R – Chelsea, Sue, Hector and Jose
standing in the Logos Bookstore we owned 1979-83. This is the photo
used in the newspaper article where we famously told the world of
our plan to "have two and adopt two" children. God was probably
laughing that day! November, 1981

*After Isaac's birth, the family grew to five – L to R – Jose,
Sue, Isaac, Hector and Chelsea – taken for Sue's parents' 25th
anniversary gift, July 1982*

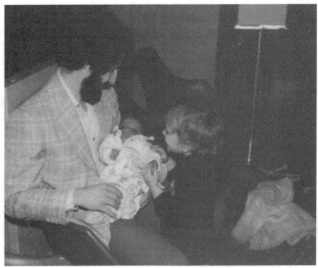

*Hector and Chelsea meeting Raj for the first time
at the airport in Boston, November 1983*

The first big family road trip took us through Niagara Falls on our way to our first NACAC conference in Chicago, Summer 1984, L to R Chelsea, Jose, Raj, Hector, Isaac

Three of our foster sons came with us on our second family road trip, where we were so small in the Redwood forest, and ate ice cream in Nevada to celebrate the truce reached when the teens agreed not to fight for the rest of the trip, 1985

By Christmas, 1986, we had 10 children – gathered here in the playroom Hector built as a Christmas surprise in our Cabot, Vt house. Back row, Isaac, George, Middle Row, SueAnn holding Raj, Flory, Joelle, Chelsea, Front Row, Jose, Abel holding Todd.

In January 1988, our church welcomed the 3 newest Badeaus – Renee, Trish and David. Back Row, Renee holding Todd, David, Sue holding Joelle, Abel, Trish. Front row, Chelsea, Isaac, SueAnn, Raj, Flory, George, Jose and Hector

JD (far left), Lilly and Fisher (in window with Sue) had joined the family by the time we were profiled in Woman's Day magazine in the December 20, 1988 issue. Here, we are lined up in front of our home in Cabot, just before moving to Barre.

1989, Bob and Dorothy Debolt came to Vermont to help us launch the adoption agency we founded, Rootwings Ministries, Inc. L to R, David Hoag (Sue's brother), Bob DeBolt, Marie Hoag (Sue's mom), Dorothy DeBolt, Sue, Hector, Jim Hoag (Sue's dad)

A photo of Alysia that hung on our refridgerator while we prayed about adding her to the family. Spring 1989

L to R Hector, Sue, Lilly, Lucie Arnaz and Larry Luckinbill when they visited us in Vermont, Winter 1989

June 1989 brought the first of many graduations to celebrate. L to R, Sue's sister Nancy, with her son Stephen, Grandpa (Sue's dad), Lilly, Fisher, Mamie (Sue's mom), Nancy's husband Bobby holding son Michael

Dylan's first visit with our family Short St. Barre, VT, Spring 1990

Wayne and Todd with Flory and Alysia enjoying a picnic breakfast soon after Wayne joined the family, just before he wandered off to help himself to food at a neighboring campsite, Summer 1991.

1991 summer trip, New Mexico, Back Row Raj, Todd, Jose, Sue; Middle Row Chelsea holding Alysia, Lilly, Trish, Joelle, Isaac, Wayne, Hector; Front Row Abel, David, George, Flory holding Dylan, SueAnn

Part II: Mountaintops and Deep Valleys

" . . . A time to weep and a time to laugh; a time to mourn and a time to dance . . . "

Ecclesiastes 3:4

15

New Beginnings

"Oh Dad, you should see this house! It's got like a million rooms and a huge yard and it's so awesome!"

I'm smiling as I listen to Abel describe the house to Hector over the phone.

After doing some research, I learned that Mt. Airy is the best neighborhood for our family in Philadelphia. It's racially mixed, the houses and yards are large, the schools are excellent, and there are churches, grocery stores, and everything else we need close by. On my first weekend here I went to several open houses in Mt. Airy and met many Realtors. My spiel to all of them was the same: "I'm moving to Philadelphia from Vermont with my husband and sixteen children. I need a house that's big enough for all of us near Henry school, and we want a yard and—oh, by the way—we don't have very much of a budget to work with. Can you help us?"

"I need a house that's big enough for all of us near Henry school, and we want a yard and—oh, by the way—we don't have very much of a budget to work with. Can you help us?"

Both Hector and I knew it would take a miracle from God for us to find a house that we could afford and that also meets our family's needs. And so I shouldn't have been shocked when He found it for us—but I was. When the Realtor led me to the house at 30 Pelham Road, I was dumbfounded. The Tudor-style stone house is enormous and beautiful. "Oh Lord, how cool is this? You remembered our dream of living in a house built from stones!"

We sign a lease-to-buy agreement, and I move in by myself in March. Hector and the family will move here with all of our things in July, after everyone is out of school and Trish graduates. For now, the kids are coming on the train every other weekend, two-by-two, to visit me. Abel and Jose are the first to make the trip and they love the house.

"This will be a road trip to remember," Hector says to me during our last phone call before he sets out in his caravan—an 18-foot U-Haul truck he's driving, followed by JD driving our 15-passenger van filled with kids, and finally our friend Judy bringing up the rear with her car and the remaining kids and boxes.

"We'll be watching for you!" David is already in Philly with me and so excited for Hector and the rest of the family to arrive. He's joined by Angelo, Antoine, Angel, and Eric—four boys who'd been "camping out" in the house when it was vacant because they had nowhere else to stay. "Only our family can buy a house that comes with kids included," I joke to Hector. "But they promise to help unload the trucks." Little did we know that these boys would become unofficial members of our family, with Angelo living with us all the way through college.

Thunder, lightning, and pouring rain greet our hearty band of travelers as they finally arrive at Pelham Road around 9 PM on July 18. David is standing outside in the rain, flagging them down and motioning them into the driveway.

"Hey Sue. Did I work on the cars last night?" Hector asks me a week later, walking up the driveway carrying a newspaper.

"Not that I remember. That's an odd question. Why do you ask?"

"I went to the store to get a paper, and when I came back, I noticed the hoods of both vehicles are open."

"That's really strange. You better see what that's about." We walk together toward the back of the driveway.

"Look at that: both batteries are gone. I guess that's our 'Welcome to Philadelphia' greeting from someone in the neighborhood," Hector says, stunned. "Great. How can we get new batteries now?"

We have several more incidents throughout the summer—lawn chairs, kids' bicycles, hanging planters, and even a mop and bucket all go missing. On top of that, I have a car accident, while making a trip back to Vermont less than a month after moving in, totaling our car and breaking two ribs and my wrist. Fortunately, the accident was near enough to Northampton that I was able to stay with our friends Dan and Pam while recuperating.

What would we do without our Mill River House Church friends? They're always there for us in any crisis, no matter what twists and turns our life journey takes. This whole episode forces us to miss the NACAC conference for the first time in years, and I'm really disappointed. But by the time the first day of school rolls around, everything has settled down.

"It's going to be a big adjustment, kids," Hector says during our annual night-before-school-starts family meeting. "But your mom and I are confident you'll be fine. You'll make friends and get used to the new routine in no time."

Seven of the kids—from Todd in kindergarten to George and Chelsea in seventh grade—are attending the Henry School in the neighborhood and will be walking to school. Dylan, Wayne, and David are in specialized schools across the city. They'll have yellow school buses in a few weeks, but to start the year, we have to drive them. Alysia will start preschool at United Cerebral Palsy in a few weeks. Jose, Abel, and SueAnn are all in high school, and they have to take the city SEPTA buses. Thankfully, Angelo and Eric have been teaching them the bus routes over the summer.

"Everyone had great report cards, so it's pizza for dinner!" Hector announces. We order ten pizzas and I mix up a big batch of ice tea to celebrate. "I hope this is the first of many 'good report card celebrations' to come."

"You're getting too stressed. It's your parents who are coming, not the Pope or the President," Hector says to me as I review the cleaning checklist one more time before my parents arrive for our first Thanksgiving in our new house. "Don't take the 'thanks' out of Thanksgiving, OK?"

Of course, Hector is right, and I didn't need to be stressed. It was a wonderful gathering, with so many of our Vermont family joining us in Philly. "I don't think my dad left that chair in front of the fireplace more than a handful of times all weekend," I say to Hector. "He loved calling the kids over one by one and having conversations with them. I thought that was really great."

"It was, and it was also nice that he gave me a hand getting the lights on the bannister and the railings for Christmas. Hard to believe Advent is about to begin."

"Did you find the book?"

"Right here." Hector holds up the daily devotional book we have used during every Advent season since we were first married. "Now it really feels like home."

"Speaking of Advent, it's interesting how they do the candle lighting here at Summit. It's a little different than how we did it at our church in Barre."

"True, but I like it." After visiting every church within walking distance, we chose Summit Presbyterian for many reasons. We feel the preaching and worship are solid, we love the music, the church is racially mixed, the people are incredibly welcoming, and there are a lot of kids at all of the ages of our kids. Hector has plunged right into the life of the church and has already been asked to be on the Session. Because our teenagers' high schools are so far out of our neighborhood, most of their close friends are from Summit and, on any given Friday night, if they aren't playing basketball at church, they're all hanging out at our house.

"What do you think the kids will say when they get home?"

"They'll totally flip! They've been wanting a horse forever. Its pretty ironic that we never had a chance to get one when we lived in Vermont, but now here we are, city-living, and we're going to have a pony in the backyard."

"What's his name?" . . . "Can we ride him?" . . . "He's so pretty!" . . . "He looks hungry, can I feed him?" George, Chelsea, Flory, Isaac, Raj, and Todd are all talking at once as soon as they see the pony in the backyard. Joelle is hovering at a distance, watching with wide eyes.

"His name is Baby and he's a pony that used to give rides at circuses and carnivals," Hector tells the kids. "He's too old for that now, so he's joining our family."

"So if he gave rides before, we can ride him, right?" George says. Not waiting for an answer, he hops on Baby bareback and starts riding him around the backyard.

"Easy, George. Let's help him get used to us before we push him too hard."

Over the next several weeks, all of the kids fall in love with Baby, and they take turns feeding him, cleaning up after him, and riding him around the yard. We're probably the only family in Mt. Airy with a pony in our yard. Chelsea and George sometimes take him out to Valley Green in Fairmount Park so they can have a real ride.

"Dad, Dad! Baby got loose! He's running down the street!" Abel comes running in the house, breathless. "I was waiting for my bus to go to school and all of a sudden Baby busts out!"

"George, go get some of his food in a bucket and you and me will go bring him home," Hector says. The rest of us are watching from the porch as Baby runs wildly up and down Pelham Road. Some children walking to school squeal, half in fright and half in delight. Finally, Baby heads for the parking lot of the Core States Bank on the corner, and Hector and George are able to safely lead him home.

"Phew, that got the old ticker pounding first thing in the morning! I think I need another cup of coffee," Hector says once everyone has left for school and Baby is settled down.

There were no more incidents with Baby for the rest of the school year, and when our friend, and photographer, Doug Farnham comes for a visit in June, he takes some amazing photos of the kids with Baby in the backyard.

"It's hard to believe we are rolling up to our first anniversary of living in Philadelphia. I never thought I'd like city living, but actually, I am starting to feel at home here," Hector says to me as we turn the calendar from June to July. "I think I'll take the kids to this Fourth of July parade in the city I've been hearing about."

"Are you kidding? You hate going into the city," I say.

"But this is different. It'll be an experience."

"I'm sure it will. Who do you plan to take?"

"Everyone."

"Even Dylan and Wayne?"

"Sure. I took them all across the country on camping trips. I think I can handle one night in the city here."

"Well, I'm not going, I'll stay home with Phillip if Trish wants to go." Trish and Phillip have been living with Michelle, helping with childcare. Renee got a similar live-in nanny position with an adoptive family in Seattle.

"I've never seen—or heard—anything like it, Sue!" Hector exclaims as the kids tumble out of the van at 1 AM when they return home. "I think there were more people on the Ben Franklin Parkway than in the whole state of Vermont—it was a sea of people. *Incroyable,*" Hector says, using the French word for incredible. "I don't know how I managed to keep all the kids together, but I think they all got home with me. You might want to do a head count to be sure!" he chuckles.

When the new school year begins, Abel tries out for soccer and Jose joins the debate team. It's good to see the kids getting involved in activities. I've found paper-making and dance classes for a few of the others, and Isaac plans to be in the school play at Henry.

"Dad!" Jose yells, coming in from school one evening after debate. "You should have seen the size of the rat I saw on the train tracks tonight. It was bigger than our cat Monster!"

"Why didn't you grab it and bring it home?" Hector asks.

"What?" Jose replies, dumbfounded.

"We could have cooked it up for supper." This elicits a chorus of "Oh Dad!", "Gross!", "Nasty!" and similar comments from all the kids.

"Don't forget your chore, chump," Hector says to Jose. "Just because you get home past chore time doesn't make you exempt."

"I know, I know."

"Rats," Hector says to me. "One of the finer points of living in the city."

"Mom, Dad, guess what? Me and Flory and Isaac and George will be singing in the school Christmas concert. And I'm signing up to take flute classes."

"That's great, Chelsea. We'll definitely make that one of our family Advent activities this year—make sure you tell us the date when you find out. Speaking of holidays," Hector says, switching gears, "now that Thanksgiving is getting closer, I want to remind everyone that Mamie and Grandpa, JD and Melissa, Aunt Nancy and Stephen and Michael and Aunt Deanna and Uncle Freddy are all coming for Thanksgiving. So everyone needs to get their rooms ready for guests."

"How come we always have to give up our room?" Abel and Jose complain.

"Because that's the way it is," Hector says. "So let it be written, so let it be done! I'll be checking all the rooms tomorrow." The kids start to file out of the living room, and Hector has one last comment for George: "And no dirty socks and underwear behind the radiator."

"What are you talking about, Dad?"

"You know exactly what I mean, George."

"Are you ready to go, Hec?" I shout. "My parents are already in the car." We're heading out to go Christmas shopping the day after Thanksgiving. My parents want to find a new set of fire-place tools for our family gift, so we're headed to a specialty shop. Thank goodness we don't have to brave the malls!

"I'll be right there—just throwing a few logs on the fire."

"Dad, I need to talk to you and Mom about something."

"Not now, SueAnn. Don't you see Mom and I are getting ready to leave?"

"But, it's really important."

"OK, we'll have time for a good conversation after Mamie and Grandpa head home tomorrow. Just don't tell me you're pregnant, and we'll be fine," he says, jokingly.

Neither of us have a clue the next bombshell is about to explode in our life.

"It can't be possible that this is happening again. Is it a family curse? JD, Lilly, Trish, now SueAnn!" Hector yells, slamming the door in front of SueAnn's school as we step outside. "Each one a little younger than the next. God, what are you trying to teach us? We are listening. Can't we get the message already so you don't have to keep sending us the same lesson?"

"She only thinks she might be pregnant," I say, clinging to a remnant of hope entwined with denial. "I'll pick up a pregnancy test on the way home and maybe it will turn out not to be true."

"Even if it's not true, if she thinks it, you know what that means," Hector bellows.

"OK, OK. We don't need to air our dirty laundry with the whole world. Quiet down, will you?"

In the car on the way home, the tension is palpable. SueAnn is in the back seat, quietly crying. Not a word is spoken until we're all seated in the living room.

"What were you thinking?"

"You're just a baby yourself."

"Is your boyfriend, Bill, the father?"

"Haven't you learned anything from your sisters? You see

how hard it is."

"Haven't you heard any of what we have tried to teach you at home and church all these years?"

We bombard her with questions, our voices rising louder and louder with each one.

"Stop screaming at me!" she yells.

"Young lady, you're in no position to be talking that way to us."

"You want to play adult? Now you have to be an adult. Are you ready to drop out of school and raise a child—or else place the baby for adoption? Those are your options, you know."

This continues for several more minutes, until SueAnn flees, running up to her room. Her sobs seem to fill the entire house.

For the next several days, Hector and I pour over the biblical book of Job, venting our anguish to God, questioning ourselves. The younger kids, who don't know what is happening, are acting out due to the tension in the house.

"That's it! I've had it!" I hear Hector yell at the same time I hear Todd, Raj, Isaac, and George fighting again. "Everyone in the living room."

"We're canceling Christmas this year," Hector says to the children gathered in front of us. "Oh, Jesus will still be born and we'll still go to church and school concerts, but that's it. Our tree is already up, so we'll keep that, but nothing else. No eggnog. No cookies. And most of all: No. Presents. The values of the world seem to have taken over our lives. Your mother and I are sick of it. No money will be spent and no presents will be under the tree. That's it. Now go finish your homework and I don't want to hear another word of fighting.

"And Abel, get in the kitchen and get those pots and pans done. It's been your chore all week and you keep putting it off. Go. Now. Isaac, Raj—out back with me. We have three deliveries to get ready for tomorrow."

To help make ends meet, and keep us supplied with plenty of wood for our many fireplaces, Hector has started a small business selling firewood in our neighborhood. He gets huge logs—often whole trees—from a landscaping friend who takes down trees and cleans up after storms. Isaac, Raj, and sometimes George are his assistants, helping with the splitting, stacking, truck loading, and deliveries. I know splitting some wood will help Hector calm down; I think the business has more value as therapy than any amount of money it brings in.

Later, the house is finally quiet and we sit in front of the fire. "I just don't know what to think, Sue," Hector says. "I'm so angry, guilt-ridden, and sad for SueAnn. What did we do wrong? I just don't know what to do. On the one hand, I want to show mercy and compassion. I look into her eyes and I see her fear and pain and I want to comfort her. But on the other hand, my French anger gets the best of me, and I just want to shout, 'You made your mess. Don't expect me to clean it up!'"

"I just don't know what to think, Sue," Hector says. "I'm so angry, guilt-ridden, and sad for SueAnn. What did we do wrong? I just don't know what to do."

"I know what you mean," I say. "I have been having many of the same thoughts. We really try to raise our children with godly values, and so why does this plague keep descending on us? And then, after I think that, I feel guilty, because—look at our beautiful grandchildren. I wasn't always happy when I learned about those pregnancies, but can you imagine a world without Kirsten, Whitney, Ashley, or Phillip? I'm sure once we get past this crisis stage, we will find the same love in our hearts for this baby too."

"Yes, I know what you say is true," Hector says. "I just feel overwhelmed and sad right now. This changes her whole life—

she's so much younger than the others were when they were in this situation. I guess we need to trust God to give us the wisdom we'll need and hopefully something good will come of it . . . " Hector's voice trails off. It's time to be still and listen.

"Great concert, kids! You did a wonderful job. I could even hear your voice, George, all the way from our seats in the back!"

"Thanks, Dad. But I didn't really know the words, so I faked it!" George laughs.

"Oh, you were in the back? I was looking and looking for you and I didn't see you," Flory says.

"I had no idea it would be so crowded," I say. "Next year we'll get there earlier. But it's great to see so many Henry parents coming out to support you kids."

By Christmas Eve, I am feeling sad about our decision not to give the kids gifts. I decide to at least write them each a card, telling them why they are special and unique. I'm still working on the cards when Hector goes to bed. I climb in a few minutes later. "It's sad not to be filling stockings," I say as I warm my cold feet against his warm legs.

"I know. We had to send a message. I'm not sure if this was the way to do it, but we had to do something. Let's just try to make tomorrow about the real reason for Christmas, and we can still have a good day."

"I know. Good night."

There's a pile of wrapped gifts under the tree. "Am I really awake, or is this a dream?"

I stand looking at the sight in front of me. Every stocking is filled. There's a pile of wrapped gifts under the tree. "Am I really awake, or is this a dream?" I whisper to Hector. The kids aren't up; they felt no need to rush downstairs on this "cancelled" Christmas morning. "Where did these gifts come from?"

"I have no idea," Hector says, looking as stunned as I feel.

Soon, the kids start making their way down for breakfast. The astonished faces and tears of joy that grace our home this Christmas morning is something I will never forget. As the kids tear into the packages, revealing dollar-store gifts, the excitement is contagious.

"Santa really came!" Joelle shouts gleefully.

"Where did these gifts really come from, Mom? I thought Christmas was cancelled." Chelsea asks.

"I don't know how they got here," I say. "But this I do know. I think we all just learned a really important lesson: Christmas cannot be cancelled. Even in the darkest of times in our lives, when it seems like nothing is going right, the light of Christmas will not stay under the bushel basket. God used some secret elves to teach us this lesson, and we can all give thanks in our hearts."

Later, quite by accident, I overhear three of my boys talking among themselves, and it is only then that I discover who the secret elves were. Secretly, they'd pooled their money. Stealthily, they'd accomplished their mission with no one—not even Hector and I—catching on. Excitedly, they'd waited until after everyone had gone to bed on Christmas Eve and then tiptoed into the living room, filling every stocking and adding a pile of wrapped gifts around the fireplace.

I decided not to share their secret. Like the very first Christmas mother, I too "treasured up all these things and pondered them in (my) heart" (Luke 2:19).

Just a few weeks after Christmas, George and Chelsea have the opportunity to go to PEEC, the Pocono Environmental Education Center, for a week-long field trip. It's a special privilege for eighth-graders at Henry School.

"Outdoor camping is going to be chilly, George and Chels. Make sure you pack your woolies," Hector advises.

"What are woolies?"

"Oh, that's another word for long johns," I tell them. And don't forget extra socks; it can be miserable if your feet get wet and cold."

"Mom, Baby won't get up. I'm trying to feed him, but he won't even move." Isaac comes inside, looking distraught.

"Hec, can you check on Baby? Isaac says he won't stand up or eat this morning."

Two days later, we still can't get Baby moving or eating, and we are very concerned. "I'm calling the vet," I say, wishing we had our friend from Vermont, Tom Stuwe, available down here.

"Everyone in the living room," Hector calls. "We need to have a family meeting."

"I didn't do it!" Abel says.

"No one did anything. We have some sad news," I say. "SueAnn, this is going to be hard for me to talk and sign at the same time, so can you sign for David as I go along?"

"Sure, Mom." She motions for David to sit across from her.

"You've all seen that Baby hasn't been feeling too well the last few days. Well, the vet was here today, and he told us that Baby is going to die. He's actually a lot older then those people from the carnival told us. There's nothing the vet can do for him. He's old and worn out, and it's his time to go."

David's hands start moving rapidly; he's clearly upset by this news. Isaac and Joelle start to cry. SueAnn gets up and gives David a hug. Everyone else sits in stunned silence.

"If you want to say good-bye to Baby, put your coat and boots on and go give him one last hug," Hector says. "The vet has to take him in a few minutes, and I want you kids inside when that happens."

"Are you going to call George and Chelsea?" Abel asks. "You

know how they are about Baby. They'll feel terrible if they don't find out 'til they get home in two more days."

"I'm not sure if I can get through to them at PEEC, but I'll try," I say.

"David wants to know if Baby is going to be with Jesus in Heaven, Mommy," SueAnn asks.

"Yes, SueAnn, I believe he is going to Heaven. God created all creatures, and I believe all of God's creation will be represented in heaven." SueAnn relays this to David, and he smiles.

"It's February, Hec. You know what that means."

"Groundhog didn't see his shadow?"

"No! It's science project time!"

"Ahhh yes. Well, that's your department. Don't get me involved."

"Thanks a lot! I was thinking this year that I'll take all the Henry kids to my office at Option of Adoption on the weekend before they're due. We can have snacks, and a sleepover, and they can all spread out and do their projects without worrying about the little kids or Monster messing things up."

Saturday afternoon, the phone rings. We've been busy working on science projects since Friday evening and we're close to being finished. "Hi Hec. What's up?"

"Have you looked out the window?"

"Not really. Why?"

"Everything is iced up. It's a mess out there. I even heard on KYW that SEPTA [the city bus line] isn't operating today. I don't know how you'll get home."

"Oh no. I guess we'll have to stay over another night. It's a good thing the kids enjoy computer games. If they finish their science projects, they'll have something to do. Hopefully, by tomorrow, things will be better."

"Mom, it looks crazy bad out there," George reports. "I don't think you can drive the car out of the parking lot."

"Mom. We have to get home," Chelsea says. "We don't have any more food here and we have to change our clothes."

"Well, it's only two miles. I guess we'll have to walk."

"I'm scared of walking two miles."

"You'll be OK, Flory. We're all going together."

"Are you OK, Mom?" I look up into five concerned faces hovering over me. I think I blacked out for a minute; I feel disoriented.

"What happened?"

"You fell on the ice."

"You passed out."

"I was really scared."

They are all talking at once.

"OK, just give me a minute. I'll get up slowly. I think I'm OK." I look around to get my bearings. We're near Upsal Street, not far from home. We'll make it. "Let's just walk extra slowly now, OK?" Chelsea and Flory stay close to my side, but George, Isaac, and Raj run ahead, freezing and eager to get home.

"I've been thinking about adoption." SueAnn steps in front of the fireplace, and blurts this news out to Hector and I after dinner. "If I did place my baby for adoption, I would want it to be an open adoption, like Todd and Darlene. But I would want the parents to be someone I already know and trust."

"You've been giving this some thought. That's good."

"Yeah, that social worker Della at my prenatal clinic has been helping me think about a lot of things. I think my birth mother was too young when she had all of us, but she didn't realize it at the time, so she tried to take care of us, and then we all had to end up in foster care. I don't want that to happen to my baby, so I have been thinking I should place her for adoption right away, when she's a newborn, so she has time to grow up in her new family and never has to go through what I went through."

"Wow, we've come a long way from the shouting matches we had when we first learned you were pregnant. How does Bill feel about this?"

"He is willing to talk about it."

"OK, did you have a family in mind? A family you can trust, as you said?" Hector asks.

"Well," she says slowly. "Don't the Kirpans want to adopt a baby?"

"Yes, they do," I say. "They want one more now that they have Sophie and Grace along with the older kids."

"Can we talk to them?" SueAnn asks.

"It can't hurt to call them and see what they think."

Later, in bed, I say to Hector, "Wow, that was a surprise, I had no idea SueAnn was even thinking about adoption. We asked her about it a few months ago and she seemed so adamant that she was not going to do that."

"Yeah, I know. I am so torn about this. I don't want her to drop out of school. I can't imagine raising another baby right now. I mean, I don't want to start raising my kids' kids, you know?" Hector says, half to himself. "But this is our grandchild. I'm not sure how I feel about another family raising our grandchild. Even our best friends. It's just a lot to take in."

"I know. I'm torn too. I wish I could be one hundred percent sure what the best decision is."

"Did I tell you about the grocery store?" Hector asks.

"No, you didn't—are you changing the subject?"

"No, this has to do with SueAnn. She came with me to get a few things, and we were in line together. Suddenly I felt like all eyes were on me. I imagined everyone looking at her and looking at me and wondering what kind of dirty old man I was to be with such a young pregnant girl. I started to move away from her. I didn't want to be seen with her."

I hear a catch in his throat; Hector is starting to cry. "And then I felt so ashamed of myself for even thinking that. And I wondered if God ever feels like he wants to move away from us when we shame him. But he never does, he always comes closer to us in those moments. Something to think about."

"Mom, Dad, I've made my decision. Can we talk somewhere quiet, please?" SueAnn asks, two weeks later.

"I want the Kirpans to adopt my baby. They've promised we'll stay in touch and have letters and visits. They told me I can name her too."

"I've thought about it and prayed about it and I know in my heart that I'm not ready to be a parent." She starts to cry softly. "I wish I could do it, but I'm too young and I know I need to finish school. My baby deserves a better life than what I'm ready for right now."

We all sit silently for a few moments.

"I want the Kirpans to adopt my baby. They've promised we'll stay in touch and have letters and visits. They told me I can name her too."

"Are you sure, SueAnn? This will be really hard to go through with," I say.

"Yes, I'm sure. I know it will be hard, but I know it's best for everyone." She rests her hand on her belly. "Especially for the baby."

"We'll help you however we can, but I think you should also go to a counselor," I say. "You need someone else besides us to talk to—someone not so personally involved."

Hector's eyes are filled with tears. "I love you, SueAnn," he says, giving her a big hug.

"I'm so excited that it is baseball season again—I love baseball!" I say as we climb to our seats on the bleachers at George's game.

"Come on George! Smack it a good one!"

"Oh no!" I scream. George has been hit by a pitch and he drops like a rock, right on home plate. He's not moving. "Oh no, oh no, oh no," I say, running toward the field.

Hector gets there before me and I breathe a huge sigh of relief when George starts to get up. "We need to take him to the hospital, Sue. The coach thinks he might have broken a cheekbone, and maybe his nose."

"Oh my poor Georgie-bones!"

"Look at that shiner!" My brother David says when he arrives the next day with my dad. "How does the other guy look, George?"

"Very funny, Uncle David. I wasn't in a fight. I got hit by a fastball. The fastest pitcher in the league—he drilled me."

"Wow, that must have hurt."

"Oh, it wasn't bad," George says with a broad smile.

Dad and David are staying with us for a few days after David's UPenn graduation, to help him move out of his campus apartment. My mom, sisters, and other family members left last night after the last of the graduation festivities ended.

"Well, speaking of baseball, I hear the Phillies are playing tonight. Let's go see if it's on TV," my dad says to George and David.

"Mommy!" I hear SueAnn screaming from the third floor. I run up to see what's happening. "My water broke!"

"OK, we'll call the doctor and see if he wants us to take you to the hospital right away. Try to relax and get yourself cleaned up." As I head down to the phone, I see Abel in the hallway. "Can you get some towels and bring them to SueAnn? She's going into labor and she needs to get ready to go to the hospital."

After I get off the phone, I poke my head into the TV room. "SueAnn's in labor. I just talked to her doctor and he said we should get her to the hospital within the next half hour or so since her water broke. They don't want to risk infection."

"I'll drive you there," my dad volunteers.

"Really? OK, thanks Dad. You guys can keep watching the game for now, and I'll let you know when SueAnn's ready to go." Glancing at the TV, I can see that the score is tied and the Phillies are at bat.

"He popped out!" Hector yells. "I can't believe it!"

Abel comes running. "What happened?"

"Oh, the Phillies lost a chance to get some runs," Hector says. "No crisis."

"Oh I heard you say 'he popped out,' and I thought SueAnn had her baby already."

"Abel, you're a nut!"

"Are you ready for this, SueAnn?" my dad says as we pull up to the hospital.

"I guess I have to be now. I'm just in so much pain, I want this part to be over with. Are you going back to the house, Grandpa?"

"Oh no, I'll stay right here. I'll find a waiting room."

"I named her Milagro, Dad. It means 'miracle' in Spanish," SueAnn says when Hector comes in, moments after the delivery.

"She's beautiful and that's a beautiful name," I say, giving her hand a squeeze.

"Is Grandpa still here too?"

"Yes, the nurses have been treating him really well. They brought him snacks the whole time you were in labor. He's down by the window, looking at the baby now."

"That's funny, Mommy," SueAnn laughs.

"I agree with Mom. That's a beautiful name. I'm so happy everything went good and you're both healthy," Hector says with tears in his eyes—and then he walks out of the room.

"My heart is breaking," he whispers to me as he slips out the door.

Bill and SueAnn are sitting under a tree in the backyard, their last few moments with Milagro before the adoption ceremony begins. I walk over to them and gently let them know it's time to come inside.

"Are you sure you want Jane here for all of this?" I ask. Jane von Bergen, a friend from church and journalist, has been chronicling SueAnn's pregnancy for an article. She has seen all of us at our best and our worst over the last several months.

"Yes, Mom, I am hoping her article will help some other girls. Maybe one less teenager will become pregnant if she reads my story."

"You're strong and brave," I say.

We have a special meal, read some poems and Bible passages, light some candles, and end with prayer. Our family gives Patty Kirpan the quilt we made for Milagro and we all are crying as we prepare to say our good-byes. Alysia goes out to the porch and begins to sob inconsolably.

"You are a miracle, little one," I whisper to the baby as I take my final turn holding her. "You are beautiful, and precious, and deeply loved. Never ever forget that."

"I can't even begin to imagine how SueAnn feels right now," Hector says to me later. "I hugged her and told her I love her, but I don't guess that helps a whole lot to ease her pain today."

"We're on the other side of adoption now," I observe.

"Yes. We have a little taste of what Darlene and the Chans went through when we came to their home and left with their child. And all the other birth parents of all our children. It hurts.

It hurts." Hector breaks down yet again. We have cried an ocean of tears today.

After he regains his composure, he says, "I knew there would be bumps along the road in our adoption journey. I just never thought there would be so many 'baby bumps.' I always talk about paying the fiddler if you want to dance. But this fiddler charges a high price—and only accepts tears and sorrow for his fee."

16

Adam and Aaron

"How does it feel to be at NACAC without the family?" I ask Hector when he calls at the end of his first day in San Jose.

"Feels good!" he says. "First time I've had my own vacation in years."

"Say hi to all our friends and don't come home with any new kids," I joke.

With so much going on at home, we decided not to do a summer trip this year, so attending NACAC as a family was out of the question. Yet we couldn't pass up the chance to combine a trip to NACAC with a visit to Renee while she's living so close to San Jose, in Mountain View. So this year, Hector is the family ambassador.

"No new kids, I promise," he says. "But speaking of kids, I'm looking forward to seeing Renee. I'm anxious to see what her living situation is like out here. How are things at home?"

"Things are fine. One of the families from Pittsburgh that I placed a baby with is going to visit in a few days. They'll be arriving the same day you get home. I've been having a ton of computer problems. I was about ready to throw the darn thing out the window, but Jose thinks he can fix it. So I'm going to let him try; he can't make it any worse."

"No new kids, I promise," he says. "But speaking of kids, I'm looking forward to seeing Renee. I'm anxious to see what her living situation is like out here."

"He'll probably surprise you. I think he knows more about computers than some of the so-called experts. Any news from JD and Melissa?"

"I just talked to them yesterday to make the arrangements for Kirsten and Whitney to come spend two weeks with us as soon as the new baby is born. Should be any day now."

"That's good. Well, it's time for me to go have dinner. I'm meeting up with Marty and Lorraine."

"Give them my love, and have a great time. If you see Maris, give her those pictures of Wayne I sent with you—the ones Doug took."

"OK, will do. Love you."

"Love you more."

Just a few days after Hector gets home, we get the call that our newest grandchild is born. "I have another girl, mom!" JD says when he calls. "She's beautiful and her name is Erica Marie. Her middle name is after your middle name."

"Oh, congratulations JD! I'm so excited for you. I can't wait to see her. For now, give her lots of smooches for me. How's

Melissa?"

"She's tired, but she did a great job. I'm proud of her. And the girls are really excited about coming to Philly."

"We're excited to have them here. It'll be a big deal for them to be here without you and Melissa. They're getting to be such big girls. Let me put Dad on the phone; I know he wants to congratulate you too."

"You can't leave on your trip while Kirsten and Whitney are here," Hector points out as I look at train schedules.

"Of course not. We only get a little time with them each year; I don't want to miss any of it. They're going home on Sunday, and I was thinking the girls and I will leave on Wednesday. That will put us in Albuquerque on Friday afternoon. We'll stay through Monday and then come home. So we'll be gone a week in total."

"That sounds good. Are you sure Abel and George don't want to go?" Hector asks.

"I've talked to them together and separately. They aren't ready for this. I don't want to push it. When they're ready, we'll figure out a way for them to get out there, but for now, it will just be the two girls and me," I reply.

It's been two weeks since we received a call from an adoption search organization. At his birth mother—MaryJean's—request, they had been searching for Abel since his 18th birthday in March. We've had a flurry of phone calls since then, getting acquainted with MaryJean and her mother and sisters. They really want to meet all four kids, but only SueAnn and Flory feel ready to take this step, so I'm taking them on a train trip to meet their birth family.

"I can't wait to show you all the pictures, Daddy," SueAnn says when he meets us at 30th Street station the day we get back to Philly from New Mexico.

"We have *soooo* many cousins, you wouldn't believe it," Flory says.

"I can't wait to hear all about it," Hector says as we start driving home.

"We had a great time, Hec, and they all want to meet you too. A really awesome family. Flory's right. I think we met about a hundred aunties, uncles, and cousins. And man, did we have some good food while we were there, right girls?" I say.

"Oh my gosh yes. I couldn't stop eating, there were so many different kinds of fajitas and homemade tortillas, and we got to help roast some chilis," Flory explains.

"We made a videotape for Abel and George. MaryJean and I talked about it, and decided it would make sense for her to tell them she understood that they needed more time, and that she's thankful that they're happy and having a good life with our family. I don't want them to feel torn between two families, so maybe when they see that she and I are on the same page, they'll feel more comfortable getting to know her."

"Sounds like a good strategy, Sue. That's what I count on you for," Hector adds.

"Go ahead and look at the pictures with the girls, and I'll just go through my mail," I say when we come in the house. Alysia runs over to greet me with a giant hug.

"I'm not sure what to think, Sue. It's only been a few months since Milagro was born. I can't even imagine adopting another child right now. I'd feel guilty."

"I know what you are saying, but this is totally different. This is a little boy with Sanfilippo Syndrome. A six-year-old with disabilities, not a newborn. Two different situations."

"I know, but I can't help the way I feel. Tell me more and I'll think about it."

"A social worker in Tampa, Florida called our friend Mary Gayle looking for a family for a child with Sanfilippo. Of course,

Mary Gayle knows we have Wayne already, so she thought of us. His name is Adam. He didn't get the same good start in life as Wayne did, though."

"What do you mean?" Hector asks.

"Besides Sanfilippo, he also has Fetal Alcohol Syndrome. He's been in five or six different foster homes already and it seems he's been abused in at least one of those homes."

"Oh, that's heartbreaking. This poor little guy has sure had a tough start in life."

"Oh, one more thing," I say. "He has a four-year-old brother named Aaron who also needs to be adopted, but the agency is planning to place him separately."

"You're kidding, right? Don't they understand how important it is to keep siblings together?" Hector asks.

"Apparently they don't think it matters when a child has this kind of disability," I say, shaking my head.

"Well, let's give it some thought and prayers. I am not sure I'm ready to commit to two terminally ill children. It's going to be hard enough when Wayne dies, and we don't really know how long Dylan will live. I'm not just thinking of my own emotions, but the other kids, too."

"I agree, it's a huge commitment, not one to take on lightly," I say.

"I do know one thing," Hector adds. "If we decide to say yes, we need to fight for his brother too. Separating siblings is not right."

"Can I be excused?" Raj asks.

"Not just yet. We need to have a short family meeting before everyone leaves the table," Hector says. "A social worker in Florida called to tell us about a six-year-old little boy named Adam who has the same disease as Wayne—Sanfilippo Syndrome. And he doesn't have a family."

"This social worker wants our family to think about adopting him," I add. "And we want to know what you kids think."

"Is he going to die, too, like Wayne?" Todd asks.

"Yes, he's actually a little weaker then Wayne, so we don't know how long he'll live," I say. "He's been moved around a lot from foster home to foster home."

"There has to be another family, Mom. Our family can't take every kid in the world," Jose says.

"You're right, we can't," Hector says. "And we don't. Remember just a few months ago an agency wanted us to adopt a girl named Monica and we talked and prayed about it and then decided the answer was no. We just have to make one decision at a time and do what we think is right for that child and for the rest of the family."

"I don't know. I think it will be hard to have another brother who's going to die. I don't know about that," Abel says.

"I think we should adopt him. It will be nice for Wayne," Joelle adds.

Flory is nodding.

"What's that, Alysia?" I ask, paying close attention as she tries to express herself.

"Yes, that's right. Adam is the same age as you."

"Oh, and I forgot to mention, he has a brother named Aaron, but the social worker says a different family is going to adopt Aaron."

"What? Are you letting them do that, Mommy? You always stick up for keeping siblings together," SueAnn speaks up.

"I know. I told them very strongly what we believe, but it seems like their minds are made up," I say.

"I'm going to write a letter to that social worker," she says.

"I wish someone was doing more research to cure Sanfilippo Syndrome," Chelsea says. "It doesn't seem like it should be so hard to find a cure."

"It's such a rare disease," I reply. "So not many people are working on it."

"I'm going to discover the cure, then, when I get older," Isaac says.

"I hope so, Isaac. That would be wonderful. Thanks for your input, kids. Your mother and I will discuss it and take all your opinions to heart. Let's wrap up in prayer and then you can be excused."

"He looks just like Wayne, Hec. It's really amazing," I say when I call home from the airport while waiting for our flight home. I have Adam, and he is buzzing around, stamping his feet and clapping.

"He's Chinese?" Hector says, sounding confused.

"No, he's not Chinese. But I mean, his features—they are so similar to Wayne's. He's a good-looking boy, but so scared. Someone hurt him badly at some point. When I started to help him put his jacket on, he backed away from me as if he thought I was going to hit him. It broke my heart." Just then Adam starts making some noises behind me.

"Is that him I hear in the background?" Hector asks.

"Yes, that's him."

"He sounds like Wayne, then. Wow, that's really interesting. So how was the rest of your trip down there?"

"Well, I really like the social worker, Eleanor. She feels really bad that they can't place Aaron with us too. She says it was not up to her. Can you believe they actually said that Adam is too disabled to even know he has a brother? That's crazy. He knows in his heart who his brother is, and I think being separated is really going to further traumatize him. And Aaron too."

"Did you meet Aaron?"

"Yes, he was there at the foster home. Oh my gosh, Hec, he is the cutest little boy. He wasn't feeling well, and he seems so sad. I just wanted to scoop him up and tuck him in my pocket. It broke my heart when he said good-bye to Adam."

"Hopefully, we can help them stay connected at least," Hector says. We have no way of knowing how soon they will be connected again.

"What a handsome little guy you are!" Hector greets Adam as he lurches off the plane. "Welcome to the family."

"Phew, that was a challenging flight. Adam didn't like much about it. He wanted to get up and move around and wasn't too happy that he had to stay buckled in his seat. We're going to have our hands full with this one, I think."

"I can't wait for him to meet Wayne. And the rest of the crew, of course, but especially Wayne," Hector says. "You're right; they do have very similar features. But I haven't seen him smile yet—does he smile?"

"Not much. I've hardly seen him smile at all. He's scared and sad. It's going to take a lot of love, and time, to help him believe he's really safe with us, I think."

"Well, with Thanksgiving just three days away, I hope all the activity doesn't scare him more," Hector says. "And speaking of Thanksgiving, I hope you're not getting stressed about your parents coming. I know we didn't tell them about Adam yet, but don't worry, it will be OK. I think by now they know that when we believe God is leading us to do something, we do it. And they're always accepting of all our kids."

I stare at him, wondering if it will go as smoothly as he predicts.

"You are going to wear a hole in my face with that glare, Sue," he says. "Relax."

"I know. I'm just thinking about my dad and how much he loves Thanksgiving. Now that his prostate cancer is really getting worse, I just don't know how many more years we have left with him, and I want everything to be perfect."

"Nothing is ever perfect, but it will still be nice," Hector says as we arrive home, with a house full of kids waiting to meet their newest brother.

"Good morning," Hector says to me the day before Thanksgiving. "Do you feel better than you did last night?"

I look at him a little cross-eyed. "What do you mean by that?" I snap.

"I heard everything," he says, barely concealing a laugh. "You were walking toward our bedroom—what was it, 1 or 2 in the morning? And suddenly I hear such a commotion. 'Everybody downstairs! Family meeting right now!' You went from room to room screaming at the kids to get up. At first I thought I was dreaming, but the longer I listened, I knew it was real. I started to get up to see what all the fuss was about when I hear you screeching at the kids, 'Who ate the crackers?'"

By now Hector is not even trying to tone down his laughter as he continues: "As soon as I heard that, I knew it was not a real crisis and there was no way I was going to go down and get in the middle of it. So I pretended to be asleep and let you have at it. Oh my—it went on for half an hour at least. 'I bought those crackers especially for my sister Stephanie. They are her favorites and she hardly ever comes to visit. And now they're gone! See this box? Empty. I found it in the trash. Empty! Someone ate the crackers. Now someone needs to confess or we're going to be here all night. I can't believe I can't even buy one special treat for my sister without someone getting into it!' Your screaming was getting louder and louder."

Hector pauses for a sip of his coffee, laughing so hard his hand is shaking as he lifts the cup to his mouth. "After about ten more minutes of this, Jose says, 'I'm sorry, Mom. I ate the crackers, I didn't know they were for Aunt Stephanie.' I don't know if Jose did it or not, but I sure was glad the drama was coming to an end. When I heard the kids scurrying up to bed, I ducked under the covers and started snoring."

Hector pulls his hankie out of his back pocket and blows his nose. "I know this is one for the books. You mark my words—the kids will be talking about 'The Case of the Missing Crackers' for years to come."

"OK, OK. I feel bad about it. I guess I was just overtired."

"You *should* feel bad. That was way over the top," Hector says. "But let it go now and let's hope you got all the craziness out of your system so we can have a good Thanksgiving. People will start arriving soon."

"Maybe you need a cracker incident every year," Hector says on Sunday night. "Everything went so well after that, it was really a great Thanksgiving. Hard to believe we had 45 people here. Good job."

"It was a team effort, and we all did a good job. I just hope it's not the last Thanksgiving with my dad. I'm worried about him."

"Me too, Sue. Me too," Hector says, giving me a kiss on my forehead.

I'm lying in bed awake, listening to Adam cough and wondering if I need to get up and go check on him again. As I lie here, I reflect on our experiences over the last three months since Adam joined the family.

Adam is definitely more sickly than Wayne ever was, and by the time the new year rolled around, we'd battled several colds, stomach upsets, and ear infections. He has a special device, called a chest port, so that he can receive medications to help him stay healthy. He's a fussier eater than Wayne, so feeding him is challenging and takes a lot of time. Joelle and Flory do a great job feeding him and are very patient with him. In some ways, caring for him is like caring for a baby—at times he seems almost colicky and he puts everything within reach into his mouth. Hector has mastered his physical care easily—we're all more concerned about his emotional needs.

Adam almost never smiles. He's not generally a pleasant child. He doesn't snuggle or even like to be hugged. He frequently flinches when someone approaches him to wash him up, change him, feed him, or even give him a hug. His body is often stiff, and his movements are sharp and flailing. He makes some sounds, but unlike Wayne and Dylan, who delight us with their peals of laughter and funny noises, Adam's verbal utterances tend to be cries or moans more often than contented sounds or laughs.

Since adopting Wayne, and even more so since adopting Adam, we've run into people who ask us, "Why would anyone want to adopt a child who's going to die?" On top of that, when they hear of the challenges we have with Adam, they ask, "Why would anyone want to adopt a cranky, unpleasant, stiff, unaffectionate, sickly, unsmiling child who is going to die?" We've heard people speculate on motives. Some think we're altruistic saints, others imagine we have darker motives—to get money or notoriety or some other tangible benefits from our children.

Since adopting Wayne, and even more so since adopting Adam, we've run into people who ask us, "Why would anyone want to adopt a child who's going to die?"

The truth is very simple. I love Adam. We all love Adam. We love him as our child. When he's sick, like tonight, I stay awake with him. When he's sad, I want to cheer him up. When I watch one of the other kids interacting with him, I get a lump in my throat, overcome by the strength of the love I have for him. Hard as he is to like at times, difficult as he can be to care for at times, we truly and deeply love him. He's unique and not like any other person—not one of our other children, not even

Wayne, with whom he shares a disease. He's precious and priceless and unique and loveable.

And loving him helps keep me grounded in the reality of what it really means to love and to be loved. So I'm thankful that we did decide to adopt and parent this "cranky, sickly, unsmiling child." And right now, I'm thankful that his coughing has subsided and he is drifting off to sleep. Hopefully, that means soon I, too, will be in dreamland.

"Don't turn the lights on, please," I whisper to Hector as he gets out of bed.

"Another migraine?" he asks.

"Same one. Fourth day. Feels worse today than yesterday."

"Seems like they're worse a lot this year. Worse than any other time I can remember."

"I know. One year in Cabot they were pretty bad, but aside from that this is definitely the worse year ever since I first started getting them when I was eleven."

"I'll leave you alone. Just rest. Hopefully you will feel better in a couple hours," Hector says, grabbing his clothes and slipping out of the room.

Never before have my migraines interfered with my work and my life as they have this year. I've tried so many prescriptions, acupuncture, diet changes. Nothing is helping, and I feel like I am going to lose my mind if we can't get to the bottom of this.

"Lord, please, take these headaches from me!" I beg.

"Hec! Hec!"

"What is it, Sue?"

"I decided to get up and all of a sudden I got dizzy. I fell and I'm scared to get up. My vision is blurry and I feel like I'm going to throw up. I think I need to go to the hospital again and get that intravenous treatment I got last time it was this bad."

"OK, I'll take you, hang on," Hector says to me, and then I hear him calling the kids: "Jose—come give me a hand getting your mother to the car—she's dizzy. She has one of her bad migraines. SueAnn: I need you to be in charge here at home until I get back; I have to take Mom to the hospital."

By the time we arrive at the hospital, I can't even see; the black spots have taken over my field of vision. "I can't take this, Hec. I'm scared. Why can't God just heal me of these headaches? Its not fair to you or the kids when this happens."

"Shhhhhh," he says. "Don't stress about all that. Just try to relax and you'll get that DHE shot and you'll be OK in a few hours. I'm going home to take care of the kids, but have someone call me when you're ready to get out and I'll come back and get you."

"OK," I say, closing my eyes to ward off the painful light.

"Any excitement while I was gone?" I ask the next morning when I'm home and feeling better.

"Let's see. Adam bit Alysia on the toe. Dylan took a good poop. Isaac and Raj had play practice. The art teacher called to complain about Todd's behavior again, and oh—one more thing . . . " Hector pauses.

"OK, don't tease me. What is it?"

"Adam's social worker called from Florida," he says.

"And?" I ask.

"Well, it looks like Aaron is not doing so well in the home they placed him in. He's acting out at school and causing all kinds of havoc, so the family that was planning to adopt him has changed their mind. So now they want to know if we'll still take him."

"Wow, that's big news," I say, trying to digest it. "Of course it's best for the two brothers to be together. I just wish they had decided that right from the beginning. Now we have to go through the whole process again. What a pain."

"Not to mention the extra trauma Aaron had to go through that could have been prevented," Hector adds. "It burns me up that they put him through one more loss in his life."

"I couldn't agree more. He's just four years old and he has had too many losses already. Well, at least Eleanor has believed in keeping the siblings together the whole time, so she'll support us. What kind of timing did she have in mind for getting him here?"

"Well, the family where he's at now wants him out right away, and Eleanor doesn't want him to be moved any extra times, so she wants to bring him here next week."

"Wow! How will they get ICPC and everything done in time?" I ask, baffled.

"She seems confident that she can expedite it."

"Did you talk to the kids?"

"No, I thought we'd do it together at dinner tonight," he says, heading toward the playroom to check on Wayne and Adam.

A week later, Eleanor arrives with Aaron, promptly at one o'clock. "Come in, come in," Hector says, opening the front door and extending his hand. "Nice to meet you in person. And you must be Aaron."

"Hi, Eleanor. Hi, Aaron. Do you remember me? I met you last fall when I visited you in Florida," I say, smiling at him.

The four of us go into the living room to talk and sign the necessary paperwork. Before we know it, the time has come for Adam's bus to bring him home from school.

"Aaron, would you like to come down to the sidewalk and help me bring Adam in from the bus?" Hector asks.

Aaron jumps up, slips his small hand into Hector's, and they head out to greet the bus. Adam will be the first one of the kids home from school today. Eleanor and I trail along behind, chatting and watching from the top of the driveway.

As soon as the bus attendant lowers the lift and Adam's wheelchair hits the pavement, Aaron runs up to him and gives him a big hug. "Tubby!" Aaron says gleefully. And then the most wonderful thing happens—Adam's face lights up into the biggest smile we've ever seen.

> **"Tubby!" Aaron says gleefully. And then the most wonderful thing happens— Adam's face lights up into the biggest smile we've ever seen.**

I gasp and tears come immediately to my eyes. I glance over and see that Eleanor's eyes are brimming over as well. "Do you see that?" she asks. "This just confirms that we made the right decision."

"Do you remember, Eleanor, when we first tried to get your bosses to agree to place the boys together, and one of the administrators said that Adam was too disabled to even know he had a brother?"

"I do remember that. I wish I had videotaped this moment to show them. If ever there was a Kodak moment to underscore the importance of keeping siblings together, I think you and I just witnessed it."

Adam and Aaron sit together, playing for the rest of the afternoon, and Adam doesn't stop smiling once.

Hector waits on the porch for the kids to get home from school. When the Henry school crew arrives, I hear him say, "Aaron is here with his social worker. Go on in to the living room and meet your new brother. Use your manners when you meet Ms. Dixon, and then you can go have snack and get started on your chores."

A few minutes later, SueAnn and Abel come in with two friends. "Oh, they're here!" SueAnn exclaims. "Look, Tanya and Dawn. It's my new brother Aaron!"

"Eleanor, I'd like you to meet Abel and SueAnn," I say. "SueAnn is the one who wrote that letter to your governor about keeping siblings together."

"I'm honored to meet you, SueAnn. I believe you have a great career ahead of you as an advocate for children. Thank you for speaking up."

I am beaming with pride as I wonder how many more opportunities our children will have to be ambassadors, speaking up for those with no voice, for "the least of these."

17

From a Father's Heart— A Day in the Journey

Beep, beep, beep . . . . . . "What, what?" I turn the alarm off: 4:45 AM. I roll over, pulling the covers over my head and starting to dose off.

"Oh crap!" I jump up, shouting: "First day of school!"

Sue startles. "What's going on?"

"I need to get up. Time to make the donuts," I say.

"What are you talking about?" Sue mumbles sleepily.

"First day of school, don't you remember?"

"Oh yeah. OK, you get started. I'll be down in about 20 minutes."

I throw on my clothes and head for the kitchen. Got to get that coffee going—one cup and I will be ready to function. I walk over to the living room to get Dylan started on his feeding.

I check on Wayne and Adam to see how they're doing. "I'll be back to get you both fed and changed in a few minutes," I tell them. Wayne is smiling. Adam is still asleep.

With my first cup of coffee in one hand and my Bible in the other, I head for the front porch. It's still a little dark, but the sun is threatening to come up. Should be nice for the kids' first day of school. I sit and light a smoke to go with my coffee. I love this early morning time—I can spend a few minutes alone with God before the "hecticness" of the day begins. After reading a few passages of Scripture, I begin to review my day, praying as I go along that God will give me the wisdom and strength I need for each item on the agenda, starting with getting fourteen kids off to school by 8 AM.

So: high school kids up by 5:45, and get Wayne fed and changed. Make eleven lunches, and then get Adam fed and changed. I take another sip of coffee. Double check on high school kids and give them their bus tokens for the week. Wake up the Henry school kids by 6:45. I'm glad we got all of their stuff ready last night, so that should go smoothly. I continue reviewing and praying my way through the day as I finish my coffee and snuff out the cigarette into the ashtray.

"Good morning, my dear," I say to Sue.

"Good morning to you. Did you make me a coffee?" she asks.

"Let me wake up the high school kids and then I will," I say as I start for the stairs.

"Yes, remind Abel and SueAnn their bus route is longer this year, so they can't be late getting out the door. Oh, and can you grab the camera off my desk on your way down? I want to be sure to get the first-day-of-school pictures," Sue calls after me as I make my way to the third floor.

"SueAnn! Jose! Abel! Let's go! Get moving!" I yell to the high schoolers as I stop by David's room to shake him awake.

"Where's my new backpack?" Jose asks.

"Mom gave it to you last night during family meeting," I reply. "It should be in your room."

"It's not in here," he says.

"Well, you must have left it in the living room. Go check," I say, thinking to myself, *Leaving stuff all over the house—it's already started!*

As I come back to the first floor, Sue is walking toward me. "I did the lunches and I heard Dylan's pump going off, so I turned it off and flushed it."

"Oh, good. I would hate for it to clog on the first day of school!"

SueAnn and Abel stumble into the kitchen. "Good morning. Have some cereal or toast before you leave for school," I say.

"I'm not hungry," they both say, almost in unison.

"I'm not hearing it. Eat something before Mom has to lecture you about the importance of breakfast."

"All right, all right, Dad. We got it."

They start their toast as David walks in. He grabs a bowl and pours himself some cereal. "You see how simple that is?" I say to the other two. "No back talk."

"That's only because David can't talk back," Abel jokes.

"OK, enough of that, wise guy. I have to go get Wayne and Adam squared away before their buses get here." Wayne's bus will come at 7:15, Dylan's at 7:25, and Adam's at 7:35.

"Sue, can you get the Henry kids moving? And if you want the high school kids' pictures, you better hurry. They need to leave in a minute."

"I still can't find my backpack," Jose says. "I looked every-where."

"I think I saw it on a chair in the dining room," Sue tells him. "And don't leave without letting me take your picture . . ."

"OK, Hec, all the high school kids except for David are on their way," Sue says, reminding me that I have to drive David for the first week until his transportation is in place.

Oh crap, I think to myself. I completely forgot about driving

David—40 minutes each way if the traffic isn't too bad.

"Chelsea, Flory, George, Isaac, Raj, Joelle, Todd, Alysia, Aaron—let's get moving!" I yell to the Henry School kids, knowing Sue has already given them their first wake-up call. "Sue, can you get Wayne in his chair? Dylan's all set and I have to finish up with Adam. Make sure you wipe his nose; it's been running this morning."

"OK, I've got him. By the way," Sue reminds me, "I hope to take the 8:15 R-8 train this morning if everyone is out the door on time."

"Isaac, tuck in that shirt. Chelsea, Flory, don't leave without Todd, Joelle, and Aaron. I'm counting on you walking them and getting them safely across Lincoln Drive."

"Dad. We know that already," Chelsea replies.

A horn honks on the street. Wayne's bus. "I'll take Wayne down. Sue, keep the other kids moving," I say as I head out the door for the first wheelchair trip down the driveway.

When I come in, I see that Raj is ready and Alysia is finishing her breakfast, just as I hear the horn for Dylan's bus. "Did you get a brush through his hair?" I ask Sue.

"Yes, he's all set. Relax!"

A few minutes later, Adam and Alysia have been buckled into their buses, all the kids except for David are out the door, and Sue is heading for her train. I sign to David to tell him to get in the car for our drive out to Lincoln High School in the northeast. With any luck, I'll be home by 10.

"That went smooth," I say to Monster, the cat, letting him out the back door as I prepare my fourth cup of coffee. I head for the porch for a breather. I have five hours to get things done around the house before the kids come home—that is, if I don't get any calls from any of the schools. . . . And sure enough, there's the phone.

"Hello, Oh, OK. I'll be right down," I say, hanging up the

phone. Flory forgot her lunch.

"Well, looks like I will have a little less time to get things done," I mumble to myself as I come back to the house, grabbing my trusty laundry basket and heading for the first bathroom. I start on the third floor and work my way down collecting towels, washcloths, and other items along the way.

As I put the third load into the dryer, I hear the phone again.

"Hello, Sue. What's up?"

"I just wanted to remind you to get David by two so you can get home before Dylan's bus gets there. I know it's tight, but I think you'll make it. Also, I took out a couple of chickens for you to boil—I planned on you making Arroz con Pollo for tonight's dinner. Not sure which train I will be on. Hopefully, I will be home by 6, or else it will be 6:30."

"Gotcha," I reply. "Everything is under control. I saw the Arroz con Pollo on the menu so I'm ahead of you. I already started boiling the chickens in between loads of laundry."

"Great, thanks. I have to get back to work now—see you later."

. . . Well, I did have the chicken boiling—but I'd forgotten about the timing for picking David up, so I am glad Sue called.

"What's for snack?" George asks as he bursts into the house full of energy, several steps ahead of his siblings, who are straggling up the walk.

"There are apples and granola bars on the counter. OK, everyone, since it's the first day back in the saddle, let's review the routine. You can have your snack and a little break. Be sure to put your backpack in your room and check the chore chart so you know your chore for the week. Isaac, you're dinner helper, so I expect you in the kitchen at 5:15. At four o'clock, I expect you all to be working on your homework in the dining room."

"No homework tonight, Dad," Joelle says. "Just all these papers for you and Mom to fill out—we have to bring them back by tomorrow."

"Well, you all know the rule: if you have no homework, spend at least 30 minutes reading a book or writing a letter or doing an art project. And give me the papers so I can have them ready for Mom to do tonight," I chuckle. I hate paperwork. Contact information in triplicate for fourteen kids. Gotta love it. It's a good thing Sue and I made that agreement years ago—she'd do the paperwork if I did the diapers!

"That's not fair! I have homework and papers to sign!" George says.

"I have homework too," Chelsea adds.

"Well, get to it, then, and make sure you let me check it before you leave the table. And no TV until 8 tonight. I don't want to catch anyone trying to turn it on!"

"Oh great. Chelsea has math word problems—my favorite," I chuckle to myself. At least Alysia's homework of circling items that start with the letter A isn't too hard. And reviewing George's spelling words with him only takes a minute. I sit with the kids a few extra minutes, hearing a little about their day as they read their books.

Luckily, today there are no dance classes, sports practices, or other after-school activities, so the kids have a little time to play between homework and dinner. That routine will start soon enough.

"OK, Isaac, let's go," I holler out to the backyard at 5:15. "Time to set the table."

I put two bowls on the counter for Wayne and Adam.

"Where are all the plates?" Isaac asks, eyeing the empty shelf.

"Check the dishwasher. I don't think I unloaded it yet today."

"Jose! Get down to the kitchen. I need your help for a few minutes!" I call.

"Yeah, Dad?" he says as he looks at the two boiled chickens

sitting on a cookie tray on the kitchen counter. "Why me? I always have to bone the chickens."

"Well, Jose, count it a blessing that you are my best 'de-boner,'" I reply.

Without a smile, he gets started.

"Smells good, Hec. I'll serve out dinner. Tell the kids it's time to eat," Sue says as she drops her computer bag in the entryway and heads for the kitchen.

I give the "time to eat!" call and it echoes throughout the house. "We really do need an intercom system in this house," I say to Sue. "Just like your dad always suggested every time he was here!"

Soon everyone is gathered at the dining room table. I snap Wayne and Adam into their high chairs. "Flory, it's your night to feed Adam," I say. "And Joelle, you have Wayne. I'll give them a little something on their tray until you're ready to feed them."

"OK," they both respond.

"Hey Mom, did Dad show you all the papers you have to fill out tonight?"

"No, not yet, but I do remember that the first few days of school there's always a ton," she replies.

"And you remember our deal about paperwork, right?" I chuckle.

"Hmmm, not really. What deal is that?"

"OK, if you don't remember the deal, you can have diaper duty tonight and I'll do the papers! I think I can smell Dylan from here!"

"Gross, Dad! We're trying to eat here," SueAnn says.

"Oh, *that* deal! Yeah, I remember it, and I'm fine with the paperwork, no problem."

The kids all laugh. "Can you picture Mom changing one of Dylan's nasty diapers?" Flory says, and another roar of laughter fills the room.

"OK, enough of that!" Sue says, adding, "It's time for everyone to share one thing you did or learned at school today."

After a few groans, the kids each share something about their day. Most of what they share has to do with the new classes, teachers, and textbooks they got acquainted with today, but then Todd pipes up. "I learned that it's a good thing Isaac has the same recess I do. He saved me from getting beat up!"

"What?"

"Yeah, this kid was about to beat me up at recess because I hit him with the ball on accident, but Isaac came over just in time and told him to back off!"

"Well, that's a good time to remind us all about 'pats on the back,'" Sue mentions, holding up one of the brightly colored papers with the outline of a hand on it. "Todd, you can write that up as a pat-on-the-back for our Sunday dinner. And everyone else should be remembering to do these all week so we will have a big pile on Sunday."

"Good reminder," I say. "And it looks like everyone is finished eating. Chelsea, can you hand me the book for our reading? I will read our passage and story and then Flory, I think it is your turn to pray."

After we finish, chairs start scraping the floor, as everyone is eager to leave the table. "Scrape and stack, everyone," I say. "SueAnn, you have after-dinner cleanup this week. And Abel, it's your laundry day today, so if you have some to do, get to it or you'll be out of luck until the weekend."

"OK, I don't have much, but I'll get it done later," Abel says.

"Another day for the books," I say to Sue as I finally kick back in my chair. "What time is it?"

"Ten o'clock. Everyone's in their room. Do you want to watch a little TV? I'm not sure what's on. I'll check."

"Doesn't matter. I just want to veg a little," I reply.

"Just think: we get to do it all over again tomorrow!"

"Ah, it beats having a boss over me any day," I reply as I feel myself starting to doze. "Besides, no two days are ever the same. "I wonder what tomorrow will bring?"

18

The White House

"You look like death warmed over, Sue," Hector says when I come downstairs the morning of David's and Angelo's graduation from Lincoln High School.

"Thanks for the compliment," I snap back. All spring I've been in and out of the hospital battling severe migraines. The worst part is missing several of the kids' ball games, concerts, and other activities, and I'm determined not to miss David's graduation, the first of our kids to complete high school since we moved to Philly.

"I'm sorry, I wasn't trying to be mean. I'm just concerned about you. I think you should stay home. It's already 90 degrees and it's going to be miserable in that gym."

"I'm not missing one of my kids' graduations. Don't even

think about it. End of story. I am just sad my parents couldn't make it down here. We'll have to find another time to celebrate with them so David can get the attention he deserves for his accomplishments," I say.

"Yes, I know they wanted to be here, but with your dad's treatments going on right now, it's not feasible for them to travel. We'll find a time that works with them. Right now, it's you I'm worried about."

> "I'm not missing one of my kids' graduations. Don't even think about it. End of story. I am just sad my parents couldn't make it down here."

"I'll go right to bed when we get home if I have to, but I'm going to the graduation. So let's get ready; we have to leave in 20 minutes to allow for traffic. Do you have coverage for all the kids at home?"

"Yes. Wayne, Dylan, and Adam are all fed, and SueAnn is going to make sure Alysia gets lunch if we don't get home in time. Everyone is set. Do you have the camera?"

"Right here." I hold it aloft.

"Oh, look at you David," I sign to him after he comes into the room. "Mom and Dad are so proud of you! You look very handsome today!"

David is beaming. He's paraded around the house, making sure everyone sees him in his cap and gown. We snap a couple of pictures now, and get in the car.

"Ugh, is this heat ever going to break?" I ask Hector a week later. Thankfully, my headache is gone, but the heat is oppressive.

"The weather report said we're going to have a heat wave this summer that might be as bad as 1993," Hector reports.

"I have that interview with the National Adoption Center this afternoon," I remind him. I'd really like to get this job. I am

ready to move from direct casework into more adoption training, advocacy, and policy work.

"*Bon chance,*" he says. "I'm going to mow the lawn. Let me
know if you want a ride to the train."

"In this heat—you bet I want a ride. I plan to take the 1:15
train into the city."

"OK, just flag me down a few minutes before you're ready to
go."

"I got the job!" I shout, hanging up the phone after accepting
the offer. "Let's celebrate with water ice! Who wants water ice?"

In less than a minute, the van is full of kids and we are singing
oldies along with the radio on our way to get water ice as a treat.
Handing Raj a pen and paper, I say, "Raj, find out what kind
everyone wants so we can order quickly when we get there."

I hear a chorus of "Lemon!", "Cherry!", "Watermelon!" and
more being shouted out as Raj gets it all down.

"It's a good thing so many of the kids will be at camp during
the heat wave," I say to Hector. We're walking back to our car
after leaving ten of our kids at their cabins at the Independent
Lake Camp. Now we prepare for the three-hour drive home.

"It sure is nice here. I wouldn't mind spending the summer
here myself," Hector replies. We've both loved camping since we
were kids. "It's been a few years since we've had a summer trip,"
he adds. "Aaron's never been on one, and most of the younger
kids barely remember the last one. I think we should plan one
for next summer."

"That's so funny. I have been thinking the same thing," I
laugh. "I love living in the city. There are so many opportunities
for the kids, but I think it does them a world of good to get out
of the city once in a while too."

"It's a good thing we are talking about this now so we have a
year to plan. We'll need a vehicle, and lots of new camping sup-

plies. Most of our other tag-sale finds have been lost or worn out since our last trip," he says.

"And this is going to be a big year—so many activities. Senior year for Abel, SueAnn, and Jose. David graduating from his program at Elwyn. Soccer, basketball, debate team, college applications. Baseball, drama club, dance classes. Isaac finishing eighth grade. Alysia's surgeries on her arms—and that doesn't even include my responsibilities at work now that my federal grant was approved."

> "And this is going to be a big year—so many activities. Senior year for Abel, SueAnn, and Jose. David graduating from his program at Elwyn. Soccer, basketball, debate team, college applications."

"I'm tired just thinking about it. We also have four more weddings lined up at the house, maybe more to come. It seems like every time we do one, three more get scheduled. Better start eating my Wheaties!" Hector jokes.

A short time after we moved into our Pelham Road home, a young couple knocked on our door asking if this was the house people rent for weddings. We said no, but then we got to thinking: Why not? It brings in a little extra money, and it's a fun way to share our home with the community. And we have become good friends with the caterers who bring us most of the business. Hector serves as the host and maître d' and my job is to pack up the younger kids and take them out for a picnic or some other activity until the festivities are over. Dylan, Wayne, and Adam love riding in the van, so we've had some good adventures on the "wedding weekends."

"It can't be possible that half the school year and the holidays are behind us already," I say to my friend Patty during one of our telephone catch-up calls.

"That's why I'm calling," Patty says. "I know SueAnn will

want me to bring Milagro down for the graduation, so I am trying to find out if you know the date yet."

"I don't think it's been announced, but I'll find out as soon as I can and get back to you," I say. "In other news, did I tell you we have another grandchild on the way? Renee is pregnant. No, no, don't ask. I'm still working it through in my own talks with God. You're the only one I've told, because I know you 'get it'. Keep us in prayer . . . Anyway, enough about me—how's everything in Vermont?"

"It's been a great year for skiing. We even got Milagro and Grace started on their first pair of skis."

"That's great. We don't get much skiing in down here, but today the high school kids are on a field trip with the church youth group, and they are skiing at a spot not far from here. It's not quite the same as Vermont, but I hope they're having a great time." No sooner are those words out of my mouth than the call-waiting signal begins to beep on my phone. I click over . . .

"I'll have to call you back, Patty. There's been an accident at the ski resort. Chelsea is hurt. I've got to go now," I tell her, frantically.

"Oh no. Keep me posted," she says.

"This doesn't sound good, Chelsea," Hector says after our visit with the doctor. We learn she has torn her ACL, MCL, and PCL ligaments—and the only solution is surgery.

"I guess there won't be any more moguls in your future for awhile," I add.

"I just hope it is healed in time for tennis season," she says, gloomily. "I guess now I can give up school for Lent."

"Good one, but not so fast. I talked to the principal and just because you have to be home for several weeks doesn't mean you can't keep up with your assignments. We have a plan," I tell her.

"Yippee," she says. "Can't wait."

"I filmed the inside of your knee while we were doing the surgery," the doctor tells Chelsea, handing her a videotape at our first post-op appointment. "I thought maybe you could use it for science class or something."

"Thanks. I'll watch it at home," she replies.

"In between soap operas," Hector laughs. With Chelsea home all day, she has more time than she needs for her schoolwork. She's been doing lots of art projects, and reading, but since she can't move around much, she's also started watching a couple of soap operas. I tease Hector that he has to be careful not to get hooked with her.

"Guess what I did today?" Chelsea asks at dinner several weeks later.

"Kissed a boy?" Joelle guesses.

"Eeeeewwww!" Todd says, as Alysia joins in the laughter.

"No, silly. I played tennis. I'm so proud of myself. There were days I thought I would never walk again, and today I actually played a game of tennis."

"Bravo—that's terrific, Chels," I say. "How did your knee feel?"

"It felt really strong, actually. I was surprised."

"That's great. Between your art projects, flute concert, and tennis matches, I don't think we'll see much of you this spring."

"Don't forget my job at The Melting Pot," she adds. Chelsea is the fifth of our kids to work at the restaurant in Chestnut Hill, and we hope the younger kids will each get a turn when they're old enough.

"Mom, I have to turn in those forms for my senior dues and cap and gown—and I need the money by tomorrow," Jose reminds me later.

"Oh Jose, I still can't believe you're graduating. How is it possible?" I ask, rummaging in my purse for a pen. "I'll sign the papers, and then you can get the check from Dad." My first son, the first child we adopted, the little boy who loved trains and hated bridges—when did he turn into this smart, strong young man?

"Abel, SueAnn, I have some news for you," Hector says. "We just confirmed that some of your birth relatives from New Mexico are coming for the graduation. Your uncle Sammy and cousin Ruth are coming for sure. Your birth mom MaryJean is trying to work out the arrangements to drive with your grandma Lucy and aunt Geraldine. Her car needs some work, but she's figuring it out. We told her we'd help cover some of her gas costs if she can make it."

"Wow, there are going to be a lot of people here," SueAnn says. "From Vermont, New Mexico . . . Lilly and Trish are coming, right? And Mamie and Grandpa? And what about Jose's special friends?"

"I don't think Dan and Pam can make it, but you're right it's going to be a grand celebration—three high school graduations, plus David's Elwyn graduation and Isaac's eighth grade from Henry. We'll need a lot of food. I better call Nancy Alston!" Our catering friend has agreed to help us with some of the food for the June festivities.

A few days before the graduation, the phone rings. "Hello?"

"Mom, is that you?" I hear Renee's voice and a lot of commotion in the background.

Suddenly someone else takes the phone. "Mrs. Badeau, I'm a doctor here in Sunnyvale, California. Your daughter Renee is in labor and she was hoping you could stay on the phone with her since you can't be here in person. She is transitioning now. I don't think it will be long."

"Oh wow, this is a new experience—long-distance childbirth coaching! Yes, of course, put the phone close to her ear, and I'll give her some encouragement and remind her to breathe," I say.
. . .

"It's a boy!" I hear moments later.

"I have a boy, Mom. I have a boy." Renee is crying into the phone. "The doctor says I did good, Mom."

"You did good, Renee. I'm so thankful everything is OK. Have you picked a name?" I ask.

"Daniel. I am naming him Daniel Jamal. He's your second boy grandson, Mom. Now Phillip won't be the only boy."

"Give him a big kiss for me. I can't wait to meet him. Get some rest now. *Nakupenda. Ichliebidich*," I say, blowing a kiss into the phone.

"*Te amo*, Mom, *Je t'aime.* Love you." We sign off by saying "I love you" in these five languages, a tradition we started when she was a teenager the first year we adopted her.

"We have a new grandson, Hec," I say when I get off the phone.

"I'm going to say some extra prayers tonight," he replies. "Prayers for Renee and this new little baby Daniel."

"That was the strangest graduation I have ever been to," Hector says on our way home from Jose's graduation.

"I've never seen adults act so rude," I say. "They were so loud we couldn't even hear the names being called. I wonder what my parents thought about it." I chuckle. They are following us home in their car with a couple of the kids.

"I hope the audience at SueAnn and Abel's graduation tomorrow night is a little more respectful," Hector says.

"I wonder if we'll be the only family who has the adoptive family and birth family of the graduate—and the child she placed for adoption—all in the audience tonight," I muse the next evening on our way to the second graduation ceremony in two days. Although SueAnn and Abel's birth mother didn't make it, their uncle and cousin did. With my parents, Lilly and Trish, and the Kirpans here from Vermont, we have quite a large contingent for the festivities.

"You have to admit, it's pretty unique," Hector adds.

A week after graduation, Hector sets out on the summer trip while Abel heads to Independent Lake Camp to work for the summer. Jose and SueAnn are also staying home to work; everyone else is in the bus and on the road.

"It's been great meeting Adam and Aaron's relatives," Hector reports on our call after his stop in Florida. "His grandmother, his sister, lots of great folks, and they are so happy to see that Adam and Aaron are together. You should see this giant stuffed animal they gave Adam. It's a good thing we have a big bus!"

They're headed west now, and soon, SueAnn and I will meet up with them in New Mexico. We're planning a big reunion with all the birth family relatives and former foster family. The trip will also include a stop in Austin, Texas at the Marywood agency where we adopted Alysia.

"This is what's so awesome about these summer trips. Not only seeing the sights and creating memories, but also keeping the kids connected to their history. You're a great dad," I say.

"I try. We're looking forward to Nashville next. All these years of being a country music fan, and I've never been to the Grand Ole Opry, so we're going to do a tour."

"That's great, take lots of pictures," I say before we hang up.

"Are you hiding?" Hector asks.

I'm sitting in the dark on a picnic table bench, several yards away from the festivities. "No, I'm just taking a few moments to soak up what's happening here. Only God could do this. Just look around. Relatives are here from both the birth mother and birth father's side of the family, and the foster family. Many of these people haven't spoken in years from what I was told. And here we all are, having a party, enjoying each other's company. It's pretty awesome."

"You're right, it really is. We do need to savor moments like this. Who knew when we started out on this journey that we would get to be part of something like this?"

After a few quiet moments I ask, "Did you come over here for a reason? It seemed like you were looking for something or someone."

"Yeah, I just wanted to check on Dylan and Wayne. Raj and David took them for a walk in their wheelchairs a little while ago and I haven't seen them come back yet."

"Seriously? Is David pushing Dylan?" I ask.

"I think so. Why?"

I burst out laughing. "I guess that's what you call the deaf leading the blind."

Hector joins me in the laughter just as we see the four of them heading back toward the campsite.

"Any news on dad?" I write in an e-mail. My sisters and brother and I have just started using e-mail as a way to get updates on my dad, whose cancer is progressing rapidly. We've just returned from our trip. Hector is buried in back-to-school preparations, and I'm swamped making the final arrangements for a huge national conference I'm in charge of.

"He's in good spirits, but not feeling great. When are you coming up?" my sister Nancy replies.

"I'm coming just for the weekend for my twentieth class reunion next week. I can't stay longer because I have this big conference at the end of the month. But I hope to come back and spend a week with Dad in early October," I write back.

"Sue Badeau, please come to the front desk for an important message." Suddenly, my name is being broadcast from the speaker system in the middle of the conference.

This is embarrassing, I think to myself. *I wonder who's in trouble at home? It must be serious if Hector's having me paged.* It never occurs to me that anyone other than Hector would be tracking me down at my conference.

"Susan." I can hardly recognize the voice on the phone.

"Nancy?" I say, uncertainly.

"Yes. It's Dad." She is crying.

"What's happened?" I ask, gripping the phone, not sure I want to hear the answer.

"He's going in and out of consciousness. Hospice is here. He's not going to be with us much longer. Can you get home?"

Quickly, I call the travel agent and make arrangements to get home tonight. Once plans are in place, I call Hector and give him the details, promising to call when I change plans in Charlotte.

On the ground in Charlotte, I call Nancy.

"He's gone." She tells me.

I'm in shock. *Noooooooo. Daddy you can't die yet. I didn't get my last visit with you. I'm coming in October.*

"David's flying in too. The Karnedys will pick you both up at the airport tonight. Be safe."

I call Hector. "What? When? I'm so sorry, Sue. I wish I could be with you." I can barely understand the rest of what he is saying; his tears are drowning out his words.

I hear a lot of noise in the background and remember that there's a wedding at our house tonight. "Go sit with Nancy Alston in the kitchen," I tell him. "She has a strong faith; she'll help you." I know that Hector loved my dad as much as I did; he's always told me that he felt my dad was the most important father figure in his life.

"I can't believe he's gone, Sue," I hear him say. "He took me in like I was his own son. The memories are just flooding down the halls of my mind. 'Hector, I'm bringing Papa home. Do you need a ride?' 'Hector, we have one piece of steak left, do you want it?' I can hear his voice as if he was beside me right now."

"I know, I know. He did love you as a son. I'm going to miss him so much." I cry.

"Just a minute, Sue." Hector puts the phone down and then comes back. "That was David. He saw me crying and wanted to know what happened. I had to put the phone down so I could sign to him. I really have to go and talk to the kids."

"Thanks for handling everything at home. I love you," I say, and then realize it's time to board my flight to Burlington. I look around at the Charlotte airport, hoping I never have to fly through here again. I have no way of knowing how many times in the years ahead I will fly through here.

I will never like this airport.

"Drive carefully," Hector says as I head out for Vermont on November 1. When I came home after my dad's funeral, I told my mom I would come back for a week in November. It's hard to believe he has been gone a month already.

For the first few days, we stay home, writing thank you notes, looking at pictures. My sister Nancy stops by each day; Lilly and Trish also visit. Trish is scheduled for a C-section for her second child, on election day.

"Mom, let's go so you can vote," I say. She's not sure she's ready to leave the house, but it's time to take one small step. After she votes, I take her home to rest, promising to come back so we can go watch the election returns with her friends Patty, George, and Nira. They've all known me since I was a little girl. I head to the hospital.

"He's beautiful, Trish. He's a little peanut, too, but not quite as small as Phillip was," I say, sitting on the edge of her bed, holding my newest grandson.

"Phillip will be so happy it's a boy. He really didn't want me to have a girl," she laughs.

"Sean Steven, I'm your nanna." I practice saying his new name, giving him "nanna kisses," as they have come to be called, all over his cheeks. "I have to leave now, sweetie. I have to go get Mamie. We're going to watch the election results. . . . Did you vote, Trish?"

"Mom, how could I?"

"I'm teasing. You didn't know this was the date in time to get an absentee ballot. Just don't let it happen again."

"Yes Mom, I know you and Dad have taught me how important it is to vote. 'People died so I could vote,'" she quotes.

"That's right. I'm glad some of my lessons stuck with you."

"Oh Mom, so many lessons you and Dad taught us stick with me all the time. Remember when I was a senior at Spaulding and it was the spring concert? I dedicated that 'Dream the Impossible Dream' song to you and Dad?"

"Of course I remember that. You embarrassed us in front of the whole audience. I was so humbled, and touched by that, I cried through the whole song."

"Well, I meant it then, and I mean it now—without you and Dad, I never would have known it was possible to believe in myself and that I could accomplish something in life. I'm not going to let you down. You'll see."

"Trish, sweetie, we've had our ups and downs, and we'll have

"Well, I meant it then, and I mean it now—without you and Dad, I never would have known it was possible to believe in myself and that I could accomplish something in life."

some more, but you've never let me down. I'm proud of all you've accomplished and I know there's a lot more to come. "Now, I do have to go. Try to get some sleep, because once you get home, you won't be getting any for a long time."

"OK, Mom. Thanks. Love you."

"Did you know, Susan, that Clinton was on the National Commission on Children in 1991? He was appointed by Reagan, so he can't be all bad," my mother's friend says while we watch the returns.

"I did know that, and I know that both he and his wife have been big child advocates over the years. I'm excited to see what he will do for kids and adoption if he wins this election," I tell her.

David is pointing to the mess on the floor and asking me, in sign language, what happened. David and I are doing the shopping for Thanksgiving when I picked up a jar of blackberry jam from the shelf—my dad's favorite. Suddenly, a wave of grief nearly knocked me over as I realized that my dad won't be with us for Thanksgiving this year. I dropped the jam and it smashed on the floor of Aisle 13 in the grocery store. "I'm sad today," I sign to David. "Missing Grandpa."

David nods and then makes the sign for Jesus and points toward Heaven. "Yes, David, you're right. Grandpa is with Jesus now," I reply as we look around for someone to tell about the mess we've made.

"Are we doing Secret Santa this year, Dad?" Chelsea asks on Sunday before church, the first day of Advent.

"Of course we are!" Hector replies. "We'll draw the names at dinner tonight after we have our tortellini soup and readings and candle lighting. Then you can all start plotting what little gifts and good deeds you can do for your Secret Santa."

"We'll also do the drawing for your three gifts and decorate the mantels," I remind her. Our Advent and Christmas celebrations are rich with traditions. With so many children, gifts are not the biggest part of the festivities. Hector and I give the kids one gift each and fill the stockings. The children each pick the names of three of their siblings to give gifts to—so each child both gives and receives three gifts. The rest of our celebration is filled with food, readings, crafts, decorating, and music.

Tonight, the kids each decorate one of the many mantels and bookcases in the house. They each have a special theme, from "Feliz Navidad, Christmas in Mexico," to "Texas Cowboy Christmas," "Angels We Have Heard on High," and "Wise Men Still Seek Him," and we also have mantels honoring Hanukah, Kwanzaa, the winter season, and New Years.

"Who's ready to do the piñata?" Hector calls out, and Todd, Alysia, Raj, and Isaac are quickly at his side. Every year on December 28, we have a tradition of breaking open a piñata on George's birthday. He's turning 18 today, so we thought he might be a little too old, but he said, "Let's keep the tradition, for the kids."

While Todd is wielding the baseball bat, the phone rings.

"Who was that?" Hector asks, a few minutes later, when I return to the festivities.

"It was Fisher. His girlfriend Jen just had a baby."

"Fisher's the father?" Hector asks, surprised.

"I guess so. I didn't even know she was pregnant. The baby is a boy, named Alec."

"I'm sure he is a beautiful child. Is he healthy?"

"Yes, everything went well. I told him we'd be praying for all of them and hopefully meet the baby soon."

"I sent that letter to the President," I tell the kids at dinner, a few days into the new year. In December, President Clinton launched a project called Adoption 2002—it has the goal of doubling the number of children adopted from foster care in five years. As part of the initiative, he put out a call for input—asking everyone from adoption researchers to regular families like ours to provide ideas and advice about how to improve the foster care and adoption system in the U.S. Our family worked on a response together and today it went in the mail.

"The. President. Write. To. Me." We all listen carefully as Alysia patiently types out her response on her Delta-talker communication device. She is still learning how to use it.

"Don't get your hopes up, Alysia. The President is pretty busy," Joelle says.

"This is the third day that I can't get Adam to eat, so I called Dr. Finkelstein." Hector is on the phone, and sounds worried.

"What does he think we should do?" I ask.

"He wants us to take him to the hospital. Finkelstein recommends Children's, but our insurance says we have to take him to Jefferson."

"OK, call me as soon as you get there, and I'll walk over. It's not far from my office. Oh, bring a change of clothes for me in case they keep him overnight. I'll stay with him and you can go home with the other kids."

"I know he has a terminal illness, but I am not going to just sit here and watch him die of starvation!" I am raising my voice at the nurse. It's our fourth day at Jefferson, and Adam is still not eating. "I know there are alternatives—tube feeding or IV nutrition. Look how skinny he's getting! He needs to get some calories in him."

"The doctor is not worried about that . . . " the nurse begins to explain, but I cut her off.

"Well, I'm his mother and I'm very worried about that. Tell the doctor I need to speak to her immediately." As soon as the nurse leaves the room, I call Hector.

"You need to get ahold of Finkelstein and our insurance. We need to get Adam transferred to Children's Hospital today. Like *now*," I say forcefully. "Jefferson is a great hospital for athletes, but I know Adam will be better served at a hospital that specializes in children. I'm not taking no for an answer."

We've learned that Adam has very high lead levels, probably accumulated during his many moves in foster care. That's why he's so unhappy and refusing to eat. The doctors are treating the lead levels, but I believe he needs nutrition at the same time. One thing I have learned over the years: no one knows my children as well as I do, and if I don't stand up and advocate for them, I can't rely on the schools, hospitals, or anyone else to do it. I don't know what to expect at Children's Hospital, but I have a feeling this is going to be a long ride before Adam comes home.

"It's so good to be eating dinner with my own family, and not eating hospital food again," I say to the kids as we sit down to eat. It's my—and Adam's—first night home after a six-week ordeal that started at Jefferson, moved to Children's Hospital, and ended with a few weeks at Seashore House to help Adam relearn how to eat. I have stayed at his side, going to work in the mornings and returning to the hospital each night. Hector spent time with him each day when the other kids were in school.

"Is Adam going to be OK now, Mom?" Aaron asks.

"Yes, he's much stronger and healthier now. The lead is out of his system, and he's eating better. He still has his disease, but we have a long way to go before we have to worry about that. Let's just be thankful now that he's healthy and happy."

"Gives that saying 'Get the lead out,' a whole new meaning," Abel, our family comedian, jokes.

"Well, guess what I did today?" Hector asks, changing the subject.

"Farted?" George asks, and everyone at the table cracks up.

"Probably a few times, George. But I did something else too. I found us a big van— well, it's more like a bus—for our summer trip. We'll be getting it on the weekend." This elicits a chorus of cheers and leads into a very joyful prayer time to end our meal.

Hector is working on the new van to get it in shape for the trip when an unfamiliar car pulls into the driveway.

"Hi Pops," Fisher says as he steps out of the car.

"Well, this is a surprise. Does Mom know you're coming?" Hector asks as the two men clasp hands and then hug.

"Not really," he says. "I wanted you all to meet your grandson." At that moment, Jen gets out of the car with a chubby six-month-old baby. "Alec, come see your poppa," Fisher says.

"Well, this is a surprise! Let's go inside and find Nanna," Hector says, taking the baby from Jen. The baby instantly smiles at Hector.

Hector walks into the living room with a baby in his arms, and I'm confused. Renee is here and Trish is visiting from Vermont. Both of their babies, Daniel and Sean, are on the floor with me. All at once, I see Fisher and Jen coming in behind Hector, and I understand.

"Oh my goodness, what a cutie you are, Alec. We finally get to meet you. Let's get some pictures with your cousins." I line the three babies up and start snapping pictures. Three new grandsons—all born in the same year.

"Oh look, Mom. You have to get a picture of these three boys too," Flory says, pointing to the couch. Dylan, Wayne, and Adam have all fallen asleep, leaning on one another like dominoes. Too cute.

"Fisher's been here two weeks since everyone else went home, and it seems like he's floundering," Hector says when we are alone in our room. "All that talk about getting a job hasn't led to anything concrete. It's been nice having him help me get the van fixed up, but he can't just be hanging around. I'm worried he is using again."

"I know. I'm worried too. He did a great job speaking on that panel about teen adoption for me at the National Adoption Center, but afterward he had to wait a couple hours while I finished work. When we met up again, I was pretty sure he was high."

"Does our insurance cover drug programs?" Hector asks.

"Yes, I've been looking into it. There is a good day treatment program near my office. Our insurance covers it."

"Well, I think he has to agree to start the program or else leave. It's not a good influence on the rest of the kids if we let him hang around with no job and getting high when he goes out."

"You're right. Let's have this talk tomorrow."

A week later, Fisher is gone. "Fisher left today. He said he's moving back to Vermont," Hector says when I get home from work.

"Oh, this breaks my heart. I was really hopeful he would stick with the program this time. Those drugs have such a stranglehold on him. He's really a good person underneath—he has so many talents in music, and a generous, caring side too. I'm so angry with him, but my heart breaks for him at the same time."

"He's not going to accept treatment until he's believes he needs it. Let's pray he comes to that realization sooner rather than later," Hector says.

"That bus is an eyesore," I say to Hector. We're sitting in the backyard enjoying one of the last nights of summer before the school routine begins again.

"Yeah, it wasn't our best investment ever," he chuckles. The summer trip had to be cut short this year; the bus kept breaking down. "Well, we did make a few new memories, but I don't think I'll take that baby on the road again."

"We've been invited to the White House to meet the President!" I announce to the kids at dinner. "Remember that letter we wrote back in January? Well, we got picked to win an award called the Adoption Excellence Award. And the President is also going to sign a new law to make it easier for kids in foster care to get adopted. He wants us to be with him when he signs it."

"When do we go?" Renee asks.

"Tomorrow," Hector says, shaking his head. He still can't believe they gave us less than a day of notice to get our whole family presentable and to travel to Washington, DC.

As I sit here now in the East Room of the White House, surrounded by my husband, brother, and 17 of my children—two on stage with the President of the United States—awaiting the signing of the Adoption and Safe Families Act, it's hard to believe it's been a year since the election and more than a year since my dad died. He really would have loved this moment.

"The kids were so well behaved," Hector whispers to me while we're lining up for the official photos with the President.

"Except for Wayne's hilarious outburst, they were quiet and seemed to be paying attention. SueAnn made me cry with her amazing speech introducing the President, and wasn't Aaron cute up there on the stage?" I say. At that moment, President William Jefferson Clinton leans down to say something to Hector.

Clasping his large hand on Hector's shoulder, he says to him,

"I'm so proud of your family. You're the kind of man we should all strive to be."

After the group photos are finished, I look around, noticing that Jose and Joelle are missing. *Oh dear, we can't have missing kids at the White House,* I think to myself: All we need is the Secret Service finding them wandering somewhere they are not supposed to be.

"Look what I got, Mom! A Presidential napkin," George says, proudly showing me. He has a White House bathroom towel signed by both the President and Mrs. Clinton. "Wow, that's a treasure, George. Don't spill anything on it."

Out of the corner of my eye, I see Jose and Joelle coming back toward me. "Where were you two?" Hector asks.

"We got pictures with Mrs. Clinton," they say.

"By yourselves?"

"Yeah, people were lining up, so we just got in line and we got our pictures with her," Jose says, "Was that OK?"

I laugh. "I'm sure it was fine. Now let's go out on the lawn. We can meet Dave Thomas. We need to thank him for paying for the train tickets so we could all be here today."

"What was the best part of the day, kids?" Hector asks on the train ride home.

"Meeting the President!"

"Meeting Dave Thomas!"

"Getting White House M & Ms!"

"My Presidential napkin!"

"Being on TV!"

The litany of favorite moments continues for several minutes. It comes to a fitting end when Renee says, "Knowing more children will get parents because of today."

"Thanks for including me," my brother David says. "It was an awesome day. I wonder what the press coverage will be like? There were at least a thousand cameras there."

"I know. A little overwhelming," I reflect.

"I hope Renee is right. I hope it leads to lots of kids finding homes."

We get the answer rather quickly.

The next morning, our phone does not stop ringing as friends and relatives call to tell us about the coverage of the event in every paper from the *New York Times* and *USA Today* to small local papers around the country. They all have Norman Rockwell-style photos of Aaron next to the President.

"Look Aaron, you're famous!" I tell him when he gets home from school, holding up the front page of the *Washington Post*. "You're in hundreds of newspapers all over the country."

"Can I take it to show my teacher?" he asks.

"I think that would be a great idea. Let's make a little story-book about your day at the White House and you can bring it in."

"Guess who's on the phone?" Hector interrupts, covering the receiver with his hand. "It's the producer for *CBS This Morning*. They want to come to our house on Thanksgiving."

"Thanksgiving? What a great opportunity to spread the word about children needing families," I say.

"They want to come at 5 in the morning," he says.

"Are you kidding?" I ask.

"No, that's when they film the show. And they want to film us in the kitchen, making our typical Thanksgiving dinner. Because, you know, we always make our mashed potatoes at 5 AM."

We're both laughing by the time he hangs up.

What have you gotten us into this time, God?

19

Geeta

"Do we have any deliveries today?" Raj asks, still in his pajamas.

"Yeah, we have three, so we have to get started by 9—get yourself ready and tell Isaac to rise and shine too."

"We're ready, Dad," Isaac says, emerging from the second floor a few minutes later.

"Great, let's saddle up. Our first stop is the Claxtons over on Durham."

"Glad you're here. We're almost out," Maria calls out as Hector and the boys back into their driveway.

"Where do you want it?"

"Over here on the side of the porch," she points.

"OK, Isaac, Raj, let's get stacking."

"Hey, I recognize you. You're the Badeaus with all those kids, right?" Maria asks.

"Yes we are. I have eight sisters and twelve brothers," Raj replies.

"Nick, come out here. I want you to meet somebody," Maria calls into her house. As her husband appears in the doorway, she continues: "These are the people we saw on *CBS This Morning* on Thanksgiving. I thought they lived near us."

"Nice to meet you," Nick says, extending his hand to shake Hector's. Turning to offer a tip to Isaac and Raj, he adds, "We have a child we adopted from India too."

"That's cool," Raj replies, heading back to the truck for another armload of wood.

"Would you have time to come in for a cup of coffee while your boys finish stacking the wood?" Maria asks.

"We'd like to pick your brain on an adoption issue," Nick explains.

"I have a few minutes before we have to get ready for our next delivery," Hector replies.

"Are you and your wife looking to adopt any more kids?" Maria blurts out as soon as Hector enters the house.

"No. We're holding steady at 21," Hector quickly responds, laughing.

"Well, we'd like you to help us find a family for another child from India," Nick says.

"Not your daughter?" Hector asks, taken aback.

"Oh, no no, no. That's not it." Maria answers firmly.

"We met another little girl, Geeta, years ago. She arrived at the airport the same time our daughter did. At that time she was being adopted by a single mom and we agreed to stay in touch. She was five at the time," Nick explains.

"We've stayed in touch all these years—she's fourteen now," Maria continues the story. "Her first adoptive mom loves her very much and has continued to be involved in her life, but felt she couldn't raise her, so Geeta has bounced around. She's been in several foster homes and three more adoptive homes, but they all fell through. She really needs a family that will stick with her."

"We really want to stay in her life, but we're not able to adopt her ourselves. So we've made a commitment to help find a family for her. When we saw your family on TV back in November, we both said, 'That looks like the perfect family for Geeta.' And now here you are on our doorstep. When I called to order firewood, I had no idea you were that family," Nick concludes. He waits for Hector's reply.

"Oh, I hate to hear a sad story like that. Every child deserves to be in one family and not bouncing around. I'll talk to Sue and we'll see what we can do to help—she works at the National Adoption Center. I'm sure they might have some resources. But it won't be our family. We're definitely not adopting again."

"Thanks for all your help, Dad," Isaac jokes as Hector returns to the porch and sees that the stacking job is finished.

"Great job, perfect timing. We need to get home and load up for our next delivery," Hector tells the boys.

Hector comes inside to tell me about his conversation with the Claxtons while the boys warm up before starting the next order. "This couple saw us on *CBS This Morning*. We knew God was up to something with that show, but I sure didn't think he was going to use it to try to get us to adopt again."

"What are you talking about?" I ask. Hector shares the story with me while I shake my head in disbelief.

"Real nice couple. The husband is from England. But now he works for the city. He thinks he may have met you at one of those DHS meetings you've been to."

"His name does sound familiar," I say, adding, "I'll talk to Chris and Debbie at work on Monday. Maybe they'll have some ideas about families for this girl."

"I got another acceptance letter!" Chelsea is waving her mail at me as I come into the house after work.

"Which school?" I ask, hoping it's Smith.

"West Chester. This isn't my first choice, but they offered me a scholarship. I just don't know what to do," she moans. Chelsea has applied to ten schools. So far, this is her eighth acceptance letter.

"That's why I only applied to one school. No decisions to make," I laugh. I remember being so relieved when I got my early-decision acceptance from Smith College all those years ago.

"Well, I'm not you," she retorts. "I'm not actually sure I even want to go to college right away. I've been looking at some other programs, things you can do for a year before college. My guidance counselor told me a lot of people are doing that these days. They call it the gap year."

"That term is new to me. What kind of programs are you talking about?" I ask.

"Some are in other countries, but the one I really like is this program called City Year. You do a year of volunteer service in a city and also get money for college."

"That sounds like something worth exploring. Let's look into it," I suggest. At the time, I didn't imagine that she'd be the first of four of our kids and five other teens close to our family to participate in this terrific program. With three kids already in college—SueAnn at Harcum, Jose at St Joseph's, and Abel at Antonelli—maybe this gap year for Chelsea isn't such a bad idea. And we're still waiting to learn if George will be accepted at Thaddeus Stevens in Lancaster.

"I can't believe this day has come, Sue." Winter morphed into spring, and summer is upon us as Hector begins getting dressed for our busy day—two graduations, for Chelsea and George. The house is abuzz as our many guests are also getting ready to participate in the festivities.

"And don't forget Joelle's eighth-grade graduation too," I reply. "We always have to miss the eighth-grade ones. I wish they wouldn't schedule them all on the same day."

"At least we have a big enough family, so she'll still have a cheering section. I was just thinking about how far we have come with both Chelsea and George. Chelsea is our first birth child to go from Gerber foods to graduation. And then there's George. Remember when that psychologist in New Mexico said he'd never graduate?" Hector says.

> "Chelsea is our first birth child to go from Gerber foods to graduation. And then there's George. Remember when that psychologist in New Mexico said he'd never graduate?" Hector says.

"Well, he proved them wrong, didn't he! I can't wait to send them a picture of him receiving his diploma tonight," I say.

"I'm so proud of both of them," Hector says. "And to see George going on to college is cream on the cake. And Chelsea heading off to Chicago for City Year; that will be an adventure. Devoting herself to community service—wonder where she gets that from?"

"I'm super proud of both of them too. But I must admit, I'm a little nervous about Chelsea going off to live alone in Chicago. She's barely 18. George will just be a couple hours away, but Chicago . . ."

"I know what you mean, Sue, but she'll be fine. She has your brains and my common sense," Hector laughs.

"Did you realize that after today eleven of our kids will have graduated from high school? We're halfway there," I point out.

"Who knew when we started this journey that our firstborn would become the middle child?"

"Sounds like you're taking a trip down memory lane." I smile.

"Actually, I was thinking about that comment I made about

Chelsea going from Gerber to graduation. I thought I was just being clever, but it kind of reminds me of that passage in I Corinthians about the milk and the meat. I think in some ways I have graduated from milk in my faith journey, but I still sometimes have a hard time chewing the meat. . . . Something to think about," Hector ponders as he pulls up to the front of the Academy of Music to leave Chelsea, Renee, and I off for the graduation.

My mom, brother, Lilly, and Trish are already waiting for us on the sidewalk.

"Each graduation is so different," my brother observes later that evening. We are sitting on the porch relaxing after a very hectic day.

"Chelsea's was more like attending a concert," my mom adds.

"Well, that's what I expected. She did graduate from the school of Creative and Performing Arts," I say.

"But I never laughed so hard as I did when we were trying to get all of us in to George's graduation," David says, chuckling.

In went this way: we had six tickets, but twice that many people. His grandfather and other birth relatives from New Mexico, Hector, SueAnn, my mom, brother, and I all went. My mom devised a plan for all of us to get in using the six tickets. It was a little shady, but it worked, and we all got to see George proudly receive his diploma from Mayor Ed Rendell.

"I wasn't sure whether to ask for forgiveness or just give thanks that it worked," I laugh.

"I'm really happy I can go to this conference with you since I can't go to NACAC this year," Hector says as we load our suitcase into the car, heading to the annual Pennsylvania State Adoption Conference.

"I know. This one is close in case there are any issues at

home. You can get back here quickly. I think our days of attending NACAC together may be over now that our kids are older and we have grandchildren in the mix. But who knows? Maybe we'll make it to one again as a family someday in the future," I reply, walking out to the backyard to give good-bye hugs to Alysia, Joelle, and our granddaughter Ashley, who is spending the summer with us.

"Bye mom!" Todd, Aaron, and Phillip shout from the pool.

"Bye. Be good. I'm not hugging you. I don't want to be all wet for my drive," I laugh.

Those boys are fish; they rarely get out of the pool all summer long. The pool has been a godsend—a survival mechanism for Philadelphia summers, especially since our house has no air conditioning. Even Wayne, Dylan, and Adam enjoy splashing around in the cool water. And we never have a shortage of kids from the neighborhood in there as well.

"Dad, we've got it covered!" Trish and SueAnn shoo Hector off to the car. He's going over the feeding schedule for Wayne, Dylan, and Adam one more time. He's always nervous leaving home, but this will just be two days and everything should be fine. Trish and SueAnn—with help, especially, from Joelle, Isaac, and Flory—are great at taking care of the kids.

"I had an interesting conversation while you were in your workshop," Hector says when we meet in the exhibit area at the end of the day.

"Interesting . . . how so?" I ask.

"I met the social worker for that girl, Geeta. The one the Claxtons told me about when we were doing a wood delivery."

"Oh good. Did they find a family for her?" I ask hopefully.

"No, that's the thing. She still doesn't have a family, and she's moved two more times since I talked to Nick and Maria."

"Hmmm. So what did you say to the social worker?"

I can see that look in his eyes.

"I told her to send us the file. The words just popped out of my mouth. What did I just do?" he wonders aloud.

"You know what usually happens when we agree to look at a file," I say. "What were you thinking?"

"You know what's weird?" I ask Hector a week later as we are reading Geeta's file in our room.

"What's that?"

"I always believed in my heart that we would one day have a second child from India. It was just kind of a thought in the back of my head, but it seemed like it was never coming to pass."

"God must have planted that seed in you, because I'm really feeling convinced that we need to adopt this child," Hector says.

"Joelle, Mom and I want to talk to you," Hector calls.

The last time we adopted teenagers, they came in as the oldest kids in the family. All the younger kids were excited about getting big brothers and sisters. This time, we are adding a teen among the youngest kids in the family, a totally different dynamic. We're hopeful that the transition will go smoothly, but we know there will be challenges.

"Geeta will be going to Roxborough, along with Dylan and you, Joelle," I explain. "I hope you can help her get adjusted."

"Sure, I'll show her around. But don't expect me to have her hanging around with me and my friends," Joelle replies. Navigating high school peer relations can be so tricky . . .

"She has different interests than you do. I am sure she'll eventually make her own friends," I say.

"But in the meantime, remember you are her sister and treat her the way you would want one of your other sisters to treat you," Hector reminds her.

"Wow, Mom. You look great," Todd exclaims as I return home from my day at the spa.

"Thanks, Todd. I had a really nice day. I got my first facial ever." I run my hand across the smoothness of my face and bat my eyes so he can fully appreciate my makeup.

"Oh, you do look beautiful, Mom. You should wear makeup more often," Joelle says, coming into the room.

"Oh, I don't know about that. I think this is about the third time I have ever worn makeup," I laugh. My mom, siblings, aunt, and uncle have chipped in for me to have a full day of pampering at one of the top spas in Philadelphia for my 40th birthday.

"How was it?" Hector asks.

"It was heavenly. I had a massage, manicure and pedicure, facial, and a fancy lunch by the pool. It was like a week's worth of vacation, all in one day."

"Well, you deserve it. And I agree with the kids, you do look beautiful," he says, planting a kiss on my forehead.

"All that time I had to sit with my own thoughts, it really hit me that I'm 40 now. In some ways I still feel like a kid, and in other ways I feel like an old grandma."

"A sexy grandma, at that. I still have a gift for you too, but you can't have it til later," Hector adds, winking.

"Ummm, sounds good. But anyway, while I was pondering what it meant to be 40, I realized there are two things I always wanted to do in my life that I still haven't done. One is to get my master's degree and the other is to publish a book. I really want to try to accomplish those goals one day."

"You've had those goals for a long time. Anything I can do to support you, count me in," he says.

"My friend Ann and I at work have been talking about writing a book together. We really want to focus on the intergenerational impact of adoption. We're going to start by interviewing her grandmother. She was orphaned as a young child. I think it will be fascinating. And I'm going to look into some master's programs and see if there is anything that I can afford—time-wise and money-wise."

"Sounds like a plan."

Several week later, Ann and I are at her grandmother's house videotaping our interview. We take a short break and I call home to check in. "You have a phone call you might want to return before you get home," Hector tells me. "It's from the director of that Kennedy fellowship you applied for."

My hands are shaking as I dial the numbers on the phone. I applied for the Joseph P. Kennedy Foundation Public Policy Fellowship. I found it while looking for master's programs. It won't give me a degree, but if I get it, I get to spend a year in Washington working for a member of Congress. I've always loved advocacy and politics since helping my dad run for the school board when I was a little girl, but I really got bit by the policy bug after our experiences advocating for the Adoption and Safe Families Act, and this seems like a perfect opportunity to further my learning and take a next step in my career.

"Please God, let the answer be yes," I whisper while waiting for the call to connect.

"It's going to be a big change," Hector tells the kids during family meeting. "Mom will be working in Washington during the week and coming home on weekends."

"Will you be sleeping in your office?" Geeta asks.

"No, I'll have a small apartment down there," I explain.

"Can we visit you?" Todd wants to know.

"Of course. I hope you'll all get a chance to visit me—it'll be fun. I'll be working for Senator Rockefeller from West Virginia. I'll be helping him work on laws that help children. Children in foster care and children with disabilities. It's very exciting."

"This really is a big change, Sue," Hector says to me later when we are alone. "I remember when we first got married, we said we never wanted to spend a single night apart. Now we'll be apart four or five nights a week."

"I know. We're going to have to make some sacrifices, but I really believe this will be a chance to make a difference in new ways. Remember when we first became foster parents? We learned about foster care and we wanted to make a difference for more kids, so we took the group home job. And then we started to understand the importance of permanency, so we started Rootwings. Moving to Philly and then working for the National Adoption Center gave us new opportunities to make a difference for more kids than the ones we could touch personally. I think this is just the next step on the same path."

"You're right. As I've always said, 'Each thing we do turns out to be a stepping-stone on the way to the next part of God's plan for our life.' But it's going to be different, and I'll miss you."

"We're having a meeting about the Independent Living legislation. I want you to come with me," my supervisor and mentor, Barbara Pryor, says. "And on the way over there, I want to go over some letters I've been receiving from adoptive families about subsidy issues." Barbara moves at the speed of light and is always multitasking. I've never had a chance to work with someone as smart as her, and I'm soaking it all in.

"I love it. I'm learning the sausage-making side of legislation. It's a little messy but fascinating. There are so many opportunities to make a difference," I tell her.

"How do you like you're new job?" It's my mom on the phone, checking in on me.

"I love it. I'm learning the sausage-making side of legislation. It's a little messy but fascinating. There are so many opportunities to make a difference," I tell her.

"Is it working out OK at home?"

"Yes, all reports I get are good," I reply. "The only things that will be a little challenging are planning Flory's graduation party and Abel and Sonya's wedding from a distance. But I have my evenings to myself, so I'm hoping to get a lot done."

"I'm looking forward to coming for both of those events. You have a busy summer ahead of you."

"Yes we do, not only in Philly, but Hector and I are also going out to Chicago for Chelsea's graduation from City Year. It's a lot, but all good stuff." We end our conversation talking about the details for her trips to Philly this summer.

No sooner have I hung up than the phone rings again. It's Hector calling for our nightly chat. "I need to tell you about this letter that came in the mail today from Lutheran Family Services," he begins.

"Oh no. We are *not* adopting any more kids," I say.

"No, no. Nothing like that. But this is something I really feel we need to get involved in. As soon as I read it, I knew that God wants us to do what we can. No need to pray about this one. I just know this is right. I feel so strongly . . . "

"OK, so tell me what you are talking about," I interrupt.

"Lutheran Family Services is helping to resettle refugees from Kosovo to Philadelphia, and they are looking for host families to take in families. We can do that. We have the big empty room on the third floor. There is a meeting on Wednesday to learn more about it. I plan to attend. God is really hitting me over the head on this one. This is a James 1:27 moment, no doubt about it."

"Wow, you are really on fire, Hec. I love the passion you have for people, but let's take it slowly. Go to the meeting on Wednesday and then you can fill me in.

"Now, changing the subject—did you figure out coverage for the kids at home for the days we'll be gone to Chicago?"

Wednesday I work late; this Independent Living legislation is really taking over my life. I'm determined to get some language in there acknowledging that even teenagers still need permanent families. Having an apartment or college fund is good, but none of that replaces a family. I've asked Hector to call me a few hours later than our usual time. . . .

"I can tell from your voice that you are still on fire about this," I say after listening to Hector describe the meeting at the Lutheran agency.

"More than ever. I can't wait until we get assigned a family. There is some paperwork, and you know that's your department, so you can do it this weekend."

In between filling out the paperwork and getting assigned to a family, we make a quick trip to Chicago for Chelsea's City Year graduation.

"I'm so proud of you, Chels," Hector says at dinner after the ceremony. "This experience really gave you a chance to shine."

"I can't believe they promoted you into a staff-level position. Very impressive," Cathy says. My cousin Cathy and her family live in Indiana and have joined us for the celebration.

"Doesn't surprise me at all. You've been a leader since you were a tiny girl. You used to boss everyone around, even back at the Mill River House Church when you were only two," I tease. "But seriously, this is a great accomplishment and will really give you a leg up when you start college at Arcadia in the fall."

A week before Flory's graduation, Hector gets the call that we have been selected as the host family for a family of refugees from Kosovo.

"Are you sitting down?" he asks as our phone conversation begins.

"Uh oh. Why do I need to be sitting down?" I ask.

"We got our assignment from Lutheran. We'll be hosting a

family of eight."

"Eight—as in eight people?" I say, flabbergasted.

"That's right. It's a mother and father, their five kids, and the grandmother. I'm so excited about this. I can't wait to meet them."

"Do you think they'll be OK all in that one room?" I ask. It is a very large room, larger than my entire apartment here in D.C., but still, there's not a lot of privacy.

"I asked the social worker about that and she said they'll like it that way. And it's only for a few months until they get settled, and then they'll get an apartment."

"OK, sounds good. When do they arrive?" I ask.

"June 18th."

"Wow—that's the same day as Flory's graduation from Parkview," I remind him.

"I know. The graduation is in the morning, and the meeting at Lutheran to meet the family and bring them home is in the afternoon. And Flory's party is not 'til the next day, so it works."

"I see you've got it all worked out," I laugh. "And don't forget, my mom and David are both arriving on the 17th for the graduation."

"We're so proud of you, Flory. You've come a long way since you were the little 'Popper' we first met in New Mexico," I say, giving her a big hug as she comes down the stairs in her cap and gown. I turn to look at Hector, and he has tears in his eyes.

"I've spent many hours in many meetings at your schools, so we could always get the best plan for you," he says, a little choked up. "And look at you now. Graduating and going on to Job Corps when you get back from Vermont." He gives her a big hug and we head out the door. Our newest grandson, Matthew, Trish's third child, was born in Vermont on Wednesday. Flory will be going to Vermont for a week after graduation to help out.

It's a hot summer evening and we can't sleep, so we're sitting on the deck of the pool after everyone else is in bed. "I can't believe the Namanis have been here for almost two months already. It's been so good to be part of their lives. I'm so glad we decided to do this."

"Me too, Hec, and you would hardly know there are five kids in the house, they're so well-behaved."

"The four girls are so adorable, and the baby, Lorik—oh, he really stole my heart from the first day. He reminds me a little of Isaac when he was a baby. He sure keeps the grandmother busy with three-year-old Renita while Zech and Sevdije are working and the older girls are playing outside," Hector says with a smile.

"Zech and the girls are really picking up English fast, especially Marigona," I add. "She is so studious. They are always reading books from our bookshelves. They'll do great once school begins."

"It'll be interesting to see how they blossom and make friends. Sometimes they act a little shy, but then you get a glimpse of their personality shining through. Particularly Miranda—she has a lot of spunk."

"Majlinda is the shy, sweet one. She makes me think of Whitney, and they are kind of close in age. I hope they hit it off when Whitney comes down for the wedding."

"Yeah, me too. It will be good for them, but sad for us, when they get their own apartment. I hope they find one close by so we can stay connected. Their home in Kosovo was beautiful. It's so sad that they lost everything except one envelope of pictures."

"I know," I say. "It's got to be so hard, starting over like that after all they have been through. They have such an amazing spirit. To me they define the word resilience. I think that is one advantage they have over kids in the foster care system here in the U.S."

"How so?" Hector asks.

"Well, they experienced devastating loss and trauma, but they all experienced it together, with their parents and their whole community. So they can all share their feelings together and heal together. But for kids in foster care, they often feel like they are the only ones going through what they've been through. Many feel they have to keep their experiences secret; sometimes they're even ashamed, even though what happened to them was not their fault. It makes it a lot harder for them to have hope and to heal when they feel so alone."

"Yeah, I can see that. I never thought of it that way," Hector says. "Well, it's getting pretty late. Let's try to sleep. All the guests from England start arriving tomorrow for the wedding."

"Finally, I get to meet my new grandson. Give that baby to me," Hector says before Trish can get out of the car. "What's his name again?"

"Dad! Don't you remember?"

"I have ten grandchildren now. I've earned the right to be a little forgetful!" he replies, then, cuddling the baby, says, "Oh Matthew, you are a cutie."

"Ha ha Dad, you did remember." Trish smiles as Sean, Phillip, and Ashley tumble out.

"Come here, Lilly. Give your old man a hug," Hector says as Lilly emerges from the driver's seat.

"Bama!" Sean runs up to me on the porch. He's the only one who has a special name for me, and it's so endearing I never plan to correct him.

"Where is my baby?" Trish asks Hector while people are getting seated for the wedding ceremony. "I thought you had him."

"I did for about a minute. But as soon as Aunt Deanna got him, she took over. I don't think you will pry that baby out of her arms all day," Hector tells Trish.

"I'm exhausted, but on cloud nine," I say to Hector as I plop down on our bed rubbing my aching feet. "It was an amazing day."

Seeing our family and friends from England, Grenada, Haiti, Michigan, and Vermont all enjoying each other was so special. And a few moments completely took my breath away. The Chans coming from New York to attend the wedding and see Wayne; Gracie Kirpan, their child with Down Syndrome, never leaving the dance floor; Chelsea's beautiful performance on the flute. Sonya looked stunning, and Abel is so happy.

"Of course there were the funny moments too," Hector adds. "Like Jose, Isaac, and your brother dancing to 'Cotton-Eyed Joe.' I haven't laughed so hard in a long time."

"Can't wait for the Jamaican meal Sonya's mum, nanna, and aunties are making for us tomorrow. . . . But for now, I need sleep."

"Me too. Good night, my love."

"Good night, my watermelon pickle," I say, using an old silly nickname from our high school dating days. The day was close to perfect, and I am still reliving the special moments in my mind as I begin to doze off. If only Hector hadn't had too much to drink, it would have been totally perfect. I hope this was a one-time thing, and not the beginning of a problem . . .

Less than a month later, when Hector calls for our nightly chat, he tells me that the Namanis have found an apartment. "We have everything worked out. I got the landlord to wave the security deposit, and I've talked to some of the deacons at church about helping them get furniture and other things they'll need. Zech's sister and her family can also get an apartment in the same building."

"Sounds perfect. And guess what? I have some exciting news too. We got invited to the White House again. It's not for the whole family this time. It's the Adoption Excellence Awards again, and we got six tickets, so you and I and four kids can come. I was thinking we should definitely bring Geeta since she wasn't with us the last time we came."

"Wow, that's great. We'll plan on it. Give me all the details, and I'll work things out on this end," Hector says.

Sitting in the audience at the White House adoption event, we are startled to hear President Clinton call us out by name in his speech:

"I'd also like to say a special hello to the Badeau family. Some of you may remember this. Two years ago, almost, Sue and Hector Badeau joined us at the White House when I signed the Adoption and Safe Families Act. They brought 18 of their 22 children they have adopted. Now, you need to know that, as if they didn't have enough to deal with, this summer they also welcomed into their home a family of eight Kosovar refugees. So if you ever need proof that there's no limit to human goodness, you can look at Sue and Hector Badeau. I'd like for them to stand. Where are they? There you go. They've got some of their kids here. Stand up. Thank you. God bless you."

"I'm stunned that he remembered us," Hector says when we stop for a bite to eat after the event.

"You could say it was his staff, but then when he talked to us afterward and asked about George running track and mentioned getting Aaron's photo book, I knew it was more than just good staffing. He actually remembered us," I say, shaking my head.

"I just pray that every time we get recognition God can use it to create opportunities for more children to get homes. I don't want the recognition for us, just for what God is doing in our lives and for the work that is still needed until all children have families."

"Amen to that."

"Say a prayer," I ask Hector, calling him before my work day begins on November 19.

"What's up?"

"Today is the last day of the legislative session, and neither of the bills I've been working so hard on has come up for votes yet. Now that the foster care bill has been named in honor of Senator Chaffee, we thought for sure it would move through. And so many people with disabilities really need the work incentive bill. Barbara says these are the kinds of bills that always pass on the last day, but it's so nerve-wracking. They have to get voted on today—or all our work will be for nothing."

"I know how hard you've worked on these, and I know how much they're needed," Hector says. "I am confident they'll pass. Keep the faith."

Later that night, I call him back.

"I can tell from your voice that you have good news," he says.

"I have lots of good news. Both of the bills passed!" I take a few minutes to describe how Barbara and I waited in the office until after 9 PM for the call from the cloakroom.

"That's fantastic, Sue. I'm proud of the work you did there, it will really make a difference."

"Well, I was just one of many people who worked hard on these bills, but I'm so excited with the outcome. We didn't get every provision we wanted, but it will be a big improvement over the way things are now. And I have more news."

"Really, what's that?"

"While we were waiting for the news about the bills, I got a call from Vermont. Jen had her baby, a little girl named Emma. I didn't get to talk to Fisher, but Jen says everything went well and she and the baby are both good. So now Alec has a little sister and we have grandchild number eleven. I called the hospital gift shop and sent some flowers to Jen's room."

"Wow. It's a lot to take in. I hope we can meet her soon. Another child for my prayer list. On another note, I have some sad news."

"What?" I say, concerned.

"The Namanis are moving back to Kosovo."

"Really? I don't understand."

"Well, you remember they always said they would go back once the government declared it was safe."

"Yes, I remember. I just didn't think it would be this soon."

"I know. I can't say I blame them. If I were in a foreign country, I know I'd want to go home too," Hector says. "But it's going to be hard to say good-bye. Let's plan a little send-off party when you get home."

As we hug each of the Namani children good-bye, I see Hector's eyes filling with tears. "I'm going to miss you so much," he says to each of them in turn.

"I hope it all works out for them. It's hard to imagine we'll never see them again," Hector says later.

"It's a small world, Hec," I say. "You never know. Maybe we will see them again one day."

20

The First Good-bye

"What do you think about Flory and Renee living together?" Hector approaches me with his idea after
everyone is in bed.

"Say more."

"Well, I think they're both ready for more independence,
and if they're together, they can help each other and share the
expenses. I think it would be good for Daniel to have another
adult around, and after Flory has her baby, she'll be needing
extra support too."

"That all makes sense, but what brought this up right now?"
I ask.

"I haven't talked to the Namanis' landlord yet, but I feel terrible that the lease was broken, so I was thinking maybe we can

just transfer it so Renee and Flory can live there."

"Ah, now I get your logic. Makes sense to me. Sure, talk to the landlord and see what kind of response you get, and then if it's a real possibility, we can talk to the girls. By the way, are you still coming down to D.C. for the ABA conference? It's just one night, but one night in a hotel is a pretty good treat!"

"I'm counting on it. We can use a little R&R. Why waste an opportunity to enjoy a free hotel room?" Hector replies.

"How long has it been since we had a date night?" I ask as we make ourselves comfortable for the evening.

"Too long. Remember when Fisher was in high school and he used to babysit once a week so you and I could have a date night? That was a real treat, but those days have come and gone."

"Yeah, it's a lot harder now. Getting care for Wayne, Dylan, and Adam is different than getting care for the other kids. And with my work schedule, date nights are few and far between, so we better enjoy. Who knows when we'll have this chance again?"

Ring, ring, ring.

"What? What's that?" I'm disoriented, until I remember that we're in a hotel. *Why is the phone ringing?* I wonder, noticing that it's two in the morning.

Hector picks up the phone, "Hello? . . . SueAnn . . . is everything OK at home? . . . . Oh, really, are you sure? Let me put Mom on." Wordlessly, he hands me the phone.

"I knew it was too good to be true," I say to Hector as I fall back into bed. "Why can't we have one date night without interruption?"

"So what's the story?"

"Well, Flory's in labor, but it's in the early stages. I told SueAnn we're going back to sleep and to call us in a few hours with an update."

"Well, that was a short vacation, but still fun," Hector says at 6 AM as we hit the road for Philly.

"It sounds like we'll get there before the baby is born by the way things are going," I say.

Sure enough, we arrive at Jefferson Hospital moments before Jasmine makes her way into the world.

"The baby is beautiful, and it sure is good to have a positive experience at this hospital," Hector says as we head home, physically and emotionally spent.

"Looks like it will be a Badeau baby for the Christmas pageant at church again. Ever since Raj played that role in 1983, we seem to have a lock on that assignment," I chuckle.

"Hey George, can you bring Adam up to bed?" Hector calls to George.

We're sitting by the fire enjoying one of those lovely quiet moments between Christmas and New Years. Adam is in his beanbag chair next to me, holding my hand. He seems particularly happy and peaceful tonight. "He's been smiling a lot tonight," I say to Hector.

"I've noticed that too. Those big, beautiful blue eyes really light up when he smiles. It's been a long road for him to feel safe and comfortable, but I really feel it now. What a change in him since that scared little boy you brought home five years ago."

"OK, Dad, can you help lift him out of his chair?" George appears, ready to bring Adam to bed.

"Mom and I have to go to the Willow Grove Mall for a couple hours to get some supplies for the Millennium Party. Keep an eye on the fires and the little kids while we are gone, OK?"

"I will," George hollers back as he climbs the stairs with Adam.

"Here's your coffee, Sue," Hector says the next morning. It's so pleasant to enjoy our coffee and panettone without having to get anyone out the door to school or work.

"Thanks for having the fire ready. It's a little chilly today. I didn't hear you get up. What time was it?" I ask.

"The usual: 5 AM."

"Oh, I thought you might sleep in since there's no school today. Are any of the kids up?"

"I heard a few kids walking around, but it's still pretty quiet. This will give us a chance to finalize the plans for the New Year's party. Nancy and Bobby and Deanna and Freddy are all driving down today, aren't they?"

"Yes, they're staying over at the Doubletree. It's supposed to snow today, so I hope they have safe travels. Jill and Kai are arriving today too." Our traditional New Year's Eve is pretty quiet. We prepare a buffet of finger foods, rent movies, and play board games. But this year, the year the calendar turns from 1999 to 2000, our extended family thought that welcoming in "Y2K" together would be special, and so relatives from out of town are all arriving for the celebration.

"Have you talked to Peter?" Hector asks.

"Yes, he and Nancy have the menu all set, and the chairs and tables will be delivered in the morning," I say. "I'm really glad the family decided to chip in for the catering. It would be a lot to do ourselves—can you believe there'll be close to 75 of us here? Almost like another wedding. And Jose has the music list; he's going to be the DJ using his computer for the music."

"Turn of the century. Hard to believe," Hector notes.

"Dad, Dad! Adam won't wake up!" Aaron is shouting from the second floor.

"Let him sleep, there's no school today," Hector replies. Turning back to me, he continues. "Anyway, where was I? Oh yes, I have to get all the living room furniture cleared out today. I am counting on Raj and Isaac and David to give me a hand with that."

"But Dad! He really won't wake up, and he doesn't look right!" Aaron shouts again. "Please come up here."

"OK, I'll come check on him," Hector says.

"Sue, Sue! Call 911 right away!" Hector screams as he bursts out of Adam's room and carries him down the stairs. "He's blue and he's not breathing. I'm going to start CPR, but call 911 quick."

Hector kicks the couch aside, throws a blanket on the floor, and lays Adam on it, urgently starting CPR.

"I have the 911 operator on the phone. I told him you had a class in CPR but have never had to use it. He's going to talk you through it." I put the phone on speaker and stretch the cord as far as I can so Hector can hear.

"Is he breathing yet?" I ask urgently.

"No, he won't breathe!" Hector replies hysterically.

By now, most of the kids have gathered in a circle around us. Some are sitting on their stairs. Several are crying softly. Jose is pacing back and forth, asking what he can do. I ask him to go up to Adam's room and get some socks we can put on him. His feet feel so cold.

The 911 operator encourages us to remain calm and promises that the ambulance is on the way.

"They're here, Dad," Abel says, opening the door for the EMTs.

"We'll take over," one of them says, roughly pushing Hector aside. Within seconds, three people are working feverishly on Adam, while two others are wheeling a stretcher into the house.

"Police are here too," Jose says. "Why are they here?"

"I don't know. Just let them in," I tell him.

"I'm sorry, Mr. and Mrs. Badeau. There is nothing more we can do," one of the medics says after several minutes. "We have to bring him to Chestnut Hill Hospital for the official pronouncement, but he's gone."

We're in shock and can't move or speak . . .

"Ma'am, ma'am. I have to ask you a few questions." One of the police officers is tapping me on the shoulder.

"I'm sorry. I have to go to the hospital to be with my son. He's so cold. I have to bring him a blanket and socks. Jose? Did you get those socks?" I ramble.

"We have to get some information, and then you can go to the hospital," the officer says.

"I'll take the kids in the living room," Hector says numbly. All of our kids, plus JD's kids, are huddled on the stairs.

"When I put him to bed, Dad, he was all happy. I didn't do anything to him," George says urgently.

"I know, George. You did everything right. It's not your fault. It must have been his time to go be with Jesus. We just didn't know it would be this soon," Hector replies, giving George a hug.

Hector's voice is cracking as he speaks to the rest of the children. "We don't know what happened. Mom and I will go to the hospital to find out more. It looks like Adam died in his sleep, and he has gone to be with Jesus. Please stay calm, and as soon as we know more information we'll call you."

"We didn't get to say good-bye," Joelle cries.

"We'll make sure everyone who wants to come to the hospital and say good-bye has a chance. This is one of those times we need to pull together as a family and support each other and ask God to give us the grace to get through this. You older kids have to look after the younger ones while we're gone to the hospital."

When we arrive at the hospital, Hector goes immediately in to be with Adam. I use the phone to call our pastor and ask him to come meet us here. When a nurse escorts me into the room where Adam lies, I see Hector sobbing, holding his hand and gently tousling his hair.

"He's only eleven years old, Sue. How can this be? He was so happy last night, almost the happiest he has ever been." Hector ekes out his words between sobs.

"I know. We knew this day would come. We knew it in our heads, but our hearts weren't ready yet," I say softly.

"Like the good book says, 'He knows the number of hairs on our head and the number of days of our lives,'" Hector whispers, continuing to run his fingers through Adam's hair.

"I guess Adam's number was up," I say, and suddenly, the tears began to flow.

Moments later Bill, our pastor, comes into the room. Together we pray over Adam and sit for several more moments in silence. I leave Hector alone with Adam for his final good-bye, while I go to the desk to make arrangements to bring the children over to say their good-byes.

We drive home in silence. Before we get into the house we can hear Alysia sobbing loudly; others are silent. A few of the kids have retreated to their rooms, but most are still in the living room. Not all want to come to the hospital, but those who do quietly put on their coats and boots and file out to the van. Each child needs the space and opportunity to grieve in their own way.

I am most concerned about Aaron, who is sitting stoically in the corner of the couch. I give him a hug, but he doesn't move.

The woman from Kirk and Nice, the funeral home, is already at the house by the time I return with the kids from the hospital. She's incredibly kind, compassionate, and patient as she guides us through the paperwork and decisions we have to make. We agree to have the funeral here at the house. They will take care of all the arrangements for the death certificate and cremation. "Ashes to ashes," I say to no one in particular as she leaves.

At the same moment, Jill and Kai arrive. Kai takes one look at me and sees the tension in my back and neck. As a physical therapist, he knows that the best support he can offer me right now is a neck rub. As he works, he soothingly reminds me of our faith and trust that Adam is now in a better place.

"What should we do about everyone arriving from out of town for the party, and all the catering we've ordered?" Hector asks me and Jill and Kai, pulling his hair back from his face.

"The party will go on," I say. "It's a blessing that we have so many of our family here. The party will be a celebration of Adam's life. I'll get some balloons we can release to send our prayers and love to Heaven for Adam, and we will give him a great send-off."

"The house is packed, Sue," Hector whispers to me just before we begin the funeral service.

"I know, and more of our friends from church are still on the porch. I just can't believe we are saying good-bye to a child. An eleven-year-old boy. I have a hole in my heart that feels like it will never be filled."

"Here you go, Aaron. You can be the first one to send a balloon up to Heaven," I say, and then, turning to all of the children: "The balloons are just a symbol of our love and prayers and a reminder that Adam is now in Heaven with Jesus."

Later, Hector and I are sitting alone in the living room. Adam's urn is on the mantel. "It's hard to believe that the day will come when all three of our boys will be on that mantel," Hector says.

"I'm not ready to think about that right now." I lean into his shoulder and the tears start to flow again.

Losing a child has been an unspeakably devastating experience. We knew Adam had a terminal illness, yet no matter what the circumstances . . . you just shouldn't have to bury a child. It never feels right.

Adam has been gone for a week. It's the middle of the night, and I'm writing an e-mail to my colleagues at Senator Rockefeller's office, explaining why I won't be at work for a week. I'm writing in the middle of the night because I can't sleep. I have this totally irrational fear that if I dare to fall asleep, someone else may die. As I've written in my e-mail, the pain is truly unspeakable. I wonder if I will ever sleep again.

21

Mourning to Dancing

Hector reaches over and squeezes my hand. He must have noticed the tears in my eyes. The three-hour Good Friday service is one of my favorites of the year. Rarely do we take three full hours to sit quietly, listening to the Word and the still small voice of the Spirit.

The opening chords of "Were You There?" begins. With the rest of the congregation, we stand.

"I needed that today," I say to Hector as we walk to our car a few minutes after three o'clock. "We've been carrying on with day-to-day life as usual since Adam died, but underneath the surface, my heart is still broken, and I'm still not sleeping. The service today was like a healing balm to my soul."

"I know what you mean. I've always thought of Good Friday as a time to remember Jesus' death as we prepare for the resurrection on Easter. I've meditated on John 3:16: 'For God so loved the world that he gave up his only son . . . ' But today I experienced Good Friday in a whole new way. We are all God's sons and daughters. So each time one of us loses a child, God not only understands, because he went through the death of Jesus, he understands because he grieves alongside of us. God grieves Adam with us. I really felt that today."

"God grieves Adam with us. I really felt that today."

"Yes, you put into words exactly what I was feeling. He grieves with us, but he also rejoices with us that the resurrection is not only for Jesus, but for Adam too. He rejoices with us, and we can rejoice. We can put away the season of grief, just like we put away the winter coats and boots. We can put on a season of rejoicing, just like our azalea tree at home is putting on its annual display of dazzling colors."

"So, what you're saying is: Psalm 30 is right—the time for mourning is finished and it's time to dance?" Hector says as he sweeps me up into a dance hold and twirls me around in the parking lot.

"Yes, yes, that's it!" The tears this time are tears of laughter. "We must look pretty silly, dancing our way out of a Good Friday service."

"Well you know that song you always liked, 'The Lord of the Dance'? What are those words? He's singing to me:

'They cut me down but I leapt up high, I am the life that will never, never die.'"

I join in:

"'Dance, then, wherever you may be, I am the Lord of the Dance says he!'"

We're getting some funny looks as we finally get into our car to drive home.

"I can't help it. I get tears in my eyes every time I watch her dance," Hector says, brushing the tears from his cheeks.

"I know. It's amazing—the girl who 'would never walk' can now dance like an angel," I add, picking up the flowers on the seat next to me as we leave the dance recital and go look for Alysia. Dance, even more than physical therapy, has helped Alysia to blossom. It not only strengthens her muscles, but her confidence, and it has become one of her primary forms of communication.

"Those social workers in Texas were right about one thing. We do need a wheelchair-accessible house. They were just wrong if they thought we would need it for Alysia," Hector laughs.

"I have good news, Mom!" Trish's excitement is evident through the phone.

"I love good news. Tell me," I say.

"I won the lottery. A million dollars and I'm going to Paris next week!" she says in her version of a French accent.

"Oh, is that right? Can I come too?" I laugh. Trish is known for her telephone pranks.

"Just kidding, But I do have good news. I won an award. It's for the whole state of Vermont, for literacy achievement. It's for the work I have done to help children read and for starting that support group for other parents who have a child with special needs. I can't believe it. I'm so excited."

"That's super, Trish. You deserve to be proud of yourself."

"There's going to be an award ceremony, and I think they said the governor is going to be there."

"Make sure you get some pictures. Dad and I are proud of you. Love you, sweetie," I say as we hang up the phone. . . .

"Hey everyone, I have some good news about Trish to tell

325

you," I say to the family as we gather for dinner. I tell them that she will be honored by the governor of Vermont.

"Now that deserves a pat-on-the-back," Todd says.

"Good idea. Why don't you write one out, and we can send it to her?" I suggest.

"While we're sharing good news, I wanted to tell you about a phone call I had from George today," Hector says.

"Great. What's up with George?"

"Looks like all those years of running everywhere . . . " he begins.

"Yeah, didn't he even run to Saul a few times?" Todd interrupts, remembering the days when George would run to his high school, three miles from our home, because he was too impatient to wait for the bus.

"That's right, Todd. Anyway, as I was saying, it looks like that has paid off because he just found out he made it to the national cross country track tournament in the NJCAA," Hector finishes.

"What's the NJ . . . whatever you said? Is that in New Jersey?" Joelle asks.

"No, it's the National Junior College Athletic Association," Hector says. "That's the association his college, Thaddeus Stevens, belongs to, and he'll be competing with other athletes from all around the country."

"That's a huge deal. When is the meet?" I ask.

"Well, that's the tough part. It's the three days right before his graduation. The school will take a bus trip to get out there for the competition, but he asked if we can get him a plane ticket back because that's the only way he can get back in time for his graduation."

"Hmmm, that might be tough to arrange, but I'll look into it," I say.

"Geeta, you have after-dinner cleanup. Joelle, you're feeding Wayne. His food is ready. I'll take care of Dylan. Todd and Alysia, you both have homework to finish up after dinner," Hector reminds the kids.

"And Raj, I'm doing groceries tonight," I add, speaking and signing. "Don't forget, you're coming with me. Isaac and David, make sure you're available at 10 when I get home to help us unload and put everything away." Although the kids all take turns as my grocery helper, Raj is the best. He's organized my shopping list on Excel spreadsheets and he also manages my coupons. I'm happy it's his turn tonight to help; we can get it done quickly.

"While you were doing the shopping, I was thinking about both Trish and George," Hector says as we finish unpacking the groceries. "You know, it's really ironic. We were specifically told about both of those two not to expect them to graduate from high school. And today we get this great news on both of them—George in college track and Trish wining a state literacy award. Talk about proving them wrong."

"We were specifically told about both of those two not to expect them to graduate from high school. And today we get this great news on both of them—George in college track and Trish wining a state literacy award. Talk about proving them wrong."

"I know. Just more confirmation of the two things we believe most strongly—with God all things are possible, and all kids thrive best in families. After so many of the hurdles and challenges we go through, it's nice to get a confirmation once in a while."

"I'm really thankful for your mom's dedication to our kids. Especially since your dad died, she's never missed a graduation or other important event, even when it means she has to travel down here twice in one summer. I know it means a lot to the kids," Hector is saying as I grab the keys from him to go pick up my mom from the airport. She is arriving for our weekend of college graduation celebrations today, and she'll be back in June for Isaac's high school graduation.

"You're right. I sometimes take it for granted. I guess I should let her know I appreciate her a little more often," I reply.

"Yeah, showing appreciation is something we can always get better at," Hector adds.

"Jose says he won't be walking in his graduation after all because he has one more credit to finish up, but we're still including him in the party this weekend. So you and David and Hector and I will all go to George's graduation." I break the news about Jose to my mom, knowing she will be disappointed not to watch her first grandson receive his college diploma.

I see the look of surprise on her face, and before she can respond, I continue, "Angelo graduates this weekend too—all three colleges on the same weekend. Chelsea and Isaac are driving up to Loch Haven for his graduation. Jose will attend the St. Joe's graduation to support his friend Pat, but we don't need to go since he's not walking. Anyway, everyone will converge back here for the parties." Angelo was one of the boys who first lived with us when we moved to Philadelphia.

"Sounds like a busy weekend. We should probably go to bed now," Mom replies, noting the time.

"Good idea. Our day starts early tomorrow with the drive to Lancaster. We have to be there by ten, and there is a lot of morning traffic on Route 30, so we have to allow extra time," Hector reminds us.

"I know, and we have to get everyone squared away here before we go. No rest for the wicked," I joke.

"Geeta, can you go get Mamie another water?" I'm a little

concerned about my mom; her face is flushed. We're sitting on our porch, just back from George's graduation, and Mom is still feeling a little dehydrated from the heat of the day.

Just as Geeta turns to go inside, Pat, still in his cap and gown, and Jose walk toward us. "Congratulations, Pat! We are proud of you!" Hector goes to shake his hand, and I stand to give him a hug.

"Thanks, Mr. Hec, Miss Sue. Now you have to crack down on this knucklehead," he says, pointing to Jose.

"Yeah, I know. He needs to get that last credit so he can get his degree," I say.

"No, that's just it—he *did* graduate," Pat says. "They even called his name today. He could have walked. Look, his name's right here in the program."

"Jose!" both my mom and I yell out at the same moment.

"Uh oh, Jose. You better run for cover, because if looks can kill, you will be dead in less than ten seconds by the look of your mother and grandmother," Pat says, bursting into laughter.

A month later, Mom is back, this time with my sister Stephanie and her family, for Isaac's high school graduation.

"It seems like Isaac has a lot of nice friends," she says while we wait for the waitress. We're taking Isaac and his girlfriend, Simmy, out to lunch to celebrate.

"I love the kids from Bodine, especially this one," I say, giving Simmy a big hug. "And of course Isaac's best friend, Adrian."

"You've had a lot of great opportunities and experiences at Bodine. I think my favorite was when the Italian students came," Hector says. In Isaac's sophomore year, his school hosted more than seventy exchange students from Italy, and we had a great time hosting all of them at our house for a meal.

"Oh that was great fun!" I reminisce. "When we have a big crowd for dinner, my fall-back meals to make are spaghetti or lasagna. I was in the grocery store ready to buy the ingredients when it suddenly hit me—these are *Italian* students. I'm not making spaghetti for Italian students! So I switched gears real fast and decided to go with fajitas. And thankfully, they loved them!"

"Yeah I remember that—it was a big hit," Simmy adds. "And then we played Frisbee on the lawn and Alysia got really excited about sharing e-mail addresses with some of them. She really wants to go to Italy one day."

"Yeah, her birth father is part Italian, so she's real interested in that part of her heritage," I explain.

"So I hear you are taking another one of your trips this summer? Where are you going?" my brother-in-law, Darian, asks.

"Well, not a whole cross-country trip, but we're going down to Myrtle Beach for a week and then taking the family to the NACAC conference in Baltimore," Hector replies. "Sue's getting an award this year. We're looking forward to it."

Everyone is still asleep when I slip out of bed; the sun has not come up yet. I have been lying in bed awake, depressed and stressed over several situations going on in the family, especially Fisher being in jail again as a result of his continuing battle with addiction . . . and now this. We've just learned that SueAnn is pregnant again, which will probably mean she'll drop out of college, although that's not clear yet.

"Why, God? Why do we keep facing these same issues again and again? Show me what we need to learn or change," I pray. I feel like the same problems keep rolling in on us and over us as regularly as the waves roll onto the shore during high tide. I am hoping that an early morning walk, alone, on the beach will give me a chance to gain some strength to face these and other challenges when we get home from our vacation. . . .

"So much for being alone," I mutter to myself, noticing that several people are already on the beach. They all have pails. I watch for awhile, noticing a pattern—they reach down, pick up a shell, look at it closely. A few shells make it into the pails, but most are dropped back to the sand. It occurs to me that these shell seekers are seeking perfect, beautiful shells to save. They examine them for cracks, holes, and other faults, casting the broken ones back and saving only those deemed perfect.

I start to pick up shells, too. There are plenty of broken ones—so many pieces of broken shells that it's hard to walk without crunching them under my feet.

And as I hold one particularly fragile, delicate, lacy piece of a broken shell in my hand, while watching the pounding waves crash and break against the shore, I become amazed. *How did this fragile little shell survive?* I wonder. Why wasn't it totally pulverized by the power of the sea? I see this broken shell with new eyes. Instead of seeing its brokenness, I see its strength, its uniqueness, its resilience. Wow—this little shell fragment has been tossed, slammed, dunked, and twirled, and yet, here it is, in my hands, like spun glass. Glistening in its beauty.

And I think again about my daughter, my sons, my children. Whose poor choices and disappointing circumstances are weighing me down, threatening to drown me—my emotions battered, tossed, pounding, and resounding through my heart and mind like the waves against the shore. I realize how amazing it is that they've survived the sea of experiences life brought their way.

Now, I clearly see that they are each like this broken shell. Exquisite and amazing. And like a shell, their lives belong to the sea, to the vast expanse of God's eternity. He has a unique plan, a plan filled with hope and possibilities—for each of them. Our home is the shore—a resting place, a healing place, a time apart from the waves of life for a few brief years, before they face again the crashing and pounding of the waves and the life of the sea.

"Thank you, Lord, for giving me that insight," I whisper, putting the broken shell in my pocket, knowing I'll treasure it for a long time to come.

"Only eight kids to get off to school this year, Sue. It will be a breeze," Hector says when we get back from our trip.

"Eight through high school, but don't forget about the two in college," I add. Chelsea is at Arcadia University, and Isaac is starting at St. Joseph's.

"That's true, but at least I'm not responsible for waking those two up every morning. I was thinking. David will be glad to have Isaac at St. Joe's now that Jose is gone," Hector says. David works in the cafeteria at St Joe's, a job he's held since 1996. We think he sees himself as one of the students; he loves joking around with them, and even though it's rare for him to meet a student who knows sign language, that never seems to present a barrier. Everyone who meets David becomes his friend immediately.

"I want to tell you about a letter that came in the mail today," Hector says at the beginning of our evening phone call. Although my fellowship in D.C. has ended, I was offered an opportunity to stay on at the Kennedy Foundation, working directly with Mrs. Shriver on policy issues related to individuals with disabilities and their families. It's an opportunity we both agreed I couldn't pass up, so I am still commuting back and forth on weekends.

"Uh oh. Not sure I dare to hear the rest of this. The last time a letter in the mail got you so excited, we ended up with a family of eight people in our house!" I laugh.

"And you loved it," he says.

"I did love the Namanis, still do. I am thankful we've been part of their lives. So what's the new letter?"

"Well, you are on the right track. It's a letter from the Lutheran agency again."

"And . . ."

"Have you ever read about the kids from Africa that they call The Lost Boys of Sudan?"

"Yes, I have. It's quite a remarkable story how all of those boys took care of each other and traveled over 500 miles to get to the refugee camps in Kenya. I read that these boys often saw their own family members shot, drowned, and even eaten by lions. The fact that they survived is incredible. So you got a letter about them? Do they need donations?"

"The letter is about them, but they're not looking for donations. Lutheran is bringing some of these lost boys here to Philadelphia, and they're looking for host families. And, of course, because of our experience with the Namanis, we are on their list. So I was thinking . . . . " Hector begins to explain.

"Let me guess—you signed us up for eight boys?" I tease.

"Not eight. Just four," he says.

"Four, huh? OK, tell me more about what we are signing up for and what you were thinking."

"We get letters all the time from Lutheran and other agencies and often I don't even read them because I'm so busy. But this one really spoke to me, and I know this is something we need to do. I'm just as sure as I was for the Namanis. So anyway, I called Lutheran, and they were thrilled to hear from us, and they asked how many we could take, and at first I said two. But they convinced me that we could do four. They'll be arriving around Thanksgiving."

"Well, it sounds right up our alley. Of course, I'm still working here in D.C., so a lot of the work will fall on your shoulders," I remind him.

"I know, and I'm ready for it. I'll just want your help with the paperwork to get them into school and all that kind of stuff."

"Oh, of course. I will be as involved as I can. It's exciting, actually; hopefully we can be a blessing to them. But also I think integrating them into our family will be such a great experience for the rest of the kids. Do we know anything about the specific kids we'll get?"

"No, not yet. We only know they'll be teenage boys, mostly around seventeen years old, and they'll be going into high school. They are supposed to be in our home for about four months, and then Lutheran will set them up in their own place."

"Set them up in their own place at seventeen!? Ugh—that's what our society does with older kids in foster care, and they need more. They need a family. We should talk about that and see if they can have a longer period of time to have the stability of living with a family."

"I know I can count on you for the advocacy work," he laughs.

"Welcome, welcome. Come in," Hector says to Peter, Abraham, David, and Jacob as I arrive home with them from the airport. Their flight was delayed and it's nearly midnight. Hector begins to motion to our David to go out to the car to get their suitcases, when I stop him.

"They have no luggage, Hec. They have the clothes on their backs and these small folders of paperwork. That's it."

"Oh, OK. You guys are so tall," Hector says to the boys. "I don't think any clothes we have here will fit you. Tomorrow we'll have to shop." We're hoping they understand; their English is very limited.

After a few moments, I realize they're asking how they can wash their clothes.

"We have a machine for that," Hector says, and begins describing how a washing machine works. Their eyes grow wide at the description.

Finally, Abraham, the youngest, asks, "Then the clothes are wet. Where do we place them to dry?"

"We have another machine for that," Hector says.

"We must see these machines!" Abraham exclaims. And so our first activity with our four newest family members is a trip to the basement to demonstrate how the washer and dryer work.

"Let's go shopping. We have to stop at the food store first, and then we'll go buy you some clothes," Hector calls to the four boys after he has gotten everyone else off to school.

Abraham jumps back, startled, as the door at the grocery store opens automatically. He steps off the mat, the door closes. He steps back on it and the door opens. After he does this three or four times, he looks at Hector in amazement. And then he says, simply: "Only in America."

After he does this three or four times, he looks at Hector in amazement.

Peter, Abraham, David, and Jacob are so frustrated that they can't start school yet. They have little patience for the slow paperwork process. They are eager to progress in their education, which they see as their ticket to a better life. So they have taken to watching TV as a strategy for learning English. Every day they ask questions based on information they are gleaning from both the shows and the commercials.

A week before Christmas, the four of them are watching TV while all of the other children are in school. Hector walks into the living room to get the fire going in the woodstove.

"Who is this King of Prussia?" Peter asks.

"Who?" Hector replies, taken off guard.

"This King of Prussia the TV talks about every day. Who is he?"

"Oh, *that* King of Prussia. That's not a person, that's a shopping mall. They want people to shop there for Christmas gifts," Hector replies, barely stifling a laugh.

"Christmas is not for gifts. It is for the birth of Christ," Abraham says.

"You're right. But when we give gifts, it's a way of being thankful for the gift of eternal life that God has given us, and also to show God's love to one another. So speaking of gifts, what would you like for Christmas? Sue and I will be giving each of you a gift."

"No gift. No gift. Your home is good enough gift," David says.

"I wish you could pass that attitude on to the rest of the family! But seriously, we want to give you each one gift. Can you think of something you'd like?"

"I want an English dictionary," Abraham says.

"Yes, school books and dictionaries—that is what we want," Jacob confirms.

"Daddy, Daddy." SueAnn comes into the room. "I think it's time. Is Mommy here?"

"Sue! SueAnn has to go to the hospital!" Hector calls up to the second floor.

"Are you sure?" I yell back down. I am sitting at my computer finalizing my Christmas to-do list and I'd really like to finish it.

"*Mommmmyyyyyyyyyy!* Yes, I need to go now!" I hear the panic in SueAnn's voice, so I save my document and grab my purse, heading down the stairs.

"Oh, Hector. Wait until you see this baby. She is absolutely beautiful. And guess what SueAnn decided to name her? Her first name is Esperanza, which means 'hope.' And listen to this: her middle name is after your mom. It's Delvina." I'm calling Hector to let him know about our newest granddaughter.

"Esperanza Delvina. Wow—that's a big name for a little girl to live up to! Tell SueAnn I love her, and everyone at home here says congratulations."

"I will. I'm going to stay with her a little longer and then I'll be home. I still have to get organized so I can go out tomorrow to finish the Christmas shopping."

Just as I start backing the van out of my parking spot in Willow Grove, my cell phone rings. "Hello pretty lady." I hear that it's Fisher's voice on the other end of the phone.

"Hi Fisher. Haven't heard from you in a while. What's up?" Fisher's been out of jail for a few weeks, but we haven't talked much. He's living in Vermont trying to get back on his feet.

"You have a new grandchild," he says.

"I know—Esperanza was born yesterday. How did you hear already?" I ask.

"What are you talking about? I mean my son, Jordan, born today."

"You had a baby today?" I ask in shock.

"Well, not me. My girlfriend, Crystal," he says.

"I'm stunned. I don't know what to say. I didn't know a baby was expected."

"Well, I didn't talk about it while I was in jail. I wanted to wait until I got out and got everything situated. But he was born today, so I wanted you to be the first to know. Tell Pops too."

After I get off the phone, I lean my head on the steering wheel and close my eyes. Time for a chat with God: "OK, Lord, when I was walking on Myrtle Beach, you opened my eyes and gave me a new sense of hope and peace about our family, and so I was really in good spirits yesterday when Esperanza was born. But now you throw this curveball at me—another new grandchild that I didn't even know about. You really are testing me, aren't you . . . ?" My prayer trails off just in time to feel the *SMACK* of another car backing into my van.

"I'm so sorry. I didn't see you," the man is saying as I hop out of my van. I look at him askance, thinking, *How did he not see a fifteen-passenger van right in front of him?*

We exchange information and he goes on his way. I call home as the tears begin welling up in my eyes. As soon as Hector answers, I start blubbering: "Fisher had a baby and the van was in an accident and I am still not finished shopping!"

"Whoa, whoa. Slow down, calm down, and start again," Hector says calmly.

Starting again—that seems to be a theme. I take a deep breath and slowly give him all the latest news.

"Who's next for the Santa hat?" Renee asks, and Flory jumps up to take her turn. We have a tradition: whoever is giving their gifts to others gets to wear the Santa hat, and I always take a picture. We try to make the giving of gifts as much fun as the receiving.

"Here you go, Dad," Flory says, handing a wrapped package to Hector.

"How about that? Another coffee mug. I think that's the fifteenth one today. Ahhh, thanks Flory," Hector says, looking a little baffled. When the kids were young and all Christmas gifts came from craft activities or the dollar store, it wasn't unusual for him to get several coffee mugs as gifts. But I'm sure he wasn't expecting coffee mugs from everyone this year. I know he's thinking, *What is this? They all have jobs, I'm sure they could do better than this.*

The entire family is laughing by the time Isaac gets up and says, "Oh Dad, there's one last gift for you."

Hector takes it hesitantly. The package looks like it could be another coffee mug. Instead, he finds a toy airplane and a map of Puerto Rico inside. Now he really looks confused.

"Do you get it, Dad?" Chelsea asks.

"Get it? I'm not sure. What's to get?" he replies.

"We all chipped in to buy you a plane ticket so you can go to Puerto Rico next month when Mom goes to her conference!

You're going on vacation!" Soon all the kids are talking at once, describing their plan to fool him with the coffee mugs before surprising him with this special gift. In January, I'm speaking at a conference hosted by NACAC and the Adoption Exchange Association. With this gift, we can turn my work trip into a mini-vacation. It'll be a treat for both of us.

"Fun in the sun was great. But now it's back to reality. I wonder how many messes I'll have to clean up now that I'm home," Hector observes, noting the stack of mail and the blinking light on the answering machine.

The big surprise is how many of the messages are from Raj's school. Except for the time he got lost on an eighth-grade field trip, prompting the class to make "Where's Raj?" into the punchline of their graduation ceremonies, Raj has always been a straight A student and never in trouble. He attends Central High School, the city's premier college prep high school for high academic achievers. His grades have taken a tumble this year, mostly due to the number of days he's been tardy or absent. Raj has found it more and more difficult to get up in the morning and out the door on time for school.

"I just don't know what we are going to do with Raj," Hector says.

"I know. He's so bright and has so much potential, but just won't go to school, and won't talk to us about it," I add.

"I'm really tired of banging on his door every morning and trying to force him to go to school. It seems like the only interaction I have with him these days is an argument, and I don't want that."

"You know, maybe high school graduation is our goal for him, and not his goal for himself. Are we just forcing our own goals and expectations on him?" I wonder.

"What are you suggesting, that we let him drop out? I can't believe you would say that." Hector is shaking his head.

"I'm saying that it's his life and maybe we need to try to find out what he wants instead of pushing him to live up to our expectations. Let's plan to talk to him and find out if he even wants to graduate, and then if he says no, we'll figure out Plan B. But if he says yes, we'll have to work together to find a way to get him through it without these daily battles."

"OK, I can see that as a starting point. And why don't we ask your brother to come for that meeting? Raj really respects David, and I think that might help the conversation to go more smoothly," Hector suggests.

"Good idea. And one other thing. Raj seems to be at his best late at night, so I think that's when we should have this conversation."

"I really want to be there to see Raj graduate; I haven't missed one yet. So you need to give me the date so I can make my travel plans." My mom has called to get the ball rolling for her trip to Philadelphia. I give her the date and explain a little of what is going on with Raj academically.

"Mom, just book the ticket. I can't guarantee that Raj will graduate, but it's looking more likely," I tell her. Ever since our late-night meeting with Raj and my brother, things have been much better. Raj expressed that he does, indeed, want to graduate, and gave us a little more insight into why he was having such trouble getting up in the morning.

We've been working with the guidance counselors to get a 504 plan in place to make appropriate accommodations so that he can take most of his classes in the afternoon and do some independent work from home. As soon as these were in place, his grades began to climb to their former levels. He still has to get through finals, but it's looking good for him not only to graduate but also to be back on the honor roll in the process. I'm so thankful for my little online prayer circle of friends who have helped me gain the wisdom and patience to navigate this unfamiliar territory.

"They're here! They're here!" Alysia excitedly punches the words into her Delta Talker. Just two weeks after Raj's graduation, Dan and Pam, friends from our Mill River House Church days, pull into our driveway leading a caravan that includes a dozen teenagers from Northampton's College Church youth group and a few other adults. They've come to spend several days with us, doing work projects on our house and having some fun in Philadelphia at the same time. They'll learn about our family and our mission to ensure that all children have homes. In turn, their work experience at our house will help equip and prepare them for future mission trips sponsored by their church.

"I can't believe all the work you've done. Everyone really deserves a break, so let's get ready to head into the city for the parade and fireworks," I say, admiring the painting job the teens have completed on two of our bedrooms, while others have completely cleaned out our basement and washed all of our windows. The days have been punctuated by hard work each morning, afternoon swims and singing, and marshmallows and devotions around the campfire in the evening. Todd and Alysia have enjoyed participating with the visiting teens.

"And don't forget Garth Brooks," Hector adds. Renowned singers perform every year at Philly's Independence Day festivities, but I've never seen Hector as excited as he is this year to see Garth Brooks in person.

"Oh, what a night," Pam says to Hector as we get the last of the teens off to bed.

"I was so disappointed that Garth Brooks only played two songs. That has never happened before; all the musicians who come here usually give us a full concert. Thank goodness for Jill Scott; she was good. And then the rain! Oh my, what a fiasco running back to the train while the fireworks were still exploding. But I think the kids still had a good time," Hector replies.

"Oh, they had a great time. It's a night they'll remember, that's for sure. And who will ever forget David, leading us all to the train by holding his umbrella high in the air? Good thing we had him or we may have lost a few," Pam laughs.

As soon as our guests leave, we have to get ready for this year's summer road trip. We're heading to Charlotte, North Carolina in a caravan of three vehicles. Everyone enjoyed going to NACAC so much last summer that they petitioned us to go again this year. Isaac's best friend wanted to come, so that added an extra driver, sealing the deal. SueAnn is going to speak on a panel and I'm teaching a couple of workshops. The kids are excited about staying in a hotel again.

Summer ends; it's time for another school year and more new beginnings. Our family from Kosovo has told us that they can't really go home again after all. One of their nieces, a teenager, died due to unavailability of medications. They are returning to the U.S. for good this time. They ask if they can stay with us again until they get an apartment and jobs lined up, and of course we say yes. We are eager to see them again and happy we can help.

With all this activity, the fall flies by, and before we know it, we're turning the calendar to 2002.

"I can't believe we're into another year already. My grandfather was right. Time really does go faster the older you get," I say to Geeta.

"I'm happy it's 2002 because I will graduate this year," she replies.

"I know, and we have to get busy figuring out what you are going to do after graduation. I was thinking about the Elwyn program where David went. That might be perfect for you. Do you want to look into it?"

"Can they teach me to be a chef?"

"Well, they do offer food service skills. That's how David got his job at St. Joe's. So let's check it out. I'll talk to Dad about calling the Voc-Rehab office so we can get the ball rolling."

"OK, Mom," Geeta says, heading off to make a snack.

Hector and Alysia walk in from her physical therapy appointment. "How'd it go?" I ask.

"Great," Alysia replies.

"They say she is a good candidate for the botox treatment, and our insurance covers it, so we made the appointment to get started," Hector explains.

"Wow, that's great. Are you excited?" I ask Alysia. I can see from her broad smile, though, that the question is moot.

A few weeks later, Hector walks into my office and sees me staring at the computer screen. "What are you doing?"

"I'm trying to figure out time zones so we can try to call Jose, Chelsea, Isaac, and Raj on Easter."

"I'm really proud of them—they're all doing great things," Hector replies. Jose is living and working in Switzerland. Chelsea is studying abroad at Macquarie University in Australia. Isaac is living and learning in India as part of a program called Let There Be Dragons. And Raj is going to Atlanta during spring break to build houses for Habitat for Humanity.

"I know. It's a dream come true. I always hoped we'd have kids interested in community service and international studies. It's just funny that all four of them are doing it the same year."

"It's always great to broaden your horizons. I learned so much from my semester in England when I was in college," Hector remembers. "These trips could be life-changing for our kids. Who knows how God will use these opportunities in their lives?"

"Here's your wine." I hold a glass out to Barbara as we sit down to relax in front of the fireplace. Although it's May and no fire is blazing, it's still the favorite gathering spot in the house.

"How was your trip up from D.C.?" Hector asks. My dear friend and mentor Barbara Pryor from Senator Rockefeller's office has come to visit us for a few hours during a trip to Philadelphia.

"Dad, I'm leaving for baseball. Are you coming to the game?" Aaron says as he passes through, followed by Joelle.

"I have play practice tonight. My friend's parents are giving me a ride, but I need you to pick me up, Dad," Joelle says as she hurries out the door.

"Mom, I need you to write me a check for my senior dues by tomorrow, or they won't order my cap and gown," Geeta yells down from the second floor.

"Dad, Todd took my laundry out before it was dry!" Alysia comes stomping into the room carrying a basket of damp clothes.

"Sorry for all the interruptions," I apologize to Barbara.

"Are you kidding? I have the best seat in the house!" Barbara exclaims. "Who needs a TV when there's all this action. I'm having a great time." Just then George comes charging in the front door. Looks like he just ran over from his apartment two blocks away.

"Mom, Patrice is having contractions. The doctor says we have to go to the hospital; she really wants you to be with her. Can you come now?" he says, his words tumbling out in a rush.

"Oh, Barbara . . . " I begin.

"No worries. You need to go. I'll stay and visit with Hector and maybe we'll finish our wine!" she laughs. "And call us when you have news. How many grandchildren will this make?"

"Sixteen, but whose counting?" I say as I get up and tell George I'll be with him as soon as I get my purse.

344

"And another one due in a few weeks, but hopefully we get through Geeta's graduation before that one comes."

Hours later I call home to give Hector the news. "Destin is one big baby. But Patrice did great and everyone is resting now. I'll be home soon. Did Barbara leave? She must think we run a crazy house."

"Yes, she had to go. She said for you to give her a call tomorrow. She was pretty amused by all the activity. We had a nice visit. Give Patrice and George my congratulations. I'll see the baby when they come home in two days."

This summer, our only road trip is to Vermont. My sisters, brother, and I have decided to host a pig roast in honor of my mom's upcoming marriage to Steve Martin, a man we have all known since we were children and our two families vacationed together in Maine. It's fitting that Mom is getting married in Maine, in a small ceremony, so the pig roast will be a chance for all of the grandchildren, nieces, and nephews to celebrate with her.

"Look at Mamie. She's so happy!" JD says to me while filling his plate.

"I know," I say. "We're all so thrilled that she has opened herself up to a new chapter in her life. She grieved so hard and long after my dad died, she deserves another turn at happiness, and Steve is a really good man. We all love him."

By the time September begins, Geeta has graduated and started at Elwyn; Chelsea has returned from Australia and started her senior year at Arcadia; David is back to work at St Joe's; Flory's second baby, Chantelle, has been born; and we are easing into the rhythm of the back-to-school routines with Aaron still at Henry and Alysia, Todd, Joelle, Dylan, and Wayne at high schools around the city. I'm back to work in D.C., and Hector is picking up two-year-old Esperanza every day from her Montessori school while SueAnn works as a hairdresser.

"I have to tell you about a piece of mail I got today," Hector says as we begin our nightly phone conversation.

"Oh no!" I groan. "We can't take any more kids or families!"

"No. I knew you'd think that. I had to say it that way," he laughs.

"OK, you got me. So what is it, then?"

"I got a flyer about a men's hockey league at the University of Pennsylvania. It looks like most of the players are alums of Penn, but you don't have to be to play."

"And you're thinking of playing? I'm not going to call it a mid-life crisis, but you are about to turn 46, you know," I tease.

"I know. It's a non-checking league, so I wouldn't get hurt. What do you think?"

"I think that's a terrific idea. I would love to see you play hockey again," I reply enthusiastically.

"The only problem is, I don't have any of the equipment, and even secondhand that can be expensive."

"Hmmm. Well, your birthday is coming up. Maybe the kids and I can chip in and get it for you. I'll talk to them if you are sure this is what you want."

"Yes, I really miss playing. This will be fun."

"So much for the non-checking league," I say as Hector winces in pain from two broken ribs.

"It was fun while it lasted. I guess I'm just too old to hang with those twenty-somethings," he says.

"It was great going to your games; brought back lots of memories. I just wish it didn't end with an injury. I remember when I had broken ribs. It's not bad as long as you don't cough. Or sneeze. Or laugh. Or breathe." I chuckle.

"Ooooh, stop. Don't make me laugh," he says, wincing again.

"I hope the kids help you out. I can't stay home this week. I have three days in D.C. for my work with the Pew Commission and two days in New York for the Longest Waiting Kids project. I just hope I keep it straight and get on the right train on the right day."

"I'll be fine, the kids will be fine. Go out there and change the world," Hector says, giving my hand a small squeeze.

A few days later, I'm sitting in my little studio apartment in D.C. waiting for Hector to call. It is later than usual when the phone finally rings. "Sue, my sister Rejeanne just called." His voice is shaking. This can't be good.

He recounts the conversation. His mother is in the hospital and not doing well. "I knew this day was coming, but I'd hoped she would rebound again like she has all the other times," he says.

His sister told Hector that his mom has talked with all her other kids. "You're the last one, Hector. I think she is waiting for you before she can let go," she told him.

"I was crying like a baby by that point, but tried to pull myself together so I could talk to my mom. So I took the phone and tried to make some jokes with her, but she didn't make a sound . . . " His voice starts to trail off, then he continues. "So I said, 'Mommy, I hope you know how much I love you, and you're the best mom anyone can have. I wish I could be there with you . . . '" He is sobbing, and we pause for a few quiet moments.

"Did she respond?" I gently ask.

"No. The next thing I know, Cecile is talking into the phone. She says, 'Hector, I think Mommy heard you because she moved her eyes and hands when you were talking to her.' Oh Sue, I hope she did hear me, because I know that'll probably be the last chance I have to talk to her. I just hope God takes her quickly now. I don't want her to suffer. I told Cecile to give her a big hug for me."

"Do you want me to see if I can find a flight so you can fly up there tonight? Or first thing in the morning?" I ask.

"No. I'm glad I had the chance to talk to her, but I'm happy remembering her the way I last saw her—happy and healthy. I'm not sure I want to see her this way," Hector says.

The next morning, I am sitting at my Pew Commission on Children in Foster Care desk in Georgetown when my cell phone rings, and I can see that it's Hector. He almost never calls me at work, so immediately I know what's happened.

"Hec, is it your mom?"

"Yes, Sue. My brother Bernie called at three in the morning. It was a short conversation. He just said, 'Mommy is gone.'"

"You could have called me right away," I say.

"I wanted you to sleep, and I needed some time with my own thoughts. If anyone ever empathized with me, raising a large family, it was my mom, and now she's gone." He starts to cry again.

"I'll be home as soon as possible," I say.

"We need to rent some vehicles to get everyone to Vermont. And we'll need places to stay once we are up there," he says.

"I'll make those arrangements, don't worry. See you soon."

We rent three vans for the trip, and thankfully my mother and sister have agreed to find places for all of us to stay—two or three each at the homes of various family and friends. I am deeply touched to learn that Aunt Deanna, Uncle Freddy, and Uncle Philip all plan to come to Barre for the funeral. *It's going to be really hard on the kids*, I think to myself, knowing how close they all were to their beloved Mamere. All of the pallbearers are grandchildren, one from each family. Isaac was chosen to represent our family.

At the end of the service, we drive past the cemetery where she will be buried in the spring. "Good-bye, Mom. *Au revoir, je t'aime*," Hector says quietly.

"I know we can't make it back up there for the internment ceremony, so I want to read you what I wrote for it. If you like it, we'll send it up to your sister Irene so it can be read at the ceremony," I say to Hector a few days after we get home from Vermont.

The power of family was vividly demonstrated when 115 family members proceeded from the funeral home to the church for the celebration of life for Delvina Badeau, fondly known to all as "Mamere."

In that procession, among her sons and daughters, grandsons and granddaughters, through birth, marriages, and adoption, were people of all ages, representing many races and ethnicities. Some are stonecutters like their grandfather and others homemakers like their grandmother. In between, nearly every profession imaginable is represented—family members engaged in medical, legal, social work, banking and business, education, engineering, sales, construction, athletics, arts, massage therapy, manufacturing and production, truck driving, ministry, politics, child care, information technology, and more.

Family members share a foundation of Christian faith lived out in many ways. Some have fought for their country, while others have protested war. Some have been married for decades; others are gay, single, or have experienced the trauma of divorce. Some never left the city of their birth, others have gone to far-flung locations to pursue their dreams.

Mamere had an uncanny ability to see and draw out the best in everyone. And so, in spite of the diversity and distance represented in this family, we all came together, by car and van, by bus and train and plane, to honor and celebrate her life. We came together because we all share a common bond—a bond of love for and devotion to Mamere. Each one of us can recount a time when we were down, or facing a struggle or challenge, and she was there as an anchor, to hold us secure until we were able to find our way again.

She accepted every child with equal affection—regardless of the circumstances of their birth, the color of their skin, or the disabilities they had. She lived a life of integrity and dignity with warmth and humor. She could press a dishtowel into service as a diaper and turn a handful of random ingredients into a meal. Whether washing dishes, sewing a dress, knitting mittens, or making soup, we could always count on her for a good story, a good laugh, and a lesson about life. Most importantly, she had an unwavering faith and an unshakable "joie de vivre."

Au revoir, Mamere, until we meet again.

"That captures her perfectly, Sue. Thank you for writing that," Hector says, and we hug silently for several long moments.

The chill of winter gives way to the warmth of spring, and it's the season for school concerts, plays, dance recitals, and baseball games.

"I'll meet you at Aaron's game after I finish up the groceries. And don't forget—we have Joelle's school play tonight," I let Hector know as he and Aaron head over to Sedgwick Field. David hops on his bike to join them.

"I remember, and that reporter is meeting me at the game; he wants to interview you too," Hector reminds me. A reporter, Michael Vitez from the *Philadelphia Inquirer*, is doing a special story on Hector for Father's Day, to be published in a few weeks.

"Oh yeah, that's right. He's not bringing a photographer, is he?" I ask, looking at my baggy sweats and stained Phillies T-shirt.

"No, not that I know of."

"Come on, Aaron. Knock it out of the park," Hector yells, while Vitez asks me questions about my job and our family life. He's particularly interested to hear more about other parents who call Hector for parenting advice.

"They know there is practically no parenting dilemma that he has not experienced firsthand. If we had a nickel for every phone-counseling session he has done with other parents over the years, our house would be paid off and we would have no problems putting our kids through college," I tell him, laughing.

The whole family loves sports, and in the years we have lived in Philly we have transferred our allegiances from New England teams to Philadelphia teams. It's no surprise, then, when Chelsea tells me that for her college graduation, instead of a party, she wants to go to a Sixers game with Hector, me, my brother, mom, and Steve.

"So tell me more about your summer internship," Steve asks on our way home from the game.

"I'll be working for Senator Landrieu from Louisiana. I'll be using my communications degree, working with her press office, but I'll also get to work on some policy issues," Chelsea says. Last summer, she had an internship with a national newspaper, *Youth Today,* based in D.C., and this year she will again stay at my little apartment while working in the Senate. When she returns, she has a job at Comcast waiting for her.

"I always knew you were going to go far, Chelsea, and it looks like you are already on that path," my mom says.

"Its been great having some time with you, Mom, and hard to believe, but we'll see you again in a few weeks for Joelle's graduation. So get some rest in between!"

"Every time I'm here for a graduation it is hot as Hades," my mom says, asking Alysia to please go get her a bottle of water.

Abraham has just arrived and we are ready to cut the cake and pass out the gifts. Joelle graduated from Roxborough today, and Abraham from Central High School.

"We're so proud of both of you," Hector says, already getting choked up. It is a running joke in the family that he can't give the graduation gifts without bawling like a baby.

"Joelle, no one expected you to live when you were born, barely weighing two pounds. And Abraham, you survived the jungles of Sudan and the jungles of Philadelphia, and now you're both headed to college. I propose a toast."

"Here here!" we all say, raising our glasses high.

"No graduations next year, Hec. I wonder what we'll find to do next summer?"

"I'm can't even imagine," he laughs.

> "We're so proud of both of you," Hector says, already getting choked up. It is a running joke in the family that he can't give the graduation gifts without bawling like a baby.

22

Dangers and Detours

"How many birthdays are we celebrating today?" Hector asks, coming into the kitchen to get his coffee and seeing that I'm already working on food preparations.

"Only three," I reply. "Chelsea, Flory, and Geeta. We didn't do Chelsea's in May because of Mother's Day and Memorial Day, so we're throwing her in with the early June ones. We'll do the rest of the June birthdays later in the month."

"OK, got it. What do you need me to do?"

"Just make sure the tables and chairs in the backyard are ready to use, and I'm counting on you to grill the burgers and dogs. Flory and Chelsea both asked for fajitas and Geeta's part of the meal is the ice cream cake, so I've got that handled inside."

"OK. When do things need to be ready?"

"I told everyone we'll be eating by 3. Oh, and one more thing, I'll need the coolers wiped down—we used them for Memorial Day and they're still sitting outside collecting rain."

"That was already on my list. I'll have time to do all of that after church. I'm going out to the porch to have my coffee. Give me a holler if you need anything."

"Did you make me a coffee?"

"It's next to the toaster." He points on his way out of the room.

I do a quick head count before we get started. Daniel, Aaron, and Todd are horsing around in the pool. Jasmine and Esperanza are on the trampoline, and Chantelle's playing in the sandbox. The adults and teens are sitting in clusters wherever there's shade. Including friends, there are 35 people. I hope I've made enough food.

"Food's ready!" Hector hollers to the kids scattered across the backyard.

"Let's sing 'Happy Birthday' to our birthday girls, then we'll pray and eat," I say as everyone gathers in our breakfast room.

"Rub-a-dub-dub, thanks for the grub! Let's eat," Hector jokes.

"Not so fast," I say, giving him the look.

"I know, I know. OK, everyone, let's bow our heads. Jasmine, Esperanza, fold your hands. Daniel, Aaron, hush. OK, let's pray . . . Dear Lord, thank you for this beautiful day and time to enjoy it together as a family. We lift up to you our family members who are not here today, especially Jose in Switzerland and Fisher in jail, and pray that you'll be with them. We thank you for the three girls whose birthdays we celebrate today, Chelsea, Geeta, and Flory. We pray they will listen to you and follow your path and that you will help them to grow both in wisdom and kindness in the year ahead. And we thank you for the food we are about to eat. Amen."

"Wait, Mom. Before you serve the food, we have an announcement to make," Chelsea says loudly, getting everyone's attention. "We know it's not your birthday, or Dad's, but we have to give you this now, and you'll see why once you open it." She continues, motioning for Hector to come stand beside me and handing us a large, thick envelope.

We open the card, which reads "Happy Anniversary" on the outside. Inside, there's a letter, several pamphlets, and signatures of all the kids, even those in Vermont.

"What is this? Our anniversary is still six weeks away," Hector says, confused.

"Read the letter, Dad," SueAnn says.

"You read it, Sue. That's your department," he says to me.

"What? Are you kidding?" I say after reading the letter, which has informed us that Hector and I will enjoy a week of camping at Maidstone in Vermont for our 25th anniversary coming up in July.

"The plans are all set, Mom and Dad. You're going back to where you had your honeymoon. We bought you a plane ticket to fly to Burlington and reserved a rental car for you to drive up to Maidstone," Chelsea says, pointing out the materials inside the card.

"But . . . Wayne and Dylan?" Hector asks.

"They're all set too, Dad. SueAnn, Flory, Joelle, and I are going to be in charge of them. We have a whole schedule figured out," Isaac says.

"Did you see the gift card to REI? There's money on that, so you can buy new camping gear—whatever you need. Just remember you have to take it on the plane, so don't go too crazy," Abel laughs.

"I'm overwhelmed. Thank you, kids. This is too much. But we'll take it!" I laugh.

SueAnn pipes up. "We did try to get you the same lean-to you had for your honeymoon, but it was already reserved, so we had to get you a different one, but it's still on the lake."

"So Dad, you have a whole week to do 'whatever' you want!"

George says.

"Well, you know what I say about that, George: 'If the room is rockin', don't come knockin'!'" Hector jokes, which elicits a chorus of "*ewwwwws*." David laughs and gives Hector a high five.

"Gross, Dad. That's TMI," Renee says.

"What's Poppa mean about the room rockin'?" our grandson Daniel asks.

"It means we like to dance sometimes," I tell him. "Now let's eat before the food gets cold, and we can talk more about this while we're eating."

"This is beautiful, Sue," Hector says six weeks later, sitting back to admire the campfire he just made.

"It sure is. And so peaceful. Look up—we can see zillions of stars. We don't get to see them like this in Philly."

"No, we sure don't. Are you interested in s'mores? I thought that might be fun, and a little chocolate is always romantic, so who knows what that might lead to?" Hector jokes.

"Who knows . . . " I say with a smile.

"It's been a great week. I'm sad to leave. It's amazing that this park has not changed one bit since we were here 25 years ago. We need to come again before 25 more years slip by," I say as we drive away, heading for Burlington and then home.

"I agree. The weather, the campfires, playing backgammon, good food—it was just like our original honeymoon week," Hector adds.

"Yeah, and swimming in the lake, watching the loons, and the canoe rides, that's my favorite part," I say.

"Mine too, although my arms are aching. I think rowing uses muscles I haven't used in 25 years," Hector jokes. "It's been great that our phones don't work up here, but I hope everything is OK at home."

"The kids knew how to reach the park rangers if there was an emergency," I say. "I'm sure they were fine. But we do have to get to where we have phone service and call them this morning so we can firm up our plans for getting home from the airport. I don't want to schlep all this stuff on the train, and the price of a taxi is ridiculous."

A few miles outside of the campground we pull into a gas station and I notice that we have cell service again. "You get the gas and I'll call home," I say.

"Are we all set?" Hector asks when we are back on the road.

"I guess so, but it was a strange conversation with Chelsea. She first told me everything is fine at home, that Dylan and Wayne are doing great, but then she said everyone's too busy to come get us at the airport. So she's not sure who it will be— maybe one of their friends."

"What? There are, what?—six, seven, drivers at home and no one can pick us up? What's wrong with these kids?" Hector fumes.

"Relax, it's been such a great week, let's not get stressed now. Chelsea ended the call by saying, 'It's cool, Mom, just go with the flow.'"

"I guess we have no choice," he says.

"Did you hear the pilot say it's 93 degrees in Philly? Oh, I miss Maidstone already," I laugh as Hector grabs our bags from the overhead compartment.

"I wonder who'll be picking us up?"

We emerge from the plane and walk toward baggage claim. "Look," Hector points.

At the bottom of the escalator where all the limo drivers are standing, one of them has a sign that says "Badeau" on it.

As we approach him, he says, "Mr. and Mrs. Badeau? Follow me." Hector turns and looks at me suspiciously.

"Go with the flow," I whisper.

"I've never been in a limo before, Sue. What are these crazy kids up to?" Hector says as we pull away from the airport.

"This driver isn't taking the most direct route to our house," I point out. "I hope the kids aren't paying him by the mile."

A few moments later, the driver pulls into the Hyatt Hotel on the Penn's Landing waterfront. "Give me a moment," he says to us.

When he returns to the car, he hands us a card and then starts unloading our luggage and stacking it on the bellman's cart.

"Dear Mom and Dad, Welcome back to Philly! We hope you loved your week of camping, but we thought you'd like one night of luxury in a nice hotel before coming back to reality at home. So we've reserved you a room here at the Hyatt and you'll also be going out to dinner at Susanna Foo's tonight. Please wait in the room for the driver, who will knock on your door at 7:10 to take you to the restaurant."

I read the card aloud to Hector, and we shake our heads in amazement. Inside the envelope are also two room keys.

"The room is on the 22nd floor. That's right up there," Hector says as we get into the elevator. "Wait, look. We each have a different room number on our keys. That's odd. Why would they put us in separate rooms?" he wonders aloud.

"This is getting curiouser and curiouser. Also, I have no idea what we'll wear to Susanna Foo's. The only clothes we have with us are camping clothes, and most of them are dirty," I say as the elevator doors open on the 22nd floor. . . .

"Oh my goodness, look at this! This is not like any room I've ever seen. Plenty of space to chase you around—and we have three hours before dinner!" Hector says, throwing his arms open and looking around in awe.

"It never occurred to me that two keys meant a suite. Oh, look. A bottle of champagne and chocolate-covered strawberries!"

"Come over here. Look out the window; the view is spectacular. The kids really went all out on this."

"Oh my goodness. The closet is full of clothes—a suit for you and a dress for me. Shoes too," I say before joining Hector by the window.

"Too much, too much. Let's have a glass of that champagne and sit out here on the balcony."

"Good idea, but I'm going to shower first. I loved everything about Maidstone except the bathrooms," I laugh, heading for the shower.

"We each have our own bathroom, so I guess I can shower at the same time," Hector jokes.

"I'm all ready. Let's head down to the lobby," Hector says at a few minutes after seven.

"No, the card said to wait in the room until 7:10. The kids have planned every detail, it seems, so we should follow their instructions," I remind him.

At precisely 7:10, there is a knock on our door. The woman standing in front of us is a hotel employee, not a driver. "I'll take you to your car," she says, but then pushes the button for the third floor when we get into the elevator.

"Why are we stopping on the third floor?" Hector whispers to me seconds before the doors open.

"*Surprise!*"

The hallway outside the elevator is filled with a sea of familiar faces. They all blur together until I see Jose. "Jose! How did you get here?"

"This is the grand finale of your anniversary surprise!" we hear Chelsea saying. I put my hands to my face and rub my eyes, looking again to make sure I'm not dreaming.

After hugging Jose, I see Nancy, one of my best friends from Smith and a bridesmaid in my wedding. There's Anne, my friend since first grade. And Courtney and MaryLee from D.C. Looking around, I see nearly all of our out-of-town family and local friends from church and work. I can't believe so many people traveled so far to spend this evening with us.

Moments later, Hector's at my side, saying, "Look who's here," and I'm swept into a hug by his friend Ricky from college, another member of our original wedding party.

Later in the evening, I'm sitting at my table watching Hector dance with each of the girls in turn. I'm trying to absorb all the precious details that made this night so special. SueAnn's handmade centerpieces and name cards, a cake designed exactly like our wedding cake, my brother's hilarious stint as stand-up comic and emcee, Isaac's toast, Renee's poem, Alysia's breathtaking dance that left not a dry eye in the house, Chelsea's video rendition of our life together.

And then the moment when Hector and I are called to the center of the dance floor for a renewal of vows, and all of the guests that were also at our original ceremony make a circle around us.

"I can't believe our kids pulled all of this off without us catching on," Hector says when we get back to our room at the end of the festivities.

"I know. I can't imagine how they did that. I'm guessing they waited till the last minute to tell a few of the kids—you know, Todd or George, the ones who always spill the beans," I laugh.

"And did you see how handsome Wayne and Dylan looked in their new clothes? They fit right in. I just don't want the evening to end."

"We still have breakfast tomorrow before it's back to reality," I say.

"And it's not a bad reality, when you think about it. Happy silver anniversary, Mrs. Badeau," Hector says.

We had no way of knowing in that moment that we were on the brink of the worst few months of reality that we'd ever faced.

> "And it's not a bad reality, when you think about it. Happy silver anniversary, Mrs. Badeau," Hector says.

We say good-bye to most of the out-of-town guests after breakfast the next morning at the hotel, but a few want to stop by the house to see the work we've had done on the front porch and kitchen. As we sit on the porch opening the gifts we've received, the talk turns to memories of other projects we have done on the house in the past.

"How's the back porch holding up?" Uncle Freddy asks, and he and Hector take a walk out back so he can look at it.

"It's held up well—it's been nine years since that work weekend, and with all the wear and tear things get around here, that's more like dog years!" I laugh. I join them with the photos from that Memorial Day weekend in 1995 when Fred and Deanna and their three kids and my brother all came to have a porchraising bee at the back of our house.

"Look how young everyone looks!" SueAnn exclaims.

"Oh, was I really that skinny?" Jose asks.

"It was amazing to get a whole porch and staircase rebuilt in a weekend. We have an awesome family," I say.

"Well, Mom, Dad, I have to get to the airport. I have work back in Switzerland waiting for me," Jose says, putting an end to the trip down memory lane. This begins a final round of hugs, and soon, everyone is gone.

****

"Can we just tear the rest of the Sundays this year off our calendar?" Hector asks despondently. Three Sundays in a row since the anniversary party —and three bombshells of difficult news.

First, Geeta tells us she is pregnant. She approaches Hector while I'm out of town attending a bridal shower for my cousin Ingrid. "I'm so sorry, Dad," she says.

"How are you going to support yourself and a baby?" Hector bellows.

"Will treats me good. He will support us."

"He has a job, that's good. But there is more to being a parent than that. You don't have any idea . . . " Hector's voice trails off.

"I help you with Wayne and Dylan. I can do it," Geeta says.

"Oh, this is not what we wanted for you," Hector says, his eyes filling with tears.

After a few moments of silence, he gives her a hug, saying, "We still love you, and we'll try to support you. We have to figure out what that means now."

When Hector calls to tell me the news, I feel as though I've been sucker punched in the gut again. The news is too fresh to discuss coherently, so he changes the subject, asking how the shower was.

"It was a beautiful shower and Ingrid is so radiant. I'm so happy for her. She's really in love, and Mark's family is so nice. But I'm worried about my mom. Ever since she left Philly after our anniversary party, apparently she hasn't been feeling well."

"Hmmm, she looked great at the party," Hector notes.

"I know, that's what's so odd. This came on pretty suddenly. She's going in for some tests next week."

The following Sunday, Chelsea lingers a little after our Sunday family dinner and asks to chat with us on the porch.

"You're not going to be happy with what I have to tell you," she begins. I brace myself.

"What is it?"

"I'm pregnant. It's not like I'm still in high school or even college. I've graduated and have a good job and Lashon and I love each other," she says quickly.

"This is so not what we hoped for you, Chelsea," Hector manages to say weakly.

"I know, and I'm really sorry. I didn't want to let you and Mom down." She's beginning to cry softly. "Sometimes life just doesn't go the way you plan."

"Speaking of plans, what are yours?" I ask.

"Lashon and I are going to get married. We aren't sure when yet. We'll work out the details, but we've been talking about getting married anyway. This will just step up the timetable."

"Are you sure, Chelsea?" Hector asks.

"Yes, I'm sure. Lashon and I are the same age you and Mom were when you had me. It'll work out."

We hug Chelsea and assure her of our love, promising to do what we can to support her, but I'm sure the disappointment shows in our faces as we say goodnight.

"Where did we go wrong, Sue?"

"I don't know, I just don't know. I love every one of our grandchildren. I do, I really do. But I just wish . . . Oh never mind. Wishing isn't going to change anything."

And now, it's Sunday again, and I have just received devastating news. My mother has leukemia. She has an appointment scheduled this week at the Dana-Farber Cancer Center in Boston; until then she won't know much about the prognosis or treatment options.

"I feel like I have to go up there," I tell Hector.

"I understand. Maybe you have some airline points you can

use and get a flight."

"Good idea. I wish you could come too, but after being gone to Maidstone just a month ago, it's too soon for both of us to be gone again. It's too much to expect the kids to take care of Dylan and Wayne and everything at home."

"You're right. Maybe one of the girls can go with you. Why don't you take Chelsea? I think the two of you need a little mother-daughter time right now anyway."

"You know, that's actually a good idea," I say, giving him a hug.

We've struggled emotionally all through September from the bombshells we received in August, but this weekend we are trying to enjoy a good time at my cousin's wedding. "They say bad news comes in threes, and we've had our three, so I hope it's all good news from here on," I say as we get dressed in our hotel room.

I didn't realize how clueless we were about the bad news that would be waiting when we return home.

"Let's go have some fun. I'm ready to dance the night away," Hector says, looking dapper in his suit.

"All hell has broken loose here," he says the minute he answers the phone. **"What is it? What's going on?"**

"Call me when you get to Philly," I say to Hector as we go our separate ways on Monday morning after the wedding. He's driving home; I'm flying directly to Ohio for a speaking engagement.

I step down from the podium on Tuesday and check my phone. I have four missed calls from Hector. This can't be good. He never calls me when I'm working. I look for a quiet corner and punch in his number.

"All hell has broken loose here," he says the minute he answers the phone.

"What is it? What's going on?"

"I can't even say I fully know. It's so confusing."

"Start at the beginning and tell me what's up."

"Well, I got home yesterday afternoon and everything seemed fine. All the kids were at school and the house was still standing. Just before it was time for Dylan's bus to come, one of Alysia's teachers calls and asks if Alysia can come spend the night at her house, saying it's a birthday party for her niece, who is Alysia's age. I said OK. We know this teacher and she has been a good mentor for Alysia. Why would I question her?" Hector pauses, his voice cracking.

"OK, did something happen at the teacher's house?"

"No, no. As far as I know she spent the night and went to school this morning. But then, I get a call from the police . . . "

"Police?" I interrupt. Now *I* am getting confused.

"Apparently something happened over the weekend while we were at the wedding. Alysia ended up getting seriously hurt, although she didn't tell anyone until she went to school on Monday. She told this teacher, and that's why she took her home Monday night. The part about the birthday party was a lie."

"I don't understand. Our daughter is hurt, and a teacher takes her home and doesn't tell us? . . . I'm very confused. And I still don't understand why the police are involved. I hope you can make this make sense," I plead.

"No, I can't. But let me tell you the rest. I guess the teacher thought either that we were directly involved in hurting Alysia or at least that we didn't protect her, so that's why she took her home."

"That was wrong," I say.

"Sure was. But then this morning, the school called the police and they came over to open an investigation. Turns out a few things went on while we were at the wedding. Not just Alysia getting hurt, but other stuff too. By the time they were finished they were arresting Abel and . . ."

Hector starts to cry. I can't understand the rest of what he is saying.

"OK, we've been through tough times before. We'll get through this. I'm done here in Ohio, and I'll get home as soon as I can. Sometimes when it rains it pours, but we'll figure it out." I'm just gushing platitudes because I don't know what else to do. My head is spinning and my heart feels as though it has stopped.

"This isn't pouring rain, Sue. This is a tornado; everything is spinning out of control. Just get home as soon as you can."

"I will, I promise." We hang up.

"OK, we've been through tough times before. We'll get through this. I'm done here in Ohio, and I'll get home as soon as I can. Sometimes when it rains it pours, but we'll figure it out." I'm just gushing platitudes because I don't know what else to do.

The next two weeks go by in a blur. We have multiple meetings with social workers, doctors, and psychologists regarding Alysia, and with police and lawyers regarding Abel. It doesn't seem possible that one weekend could lead to such tragic outcomes for not one, but two of our kids. And all of the other kids are reeling from the shock, grief, and confusion. We still don't know fully what happened and have come to accept that perhaps we never will. We love them both so much and feel utterly useless. We cry out to God, but feel as though he's not listening.

"I've never before felt so much like a failure," Hector says as we numbly walk out of the courtroom after Abel's hearing. "When we adopted him, he seemed so grown up as a ten-year-old, but he was really just a little boy. A little boy who had been hurt and deeply scarred in his life. I feel we tried our best to give him a good home, love, prayers, nurture, support. And he has been a wonderful son—helpful, funny, kind.

"Yet now, this, and he has to go to jail for eight years. I am scared for him and I feel that somehow I must have let him down, let God down . . . wasn't a good enough father for him over the years. My heart is breaking."

Hector slumps against the wall and begins to sob openly.

I go to him and try to give him a comforting hug, but he brushes me aside.

"And then what about Alysia? We adopted her as a precious one-year-old. She had never been a victim of abuse or neglect. She has disabilities. It was our job to raise her well and protect her. And yet she gets hurt in our own home, under our own roof, on our watch. How did this happen? How did we fail to protect her? Why does she now have to suffer a lifetime of consequences because we failed as parents? Why did God allow this?"

Hector's sobs are getting louder; people are turning to look at us.

"Why did God call us to adopt these kids if He knew we were not fit for the assignment?" he says despondently. After several long minutes, he stands up and we walk out of the building.

> We both go through the motions of daily life, but it's almost as though we are watching from a distance while one-dimensional actors are play-acting our parts.

For the next several weeks, I feel numb. We both go through the motions of daily life, but it's almost as though we are watching from a distance while one-dimensional actors are play-acting our parts.

I have one close friend, another adoptive parent, who has been through something similar in her own family.

Yet I don't reach out to her because I feel too guilty for how little I did to support her when she was in that dark valley.

I try to explain my jumbled feelings by writing an e-mail to a friend:

You know that nursery rhyme about Jack and Jill? I feel as though I am the parent of both Jack and Jill. Two of my children have fallen down and cracked their crowns, and I can't help them, can't stop it and now, I can't heal them. I am seriously depressed. I don't mean a little bit bummed out or down in the dumps. I mean truly, seriously depressed. I've never felt this way before even in the worst moments in my past. I try to pray but I feel like I am praying into a black hole. Reading the Bible does nothing more for me than reading the newspaper. Cognitively, I have not lost my faith, I still "believe," but I feel nothing, no connection to God, no reality of the Holy Spirit in my life. I want God to be there, but I feel like I'm totally separate from him – oh yes, this must be what Hell is like. It's horrible. Half of me feels like crying out, begging God to revive me, wake me up, bring me back to life, and HE is the one not listening, not responding, turning away from me. The other half of me feels like God MUST be reaching out to me – calling me out of my tomb, just as he called Lazarus out, and the problem must be me – somehow I'm not listening, not responding, turning my back. But I don't know how to turn around. I think I am trying to listen – I don't know what else to do. I feel like I'm Lazarus in the tomb and I'm stuck there and can't get out.

*Todd with Baby the Pony, Summer 1993 in the backyard
of our home in Philadelphia*

*Adam and Aaron, so happy to be
reunited the day Aaron joined the
family, May 1995*

*SueAnn and Patty Kirpan share
a private moment on the day of
Milagro's adoption, June 1996*

*Exciting moments from our day at the White House for the signing of the
historic Adoption and Safe Families Act, November 1997. Top left, Aaron
and the President, top right, President Clinton pats SueAnn on the back
after she spoke and introduced the First Lady, Hilary Rodham Clinton.
Bottom, the family poses with the President*

The five youngest children enjoying Halloween, in chairs, Wayne, Adam, Dylan, in front, Alysia and Aaron, 1997

Christmas, 1998, everyone acting silly for the first family photo after Geeta joined the family. This is one of the only family photos that includes both Fisher and Adam before Adam died and Fisher began his time in prison.

Members of the Namani family, the family we hosted from Kosovo, visit DC while Sue was working for Senator Rockefeller, July 1999. Back row Zechir Namani, Senator John D. Rockefeller, IV, Sevdije Namani, Hector. Front row, Majlinda, Miranda and Marigona Namani, and Sue

In 1999, the family photo taken at Abel and Sonya's wedding became our Christmas card

Our young men from Sudan joined us in time for Thanksgiving, 2000. Abraham is pictured here with Todd

Sue & Hector dance at the25th anniversary celebration orchestrated by our kids, 2004.

2007, our very large family, including many of the grandchildren, gathered to celebrate SueAnn and Roberto's wedding

Many of "the girls" – daughters and granddaughters,
at Flory and Larry's wedding, July 2008

Some of "the boys" – sons, sons-in-law and grandsons
at Isaac and Simmy's wedding, October 2008

Simmy wearing the
same wedding gown
Sue wore in 1979

One of Sue's "Prayer Collages" – Photos of Children and Grandchildren who live far away or who are not seen as often as others, a visual reminder for daily prayer.

All of the local (and half of the total) grand and great-grand children celebrate Tiana's 6th birthday, May 2013

In Memoriam

Adam Joseph Badeau 1988-1999

Dylan Ryan Badeau 1986 – 2010

Nalana Elum 2010 – 2011

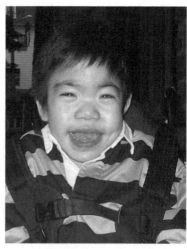

Wayne Chan Badeau 1987 – 2012

"Yet those who wait for the Lord will gain new strength; They will mount up with wings like eagles, They will run and not get tired, They will walk and not become weary." Isaiah 40: 31 (NASB)

Part III: Rivers to Cross

"... a crown of beauty instead of ashes,
the oil gladness instead of mourning ... "

Isaiah 61:3

23

Brides and Grooms

"Congratulations, Chelsea and Lashon!" Hector gives them each a big hug at the end of the short church ceremony. Wanting to be married before the baby is born, they've chosen to have a simple ceremony with just a few people in attendance. They're planning a big reaffirmation of their vows and reception at our home next August.

Little by little, God has burned off the fog that had settled around us this fall, gently reminding us of His faithfulness and keeping his promise to walk with us through the darkest valley, restoring our souls. Finally, today, we feel genuinely joyful for the first time in months, perhaps since our anniversary.

"The reservations are in my name," Chelsea says as we head for our cars. We are going out to eat with the newlyweds and

Lashon's parents.

"It was a sweet, lovely ceremony," I say on the short ride to Chestnut Hill.

"It was. Chelsea and Lashon are going to do just fine," Hector says. "He comes from a wonderful, supportive family. They both have good heads on their shoulders and a strong faith. It's going to be fun planning for their big celebration in August." Hector is grinning as he thinks about it.

"I can't wait. It's been six years since the last wedding we planned. I'm ready—I think the whole family is ready for a season of celebration," I reply.

"Yes, I'm just a little concerned about how we'll pay for it," Hector says.

"Chelsea and I plan to use Craigslist, Freecycle, and our combined creative genius to have a fabulous wedding on a shoestring. SueAnn's going to help; she's super creative when it comes to these kinds of events. You'll see. It'll work out."

"**Miles to go," I repeat, echoing our favorite answer to the familiar question, "Are we there yet?"**

"That's good. I knew I could count on you," Hector says. "In the meantime, we have plenty to keep us busy. A couple of birthdays, Christmas, and more . . . . miles to go."

"Miles to go," I repeat, echoing our favorite answer to the familiar question, "Are we there yet?"

We barely blink and it's New Year's Day.

"What time are we starting the fondue?" Hector asks.

"I told everyone to be ready by 3," I reply. Hector and I started having fondue together on New Year's Eve while dating in high school. My parents would go out to a party, and we'd have babysitting duty for my baby brother David. A romantic fondue dinner was the perfect stay-at-home date, and we carried the tradition into our early years of marriage. Once the kids came along, we shifted gears and transformed the tradition into a daylong New Year's Day extravaganza.

"OK, I'll have all the pots set up and ready to go. The kids can help you with all the chopping. I'll keep the fires going, but don't count on me for anything else," Hector laughs. For years we crowded around three fondue pots, and then last year, SueAnn gave us a set of seven, which we can spread along our entire dining room table for the festivities.

By noon, I'm in the kitchen chopping vegetables. Soon, I'm joined by Simmy and Renee; others will be along shortly. The atmosphere is festive as cheeses are grated, fruit sliced, and bread cubed. Chelsea arrives shortly before 3 to start making the cheese fondues—Swiss, cheddar, and fiesta. Ever since she worked at the Melting Pot, she's been in charge of the fondue making. "The one time a year I cook for the family," she's happy to remind us. SueAnn starts putting all the sauces into the little bowls.

David and Todd help Hector get all the pots ready to go, and Daniel and Aaron are charged with gathering the chairs. Finally, all is ready and it's time to begin. "Fondue is ready—everyone in the dining room!" Hector calls.

"OK, don't forget the tradition. While we eat the cheese, meat, and vegetable fondues, we all talk about the highlights and things we are most thankful for from the year that just ended," I remind everyone.

"And then when we have the chocolate fondue we all share what we are looking forward to in the year ahead," Isaac says. "We remember, Mom. So let's get started."

"Mom, even though I have Lashon to be with me, I want you there too." Chelsea is asking me to be at the hospital with her when the baby is born.

"Of course I'll be there. You can count on me," I say. I'm home more these days now that the grants for both the Pew

Commission and the Longest Waiting Children projects have ended. I get speaking requests quite often, but at least I'm not away from home five days a week like I have been over the past several years.

Lashon has just called to give me the update. "Chelsea's been having contractions at home for hours now, and her doctor wants her to come in. Do you want to ride with us or take your own car?"

"I'll ride with you so our car is here in case Hector needs it. Just pick me up. I'll be ready," I reply.

"How's it going up there?" Hector asks when I call him from the cafeteria—cell phones aren't allowed in the rooms.

"Looks like it's going to be a C-section. She's having contractions but nothing is progressing," I tell him.

"Oh, sorry to hear that. Tell her I'm praying for her, and give her a hug for me."

"Will do. I better get back up there with Lashon's food. I'll call you when I know more."

A few days later, Chelsea, Lashon, and our newest granddaughter, Chloe, are home in their apartment around the corner from our house. "She is so precious, Chelsea. I can't get over how much she makes me think of you when you were a baby." I'm falling in love again as I rock my newest granddaughter, breathing in the sweet newborn smell. . . .

As soon as I return home, Hector calls me to the living room.

"Sue, is that you? Come take a look at Wayne. He's burning up and limp. I've never seen him like this."

"Oh no. We need to get him to the hospital right way!" I gasp.

"I agree. I've already told Isaac to keep an eye on Dylan. I was just waiting for you to get here with the car—let's go."

"You have a very sick little boy here," the emergency room doctor says when he finishes examining Wayne. "We need to admit him immediately. We need to get some information from you about what's been going on at home."

"He's been having more and more trouble eating. He loves eating; it's always brought him such pleasure. We hate to face the fact that maybe he has reached the stage with his Sanfilippo Syndrome where he's losing his swallowing capability, but I'm afraid that could be what's happening," Hector states.

"Sanfilippo Syndrome? That's one I'm not familiar with," the doctor replies. "I'll have to consult with some of the other doctors here. But in the meantime, I can see that he needs antibiotics and hydration, so let's get him set up in a room."

"I'll stay with him, Hec. You can go home with the other kids. I'll let you know as soon as there is any update." This is our routine when any of the kids are in the hospital.

"OK. I'll come back in the morning after I get the kids off to school. Do you need anything?"

"I'll need a change of clothes and bring my laptop. I can work from here, which will be a lot easier than schlepping back and forth to an office like I had to do when Adam was in the hospital."

On Wayne's eighth day in the hospital Hector comes in around 10 AM, juggling two coffees, just as his cell phone rings. "Ooops. I know it's not supposed to be on in here, but can you answer it quickly?" he asks.

"Really? . . . OK, which hospital are you at? . . . Is Will with you? . . . . OK, I am at the hospital with Wayne, but I'll come over in a little while."

"Was that Geeta?" Hector says, hearing my reference to Will.

"Yes, she's in labor. She's over at Hahnemann. She wants me to come over, but I hate to leave Wayne. I'm torn."

"I'm here with Wayne, you go be with her. And then take a

break and go home for awhile. You've been here for days. To-night, I'll spend the night and we can switch back up in the morning. I'll call the house and make sure Isaac can get Dylan's feeding started," Hector says.

"It's another girl!" I announce to Hector a few hours later. "And she's a beauty. They've named her Titianna, and she's got the cutest little round face. She's only about half the size of Chloe," I laugh, not realizing that soon she'll be twice Chloe's size.

It was nice to spend a night at home, I think to myself as I head back to the hospital on Super Bowl Sunday. Before head-ing in I prepared some snacks for the crew at our house. The Eagles are playing in the big game, and the living room is filling up. Isaac, George, Daniel, and Renee are all there already, and Chelsea is bringing the baby over for her first outing—a Super Bowl party. Joelle comes to Children's Hospital of Philadelphia with me; we bring an Eagles shirt for Wayne and some green balloons for his room.

"He looks so thin, Mom," Joelle says, concerned.

"Yes, I know. He's not been eating. They are doing a swallow-ing test on Monday and, depending on how that goes, he might need a feeding tube, like Dylan has."

"That will be so sad for him. Wayne loves to eat," she says.

"I know, it breaks my heart too. But we can't let him just waste away."

"Wayne's home, everybody!" Hector calls out when we ar-rive home four days later. Soon kids are coming from the sec-ond and third floors to see how he's doing.

"His pump looks different than Dylan's," Isaac observes.

"You're right, it's a different kind. I'll have to teach it to you and SueAnn so you can be my backup for him, like you are for

Dylan," Hector says.

"That was a close call," I say to Hector later. "He looks good now, but those first few days in the hospital were touch and go. It scared me."

"Me too. I've been thinking—we need to get to know the hospice people. When the time does come for Wayne, or Dylan, I want them to be here at home, not in the hospital."

"I agree, Hec, but I hope that's a decision we don't have to make for a long time."

"Now that Wayne is doing better and both babies are here, we need to really focus on the wedding plans. August will be here before we know it." Hector is surveying the yard and thinking about all the work he has to do before we host 200 of our closest family and friends in a few months.

"Wait 'til you see the spreadsheets I've created to organize all the to-do lists!" I laugh. "We have to meet with Peter Alston soon to get the catering nailed down. That's one of the few budget items I can't get from Freecycle. But changing the subject: I have to tell you about a very exciting invitation I got today."

"What is it?"

"My friend Kerry Hasenbalg called. She's organizing a trip to several orphanages in El Salvador and some meetings with the First Lady there, to help her on some child welfare and adoption policy work. She invited me to go, to share some of the work I've done through the Pew Commission, helping courts and agencies work together better for kids. There will just be four of us— including MaryBeth Chapman!" I say excitedly. Chapman is the wife of Christian recording artist Steven Curtis Chapman.

Ever since our adoption of Jose, I have yearned to go to El Salvador. What an answer to prayer!

"Wow, what an opportunity. When is the trip?"

"It's right around the corner, in May. I can hardly believe it.

You know how passionate I am about the children of El Salvador. God put that seed in our hearts twenty-five years ago. I feel so honored and humbled to have this opportunity. I really hope that I can offer something of value to the people we will meet with while there."

"If God is giving you this assignment, then you have a purpose there. You'll be of value to them, don't worry," Hector reassures me.

"My head and my heart and spirit are so full—overflowing from this trip. It will take me weeks to unpack it and share it all with you!" I exclaim to Hector when he greets me upon my return from El Salvador.

"Can't wait to hear all about it. And I've missed you," he says, wrapping me in his arms.

"My head and my heart and spirit are so full—overflowing from this trip. It will take me weeks to unpack it and share it all with you!"

"I've missed you too, and the kids. Can't wait to hear how things are at home too, and it's the final countdown for Chelsea's wedding planning. But first, I just have to tell you this one thing. Part of the reason the First Lady wants our help is for a project she's doing to make it easier for all children in El Salvador to have their own birth certificates. Many, many children there do not get birth certificates, and this makes everything from health care to school enrollment to family reunification to adoption very difficult."

"I can only imagine the problems that creates," Hector says, listening.

"Anyway, she involved us to help kick off the campaign, but part of it included a PSA with two young children singing a little jingle. You won't believe the words: *no se, no se, me llamo Jose,* one little boy sings. 'I don't know, I don't know, but my name is Jose'. It gave me chills—those words were nearly identical to our Jose's first words when he got off the plane. And it helps me to understand better why he never had a birth certificate of his own. I can't wait to tell him what I've learned.

"But now, back to our regularly scheduled wedding planning."

"Butterflies?" my sister asks, astonished.

"Yes, Chelsea plans to have butterflies released when she and Lashon affirm their vows. She's read about it and she's doing it in the most ecologically friendly way."

"I would expect nothing less. But tell me again what you want me to do?" Nancy asks.

"She needs the butterflies to be kept safely overnight and then delivered to the ceremony. Can you guys keep them in your hotel room and then bring them over on Saturday?" Chelsea's wedding has turned into the ultimate family affair—all of her siblings, even Dylan and Wayne, will be attired as part of the wedding party. She's involving both of my sisters' children, my brother, and Lashon's family as well. She also has friends from the Gospel Choir at Arcadia singing and another friend playing a harp. The service will be Christ-centered, multicultural, and artsy—totally reflecting Chelsea's unique personality and gifts.

"I'm sure between the four of us we can manage that. I hope it's not too complicated. Is there anything else you need me to do?"

"Not at the moment, but don't worry. I'm sure we'll think of something! Anyway, you called me, and you didn't know about the butterflies when you called, so is something else on your mind?" I ask.

"Yes, I wanted to let you know that Mom and I have decided to come down for Chelsea's bridal shower.

"Wow, that's a lot for you both to make two trips here in such a short amount of time."

"I know, but we've really thought about it and Mom would

like to do this. She thinks it will give her more quality time to visit with you and Chelsea and the rest of the family. And just between us, it looks like her remission may be over; she's probably going to have to start treatment again, and the prognosis the second time around is not as good. But don't tell Chelsea or the others. She doesn't want anyone to know yet and she doesn't want to put a dark cloud on Chelsea's wedding."

"Oh no." I sink into my seat. Mom had a rough fall, but her treatments were successful and she's been in remission. She and Steve have traveled and she looks wonderful. Can the cancer really be making a comeback so soon?

"Go ahead and bring these appetizers outside," I say to my sister and Chelsea's friends, who are helping with the bridal shower. I stand alone in the kitchen, taking a quick look at the to-do list to make sure I haven't forgotten anything. Suddenly, I am overcome with emotion, realizing how lucky we are to have my mom with us and how possible it is that she won't be with us much longer. I can't stop the tears that begin to flow.

Lim, one of Chelsea's good friends, walks in at that moment. "Miss Sue, what's wrong?" she says, giving me a big hug.

"Oh Limmy," I say, hugging her back. And then I break down and tell her about my mom, sobbing on her shoulder. "And I can't let on. My mom doesn't want anyone to know, and I don't want to be all teary for Chelsea's shower."

Lim comforts me, saying little in words, but much in spirit. I will never forget this moment of kindness and compassion. God uses her to revive my heart, and I'm ready to join the guests for this joyful occasion.

The wedding day comes and goes far too quickly, and before I know it, summer is over and my fall schedule is filled with travels for speaking engagements across the country. It's a balmy December evening in San Diego when I finish my work for the day and call my mom to check in on her. I'm immediately struck by how weak her voice sounds. She's back in the hospital. I try to give her words of encouragement and hope, but I'm deeply saddened by this call. I feel in my bones that the end is coming for her.

Sooner than I expect, I get the call. My sister Stephanie is on the phone the next morning. As a nurse, she is often the one we all turn to when we need to understand complex medical realities. "What is it, Steph?"

"Mom has decided to stop all treatment. It's her time, Susan. She's going to go home tomorrow, with hospice care. I know you're in California, but we wanted you to know right away."

"I'll change my flight—I'll be there," I say. I missed the chance to be with my dad when he died; I am not going to let that happen again if possible. Thankfully, I arrive in Vermont in time to be with Mom and the family as she leaves the hospital and gets settled in at home.

> "*Labor* is the word that has been in my mind too. This process of dying—somehow it reminds me of the birthing process. It's labor, and a transition to a new life."

We put her bed in the living room, where she can see the beautiful Vermont winter landscape through the picture window. Her brothers and Aunt Deanna are both there, my sisters, brother, and Steve. We talk, share funny stories and memories, sing, pray. Night falls and yet no one leaves her side. No one sleeps.

"Her breathing is getting so labored," Deanna says, with tears in her eyes.

"I know," I say. "*Labor* is the word that has been in my mind too. This process of dying—somehow it reminds me of the birthing process. It's labor, and a transition to a new life. I never thought of it like that before." We all sit quietly for several more moments holding Mom's hand as she takes her final breaths.

"I'll make arrangements for everyone to have a place to stay—you figure out the rental cars," I say to Hector when I am finally composed enough to call home. He will bring the entire family, except for Geeta, who has a sick baby to care for, and Flory, who is due to deliver her third child any day and cannot travel.

As I prepare my remarks for her service, I can't stop remembering that the last time we were all with her was at Chelsea's wedding. She was so radiant and beautiful that day, and she loved the entire service, especially the butterfly release. It strikes me that the life of the Monarch butterfly is the perfect metaphor for my mom's life, and so I compose my thoughts:

The life cycle of a butterfly provides a vivid, marvelous image of transformation, of new life arising out of death, freedom taking flight out of confinement, beauty dazzling us as it emerges from the dowdy, plain shell of the cocoon. It is also joyous, flirty and fun – all attributes of our mom's personality. And the Monarch is royalty – I have learned from her friends in these last few days that one of Mamie's nicknames was "Queenie" – gently teasing and honoring her for her regal bearing, her love of all that is beautiful.

Many of us go through life on the ground, never looking up, knowing only the existence of the caterpillar – never having the faith, hope, or courage to believe that one day we, too, can become butterflies. Others have faith; we believe we'll be transformed. Yet we also understand that we must pass through the cocoon stage. And we avoid that. We don't want to give up what little freedom we have as a caterpillar to be confined in the dark, scary cocoon before emerging as the butterfly we carry without our souls.

The last two years, Mom, as you battled AML, was

your cocoon time.

Yet, Mom, you lived your life as a Monarch, as a regal butterfly bringing beauty and fun everywhere you traveled. It's a remarkable way to live, to BE the butterfly even while the world says you're still a caterpillar. This was a gift you shared with us. And now, having suffered through the dark night of the cocoon, you have emerged – your inner butterfly has been released. We will think of you every moment, every day, and the butterflies we see in the gardens and fields of our lives will forever be known as "Mamie's Monarchs."

"It's been two weeks since you got back from Vermont, and this baby is still not here. I could have gone to Mamie's funeral," Flory laments as I drive her to her doctor's appointment. She was particularly close to my mom and heartbroken to miss the funeral.

"She knew you were there in spirit, and besides, you were following doctor's orders. You had no way of knowing when the baby would come," I say, consoling her. . . .

Laurie Marie is born the next day; she is the third of my granddaughters to have the middle name Marie after both my mother and I. She's a strong, feisty little baby ready to find her place among two older sisters and a growing brood of cousins.

"Three graduations this spring, and my mom won't be at any of them," I say to Hector as we look through the mail. Todd will complete City Year, Dylan finish at Roxborough, and Alysia graduate from Hope Charter School.

"We'll have to find a way to make these graduations special anyway. They all deserve to be celebrated for their accomplishments. For a while it looked like Todd wouldn't ever have a graduation for us to attend, and who knew if Dylan would live long enough for his? And then, Alysia, after all she's been through—I'm so proud that she is graduating and heading off to Berkshire Hills Music Academy in the fall.

"My sister and my cousin Jill are going to come down for the graduation," I continue. "And Lilly and Trish will be here too. It will definitely be festive—but I'll still miss my mom," I reply.

"I'll bet we see a butterfly that day," Hector muses.

"Maybe so, maybe so."

"My 50th birthday is coming up, soon. It's one of those times you really stop and think about your life," Hector says as we sit on the porch with Lilly, Trish, and JD, who are all enjoying their annual summer visit in Philly.

I survey the porch, noting that the other chairs, stoops, and steps are filled with George, Chelsea, SueAnn, Flory, David, Renee, Todd, Aaron, Phillip, Daniel, Joelle, Geeta, and Isaac. Wayne is in his wheelchair next to Hector, while Alysia, Kirsten, Whitney, Ashley, and Erica are on the lawn in front of us. Smaller kids are crowded onto the hammock.

"Looks like we have a quorum. Should we have a family meeting?" I joke.

"Oh, Mom," and "No, not a family meeting, Nanna," come the groans.

"I want to hear more about dad turning fifty. Keep talking, old head," JD says.

"Who you calling old, JD? You are not that far behind me, you know. Anyway, with the kind of life and jobs we've had, your mother and I don't have a real retirement fund," Hector continues.

"Isn't that why you sent Jose to make the big bucks in Switzerland?" Isaac interrupts.

"Very funny, Isaac. Seriously, we've been wondering what we should do in our old age—not that we are there yet, but you know, we have to start thinking and planning. We've always loved camping and we believe that people who raise children with special needs deserve to have breaks once in a while . . . "

"Its called *respite*," I interject.

"Right, respite," Hector continues. "Anyway, we put the two ideas together and we're thinking that maybe our next calling, after everyone is graduated and launched, might be to develop a respite ministry, maybe run it out of a campground. We're just thinking, but next week we're going to look at a campground that's for sale, just to put a toe in the water."

"A campground, how perfect—hope it's on a lake. So many great family memories of camping and lakes," SueAnn says.

"Yeah, like the time we were all at Lake Caspian and David started walking around with a condom he found on the ground hanging off a stick?" JD remembers, bursting out laughing.

"Oh, I haven't thought of that in years. That was so gross," Renee adds.

"I think he thought it was a balloon," George says.

We're all rolling with laughter as some of the kids shout, "Ewwwww" and "Oh gross!"

"Speaking of memories: how about the time you left me at Disney?" Chelsea pipes up.

"Oh, here we go with all the 'I remembers'—I love it," Hector says. He adds, "I sure do, Chels, and you stuck to me like white on rice for the rest of that trip."

"Well, it wasn't only me, the next time we went to Disney you lost Todd," Chelsea says for emphasis.

"It's a good thing they have a great lost and found system," I laugh.

"I take responsibility for leaving Chelsea when she went to the restroom, but Todd wandered off on his own," Hector says with a laugh.

"Right, Dad. He was only three at the time!" SueAnn reminds him.

"It's a good thing Renee and Trish found him just a few minutes later."

"Speaking of losing three-year-olds, what about the time Nanna lost Erica at Wildwood? She was only three then, right?" Kirsten has come up to the porch to join in the fun.

"Oh, that was one of the worst days of my life!" I shiver, just thinking about it, I watched her walk no more than 50 yards from the blanket we were sitting on to where Poppa was standing, and all of a sudden she disappeared. I went from thinking she had drowned to being kidnapped at least a hundred times in my mind before the lifeguards found her *waaaaaaaay* down the beach. I still can't understand how she managed to get so far from us. I never took my eyes off of her."

"Well, I guess you need your eyes checked, then, Mom," JD teases.

"There have been so many times you did crazy things over the years, like letting Jose hold a live rattlesnake on a stick so you could take a picture by the 'Beware of Rattlesnakes' sign in New Mexico. What on earth were you thinking?" Flory chimes in.

"OK, OK. Is this a 'mom roast' or are we going to talk about camping memories?" I say, tears rolling down my eyes from laughing so hard.

"You remember that pancake breakfast we used to go to, Mom. Where was that?" George asks.

"It was in Cheyenne, Wyoming. You used to love watching how they would fling the pancakes over their shoulders to the Boy Scouts with the trays."

"I remember being so scared in Yellowstone," Joelle pipes in.

"Why was that?" Hector asks.

"Don't you remember when the buffalo walked through our campsite and you made us all hurry up and get into the van?" she says, shaking her head.

"And then you said, 'Let's go out and feed him,' and me and George and Jose started opening the door of the van. That's when you really screamed, Joelle!" Isaac adds to the story.

"That must have been funny. I was so little I hardly remember some of these, but I do remember the day Mom got caught with her pants down!" Todd chimes in.

The laughter is getting rowdier, and the grandchildren are all looking at me with bug eyes. "Oh, it sounds funny now, but it was not funny at the time," I say. "I was using the restroom, and I had all of our money in one of those fanny-pack type of wallets. When I pulled my shorts down to sit on the toilet, someone stuck their hand under the door to grab the wallet, and they got my shorts and underwear too."

By now, everyone is hooting and rolling with laughter; even Wayne is cracking up.

"We found your shorts and underwear in the bushes, but the money was all gone," SueAnn adds.

"At least you were there so you could go to the van and get me some clothes to put on. I was worried I was going to have to walk out of the restroom butt-naked. Oh my, I went to tell Dad what happened and I said, 'Hec, I have bad news,' and he looked at me and said, 'Don't tell me you're pregnant!'"

"Oh, I forgot about that. I used that line a lot over the years; it was my version of gallows humor," Hector says. "Anyway, you said, 'No, worse. We lost all our money and we have no way to get home now.'"

"It's a good thing the Luckinbills came to our rescue that time. That was the year we got to go to their house and had a barbecue by their pool," Joelle remembers.

"Yes, God has always shown up, sometimes in unexpected ways, whenever we have a crisis," Hector says.

"How many times did you go on those trips?" SueAnn's boyfriend, Roberto, asks.

"Five or six times at least—all the way across the country, and then several other shorter ones, like down to Myrtle Beach," Hector replies. "We always tried to tie them in to the NACAC conference, wherever it was being held. As a result, we've been to all of the states except for Alaska and Hawaii, and several parts of Canada. Good memories . . . "

"I wish I could go on one of those trips," Ashley says wistfully.

"I do hope to take a trip with grandchildren," Hector says. "We'll have to see if we can make it happen someday."

"Well, I get to go to California this year," Daniel says. Renee and I have started a new tradition. Now that the whole family can no longer realistically leave home, jobs, and kids to come to NACAC, she and Daniel have been coming with me, making it their own vacation time.

"That's right. NACAC at Long Beach in two weeks. It'll be fun," I say, getting up to go inside and get dinner started. Both Hector and I love these family reminiscing sessions. They remind us that no matter how many valleys we pass through, we always have a storehouse full of good memories to remind us of all the times God has provided for us, encouraged us, taught us, and strengthened our bonds of love along the way.

"Happy Birthday, Hec. You old man—50 years old today!" I walk out onto the porch, where Hector is enjoying his morning coffee, and give him a big hug, surprised to see several of the kids already gathered on the porch.

"Oh, you think I'm old? I'll show you tonight just how old I'm not," he laughs, a gleam in his eye.

"Hec, the kids are here," I say, embarrassed.

"So? They're all adults. I'm sure they know the facts of married life and how we got to have so many kids—all different colors too. Boy, I'm good."

"Stop, Dad! You're grossing us out—go get a room!" SueAnn says, laughing.

"Look at Miss Sue. She's all red." Simmy joins in the fun.

"It's great to see all of you here, but I don't understand why you're here so early," I ask, looking at SueAnn, Roberto, Simmy,

Isaac, Flory, and Larry.

"Welllllll . . . " Flory begins, laughing.

"We thought we should tell you all at the same time," SueAnn says.

"Tell me what?" I look from face to face trying to figure out the big secret.

"We're engaged!" SueAnn says, and suddenly, SueAnn, Flory, and Simmy are all holding out hands with rings on them.

"What? All of you? All at once? Wow, I don't know what to say! Congratulations, of course! But wow, this is a big surprise."

"Really, Mom, you are surprised? You know how long we've all been dating; you must have seen this coming."

"Well, of course, I had hopes marriage was on the horizon for all of you. But I didn't expect three engagements at once! Are we going to have a triple wedding?"

"No way!" Flory says. "I want my own special day."

"We all do, Miss Sue. That's why we want to talk to you so we can figure it out," Simmy says.

"I hope you're giving us at least a year. We are just recovering financially from Chelsea's wedding," Hector adds. By the end of the conversation, we have decided on a plan for staggered wedding dates over the next two and a half years.

"Well, after that morning excitement, you should really be ready for your birthday surprise," I say as Chelsea, Joelle, and Geeta walk up to join the action on the porch.

"We're giving you a day at a spa, Dad," Joelle blurts out.

"You even get a pedicure," Alysia says, stepping onto the porch just in time.

"So let's get going, I'll drive you. We have to be there in less than an hour," I tell him.

"Ahhhhhhh. That was unbelieveable," Hector says when he greets me at the end of his day.

"Oh, so glad you liked it. The kids, especially the boys, weren't sure if you'd really get into a spa day, but we all felt you needed a day of total pampering."

"I wasn't sure what to think at first, and don't tell my brothers or I'll never hear the end of it. But seriously, it was incredible. The woman who gave me the massage noticed that I had a lot of tension in my shoulders. I told her she'd have a lot of tension, too, if she had 22 kids and—what is it now—20 grandchildren? She couldn't believe it, and she said I was actually less tense then she would have predicted if she knew that ahead of time," he chuckles.

"That's wonderful. Oh, and it's 21 grandchildren counting the newest one, Nicoli. Actually, he is getting out of the hospital today, so we'll finally get to hold him," I add. Nicoli, Todd and Nina's son, was born weighing barely a pound and has been in the NICU for three months. We've visited and taken pictures, but not been allowed to hold him.

"Twenty-one—that's right. But now that you're counting, I think it's actually 22—so we have the same number of grandkids now as kids," Hector says.

"Who did I miss?" I ask.

"Angel. Now that SueAnn and Roberto are getting married, Angel is definitely one of our grandkids," he says, reminding me of Roberto's first child.

"Oh, I always count her as a grandchild. In fact, she makes me think of a little me—she is so much like I was when I was her age. It's hard to believe she's not biologically related to me," I laugh.

"Well, anyway, I felt sorry for the lady who did my pedi-

cure—she said she'd never seen feet like mine, poor woman."
Hector cracks up.

"Yeah, your feet are a mess," I agree.

"Well, not anymore. I'm so relaxed, I'm ready for a nap as
soon as I get home."

"OK, that sounds like a plan," I say, smiling to myself.

"Surprise! Happy birthday, Old Head!" A chorus of greetings
and cheers ring out as we enter the house. Friends and family
from Vermont, Rhode Island, D.C., and, of course, Philadelphia
have gathered for a "'50s"-themed birthday party.

"What? I thought the spa was my gift. This is too much!"
Hector gasps, stunned.

"Are you really surprised? No one let the cat out of the bag?"
Chelsea asks.

"I'm really surprised," he says, looking around and laughing
at all the great '50s costumes our guests are wearing. I sit back
in the rocking chair, snuggling my newest grandson and watching the festivities. I'm super proud of my kids; they are all so
thoughtful and generous, I think to myself.

"'Don't have that baby until I get back!' Weren't those my
last words to you before I left for Pittsburgh?" I say to SueAnn
on the phone.

"Yes, Mommy. I know she wasn't due until Valentine's Day,
but she's coming early. Do you think you'll be back in time?"

"I don't know. My conference just ended, but my flight is not
leaving for another four hours, and I'm not going to change it
because I made plans to get together with Patrice and Destin
and she's bringing Davon, too. I haven't seen him in a couple
years," I explain.

"Well, just hurry. I really want you to be here."

"I know, but at least Roberto is with you, and Esperanza will be fine with Dad. Just remember to breathe and I'll come right to the hospital when I get home. I have to go now. I see that Patrice is here."

"Nanna!" Two little boys run to me for an embrace. I'm delighted with this welcome, since they haven't seen me in some time. Of all our grandchildren, these two boys in Pittsburgh, George's son Destin and Abel's son Davon, are the two I see the least. I do a double take when I see that Davon's mom, Viola, is also with Patrice. This is a surprise.

"Look what I made for you, Nanna," Davon says as he unfolds a picture he's colored.

"Oh, you are a good artist, just like your dad," I tell him, feeling the stab of pain that his dad is still in jail.

"I have something to show you too, Nanna," Destin chimes in, thrusting his preschool report card in front of me.

"Will you look at all those good reports from your teacher! You're so smart," I exclaim, scooping him up into a big hug. Both boys are beaming.

I don't make it back for the delivery, but I still go to the hospital to visit SueAnn and Roberto. Roberto hands me the little package as soon as I come into the room, and I gaze down at this bright-eyed little face.

"Oh, she's breathtaking, SueAnn. I still wish you two had waited until after the wedding for this, but we're just going to love her up anyway," I say, giving the baby my traditional Nanna kisses.

"Speaking of the wedding, we have a lot to do when I get out of the hospital. Do you think I will have time to lose enough weight so I won't look like a cow on my wedding day?" she asks.

"I think you will be a beautiful bride, SueAnn, and I'm sure Roberto will agree. Say, what was your final decision about the baby's name?"

"Allegria Marguarita," Roberto says.

"Well, I'm glad she has a big name just like Esperanza does. Fair is fair," I chuckle.

"Allegria means *joy* in Spanish, and Marguarita is after my mom," Roberto explains.

"She'll get to ride in the antique carriage at the wedding, just like Chloe did," I muse.

With wedding planning in full swing, I'm grateful that my current work project is local. I have been appointed by the mayor to direct the Philadelphia Children's Commission for the remainder of his term.

"This is such a fantastic opportunity, another stepping-stone, as you'd call it, Hec," I tell Hector the day I get the job. "Although I am still committed to adoption when it is the right plan for a child, I know that many children would never have to be in foster care if we did a better job supporting struggling families in the community. I've learned so much since we started Rootwings, and I really believe we have to work harder to keep families together in the first place, and when that isn't possible, support their relatives to care for them. And finally, consider adoption if none of the other options are possible. This job will give me the chance to focus on all of the front-end supports for families. I'm super excited."

Now, as Hector calls me at the office, I'm wishing that some of those front-end supports had been more successful with our daughter Geeta. "You're kidding, right? This is a joke?"

"No joke. She has a new baby. Another girl and she named her Tianna. I just got off the phone with the hospital social worker," Hector says.

"She never even told us she was pregnant, and she didn't really look pregnant last time we saw her," I say, thinking back.

"Chelsea and I thought she looked pregnant, but she swore she wasn't," Hector reminds me.

"I guess this is payback for all those times we showed up with a new child, or four or six, and we hadn't told my parents we were adopting again," I chuckle.

"I keep wondering if my heart can stretch any further, but God always shows me that it can," Hector says. "I'm sure we will love this little one just as much as the others."

"It's nice to hear you taking this in stride and not getting all worked up."

"Yup, I'm trying to learn to 'accept the things I cannot change,'" Hector says, quoting the famous Serenity Prayer.

"That's a whole lot harder than it sounds. Why don't you take the train down to the city, and we'll go over to the hospital together after I get out of work and then we can grab a bite to eat and go home."

"Sounds like a plan as long as Isaac or Joelle can watch Wayne and Dylan. I'll let you know."

"Can you believe it? Wayne wasn't supposed to live past the age of 13, and now he has finished high school and he's 20 years old. And he still blesses us every day with his amazing spirit," Hector says as we load up the car for our trip to Vermont the day after Wayne's graduation from Martin Luther King High School.

"Milestone upon milestone, it's quite the ride we are on in this life, and now off to Vermont for the first graduation of one of our grandchildren," I add. "Can we possibly be old enough to have grandchildren graduating?"

"Another one for the books," Hector says as we walk around the backyard picking up stray plates and cups the morning after SueAnn's wedding.

"There were so many precious moments yesterday; I'm thankful Laurie Beck was the photographer. She's known our family for 15 years, so she knows how to capture the important moments," I say, looking forward to seeing the pictures and re-living the special memories.

"SueAnn put so much thought into all the little touches," Hector says. "The wedding really reflected her personality. But I think one of my favorite moments was watching all the little girls in their flower girl dresses jumping on the trampoline."

"Yes, that was adorable. Speaking of little girls, we have to get ready for the one who's arriving today. Is the bedroom all set for Shawna's family?"

"Yup, I made sure it was ready before the wedding because I knew we'd be too exhausted to do it today," Hector says. Fisher's fourth child, our granddaughter Janessa, is blind, possibly autistic, and has other challenges. I've visited her on several of my trips to Vermont, but this will be the first time she comes to Philly and the first time for most of the family to meet her. Her mother is remarried and arriving today with her entire family for a few days, and Janessa will stay on for an extra week.

"It never lets up, does it? We just roll from one thing to the next. They'll arrive later this afternoon, but in the meantime, our brunch guests are arriving in an hour, so let me go inside and finish up the quiches while you take care of the backyard," I say to Hector.

"It's been an extraordinary year. I can't wait to see what 2008 has in store—we have two more weddings on the docket," Hector says as we sit quietly in our room reflecting on the memories of 2007.

"And another granddaughter graduating from high school and two college graduations—both girls that others thought would never make it this far in life," I add. Whitney, Joelle, and Alysia will all walk in caps and gowns this spring. Whitney has been living with us since her junior year, and we are so proud of her accomplishments.

"And who knows how many more grandchildren 2008 will

bring us?" Hector wonders aloud.

"Oh, don't say that. Everyone is stable and in good places in their lives. And no new babies are on the way as far as I know," I say, hoping it's true.

"Well, don't forget the biggest milestone of 2008 to look forward to," Hector says with a twinkle in his eye.

"What, something else besides what we have already mentioned?" I ask.

"Oh yeah—you get to join the AARP along with me," he laughs.

Ah, yes. My 50th birthday looms.

"Hector, can you come in here?" I call out as I hear his footsteps in the hallway less than a week later.

He looks from me to Joelle and back, saying, "What's up?"

"Joelle has something to tell you," I say, nodding at Joelle. "Go ahead, Joelle."

"I'm pregnant," she states simply.

I can see Hector's temperature rising as blood-red color flushes his face. You'd think we'd be used to this scene by now, but like a stealth attack, it takes us by surprise every time.

"There goes your whole future," he says, his voice starting to rise. "What happened to your plans for using your communications degree in New York on TV? Oh jeesh, I can just picture it. You'll be waddling across the stage at your graduation with a big belly." Deflated, he sits down on the bed.

I was having the same thoughts about graduation, and I am disappointed to see that we are both more caught up in our own humiliation and shame rather than Joelle's welfare.

"And don't tell me the father is who I think it is," Hector booms.

"Yes, Dad, it is," she meekly replies.

"Haven't any of the values your mother and I have tried to teach you meant anything? Haven't you learned anything from your sisters and brothers?" He is yelling now and gets up to walk out of the room.

"Slow down. Calm down, Hec," I say.

"I can't. I feel like I'm going crazy. I've pleaded with God to put a hedge of protection around my kids and to give them the wisdom to make better decisions and, every single time, one by one, we get this news. But of all of them, I really least expected it from you, Joelle."

His voice has lowered to almost a whisper, and he starts to cry.

"I have to get out of here for a few hours. I need you to take care of Wayne and Dylan for the day. I'm just going out," he says, leaving the room.

Late that night, Hector walks into the living room. "Are you OK? I've been worried," I say quietly.

"I decided to buy one of those day passes and just ride the train. I rode to Trenton and back and all over Philly. I had plenty of time to think and pray," he says walking over to check on Wayne.

"At first, I was so angry. I was just yelling at God, saying, 'Why? Why? Why can't we get one of our kids to wait until they are married to have children?'" he continues, now walking to the other side of the room to check on Dylan.

"And then, God reminded me of John 8: 'Let any one of you who is without sin be the first to throw a stone at her.' And I was humbled.

"How is she doing, anyway?" he asks.

"She's pretty shaken up by your reaction," I say.

"For the rest of my train ride, I was thinking of what a miracle it is that she's alive at all, considering the start she had in life, and all the great memories of her as a little girl, creating restaurants for us at home, acting in school plays, always so tender with Adam, Dylan, and Wayne . . . Such a good sister to Alysia . . . . I'm so proud of her in so many ways and how far she has come since she was that little two-pound baby, and now she's about to graduate from college in a few months. She really is a wonderful girl."

"I know you love her, Hec. But tonight, I think she needs to hear it from you."

"I know you love her, Hec. But tonight, I think she needs to hear it from you."

"Mom, we have so many things going on this year. I think we need a meeting, a budget, and a plan," Chelsea says to me a few weeks later, ticking off Joelle, Whitney, and Alysia's graduation parties, bridal showers for Flory and Simmy, and a baby shower for Joelle.

"I agree. Let's go out to breakfast on Saturday morning and come up with a calendar and game plan." By the time we finish our breakfast, we are less stressed about everything on our plate in the months ahead. There is just something about getting it down in writing that makes what sounded crazy feel manageable.

Berkshire Hills Music Academy is in Massachusetts, so many of our New England family and friends are able to join us for Alysia's graduation. Hector's tears are already flowing when she takes the stage to recite her remarks and receive her certificate. By the time she is finished, most of our family members are wiping away their own tears. If ever one person exhibited strength and grace in spite of many setbacks, it's Alysia. She is an inspiration to all of us.

As we walk to the cars at the end of the day, my sister Nancy turns to me: "I'm going to come down for Flory's shower."

"Really?" I say. "Oh that will be so special. It meant so much to have you and Mom at Chelsea's shower. Flory will be thrilled to have you at hers."

One by one, the events approach, and one by one, they go off beautifully. Each person has their moment to be surrounded by the love of family and friends and to be celebrated for their accomplishments.

I stand on the edge of the dance floor with my friend Patty Kirpan as we watch Hector and Flory dance to "Butterfly Kisses." Tears are filling my eyes as I remember the scared little girl we first adopted, the one who sometimes hid under her desk at school. Today she is a radiant bride and confident young woman.

"I couldn't have made it through these weddings without you, Patty. I'm so thankful for you," I tell her, squeezing her hand.

"We've been through a lot together in this friendship," she acknowledges. "It's been an amazing day."

"I agree. My favorite moment in the ceremony was when Flory and Larry jumped the broom together." She'd told him the day before: "You can jump. I'll have on heels; I'm just going to step over it." But when the moment came, they held hands and she jumped gleefully.

I love the way each of the family weddings has embraced history, tradition, culture, and faith in their own unique ways.

Just days after the wedding, I am taking my granddaughter Erica to the Pennsylvania State Adoption Conference. Hard to believe my tradition of "special days" is now extending to another generation. It'll be so much fun to have this one-on-one time with her; she's growing up too fast. In a month, I'll be headed to NACAC in Ottawa with Renee and Daniel. I do love being a Nanna even if it's overwhelming at times.

Chelsea and I didn't put anything on our special events calendar about my 50th birthday, and with all the other festivities this year, I'm hoping it will slip by unnoticed. Of course, Hector will remember, but maybe he won't stir the kids up to do anything special. As the day approaches with no hints of any activity, I'm confident that it will be a quiet day. . . .

"I'd like to take you out to lunch after church today for your birthday," Hector says.

"Oh, that sounds nice. Where do you want to go?"

"Well, remember what a good time we had when we went on that *Spirit of Philadelphia* boat for our anniversary one year with JD? Well, they offer Sunday afternoon brunch specials, and I thought that would be fun."

"Oh, that was a great time. I remember it fondly. Yes, let's do it; that will be fun."

As we drive up to the launching area for the brunch cruise, I point to the Chart House restaurant. "I'll never forget having brunch there with my dad and Nancy and David when my brother was still in college. It was much colder that day. I don't think I've been treated to brunch since then—that was like 23 or 24 years ago." I laugh—and then stop abruptly—when I see SueAnn's family walking across the parking lot. *What are they doing here?* I wonder. . . .

"You tricked me!" I say to Hector. "I thought this was going to be just a quiet brunch with me and you."

"Really, Mom? In our family, you thought you could escape with a quiet brunch on your 50th birthday?" George says loudly.

"Shhhhh, George. The whole world doesn't have to know I'm 50!" I laugh.

All of the kids who live in Philly are here with spouses and children, plus Angelo, Mohan, and Azeb, our unofficial kids. And I'm shocked to see Jose. "You came all the way from Switzerland?" I ask, deeply touched.

"You're worth it, Mom," he replies.

"Good answer, Jose," Isaac laughs.

"You look beautiful, Miss Sue," Angelo says, giving me a kiss on the cheek.

"Not too shabby for a great-grandmother, eh?" I say. Our first great-grandchild, Isaiah, was born to our eldest granddaughter, Kirsten, just weeks ago. I glance at Hector; he's smiling broadly as he holds Joelle's two-month-old son, Mackell. *Oh, he is smitten again,* I think to myself. . . .

"Why is Nanna so happy to get a doll for her birthday? Isn't she too old for dolls?" I'm overhearing Esperanza and Jasmine whispering to their mothers.

"These are special dolls. They were hers when she was a little girl, and they were falling apart, so we got them all fixed up for her birthday."

"Why is she crying, then?"

"These dolls remind me of happy memories of when I was a little girl, but also they remind me that God makes all things new, just like these dolls have been made new," I say to Esperanza and Jasmine, overhearing their question. "So I'm crying happy tears."

"If you like the dolls, wait until you see what's next," Todd says.

"Hush. Don't give it away," Roberto shushes him.

"Oh my!" I'm utterly speechless. Over the years I've joked that I would love a "mother's ring" with a birthstone for each child, but that in my case it would be too heavy to wear. This year, the kids have created a special ring custom-made for me. The birthstones are tiny, so they all fit on the ring—all 22 of them. It's one of a kind —just like my family.

"You are all my jewels! More precious than rubies and sapphires. You are always in my heart, but with this ring, I will have you all with me everywhere I travel. I don't even know how to say thank you." I sit silently, with no more words coming to me.

"Write it down quick—this is the day Mom ran out of words!" Jose laughs.

"I'm so thankful for this amazing weather," I whisper to Hector as we sit watching Isaac and Simmy get up to take the dance floor for their first dance.

"I know. Planning an outdoor wedding in October was a little risky, but it's turned out beautiful," he says.

"I also want to say: I know the night is still young, but so far, you haven't been drinking much, and I really appreciate that." I am gently pointing this out. He ignores me, so I continue: "Look how beautiful they are together. I can't tell you how much it touched me that Simmy wanted to wear my wedding gown. She truly is a daughter to me. I hope she knows how much I love her."

"They are the perfect couple. They've dated even longer than we did before we got married," Hector says.

"Can you believe we pulled off four weddings in three years and they were each so unique and different?"

"I still remember pacing around the living room in our Short Street apartment all those nights when Isaac wouldn't go to sleep as a baby. Where have the years gone?" Hector says.

"I still remember pacing around the living room in our Short Street apartment all those nights when Isaac wouldn't go to sleep as a baby. Where have the years gone?" Hector says.

"We had no idea our journey would take us to some of the places we've been, and who knows what lies ahead? But for now, I'm just loving the moment," I say, leaning my head onto his shoulder.

"I was just watching the expressions on all the little kids' faces as they watch the dancing," Hector says. "You know, I wasn't happy about many of the pregnancies, but I can't imagine my life without these grandkids. They each have a piece of my heart."

"I know what you mean, Poppa. Who would have thought that on our wedding day, almost 30 years ago, we'd get to this point? Looking around at our family makes me think of Psalm 127—'how blessed is the man whose quiver is full' of children."

"Well, I must be super blessed, because I think I have at least ten quivers full!" he laughs. "And who knows how many more grands and great-grands are in our future? . . . Look, they're opening up the dance floor. May I have this dance, Mrs. Badeau?"

"I'd be honored, Mr. Badeau."

24

From a Father's Heart—Redemption

"OK, OK, Sue. I'll be there. You come in on the 11:15 R-8 train; don't worry. I'll be there."

"I hope so. Please don't fall asleep on the couch in front of the fire again. It's freezing rain outside and I don't want to have to walk up the hill with my suitcase in that rain."

"I'll be there. Don't worry. Good-bye."

Next thing I know, the front door is slamming. "Thanks a lot! I knew you'd been drinking, and you'd fall asleep again. I was hoping I'd be wrong, but I just knew this would happen."

"I'm sorry, Sue. I didn't mean to fall asleep," I say as I try to hide the beer can under the couch.

"I'm soaking wet from head to toe, and my computer better

not be ruined! I'm going to bed," Sue says as she storms up the stairs.

"I said I was sorry. I'll be right up. I just have to check on Wayne and Dylan and put some wood on the fire."

"Don't bother coming up—you can stay down there on the couch," Sue yells back. "I have to catch the early train in the morning to head to D.C.—don't bother getting up. I'll just walk to the train."

Once again, I'm in the doghouse. She's angry. *Very* angry. I check on Wayne and Dylan and they're fast asleep. Throw some wood on the fire and lie down on the couch to sleep. What's that verse from Paul? Romans 7:15? "For what I am doing, I do not understand; for I am not practicing what I *would* like to *do*, but I am doing the very thing I hate." *That's the story of my life*, I think to myself as I drift off to sleep.

The phone is ringing and the caller ID says it's Sue. "Hey, you should have woken me up . . . " I start to say. But I'm cut off.

"I just got mugged," she says. I can hear that she's crying. "This guy just ran right up to me at the train station and grabbed my bag and knocked me over." She's sounding hysterical.

"Are you OK?" I ask.

"Not really!" she yells into the phone. "Good thing there were other people here and they chased him off before I got more hurt. My back hurts and my shoulder too from him pulling my bag."

"Hang on, I'll be right down." I hang up, throw on my coat and shoes, and grab the keys. It's just a minute drive to the station, and by the time I get there, Sue is inside. After a few minutes of discussing this . . .

"You sure you're OK?"

"I'll be fine. Just go home."

"You should have woken me up."

"I did," she cuts in. "But you know how you are after you've been drinking. Cussing and hollering at me when I tried to wake you. I gave up and decided to walk."

"I'm so sorry, Sue."

"Sure you are. When I get back from D.C. this weekend, we need to talk. I'm done with this."

Sue's train arrives and she gets on without a good-bye or kiss. I drive home feeling like crap—emotionally and physically. I need some Advil; my head is killing me.

The next few days go by slowly. I take care of Wayne and Dylan, feeding them through their G-tubes every few hours, changing them as needed. I try to spend time with them each day now that both of them don't get out of bed much due to how painful it is for them to sit up. Some of the kids call and stop by to see how things are going or to stock up their refrigerator by raiding ours. Sue calls every night, but our conversations are short and chilly.

"How was your day?" I ask.

"Fine," Sue answers. "How are Wayne and Dylan?"

"Fine," I say. Then silence. Boy, am I dreading this weekend. Here we go again.

Friday night rolls around, and this time I make sure to pick Sue up as she arrives on the 9 PM train. I take one look at her face and I know I am in for it. I don't think she has cooled down at all. We get home and I carry her bag in, offering her some of the Shepherd's Pie I made for dinner.

"No, I'm OK. I ate on the train. I just need some water, watch a little TV, and then hit the sack."

"OK, then you do that while I finish up with Wayne and Dylan and tend the fires."

So, I do my thing and Sue does hers. *Not much conversation going on here, Hec,* I say to myself. I wonder when the other shoe is going to drop. We get into bed at 11, no saying goodnight, no kiss, no hug. I remember the promise we made when we were first married, from Ephesians 4:26: "Do not let the sun go down while you are still angry." We haven't broken that promise often, but it's never good when we do. We lie next to each other in hurt and angry silence, and neither of us sleeps much.

I'm up early Saturday morning to start Wayne and Dylan eating. This has been my morning routine for so many years that I can't remember when I've been able to sleep past 5 AM. They both used to eat orally, but through the years they've both needed to have the G-tubes so we can be sure they get enough nourishment. The tradeoff is that it takes hours each day to feed them.

"Hector!" I hear Sue holler. "Could you come up, please?" *Oh no, here we go,* I think to myself. I think that other shoe just dropped.

"I'll be right up."

I walk into our bedroom. The air is cold as ice and that is not just because we don't get much heat in our room.

"Sit down, we need to talk." Sue motions me to a chair.

"OK. What's up?" I ask, knowing exactly what I am in for.

"The past few days while I was in D.C., I've had plenty of time to think and pray about what's going on in our relationship, or lack thereof. I can't take it any more; your drinking has become too much for me to deal with. You are not the person I married when you drink. Everything about you changes; you become a different person. To say nothing about how it affects the kids."

"I'm listening," I say as her words start penetrating.

"The money you waste, the lies you tell me, and your lame excuse for drinking I can't take. The fact is you have a problem—we have a major problem. It can't go on like this."

I try to say something, but Sue cuts me off. "I'm talking now," she says. "Listen and listen carefully."

All of a sudden the room seems to be getting warmer; I'm pretty sure it's because I'm on the hot seat.

"Go on," I say.

"I can't stand it when you drink. I've had to tolerate it all these years. Sure there were times when you didn't drink, especially when we first got married, but even during those first ten years or so, if you got the chance to drink, like at a wedding, you'd get drunk. Moderation has never been in your vocabulary. The last five years has been like hell for me. Four of our kids got married and I was not able to enjoy those weddings to the fullest because of your drinking.

> "I'm talking now," she says. "Listen and listen carefully." All of a sudden the room seems to be getting warmer; I'm pretty sure it's because I'm on the hot seat.

"Every holiday or special times we've had, you have a need to drink. Sure, the kids don't say anything to you because they worship the ground you walk on. Anyway, if they wanted to, they'd be afraid to confront you. Some even make excuses for you. But some of the kids talk to me about your drinking and are concerned." She pauses for a moment. "Are you *listening???*"

"Yes, yes, I hear you," I respond, but my mind is wandering a bit, thinking of what I should say—whether to fight back or to just take it. I'm not sure how to respond this time; this is different from her other lectures. I think she really means it this time. There is no screaming. Just straight talk.

Sue continues. "Like I said, I'm not dealing with this anymore. You have a lot of good qualities. You've always been there for the kids, you work hard, and you have given your life to serving people. I know you are a Christian and have faith in Jesus. However, alcoholism is a disease, and you have it. I know right about now you're probably thinking, 'Don't confuse me with the facts,' but the fact is that your father was an alcoholic, and many of your siblings have battled alcoholism. You're not the person I married anymore, the person I fell in love with—I want that man back."

I feel like I've been cut down so low by this time, I could play handball off the curb. As hard as it is to admit, Sue is right in what she's saying. She always has all the bases covered when we argue.

As hard as it is to admit, Sue is right in what she's saying. She always has all the bases covered when we argue.

But she's not finished. "I've made a list of things that need to change. Look it over and decide what you're going to do. "

Strangely, a funny thought comes to mind—something I once read, a quote by Einstein: "Women marry men hoping they will change and men marry women hoping they will not. So each is inevitably disappointed." I tune back in to Sue as she goes on.

"In three months we can talk again and we'll see what progress has been made. At that time we'll reassess and make some decisions. You need to know I'm ready to leave, as painful as it will be. I feel I have no choice."

I don't say much, just, "OK, I understand." I take her list and look it over. One of the items on the list is to go to counseling. Most of the other items on her list are doable.

"Thank you for sharing this. And I really am sorry," I say as I start to walk out of the room.

"The proof will be in the pudding, as they say. If you're really sorry, I'll see it in your actions. Words are cheap right now."

The next three months are very intense. Sue does a lot of traveling for her work. We have our evening phone conversations, but they seem more like Headline News than real conversation. In the early weeks after Sue gives me these "marching orders," as I call them, I experience a range of emotions—guilt, anger, shame, self-pity. *Who does she think she is?* I think to myself many times. *I could make a laundry list for her too. After all the diapers I've changed and foot rubs I've given her, how dare she tell me what I can and can't do.*

Yet something stirs inside me and I decide to keep my mouth shut and work on the list.

"I called the counselor we saw a few years ago," I tell Sue.

"Great. What did he say?"

"He gave me the name of a woman who specializes in addictions."

"Did you call her?"

"Yes, I did. I left a message for her." I imagine Sue thinking: *Oh, here we go with the "I left a message" routine.*

"Good morning, Mr. Badeau. Come in," Mrs. Brown says to me as I enter her office a week later.

As I walk in I am thinking, *I never thought I'd be the one in the family seeing a shrink.* "Good morning," I reply.

"Sit, sit. Let me tell you a little about myself and my approach, and then you can tell me what is going on with you," Mrs. Brown says.

After I listen to her for about 10 minutes, I feel more at ease. She seems caring and she's a Christian. *OK, this might work for me.*

"All right Hector, if I may call you that. Tell me about the family you grew up in and your family now."

Oh no, not again. She knows not what she asks, I think.

"This could take days," I say.

"Excuse me?"

"It's just that I come from a large family, 16 kids. And my family now? I have 22 kids."

"Oh my!" she says in amazement. I've seen that look before, the look of unbelief.

So I begin. After about 35 minutes, Doctor Brown stops me

and states, "I think we are going to need a number of sessions. I'm not sure I have all the answers, but I do have a few ideas we can discuss."

I'm feeling much more at home. I like this woman's approach.

"You say alcohol was a big part of your growing up. Your dad drank a lot, as did your siblings. I'm afraid I have to agree with what your wife told you: 'Kids who grow up in an alcoholic environment tend to drink when they get older.'"

What can I say? It's so hard to face facts. We continue our conversation until the end of the session, and I schedule the next appointment for the following week. In the meantime, Doctor Brown suggests a few herbs and vitamins for me to take to help with my energy level and depression. I feel good driving home; maybe this was the beginning of the U-turn in my drinking journey that I need, the one setting me back in the right direction.

"Was tonight hard for you?" Sue asks. It's May 2009, and we are back in our hotel room after a fun evening celebrating our nephew's graduation from Boston College.

"Hard? No, it was fun. Good dinner, proud of Michael. Fun to see everyone. Why would you ask me if it was hard?" I reply.

"Well, this was the first really big celebration since you completely stopped drinking. And there was plenty of wine and beer available. It was so great that you didn't drink, but I was thinking it might have been hard for you," she explains.

"Hmmm, you're right. There was a lot of beer and wine around, but I hadn't thought about it that way. I really enjoyed the evening, and I'm especially enjoying spending time with you now and not feeling guilty about anything," I say as I grab Sue up in one of my famous bear hugs.

Over the last six months I've continued to meet with Doctor Brown. She's helped me get a grip on a lot of things, especially my anger with my own father. I haven't had a drop of alcohol now in a year—and I feel great. Things haven't been perfect, but I am so thankful I made that U-turn, because I know we are definitely on the right road.

And it feels good to be traveling together again. With God all things are possible, indeed.

25
Building Bridges

"I think Aaron's finally in a place where he has a chance to get the help he needs," I say to Hector upon returning from a meeting of the Governor's Commission on Children.

"What makes you say that?" he asks.

"Abraxas did a presentation at the meeting I was at today, and they say they offer trauma-informed care using the Sanctuary Model. I really hope it's true; I've been pushing for Aaron to have trauma-focused services for a long time."

"I hope it's true too. I just wish it wasn't so far away. It really makes family involvement difficult. I hated that St. Gabriel place, but at least it was close enough for us to visit every week," Hector says.

"I know. Some of these places act like the parents are the

enemy. I wish they'd actually look at the research that demonstrates how critical family involvement is if you want a kid to succeed once he gets out," I say. This is a familiar theme of mine.

"Back when we directed the group home in Vermont," Hector says, "it never occurred to me that one day we'd have a son caught up in the juvenile justice system."

"I know, and we were naïve to believe that systems designed to help our children would do so. From the minute that Fisher first got tangled up with the justice system, to the day Aaron had to go to juvenile hall, it's been a nightmare."

"You're right, Sue. The wounds aren't always visible, but the scars are real. I wonder, if we'd been able to get real help for Fisher when his addictions first started . . . " Hector doesn't finish the thought; he doesn't have to.

"Even then, that might have been too late. What I know now that I didn't know then was that he really needed help addressing the trauma from his early years. If he'd gotten that kind of help, maybe he wouldn't have traveled the addiction path at all," I say.

I can't help but wonder what might have made a difference for Fisher, and pray that we can find the key to making a difference now, for Aaron.

"No one realizes that the parents live the nightmares along with their child," Hector says, visibly moved. "The ache in my heart for both Aaron and Fisher is so strong. I wish I could take their pain from them."

"I know. We believe in a God who can do just that. I just pray that one day they will each discover that depth of faith and opportunity for healing themselves. In the meantime, I hope Aaron can graduate while he's at Abraxas, and when he gets out,

I hope he can find acceptance in the community."

"It's going to be a rough road for him, that's for sure," Hector says.

"Speaking of roads, it's time for me to hit the road. I have that meeting on Tribal Courts in Reno this week," I remind Hector.

"Do you need a ride to the train?"

"No, the train schedule doesn't really work well with the flight schedule on Sunday nights, so I'm using a car service. They'll be here in a few minutes. I rarely do this, but if I have to travel on Sunday night for work, it doesn't seem unreasonable."

"I agree. Travel safely," he says, leaning in to give me a kiss before I put my coat on.

"Nanna, please call me back right away." There is such an urgency in Kirsten's voicemail message that I leave my meeting immediately to call her back.

"What is it, sweetheart?"

"It's Nalana. She's in the hospital. They're working on her. I don't know what's going on." My granddaughter explains that the baby's father was caring for her while Kirsten was at work and she got a call to come to the hospital. Nalana wasn't breathing, but has been revived. Something has gone terribly wrong, and I know I have to get home from Reno as soon as possible.

This turns out to be the beginning of a very long road that becomes the focal point of our entire spring. Nalana's father has been arrested, and the rest of us take turns spending time with the precious baby at the hospital, holding, rocking, cuddling, talking, hoping, and praying for a miracle. Rejoicing each time she opens her eyes or smiles. Helping Kirsten navigate the many decisions about feeding tubes and DNR orders.

This turns out to be the beginning of a very long road that becomes the focal point of our entire spring.

We pull together as a family, developing a care plan so that Nalana can safely come home with Kirsten when she leaves the hospital. Hector and I, along with SueAnn, Flory, Chelsea, Whitney, and Roberto's brother Cochise all become part of the team supporting Kirsten and advocating for little Nalana.

Easter comes and goes and she's still in the hospital. Finally, by Mother's Day, she's home, and we hope the worst is behind us.

I'm savoring my Mother's Day cards and a last bite of my dessert when the phone rings.

"Mom, Dad, I did it!" Aaron's voice is excited over the phone. "I graduated and got my diploma."

"That's wonderful, Aaron. We're really proud of you. It took a lot of work and you had a lot of ups and downs . . . "

"Mostly downs," he interjects.

"Yeah, the last few years since your eighth-grade graduation at Henry have been challenging for all of us," Hector says.

"Which is even more reason to feel good about this accomplishment," I say. "When you get home in the spring, we'll throw a graduation party just like we have for all your brothers and sisters. How's that sound?" I ask.

"Sounds great, Mom. I can't wait to get home. I don't want to be here anymore."

"I know, Aaron," Hector says. "Your time is almost finished."

"Speaking of time, my phone time is finished now, I have to go. I'll call again next week."

"Hopefully, this is the beginning of better days for Aaron," Hector says when we get off the phone. "Does he get back to Philly before or after we go to Vermont for Ashley's graduation?"

I look at the calendar. "He gets back two days after Ashley's graduation."

"I guess that means we'll be making a quick trip this time."

"That's OK. Trish and the boys are coming back to Philly with us, so we'll have some time with them, and we pick up Janessa on our way back through also. And don't forget your sister Irene is coming for a week. I hope she likes the hotel I've reserved for her. I'm thankful we have those points to use. She'll be much more comfortable in the air conditioning than our hot house!" I laugh.

"And you'll be gone at least half of that time, right?" he asks, knowing the answer already.

"That's right. I'll be heading to Seattle right after we get back from Vermont." My new job at Casey Family Programs was billed as a "work from home" opportunity; they even set me up with state-of-the-art home office equipment shortly after I started a year ago. But it quickly turned into the traveling road show. One week blurs into the next and the seasons change while I traverse the country from time zone to time zone working with my Casey colleagues and public child welfare systems as they seek to increase permanency for all children in foster care.

"Speaking of travels, what time is your flight tomorrow, and do you know where you're going?" Hector asks. I've had the unfortunate experience of missing flights or going to the wrong airport on the wrong day, so Hector has taken it upon himself to help me keep it all straight.

"I leave on a 6 PM flight. I'll be in Birmingham, Alabama for three days."

"Remind me, is that in our time zone, or . . . "

"Nope. One-hour time difference," I remind him.

"OK, will you be up in time for our morning call?" he asks. We do a Bible study together every morning, in person when I'm home and by phone when I'm on the road. Our evening call is for catching up on everything else.

"You bet. I wouldn't miss it. But speaking of missing things, I better get packed and check the train schedule to the airport so

I don't miss my flight."

"Good plan. Let me know when you want a ride to the train."

"Do you know, Hec, that in 2009 alone I did my Permanency Values training over 200 times?" I remark during our evening call several months later. "I wish I had some way to know how many children moved closer to permanence as a result of all that work."

"Even if you never find out, you know you're making a difference and storing up treasures in Heaven," he says. "But I have to be honest and tell you that I liked it a whole lot better when we took our road trips together."

"I agree. We should plan a trip for this summer. I have accumulated plenty of vacation time; we just need to figure out how and when to use it."

"Funny you should mention that. I have two things to tell you. Remember when I applied for that Medicaid waiver for Dylan and Wayne and we were on a waiting list? Well, we finally got off the waiting list, and they're both approved. One of the things we can get through that is respite."

"Woohoo! That's super. Respite care—how about that? We've been at this how long? Over 30 years now—and never had respite even though we advocate for it. That's awesome news.

"You said you had two things to tell me. What's the second one?" I ask.

"I had a nice long conversation with Jose. He wants to treat us to a trip to Switzerland. It's been seven years since the first time we went; can you believe that? Anyway, he wants us to pick some dates so he can start planning."

"Oh, that would be terrific. I've been missing him. It will be great to see him and spend some time in Switzerland again. The chocolate . . . the cheese . . . yum. I'm ready. What were you thinking about for dates?" I ask.

"What do you think of this idea? If we get the ball rolling on the respite program, I can get someone in place by mid-summer. Then, NACAC this year is in Hartford, Connecticut, so we could go up there for four days. It would be a test run of the respite provider. If it all works out, we can take our trip to Switzerland in late September."

"Wow, you've got it all mapped out. I love it. And since NA-CAC is in Hartford, a lot of the kids from Philly and Vermont could come. We could even sign up the grandkids in the children's program. Wouldn't that be fun?" I add.

"Oh, that's too weird," he says.

"What's weird about it?" I ask.

"What's weird is how much we think alike—scary. I was thinking the same thing. In fact, I even talked to SueAnn about it earlier today, and she's on board. She thinks it would be awesome for her kids to have the NACAC experience."

"Perfect, let's work toward that goal. I'll put in for time off in September and you get back to Jose."

"Will do. And don't forget, paperwork is still your job, so when you're home this weekend, you'll need to do the paperwork required on this Medicaid waiver program."

"Yeah, yeah, I know. As long as you don't expect me to change any diapers, we're all good," I laugh as we say our goodnights.

"I talked to Jose, and we are all set for those dates in September. They work for him," Hector confirms, three nights later on our call.

"That's great. I already requested the time off too, so it looks like it will really happen. Are our passports still good, or do they need to be renewed? I can't remember."

"They're still good; I checked. Changing the subject: can you help me do a count of how many people will be with us for Easter dinner? I want to get the reservation made today."

"Oh, good idea," I say and we start listing the names of all of our children, grandchildren, spouses, friends, and dates who will be joining us for Easter dinner. Easter is the one time each year when we take the entire family out to eat.

"There we go. The last of the baskets are finished. Let's go to bed. That sunrise service is going to come early," Hector says on Saturday evening. We make small Easter baskets for each child and grandchild with items in them related to an Easter theme, and some candy, of course. They have to answer the questions on a Bible quiz before they get their baskets. This year's items include small roosters, soap and washcloths, and a packet of seeds.

In the morning, Hector and I go alone to the brief but lovely outdoor sunrise service at church and then come home to make a pancake breakfast. Soon, everyone will be here to open their baskets before church. As a family, we'll go to the big service and then head out to the restaurant for dinner. Our day will end with a lively Easter egg hunt on the front lawn.

"He is risen!" Esperanza says immediately when I open the front door.

"He is risen, indeed!" I reply, grinning.

"Say it Ally!" Esperanza encourages her little sister to get in on the tradition.

"Indeed!" three-year-old Ally says to me, beaming.

"Look, Ally. I want to show you." Esperanza takes her by the hand and brings her over to the tomb of stones that Hector made on Friday with all the grandchildren. "Look, the stone is rolled away, and Jesus is not in there anymore."

"Wow," says Ally.

"I love the genuine wonder the little kids have when they see that," I say to Hector.

"Do you remember the year it was only Jose and Chelsea?" Hector recalls. "We had set the tomb up next to a window. When they got up in the morning and saw that Jesus was gone, Jose said, 'He flew out the window!'"

"I'll never forget that," I say, chuckling.

Chelsea and Flory arrive with their husbands and kids, so we are ready for the quiz and the baskets.

"What does a rooster remind us of?" I ask first. All of the kids' hands shoot up into the air, begging to be called on first, as Todd shouts out "Jesus!"

Everyone bursts out laughing. When the kids were small, Todd knew that he'd be right a good part of the time if he answered "Jesus" to any question. It's a family joke now.

"OK, Titianna. What's the answer?"

After several kids offer their guesses, Isaac finally provides the answer: "Peter denied Jesus three times before the rooster crowed," he tells them.

"Great. Now who knows what the soap and washcloth are for?"

"Oooh, ooooh. I know that one!" Jasmine says.

"OK, go ahead, Jasmine.

"Because Jesus washed the disciples' feet," she says softly.

"Bravo! You got it on the first try. One more question: what do seeds remind us of?"

"Things that grow," five-year-old Chloe offers.

"That's part of the answer, Chloe, good try. Who else can add a little more too it?"

"Um, I remember something about the seeds dying in the ground before they grow," Esperanza adds.

"Perfect. That's exactly right," I say, explaining the rest of the passage.

"OK, pancakes are ready!" Hector calls from the kitchen. "Come get 'em while they're hot!"

An hour later we're sitting in church—filling four pews. I close my eyes for a moment to enjoy the music of the bell choir when Amber taps me on the shoulder.

"I think I need to go to the hospital," she whispers.

"Right now?" I whisper back—but one look at her face and I know she's right. Quietly, I let Hector know what's happening, and then Aaron, Amber, and I slip out as gracefully as possible.

. . .

I text to Hector just before pulling out of the hospital parking lot: *Dr. ck'd Amber – def. in labor but long way to go. I'll come Easter din and bk to hosp. later.*

A few days after Easter, and the birth of our newest grandson, Aaron Junior—or AJ—and I'm back on the road. When it's time for Phillip's graduation, I'm in Chicago, scheduled to fly to Vermont and meet Hector there on Friday night.

"It's pouring rain, and thunderstorms," I tell Hector over the phone. "So far, my flight has been delayed for an hour. Let's pray it's not more than that."

"Well, I made good time driving," he says. "I left Renee and Daniel off with Trish, and I'm in Burlington just waiting for you."

Two hours later I have to call Hector with the distressing news that my flight has been cancelled. I'm doing all I can to work out the next, best available flight, I tell Hector, trying to exude more confidence than I really feel.

"Is Mom going to make it, Dad?" Trish asks Hector. They're already sitting in the stands, and the ceremonies are about to begin.

"She should be pulling in any minute now," Hector tells her.

After my flight from Chicago was cancelled, I ended up on a flight to Manchester, New Hampshire that landed just more than two hours before the graduation started. I had to get a rental car and drive to Barre—all on coffee and adrenaline because sleep was out of the question. On a wing and a prayer, I pull into the parking lot just as the processional music begins.

"Do you at least get to go home now, Susan?" my sister asks while we enjoy the graduation party that Trish has orchestrated for Phillip.

"No, I'm back on the road. I have three more trips before our family all meets up in Hartford, Connecticut in a few weeks for the NACAC conference."

"Isn't the travel getting to be a little too much?"

"Weeks like this, it sure feels like too much," I agree. "But I do love the work I do."

I arrive in Hartford before the family. Not only are Hector, David, Renee, SueAnn, Chelsea, and their families coming up from Philly, but Trish and her boys and Patty Kirpan with Milagro and Grace are coming down from Vermont. My online adoptive mom friends Karen and Judy are coming too. It's going to be a great conference.

"Did you have a good trip?" I ask Hector as we get seated in a pizza place for dinner.

"It was fine. Not too much traffic."

"And you feel comfortable with the respite person?"

"Yes, she seems quite competent, although I still worry a little. We've never left Wayne and Dylan with anyone but family before."

"Relax, they'll be fine," I say, squeezing his hand. "And you deserve this break."

How could I know the trials that lay ahead in the next four weeks?

26

From a Father's Heart—
Long, Hard Road

"Sue, wake up."

"What? What is it?"

"It's Dylan," I tell her. "Something's wrong with him. I got up to feed him and he had vomit all over him and his stomach is totally distended. He's running a fever. We need to get him to the hospital."

"OK, I'm getting up. You get him ready," Sue says.

I head downstairs to change Dylan, shaking with fear. *I've seen Dylan through some rough times before, but this time, I'm not sure,* I think to myself. Last time he was in the hospital we almost lost him due to a virus. He was also losing his ability to eat due to the cerebral palsy caused by the head injury he sustained as a baby. The last time in the hospital, they put in the G-tube feeding apparatus to keep him alive.

"OK, Dylan, we're taking you to the hospital," I tell him as I change his diaper and clean him up. Poor kid is so limp. I dress him and holler to Sue, "Let's go!"

Sue walks into the room, takes one look at him, and says, "Oh no, what happened?"

"I'm not sure what that nurse did. His tube has been re-taped and looked like it was pulled out some," I say. We'd left Wayne and Dylan in the care of a respite nurse for three days while we went away to the NACAC conference in Connecticut.

"I'll grab the notebook so we can read the notes the nurse left," Sue says as we head for the door. . . .

Sue drives while I hold Dylan in the back seat. It's 6 AM on a Sunday morning, so thankfully there is not much traffic on the way to Children's Hospital. With each bump in the road, somehow Dylan manages a smile. "He still gets a kick out of the bumps when you hit them, in spite of how he feels," I say. "He could be on the verge of death and still show a smile."

Little did I realize how close to the edge of death he was.

Sue drops us off at the door and goes to park. I carry Dylan into the emergency room. The nurse at the counter listens to me describe what's going on and says, "Bring him right back." I follow her to a large room and ask her to let Sue know where we are. I lay Dylan on a table.

"He looks like he is in so much pain," Sue says when she arrives moments later. Within minutes the room is swarming with doctors and nurses. They bring in X-ray equipment, and the doctors are checking Dylan's eyes, pulse, heart, and more.

"I don't know what to think, Sue," I say as I fight to hold back tears. I'm a crier. My kids will tell you that I cry at happy times, sad times—any kind of emotional time.

Sue looks on, a bit in shock. "Let's just wait and see what the doctors tell us."

After what seems forever, a doctor walks over to us. "Your son is very sick. He has a tear in his intestines and feces has gotten into his lung and other parts of his body." He asks us to describe what happened over the last 24 hours—what he ate, what medications he took, and if he had any urine or bowel movements.

"We don't know," Sue says, her voice tight with anger. "He was in the care of a respite nurse and we left her with his care notebook. She was supposed to write everything down, but look, the pages for those days are blank. Nothing is written. And she's not answering our calls. Her supervisor hasn't returned our calls either."

These facts haunt both of us. We have no way of knowing what happened to Dylan in the few days we were gone. We don't know what pain he experienced or how scared he might have been. Our fears about what is happening right now in front of us are tinged with guilt over having left him for three days.

The doctor explains some of the issues going on with Dylan's body and then asks, "Do you have a DNR (Do Not Resuscitate) order for him?"

This hits me like a brick to the head. "You mean to tell me he's that sick?" I just can't believe this. Four days ago he was great just before we left.

"We need an answer now, Mr. and Mrs. Badeau," the doctor gently says.

Sue is always cool and calm under stress, it seems. "So, what do we do, Hec?" she asks me. "We've talked about this before; we've agreed that a DNR is the best plan. Of course, with three terminally ill children, we've had many of these conversations over the years. But it's one thing to say it and another to have to really go through with it," Sue adds with tears in her eyes.

"We've prayed about this, Sue. We agreed: no extraordinary measures to keep him alive. The feeding tube added eight years to his life, but that wasn't an extraordinary measure, and I'm thankful we did that. This seems much different. We don't want him to suffer."

After a few more moments of talking and a brief prayer, we tell the doctor what we want. "Yes, please. We agree to a DNR order, and do not take any extraordinary measures to keep him alive." It appears that the doctors and nurses in the room agree we have made the right decision, although they say nothing to influence us. It's a matter of moments before the paperwork is ready and, with shaky hands, we both sign it.

In the meantime they've made Dylan as comfortable as possible. They have him on oxygen and have started IV fluids and antibiotics. "We are going to move him to the ICU room and you and your wife can follow him up to his room," a nurse tells us. Three hours have passed since we arrived at the emergency room. I wonder if this is the beginning of the end of Dylan's journey of life. He turns 24 on September 9. Today is August 8. Will he make it to his birthday?

Sue and I follow the nurse pushing Dylan's bed and squeeze into the elevator to the sixth floor. Neither of us says much as we hold Dylan's hands. We arrive at his room, and again there is a flurry of activity with nurses and doctors bustling in and out of the room to get him settled. One of the doctors says, "We need to insert a tube into his bladder so we can measure his urine output and the color." Meanwhile, poor Dylan keeps crying out in pain.

It takes about a half an hour for him to doze off to sleep and for things to calm down in the room. "Well, Sue, here we are again," I say. "Dylan is trying to give me more gray hair! He's always had a sense of humor, you know."

Sue manages a smile, but says, "It's not so funny this time. Oh my goodness, do the other kids even know we're at the hospital?" she asks.

"I told Todd to keep an eye on Wayne, but the rest of the kids don't know what's going on yet. It was so early when we left the house. I know Todd's doing a good job, but I feel I need to get home and check on Wayne and get him started eating."

"I'll stay here with Dylan," Sue replies. "It is already ten and Wayne needs your attention."

"Yes, you're right, I should get going. But I really don't want to leave."

"I know, I understand. But I think you'll feel better once you've made sure Wayne is OK. While you're home you can make some calls and let the others know what's going on. Come back as soon as you can, but don't worry."

"All right," I say, getting up. I give Dylan a kiss and hug Sue. "I love you. We knew this day would come, but this is not how I expected it."

Somehow we both knew our faith was about to be tested again.

"Time to send up a few more prayers," Sue says as I leave.

"I will."

Somehow we both knew our faith was about to be tested again. "Time to send up a few more prayers," Sue says as I leave.

Reaching the car, I begin to pull out my cell phone to call the kids, but decide it's better if I just drive.

Memories of our "Big D with the little d" flood my mind. He was only three when we adopted him. That smile of his could charm anyone. How he loved his Smurf music! And those diapers—oh my, they got to be pretty nasty at times. I think I have changed more than a hundred thousand diapers in my life, and Dylan was a big contributor to that count!

I'm snapped out of my daydreaming by the ringing of the cell phone. Caller ID says it is Alysia.

OK, one less call I'll have to make at home, I think as I answer. "Hello Alysia, what's up? But before you answer, I need to tell you I'm on my way home from the hospital. Mom and I had to bring Dylan in early this morning. He's very sick."

"Is he going to be OK?" Alysia asks.

"I'm not sure yet."

Then Alysia starts to talk—without realizing the seriousness of the situation, I think.

"I have some good news! I'm pregnant!" she says. I cannot believe my ears.

"What??? You're pregnant?" If the angry energy that welled up in me at that moment could have been bottled, I could have heated our ten-bedroom house for a year.

"You've got to be kidding!" I yell into the phone. "Did you hear what I just told you about Dylan? He may die and you just had to call me with this news? You sound like I'm supposed to be happy about it." I feel myself about to lose it. *Dear God, how much can I take?* "You have all you can do to take care of yourself and now you are going to have a baby? And you couldn't wait to tell me later after you heard what I told you about Dylan?"

I have to let up on the gas because my anger is causing me to speed without realizing it.

"What did you say?" Alysia is hard to understand sometimes because of her cerebral palsy, which affects her speech. "You say you are three months pregnant already? Great. That's just great. And how many times have I seen you in the last three months when you could have told me? But no, today had to be the day." *When it rains, it pours,* I think.

"Well, Alysia, if you are looking for a congratulations from me, forget about it. As a matter of fact, I'm really mad right now. I'm done with this conversation for now. I have something more important to deal with today—my son, your brother, is dying. So good-bye. We'll talk about this another time." And without waiting for her to reply, I hang up.

I feel like a house just fell on me. I'm crushed.

I finally make it home without getting a speeding ticket or wrecking the car. I head for Wayne's bed and see Todd.

"How's Dylan doing?" he asks.

"Not too good. I'm not sure how long he has to live," I say, feeling the tears starting again.

Todd, who is the same age as Dylan, wants to know if he can go and see him.

"Not yet. I need you more here, and he's in intensive care right now, so he can't have too many people in the room. I'll be going back to the hospital and I need you to stay here with Wayne."

I feed and change Wayne. I call some of the other kids to take turns helping with Wayne while I go back and forth to the hospital.

"'I'm not sure how long I will be each time I go to the hospital. Mom will stay with Dylan the whole time, " I explain to Todd.

"OK, I've got you covered, Dad," Todd replies. I don't say a thing about Alysia.

I've made all the calls to family members, our pastor, and a few close friends. Wayne is content in his bed eating through his tube. I check in with Sue at the hospital and she says that Dylan is the same as when I left. It's only 1 in the afternoon, but I already feel as though I've been up for days. I sit in Dad's chair, as the kids call it, and rest my eyes for a few minutes before going back to the hospital.

As I close my eyes the song "Mama Said There'd Be Days Like This" comes to mind, but *Lord, really? Why so many days like this?* I thought I knew what we were getting into when we started this journey. Sure there would be bumps in the road and a few sharp turns, but . . .

I was even confident that I would be able to handle it when it came time for Adam, Dylan, and Wayne to die. I have always relied on the verse: "My grace is sufficient for you, for my power is made perfect in weakness," found in 2 Corinthians 12:9.

It was a shock the night Adam died. I said goodnight to him

that night and he was smiling away, more than usual. Maybe he knew something was going on and it was the last thing he wanted Sue and I to see. I'll never make that joke about "going to bed and waking up dead" again. Doing CPR on Adam still haunts me after learning that he had probably already been dead for a few hours. His heart just stopped. December 30, 1999—the turn of the century. I'll never forget how hard it was for the whole family, but God gave us the strength we needed.

Now Alysia; I did not need that call today. The last of my girls to get pregnant. Sue and I had some great expectations for the kids, and ourselves. "We're going to break the cycle," we believed—the cycles of addiction, pregnancies, and other challenges. But the pregnancies just keep on coming. First JD, then Lilly and Trish, and right on down the line. So much for our great expectations. I'm not sure who we thought we were. Some of the pregnancies hit me harder than others. Because of the hopes and dreams they had expressed for their own lives, I really did not imagine Chelsea or Joelle would join the pregnancy train. The day that each of them told me they were pregnant, I was totally overwhelmed. I remember riding the train all day after Joelle told Sue and I that she was pregnant. Just bought a ticket and rode from one end of the line to the other and back again.

What did we do wrong? Sometimes life can just be out of our control and we need to trust God. I love all the grandkids and can't imagine my life without them now, but still, this news.

Both Sue and I felt like failures as parents each time one of the kids told us they were expecting. What did we do wrong? Sometimes life can just be out of our control and we need to trust God. I love all the grandkids and can't imagine my life without them now, but still, this news about Alysia . . .

The phone rings; I startle. I didn't realize I had dozed off.

"Hi, Sue."

"When are you coming back to the hospital?" she asks. I tell her that everything is covered at home and that I'll be there in about half an hour.

For three and a half weeks, Sue stays at the hospital and I go back and forth between the hospital and home. It is a long and hard road. Dylan is struggling and nothing the doctors do to get him to eat is working. He seems to be in so much pain, especially each time they feed him; it's breaking our hearts. One of the tests revealed that he has a kidney stone, but the way it's positioned and with all his other complicating factors, there aren't really any options for doing anything about it.

We all agree that the time has come to bring Dylan home.

When his pain gets out of control, they agree to stop trying to feed him for a while, and then he calms down. But then, just when he is resting and comfortable, they decide it is time to try another feeding, and the shrieks of pain begin again. I have never seen anyone in such pain—I wish I could take it onto myself, and away from him. I wish I could just make it stop.

Sue gets up to give me a hug as I come into Dylan's room. She shows me a card and some materials left by the Pediatric Advanced Care Team. "You just missed them," she tells me. "They're so compassionate. They were explaining all of our options now that there's not really anything left the hospital can do for Dylan. They encouraged us to discuss the options with our family doctor and other people we trust before we decide what to do next."

After many prayers, several heart-wrenching conversations with the doctors, our family, our pastor, and a new friend, Abby—who God brought into our lives like an angel, just in time to help us advocate for Dylan—we all agree that the time has come to bring Dylan home. He's not going to get better, and he's just so unhappy here.

"Are you sure this is what you want to do?" one of the head doctors asks Sue.

"Yes, we've talked with our family doctor, who has cared for Dylan for almost twenty years. We understand what's happening. All of his systems are failing and he's not eating. We don't want him to continue to experience this excruciating pain."

"I understand," the doctor replies. "You've given this a lot of thought, and we want to support you. I'd like to make a referral to hospice, if that is OK with you."

"Yes," Sue answers. "That's what we want. We've experienced hospice before and they're wonderful. When it's Dylan's time to go, we want him around the family, people who love him, and in a place where he feels comfortable."

The doctors agree and hospice is set up. Dylan comes home on September 2, seven days before his 24th birthday.

"Dylan's home," Sue announces to all the kids and grandchildren who have come over to greet him.

The hospice nurse goes over all the medications for Dylan. "If he's in pain," she explains, "you can give him a little more of the morphine." She also shows us the notebook for writing everything down. We all want Dylan to be comfortable.

And so begin the final days of Dylan's life journey. He came into this world and was abused as a baby, and as he prepares to go out, he has suffered great pain again—perhaps because of neglect. Sadly, we'll never know for certain. It doesn't seem fair, and yet I know that God has both a plan and a purpose for his life. He brought great joy to everyone who knew him.

"I hope we made the right decision, Hec," Sue says on the fifth day at home.

"I know. It's been hard," I say. "I had a few doubts on the first day he came home—he was smiling and actually looked better than he did in the hospital." Of course, I knew that the reason he was more content was because the painful feedings had stopped. "Remember how he screeched in pain each time they tried to feed him in the hospital? His system just couldn't take it."

Each day when the hospice nurse goes over everything with us, it only confirms that we made the right decision. We're trusting God and savoring each moment we have left with him. When you sit vigil with someone who's dying, it's like you are in a bubble. The rest of the world doesn't exist. Friends slip in and out, some bringing food. The hospice art therapist does an arts and crafts activity with some of the smaller grandchildren. The hospice music therapist comes and spends an entire afternoon playing hymns and other favorite songs. It feels like the world is standing still and nothing else matters except what's happening in this little corner of our living room.

"I got ahold of everyone," Sue says to me on the morning of September 8. We've decided to have a little birthday celebration for Dylan and give everyone in the family a chance to say their good-byes.

We're amazed that Dylan is still with us, but we have come to the conclusion that he is holding out for his birthday. "He just wants one more party!" Sue said last night, and I do believe she's right.

"We'll have a party and I'll even make sweet potato pie for him," Sue adds. Sweet potatoes were Dylan's favorite food when he was able to eat before the feeding tube days.

"Great idea," I say. "I'll put a little on his tongue so he can have a taste of it. Maybe it will bring back some good memories for him."

Sue puts the birthday candles in the sweet potato pie as Chelsea turns on the video camera. "OK kids, gather around Dylan, and let's sing 'Happy Birthday!'" Everyone gathers around with some of the smaller grandchildren on his bed. After finishing "Happy Birthday," we sing a couple of verses of "Amazing Grace," and then, one by one, Dylan's brothers and sisters, and nieces and nephews, all say their final good- byes, tears flowing freely.

Alysia and Bernard also come to say their good-byes. Alysia gives me a big hug. Yes, we will have issues to work out in the months ahead, but at a moment like this, we stop and reflect on what truly matters, and the bonds of love we have for one another are far stronger than any difficulties or disagreements we experience.

Soon, only Sue and I are left with Dylan. I look at the fireplace mantel, saying, "Well. Adam, I think Dylan may be joining you tonight." Adam's urn sits on the mantel with his picture and his baptism Bible. Sue is at Dylan's bedside, and it's my time to take a little nap.

"It's your turn," Sue says as she wakes me. "It's after midnight. Dylan made it to his birthday."

"Happy Birthday, Big D," I cry as I give him a big hug. "Stretch out on the couch and try to get some rest, Sue. Two hours goes by fast." For the last seven days we have been taking turns sitting with Dylan and resting in two- or three-hour shifts. Even when the hospice nurses are here, we cannot bear to leave his side.

"OK, Dylan. Let's check that diaper." I change him and give him some pain medication. He feels impossibly light; he's so thin now.

"Sue, wake up. It's 1:15. Dylan is gone. He's in Heaven now with Jesus and dancing with Adam." Just then Wayne stirs a little in his bed.

"It's like he knows," Sue said. "He's the last of our three Musketeers still with us."

I give her a hug, and we both softly cry.

27

Twists and Turns

"So, tell us more about your plans." Angelo and my brother David look at us expectantly as we all sit down to lunch with Chelsea in the Comcast dining room high above the city of Philadelphia. It's the day after Thanksgiving, and we've invited them both to join us for lunch so we can share our plans with them.

"Well, after Dylan died, our friend Abby had this great idea that we could do something with the house as a lasting legacy in honor of Dylan," Hector begins.

"So, little by little, as the fog of grief began to lift, we realized that God was using her voice to help us hear his voice," I add. "The respite program we'd been dreaming of for several years can become a reality. And several of the kids—especially Chelsea, Isaac, Jose, and SueAnn—have been trying to convince us for a couple of years now to create a business, maybe a bed and breakfast, out of our house rather than selling it, now that most of the kids are grown up and on their own."

"So we started to imagine ways to put the two ideas—bed and breakfast, and respite—together, and we're at the point of creating a business plan," Hector continues.

"And that's where you two come in," Chelsea explains. "You both have experience with business plans, so we want your advice. Abby has hooked us up with her friend Teresa, who helps people starting new philanthropic projects, and she's been incredible. She also has a program called Women's Night Out, and Mom is going to be speaking for her in February. So we have a lot of balls in the air, but we need to get more organized so they don't just all fall on the floor."

By the end of lunch we're feeling encouraged and hopeful. Angelo and David both think our plans are exciting and agree to help make them more concrete.

"We needed this outing," Hector says, holding my hand as we walk back to the train.

"I know. We haven't really been out together at all since Dylan died," I reflect.

"I still can't believe he's been gone for three and a half months. I miss him so much."

Dylan's death has been hard on all of us, but especially so for Hector, whose daily routine for years has revolved around Dylan and Wayne's feeding schedules.

Both he and Wayne have had to adjust to a new daily routine. Thankfully, the holiday season, with the bubbly enthusiasm of all the grandchildren, has helped lift our spirits a little.

"What's on your agenda when we get home?" I ask.

"I'm going to work a little more on the woodwork," he says. "I need to feel like I've accomplished something before we start decorating for Christmas."

"Yeah, you're such a slacker," I joke.

"Look how much she's improved since last year," Hector says as we watch Esperanza's performance in the Pennsylvania Ballet's production of *The Nutcracker* three days after Christmas.

"I know. She really looks like she belongs up there on stage with all the professional dancers, doesn't she?" I add.

"Shhhhhh," someone behind us admonishes, and we both stifle a laugh.

Before we know it, the holidays are behind us and a new year has begun. I've accepted a special assignment from Casey, to serve for a year as a Senior Fellow in the Office of Juvenile Justice and Delinquency Prevention in D.C. So begins another year of commuting back and forth on weekends.

"How's the new apartment?" Hector asks on the first of our nightly calls when I get to D.C.

"Much nicer than the little studio I had when I did the Kennedy Foundation fellowship. I can't believe that was really twelve years ago. Funny, that fellowship is really what got me started on policy work. It opened so many doors for me. I wonder what this fellowship will lead to?"

"That's the exciting thing about our lives; we never know from year to year what lies ahead," Hector says.

"I know I'll be gone five days a week again, but at least I won't be in so many different time zones, and hopefully you can come visit me down here."

"I'd like to, but I'm not sure about leaving Wayne," Hector reminds me. He's been skittish about leaving home for even a day ever since Dylan's death.

"Well, let's think about it. Jose wants us to reschedule the Switzerland trip we didn't end up taking last fall, and I think we'll need that break. So we'll have to work something out so you can feel safe leaving Wayne. We'll go back to setting up a rotating schedule with the kids being in charge instead of relying on respite," I propose.

"I know," Hector says. "And I can't be too harsh on the nurses; we have had some really good ones too, Gladys and Carmen especially. I wish they'd been the ones here when we went to that NACAC conference, and maybe Dylan would still be alive."

"Maybe, but then again, we have to trust that Dylan is exactly where is supposed to be right now, and just work harder to create a legacy for his life so that other children and families in the future don't have to suffer like he did."

"You're right, it does no good to look backward. That has never been how we've operated," Hector says. "We always look ahead, looking down the road, waiting to see what is around the next curve. And speaking of curves, I'm looking forward to spending some time with your curves this weekend when you get home," he teases.

"Well, now you're really sounding like yourself," I laugh.

I've had three missed calls in a row from Hector while sitting in this meeting. That's our signal, if it's a real emergency; he calls three times and hangs up, and that's how I know to step out of whatever meeting or event I'm involved in and call right away. I step out to return the call, and the battery on my cell phone goes completely dead.

"Annie," I whisper to a friend and coworker sitting near the back row. "Can I borrow your phone? Mine just went dead and I think there's an emergency at home."

Annie quickly walks out into the hall with me, giving me her phone and fishing for a charger, plugging my phone into the wall.

"Oh, my God. . . . . Oh no. . . . Where is he? . . . I don't know, I'll check the train schedule. . . . No, my supervisor at OJJDP is amazing, she'll understand. . . . OK, I'll call you back." I numbly hand the phone back to Annie.

Without a word, she senses that I need a hug and wraps me in a strong one. "OK, tell me what's going on, and what can I do to help?" she asks.

"It's my son George . . . He's in the hospital. No one really knows what's going on. He works at an autobody shop, and sometimes when he works late at night he sleeps on the couch there instead of going to his apartment," I explain. "This morning, his boss came in to work and found George unconscious and they couldn't revive him. He's at a hospital in New Jersey, Camden—that's where he works. He's still unconscious." My words are running together in an incoherent stream.

"You need to go up there," Annie says. "Do you need help figuring out the arrangements?"

"No, I'll go to the train station. Can you explain to Constance and the others what's happened?" I ask.

"Of course. Just go—go now." She hugs me again and pushes me toward the door. . . .

"Oh dear Lord. We just lost one son last fall. Please don't take another son from us," I pray, urgently, on the train ride home.

"You gave us quite a scare, Georgie-bones," I say, using his childhood nickname, two days later when he finally regains consciousness. Hector and I, along with SueAnn, Roberto, Chelsea, Flory, and Joelle have been taking turns keeping vigil here at the hospital.

"Mom," he says weakly. "Patrice, Destin, come give Daddy a hug."

"I'm going to give you guys some time together," I say. "I'll go down to the cafeteria and get some coffee and call Dad and let him know you're awake now."

"The details are sketchy, but it appears that George had a really bad reaction to some painkillers for that problem he's been having with his back." I'm trying to fill Hector in on the update I've received from the doctors. "You know his job doesn't provide health insurance, so apparently he's been getting these painkillers on the street instead of from a doctor. He could've died."

"He works so hard. You'd think he could have health insurance. This is crazy," Hector replies.

"I know. Don't get me started on the politics of it. I just want to focus on my son for today. That's a battle we can keep fighting tomorrow," I say with a sigh.

"Well, I have some good news to cheer you up," Hector says.

"What's that?"

"JD passed the exam for his plumbing license."

"Oh, that's fantastic news! I'm so proud of him. He's worked so hard to reach this goal. Good for him. I'll have to call him later," I say.

"When do you have to get back to D.C.?"

"Melodee is being so supportive. I can take all the time I need. But there are some important things going on, so I shouldn't be gone too long. I plan to stay a few more days and make sure George is really out of the woods, and then I'll head back."

"OK, well, give George my love. When you come home, I'll go in a little later with Chelsea and Flory. I think Joelle wants to come with us too."

"Sounds good. Love you," I say.

"Love you more."

A few weeks after George is back on his feet, I'm standing next to a hospital bed again. This time, it's the maternity ward. SueAnn and I are at Hahnemann Hospital, supporting Alysia through her labor, along with her boyfriend Bernard. Everything goes smoothly, and by morning Ahmir is born. He's a perfect, beautiful baby with soft, dark curls.

"I'm glad I got to be here with you, Sweetie. But now I have to get back to D.C.," I tell Alysia, giving her a kiss on the forehead. "I'll see you this weekend when I come home." I head out in time for my train. . . .

Accept the things you cannot change, I remind myself as I sit on the train, worrying about how Alysia will manage motherhood along with her own special needs. At least the baby is healthy, and Alysia has taken the initiative to sign up for a visiting nurse. This is the one thing none of our pre-adoption classes or NACAC conference workshops ever prepared us for: the challenges of parenting your kids when they become adults— especially kids with special needs of their own. Whether it is new babies, like this one today; or a hospital emergency like George's; or just the day-to-day advice and support many of them need with their budgeting, children's school issues, legal skirmishes, or just navigating the ups and downs of life, there's a lot more involved with parenting adult kids than I ever imagined. *I think I'm going to propose a workshop next year for NACAC on this very topic*, I resolve to myself.

Three months later, to the day, I am on the Duke University campus in North Carolina for the annual meeting of the National Child Traumatic Stress Network advisory board. Hector calls late in the evening. We've already had our usual evening chat, so I'm a little concerned as I groggily answer the phone.

"Chelsea wants you to know they've pushed up her schedule for the C-section. The doctors are concerned that the baby's heartbeat is irregular. Do you think you can get home sooner than planned?" he asks.

"Oh no. Chelsea must be so scared. I'll be there; I'll make it happen. Let me contact Mary and see what magic she can work with my flights."

The next day, I'm sitting in the waiting room at the hospital with Lashon's parents, sister, and Chloe while we wait for news from the operating room. I'm drawing little circles on a piece of paper when Hector calls to check in.

"No news here, but you know what I just realized?" I ask.

"What's that?"

"You know that big dream catcher SueAnn made for me on my 50th birthday, the one with pictures of all the kids and grandkids?"

"Yeah. It's hanging on the wall above your desk."

"Right. Well, I was sitting here realizing that as soon as this baby is born, there will be nine new babies that are not on that dream catcher—all born in the last couple of years."

"Nine? Are you sure?" Hector asks.

"Yup, unless I missed any. There's Antonio, Rosario, AJ, Kaylen, Nicole, Saphira, Nalana, Ahmir, and now this new baby. That's quite the little population explosion, don't you think?"

"I think my head is spinning," he says.

"And what's more amazing is how individual and unique each one of them is. I mean, when people hear about how many kids and grandkids . . . "

"And don't forget we're now up to four great-grandkids," Hector interjects.

"Right. Anyway, when people hear about how many we have, they often ask me if I can remember them all or keep them all straight. I may call out the wrong name from time to time, but I don't get them mixed up at all. They're each totally unique little creatures."

"You're right, and who knows what they'll accomplish in

their lifetimes? Anyway, keep me posted when you have some news about Chelsea."

"Oh, hang on. Lashon is coming in right now."

"It's a girl!" he says with pride. "Her name is Zara, and she is perfect. Her heart is fine and she's beautiful!"

"Yes!" Lashon's family and I start to cheer with relief and gratitude—but Chloe bursts immediately into tears.

"I wanted the baby to be a boy," she wails. We all have a good laugh, confident that Chloe will come around and eventually be happy with a sister.

"Are you still there?" I say into the phone.

"Yup, still here. I heard the news—that's great! Tell Chels I love her and I'll get down there to visit as soon as I can. You know, it's funny: our last two grandchildren took us from A to Z—Ahmir to Zara. Maybe that means this is the end of the line." Hector laughs.

"Maybe," I say, "but I wouldn't hold my breath."

"You'll never believe who called me today," Hector says, starting off our evening conversation.

"Ah, let me guess. The President," I reply; this is our standard joke.

"Not this time. Actually, I had two amazing calls. The first was Abel. It's all worked out, he's really being released, and he wants me to go pick him up tomorrow."

"Wow, that's fantastic! It's a four-hour drive, right?"

"Something like that."

"And . . . So, who was the second call?"

"It was Raj. Not only that, but he called me Dad and said he wanted to come talk. We talked for over an hour and he's going to come for the ride with me when I pick up Abel."

My jaw drops. I'm speechless. This is the call I've been waiting and praying about for more than five years. My mother's funeral—December 2005—was the last time Raj participated in any family event. He lives with David, so we hear news about him secondhand, and we exchange emails—mostly about the apartment lease and related matters. But this is real, genuine communication.

"I'm beside myself with joy right now," I say quietly. "I never, never gave up hope that our relationships with both of these prodigal sons of ours would be restored. But who could've imagined it would happen on the same day?"

"You know that proverb about good news from afar?" Hector asks.

"Like cold water to a weary soul," I quote. "Proverbs 25."

"That's the one," Hector says. "Today my weary soul got a tall glass of cold water."

"Amen to that. Just goes to prove two things we've always believed. Never, ever give up hope, and families really do matter—not just for kids, but for adults too."

"My turn to say Amen," Hector replies.

For the rest of the summer, I'm deeply immersed in the work of the National Forum on Youth Violence Prevention, participating in several site visits to communities around the country. Meeting with families whose children have been lost to senseless street violence is heartwrenching, but I'm thankful I can work with such amazing people who are trying to stem the tide and bring hope and healing to their communities.

"You should see the incredible work this group of mothers are doing in Salinas," I tell Hector when I return from my most recent site visit. "These are mothers whose children have died, and yet they're standing up and working to make their communities safer for all children. I am so humbled to know them."

"I can't imagine their pain," he replies. "Thankfully, in spite of all the challenges we've faced, none of our children have suffered the kind of attacks you're hearing about."

We sit silently for a moment, and then I change the subject.

"Should we have our Labor Day barbecue on Sunday or Monday this year?"

"I've been talking to the kids, and they all say Monday is best. I told them we'd probably do it around four o'clock."

"That sounds good. I hope everyone can make it. It's been awhile since we've had a Sunday family dinner. Do you want to do the grilling?"

"I'll get it set up. David and Todd can help with the actual cooking."

"Great. Sounds perfect."

Tuesday morning finds me on the train back to D.C. It's always hardest to leave after a really good weekend with the family. But at least it's a short week and I'll be home again soon.

Ring. Ring. Ring . . .

I slowly realize I'm not dreaming and reach for my phone.

"Sue, wake up."

"What? What is it?" I say, looking at the clock. Three in the morning. My heart is gripped with fear.

"It's Aaron. He's been stabbed."

I sit straight up in bed, now fully awake.

"Ohmigod. Is he . . . ?"

"He's at Einstein Hospital. I'm here now in the waiting room. SueAnn is with me. We don't know anything more. We don't even know if he's going to be OK." Hector starts to cry.

"Start praying, and I'll figure out the earliest train I can take. I think it's around 4 AM. I'll go now so I can make the train, and then you can fill me in more. I need to know what happened."

I hang up the phone in a daze. Wasn't it just three days ago that I was giving thanks that none of our kids had ever been the victim of street violence? What did Hector say: he couldn't imagine how those parents feel? *Why Lord? Why do you have to give us every imaginable experience? Isn't it OK for us to say we can't imagine something and leave it at that? Do we have to experience everything firsthand?*

As soon as I confirm Aaron's status, I know I need to take a few days off work. I compose an email to send to my boss and coworkers. In the subject line, I write, "Youth Violence Hits Home."

I am writing today to let you know that our youngest son, Aaron, age 21, with multiple cognitive delays and mental health issues, was violently attacked last night by a gang of 8 youth, beaten badly and stabbed 3 times. Nearly died by bleeding out on the way to the hospital once an ambulance was finally called. One of the stab wounds punctured a lung and he's still in the hospital, although now they say he's "stable" (physically) so he may be discharged any day now. He's going to recover from his physical wounds. The mental and psychological wounds are the ones I'm more worried about. He's the classic example of a child that experienced extreme early life trauma in his first several years of life – every kind of trauma you can imagine and some you probably can't. Not to mention fetal alcohol syndrome. So, he's in a rough state, mentally and emotionally. I'll be taking a few days off and I'll write again when I know more. Thank you for your patience and understanding. If anything under-scores the critical importance of the work we do, this is it. Thank you to all of you for your dedication and com-mitment to making our communities safer for all of our children. You make a difference and it does matter.

"We'll take care of everything at home. You and Dad really need to go on this trip." Isaac is imploring us not to let recent events stop us from taking our trip to Switzerland. We cancelled last year after Dylan's death and are considering canceling again in light of Aaron's recent attack.

"It's just a lot to expect all of you to manage. It was one thing to take care of Wayne, but now Aaron needs care and support too," I say.

"We've got it. Really, Mom. Right, SueAnn?" Isaac pleads.

"Yes, you know you can trust us. We won't let anything happen to either of them. I promise," SueAnn says.

Hector and I look at each other, each waiting for the other to speak first.

"Well, the tickets are paid for," Hector points out.

"And Aaron is recovering well. He listens to SueAnn, so he'll be in good hands," I add.

"Good. That settles it. You're going." Isaac says firmly, ending the conversation.

"The only bad thing about this trip is that it's ending too soon," I say to Jose on our last morning in Switzerland.

"I agree. Can we stay another week?" Hector asks.

"You know it's fine with me," Jose says.

"I wish . . . But reality is calling. How much longer before we have to leave for the train?"

"About five minutes."

"Well, let's start walking then," I say, moving toward the door. Our week in Switzerland has been restful, restorative, and just plain fun. Jose has treated us to great meals and spectacular sights. Looking at the world from high up in the Alps gives a fresh perspective on life. I'm glad we decided not to cancel.

We return to Philly and distribute chocolate souvenirs to all our children and grandchildren. October begins, cool and crisp, and my brother David arrives to visit, bringing Mark to meet our family. Refreshed, we plunge back into the plans to develop our respite ministry. I work with Chelsea and our friend Teresa to create a website, develop the mission and vision statements, and look for a pro bono lawyer who can help us move forward.

Hector begins tackling the enormous job of restoring the

house. After twenty years raising twenty-two kids, hosting weddings, funerals, birthday parties, barbecues, and countless other events, the house is in need of loads of TLC. The biggest problem is that the furnace died several years ago. Without a central heating system, heating the house is an exhausting task, as Hector has to keep woodstoves and kerosene heaters stoked day and night. But replacing the furnace is out of reach for now, so Hector decides to begin by working on the woodwork in the main entryway. It's a laborious project, but one that he loves. . . .

"Working on this wood gives me a lot of time to think," he says on a Friday evening when I come home. "I started out wondering why anyone would put layers and layers of paint on this beautiful woodwork. The paint is so much uglier than the natural beauty of the wood underneath."

"I know. I just don't get it, but I guess it was the fashion at the time," I say.

"Right, exactly. Someone did it because they thought they were improving upon the original, making it more beautiful than it was before. And layers got added on top of layers, so it becomes a slow and tedious process to remove it all."

"I'm glad you're stripping it; it'll be so much nicer when you finish. Just look at this section that you've done. It's so lovely," I say, running my hand along the panel.

"I'm happy about it too, but I want to share with you the spiritual truth I'm gleaning as I work."

"OK."

"You see, in our own lives, we're often like the people who added layers of paint, covering up the natural wood. How often do we pile stuff onto ourselves, or our kids, thinking we are making improvements, when all we are doing is hiding the natural beauty within? Then, when we finally realize that all this added junk has to come off, it's such a tedious process, removing all the gunk, so the natural beauty has a chance to shine through again. Sometimes I think God is working on me little by little, slowly scraping off the layers of stuff I plastered all over myself, thinking I was making improvements. Through all my life experiences, God is showing me that it's what's underneath all the stuff that matters. He has to keep working on me because I've added a heck of a lot of layers over the years."

"You know, that makes a lot of sense. I'm sure the people who painted this wood thought they were doing a good thing and didn't realize people like us would later come along and say, 'What were they thinking?' Just like we sometimes do really stupid stuff thinking it makes total sense, while others are shaking their heads and saying, 'What were they thinking?'"

"Exactly. And even when it looks like I'm done, there is still more gunk in the little grooves. It takes special tools to really get deep down in those grooves and get the gunk out. It would be easy to say it's not worth it or it doesn't matter—but come here, let me show you something."

He walks me over to another part of the room.

"Look at this panel. This one is completely finished—even the tiniest grooves. Now what do you think?"

"Spectacular. And yes, what a difference. It really was worth all your effort to get every last bit of gunk out. You've really given me something to think about."

"I try to do that once in a while," he laughs.

"Do you remember one time, way back on Short Street before we moved to Philly, we were talking to the kids about something, and I said we had lots of ups and downs in our family life, and Isaac said, 'like a roller coaster?'" I say, calling Hector late one night.

"Vaguely," he replies.

"He was a little boy, maybe eight years old. And he started making the hand motions to imitate a roller coaster."

"Yeah, I think I remember. Why are you calling me at 10 at

night to tell me this? We chatted just an hour ago."

"Well, if we've ever had a roller coaster year, I'd say this year takes the cake. The last low point was when Aaron was stabbed, but then we had the high point of our trip to Switzerland. And things going well at home as we work on our business plan."

"Right," Hector says, still sounding confused.

"Well, our roller coaster just careened to another deep, low point." Suddenly, I am crying, unable to hold the tears back any longer.

"What happened? You seemed fine just an hour ago." Hector is suddenly very concerned.

"I was fine just an hour ago. I was fine until ten minutes ago. I just got off the phone with Mary Gayle. Nalana has died."

"No."

"Yes."

We both sit in stunned silence, punctuated by sniffles and tears. Finally, Hector breaks the silence, asking, "What happened?"

I fill him in on everything I've learned, and we cry together for a few more minutes. "I wish I was home, so you could hold me," I say, finally.

"Me too. Come home soon."

"I'll take the day off. I'll be home in the morning."

Once again, my day starts with writing a difficult email. I try to give meaning to a deeply painful personal event by tying it to the work I do every day. I write to my colleagues from the train:

> You may remember that 20 months ago, my great-granddaughter Nalana sustained severe injuries in a "shaken baby" incident at the hands of her father (the then-boyfriend of my oldest granddaughter, Kirsten). For 20 months, Nalana was gaining in strength and responsiveness, she was a cherished and valued member of the family. So it is with a heavy heart that I write today to tell you that she passed away yesterday after a series of sei-

zures from which her fragile little body simply could not recover. Her heart and breathing stopped and she left this world. I have faith and believe she is free now from her suffering and dancing in the heavens with our sons Dylan and Adam. All three of these children's lives had meaning, value, and purpose. As a friend of mine once said, "even if your life purpose is simply to love and be loved, that is enough." And in that respect, Nalana, like Dylan and Adam, was deeply loved and taught love, compassion, and tenderness to everyone who had the privilege of knowing her. Now, nothing can give Nalana's life more purpose and meaning than for me and all of us to further dedicate ourselves to the work we do everyday to make this world a more peaceful and safer place for every child and to support every parent in their efforts to raise children who are safe and free from the impact of violence in their lives. Feel free to share this email with others in our shared work efforts if you think it will provide further inspiration for them in this sacred work we all do.

How many more times, Lord? I am asking in prayer.
How much more sadness can one family bear?

28

Shifting Gears

"You know how we always refer to our life as a journey? We've never extended that analogy to describe what kind of vehicle we're traveling in, but I've come to the conclusion that it's a standard-shift car," Hector says to me over coffee a week after Nalana's funeral.

"OK, I'll bite," I say. "What brought that idea to mind just now?"

"Shifting gears. I was thinking about all there is to do to finish getting ready for Christmas, and I realized it's going to take some serious gear shifting to go from grief to joy. It's not the first time we've had to do that."

"You're right, and it won't be the last, I'm sure. Last night I sent a reminder email to all the kids with this year's theme question. Sent it to you too. Hope you got it."

"I did. That's what made me start thinking about Christmas. Favorite story, eh? There are so many . . . "

Every year, I ask all of the kids, their spouses, and children a "theme question." The answer guides my shopping for their gift from Hector and I.

"A few of the kids replied when I first sent it around, at Thanksgiving, but I'm still waiting on the others," I say. "I'm really excited about a few of the gifts I've found so far. Chelsea's favorite story is on the theme of community, and I got her this beautiful pendant from a fair trade store. It's made from the wings of butterflies after they die. The whole community is involved and the project helps sustain many families. Plus, it reminds me of her wedding.

"Chantelle loves the Big Nate books because she can draw in them, so I found her a cool 'create your own book' kit. And then Kaylen's favorite story is *No Visitors for Bear*, but we also know she loves to help cook, and I found her this adorable cupcake-making set with a teddy bear theme. Oh, and the last one I want to tell you about is Roberto's. Who knew that rough, tough Roberto would tell me that he couldn't quite chose between two Shakespeare plays for his favorite story? So I found him some really cool items—a calendar and mug—at the Shakespeare Theatre Company gift shop in D.C. That was a fun one to buy."

"Sounds like you've already shifted gears; that's great."

"Well, I have my moments when I feel like I can't breathe, or something I see in a store makes me break down and cry on the spot. But overall, I'm trying to focus on the memories we want to create for the kids, memories of joy rising out of sadness. If we don't set the example, who will?"

"Exactly. That's why I'm going to take the grandkids to the dollar store today for cousins day, so they can carry on the Secret Santa tradition," Hector says.

I lean over to give him a kiss, saying, "They'll love that! OK,

I really have to get going, but I almost forgot there's one other gift I wanted to show you. I have it here in my purse; I just found it last night. It's for Simmy. Her favorite story is *Where the Red Fern Grows*, because she loves the theme of someone who helps his family in times of trouble. I found this red journal with a fern embossed in it and then this . . . " I pull a delicate necklace out of a small velvet bag. "Let me read to you what the card says about it: '*Rajana artisans symbolically resurrect life from the damage of war. This handcrafted tree is made from one of the many bomb casings still found across Cambodia. A gift of life and hope.*' Isn't that perfect?"

"It's beautiful. Resurrecting hope—that's what we all need this Christmas."

"Amen to that. There's an online organization that supports adoption called Many Hearts, One Beat. I've bought gifts from them before. I'm going to go online and find something from them to give Kirsten in honor of Nalana. And then, I need to head out to buy some groceries before I look for any more gifts."

"Wayne just didn't seem himself yesterday," Hector says on New Year's Day, as we start to prepare for our traditional fondue gathering. "I'm getting concerned about him. He seems to have more rough days than he ever did before."

"I've noticed that too. His whole life he has been happy almost no matter what the circumstances, but lately he seems to be making more unhappy sounds, especially in the evening, like something is bothering him. It breaks my heart to see him that way."

"Hopefully he'll be happy today," Hector says. "He usually loves it when all the grandchildren are around. They climb on his bed and give him lots of attention. He seems to enjoy all the commotion."

"You're right about that. I'm looking forward to our fondue, because I have a really busy couple of months at work. So I'm not sure I'll get to do many family activities between now and Easter, with the summit coming up."

I remind Hector of the major national Summit on Youth Violence that I'm helping to coordinate as part of my fellowship in D.C. I've pressed several family members into service; my nephew Alexander created the artwork and my cousin Brett paid for the T-shirts for the youth participants. Chelsea got Comcast to donate cameras for all the youth, and she's going to come down and volunteer to help on-site. Even Zara will get in the action; I plan to bring her onstage when I deliver my remarks in one of the plenary sessions. This summit should prove to be one of my career high points— it'll be a lot of work, but I'm looking forward to the opportunity it provides to make a difference.

"You kids would be so proud of your mom," Hector says as we gather on the porch before going out for our traditional Easter dinner. "She made sure youth and families had a voice during this big meeting in D.C. The attorney general and other bigwigs were there, but they all took a backseat to listening to the teens and the parents."

"Yeah, Mom!" "Yeah, Nanna!" comes a chorus of voices around me.

"It was a team project, a lot of people helped, but I'm thankful that God gave me the opportunity to be one of them," I say. "How are we ever going to stop violence in this country if we don't listen to the children and the families that are most affected by it?"

"Preach it, Mom!" Todd laughs.

My heart is sad that Wayne's not well enough to come out to Easter dinner with us, but also joyful that Raj and Abel will both be joining our celebration for the first time in many years.

"OK, OK, enough. Nafra'ah's here to stay with Wayne, so let's load up in the cars and get to the restaurant." My heart is sad that Wayne's not well enough to come out to Easter dinner with us, but also joyful that Raj and Abel will both be joining our celebration for the first time in many years.

"It was so great to have Raj join us," I say to Hector on the way home.

"Did you hear Ally when he walked in? She pointed to him before he got close to our table and yelled out, 'Look, it's Raj! I just love Raj!' She was so excited."

"I know, that was so cute. I love how he's really connected with SueAnn's kids. I hear he's even been helping Esperanza with her homework lately."

"Loved his shirt, too, that rif on a Reece's cup, but it says 'Reason' instead. That was a good one," Hector adds, highlighting Raj's passion for science, logic, and reason.

"It was great to meet his friend too. Anyway, I can't stay for the egg hunt. I have to get to the airport to take that 6 PM flight out to Seattle. It's going to be a busy week out there. Besides my regular work, it's my annual evaluation. Isaac says he'll drive me, if you don't mind letting him use the car."

"OK, that's fine. I had Nafra'ah get the eggs ready for the hunt, and Daniel wants to help me hide them, so we'll be all set."

"Sue, I got ahold of Dr. Finkelstein, and we had a good, long conversation about what's going on with Wayne," Hector tells me Monday evening during our phone conversation. The cold that Wayne developed shortly before Easter is getting worse, not better.

"What did he say?"

"He agrees with our decision not to send him to the hospital, so he's going to call Keystone Hospice and they'll send a nurse over to evaluate him. In the meantime, he told me to keep doing what I'm doing. I feel so bad for him; he just keeps coughing and coughing and nothing I do seems to make him comfortable. I'm scared, Sue. I think he may be entering the final leg of his journey here."

"Do you think it might be pneumonia?" I ask, choosing not think about the implications.

"I'm not sure. That's what I hope hospice can tell me. I do know that I have to suction him every half hour or so, and it seems to get worse whenever I feed him.

> "I'm scared, Sue. I think he may be entering the final leg of his journey here."

"Oh, I have a call coming in; it could be Keystone. I'll call you back later," Hector says, hanging up quickly.

"I know you knew this was coming, Mr. Badeau, and you were right. Wayne is declining. His lungs are filling up and his body isn't coping well. We have some medications to try for a few days, so we can see how he responds," the Keystone nurse tells Hector. They order oxygen and pain medications to help keep him more comfortable. . . .

When Hector calls back to tell me the news, I know that I can't stay in Seattle for the week. I promise to speak to my supervisor first thing in the morning and get out as soon as I can. I need to be home.

Surprisingly, Wayne looks a little better than I expect when I come in. "The medication has been working a little. His lungs are clearer today than they were yesterday," the hospice nurse explains, "so we're going to try feeding him today and see how he responds to that." She leaves, promising to be back in a few hours.

"Sue, come take a look." Hector calls me over, a half hour after he starts feeding Wayne. "He's getting worse again; he can hardly breathe. He's all congested."

I sigh deeply. I can't help recognizing the pattern—it's so

similar to what happened with Dylan. "Let's stop the feeding so he doesn't suffer, and call hospice again."

The nurse arrives with the hospice doctor. After the doctor examines Wayne, he turns to us, saying, "It appears that Wayne's whole system is breaking down. His lungs are filling up again." He continues to explain Wayne's status in medical terms.

With tears in my eyes, I turn to Hector. "It looks like Wayne's time has come."

"I think so, Sue. I've seen some of the signs over the last few months, but didn't want to believe it. Let's do everything we can to keep him comfortable," Hector says, his voice breaking.

"Do you want a nurse at night so you can sleep?" the hospice doctor asks.

"No," Hector answers. "We want hospice to be checking on him and us regularly, but we'll sit with him, day and night. We've been through this with our other son, and we don't want him to be with a stranger when he passes. No offense; we love hospice. But we want to be sure he has one of us with him at all times."

"We understand completely, Mr. Badeau. We're here to support you and the family. We'll be checking in regularly and providing all the pain medication, oxygen, and other supplies you need. Is there anything else we can do for your family?"

"The art therapist was great with our grandchildren when our son Dylan died," I say. "If she has time to come over next week, I think we'd like that."

"So, this is it, Sue. The last of our 'Three Stooges' will be gone," Hector says in a voice choked with tears.

"I'll try to set it up. And remember, call anytime you need anything. We're very close by."

"We know. You folks are a godsend. Thank you so much," I say, walking them to the door.

"So, this is it, Sue. The last of our 'Three Stooges' will be gone," Hector says in a voice choked with tears.

"Shhhhhh. Don't start that yet. Wayne's still with us, so let's savor every minute with him and make him comfortable," I say.

"You're right. We need to let all the kids know what's going on to help them prepare. They're all going to take it hard, but Joelle, Isaac, and SueAnn especially have been my helpers with Wayne through all the years. We have to be sure to give them time to come and be with him," Hector says, still fighting off tears.

"I'll start making the calls. And I'll email my boss, letting her know I'll be taking some time off."

"While you're making calls, we should probably call Kirk and Nice so they'll be on standby. They were so helpful after both Adam and Dylan died. I wonder if we'll get a discount this time. You know: 'three for the price of two'?" Hector makes a weak attempt at gallows humor.

"Not funny," I say. But it makes me laugh in spite of myself.

Once again, time stands still. The world beyond the first floor of our house doesn't exist. All of the kids and grandkids come in and out, spending as much time with Wayne as they can. Friends from church and Abby bring meals. The hospice presence is constant but unobtrusive. Hector and I try to spell each other in three-hour shifts each night, but neither of us gets much sleep.

"The art therapist is out this week. She can come next Tuesday," I say to Hector, getting off the phone with hospice.

"I'm not sure Wayne will still be with us by Tuesday," Hector says.

"I know. I was thinking the same thing. But I think it's important to do an art activity with the kids; it really helped them last time. Remember, they made those bracelets with Dylan's name on them?"

"That's right. I do remember," Hector says.

"So I'm going to Michael's and buying some of those alphabet beads and other supplies. Tomorrow when the kids don't have school, we'll have them over and we'll make bracelets."

"That sounds like a good idea, Sue."

"Look Nanna. I made one with my name and one that says Wayne's name!"

"Beautiful, Laurie. And what are you making, Chloe?"

"I'm putting lots of flowers and stars and trees on Wayne's bracelet so he can feel like he's out in nature."

"Nanna, I found a bead with a peace sign on it, so I'm putting that next to Wayne's name so he can have peace," Esperanza says.

"Can I make one to put on Wayne's wrist, and one for my wrist too?" Chantelle asks.

"Of course you can, Sweetheart."

By the end of the afternoon, Wayne has several bracelets on his arm, and each of the children has one to keep to remember Wayne by. Adults got into the activity as well; making something with your hands seems to have a healing effect on all ages.

Just as we are cleaning up from the bracelet making, Alysia arrives. "I'm so glad you made it," I tell her. She and Wayne are close in age, and as we were going through the pictures, there are so many of Alysia and Wayne playing together—in the sandbox, at their older siblings' baseball games and track meets, on camping trips, on Halloween, and posing for the first day of school. "Look at all these pictures of you and Wayne together," I point out.

Alysia spends several moments with Wayne and then makes a bracelet before leaving.

"Mom, I want to make a drawing of Wayne," Abel says. "I

want to picture him with one of those big, bright smiles we all love so much."

"I'd love that. If you get it done in time, we'll use it for the program for his memorial service," I reply. Each child contributes and copes in his or her own way, using the special gifts and talents God has given them.

"After church tomorrow we should have a little party for Wayne," I suggest to Hector. "I know it's not his birthday, but I think it'll be good for him and for all of us to celebrate him one last time while he's still with us, and not just wait for the funeral."

> Each child contributes and copes in his or her own way, using the special gifts and talents God has given them.

"Good idea. I'm not going to church; I'll stay with Wayne. But you can plan the party with the kids."

"It will be simple. I'll just make his favorite food, chicken, and we'll sing some songs and pray." We both laugh, remembering how much Wayne loved chicken when he was able to eat.

"I think Wayne needs a change, and then I'll give him his meds and check his temperature," Hector says.

"OK. Just read it out to me and I'll jot it down in the notebook."

"Can I help?" Mackell asks. The three-year-olds, Mackell and Kaylen, love donning the blue exam gloves and "helping" Poppa with Wayne.

"Sure."

Mackell slips on the gloves and hops on Wayne's bed. He begins chattering, bringing a smile to Hector's face. I'm always amazed at how small children seem to instinctively know exactly when a smile or laugh is needed.

"Everyone's here. Let's gather by Wayne."

I call the family together and ask Chantelle to pass around the platter of chicken drumsticks. We place one on Wayne's bed and wrap his fingers around it. After we sing a few songs, it's time to pray. Several of the children pray in turn, and then Hector closes: "Dear Lord, thank you for all the joy Wayne brought to all of us and how he changed our lives . . . Thank you for his smile and his funny little sounds . . . Please take him safely to the other side now. Greet him with open arms and give him a big hug for us . . . Reunite him with Adam and Dylan . . . "

Hector is crying too hard now to continue.

"Amen," I say softly.

"Amen," each of the children say. The room is warm and the only sounds are tears and sniffles.

One by one, the kids have their individual turns at Wayne's bedside, holding his hand, leaning in to talk softly to him, hugging him, saying good-bye.

"This is too hard to watch," Hector says, crying as he steps out of the room.

"I know. My heart is breaking. Every one of them loved Wayne so fully and deeply. They'll all miss him so much."

"He looks so thin, Dad," Chelsea says as she prepares to leave.

"I know. I think he's going home tonight," Hector tells her as they hug fiercely in their shared grief.

"Call me whenever it is—even if it's the middle of the night. Don't wait 'til morning," Chelsea says.

"OK, we will," I promise.

I take over the vigil a few minutes after 2 AM so Hector can get some rest. I sit by Wayne's side, holding his hand, listening for his breaths.

The seconds between breaths are longer and longer now. It

won't be long. . . .

"He's gone, Hec," I say, gently, after I realize it's been minutes this time, not seconds, with no breathing. "He passed so peacefully in the end. He's with Adam, Dylan, and Nalana now."

And then the tears start to flow.

After several moments of hugging and crying, Hector looks over to the mantel, where the urns belonging to Adam and Dylan sit. "Your brother is with you now, boys. The last of our Three Musketeers. What a long, beautiful journey we had with you. But we've reached the end of this road."

Epilogue: "Miles to Go"

"And what does the Lord require of you,
but to do justice, to love kindness,
and to walk humbly with your God?"

Micah 6:8

If there's one thing we learned about road trips, it's that they never really end. Each time you think you've reached the end of the road, it's really just a corner that you need to turn so you can go on to the next part of the journey.

After Wayne's death, there were days when we felt we could not go on. Could not take one more step. The road trip we started when we began our family had come to an end. All of our kids were grown, living their own lives, and the three that needed us most had all passed away. We spent days in a fog of grief.

Our friends Rob and Peggy own a cabin on a lake a few hours outside the city. For years they've offered us the opportunity to take a few days of respite up there, but we've never taken them up on it. Now, in the wake of Wayne's death, they come to us, insisting that we go to the cabin.

This time we agree.

> All of our kids were grown, living their own lives, and the three that needed us most had all passed away. We spent days in a fog of grief.

"It's beautiful here," I say as we walk from our car to the waterfront before even going inside.

"I can tell already: this is just what we need," Hector says.

We sit in comfortable silence, facing the water for several minutes, and then Hector says, "It's hard to believe it's already been a month since Wayne died. It seems like only yesterday we were getting the 'Wild Man' from the Chans. It feels strange to be able to get away and not worry about anyone at home. Each morning, I get up and no one needs to be fed or changed. I wonder why I even get up—I feel like my days have no purpose anymore."

"I know. I can't imagine how hard it is for you, twice as hard as for everyone else. You've not only lost a son, but in a way it's like you lost your job on the same day. It's a turning point in our life journey, that's for sure."

"I hope while we're here, God will give us the roadmap for the next part of our journey. Because right now, I just feel lost," he says.

"Five days flew by," I say as we lock up the cabin and get into our car for the drive home. "It was a really good time we had together, Hec. I loved the Bible studies you planned, and I really feel a sense of peace about our plans going forward."

"The Spirit was definitely here with us. I'm confident we're moving in the right direction. I don't feel lost anymore. I know I'll still have days filled with grief, but I feel hopeful, too."

> **"I'm confident we're moving in the right direction. I don't feel lost anymore. I know I'll still have days filled with grief, but I feel hopeful, too."**

"We're going to be too busy in the next few weeks to get caught up in grief," I say. "Alysia's new baby will be born any day now. Then we've got the Vermont trip, Erica and Milagro's graduations, and then Alec, Emma, and Janessa coming down for their summer visit. Before we know it, it'll be time for NACAC in Virginia, and I'm so glad Trish and the boys are coming down for that, and lots of the other kids and grandkids will be joining us. Then it'll be time for the youth group to start up again and the cool days of fall will descend on us. The cycle of life. The journey continues."

"I'm looking forward to all of those things. And I feel really good about the plans we have to develop the house into a respite ministry. It'll be a great way to honor the memory and legacy of all three—Adam, Dylan, and Wayne. If anyone can relate to parents going through tough times, who better than us?"

"I'm excited about that too. I'm feeling a new sense of direction and energy," I add.

"I have to admit, I'm a little nervous about putting myself out there into the job market, but I'm excited too. It'll be the first time in over 20 years that I'll have a boss to answer to—well, besides you that is," Hector says playfully.

"Very funny."

Soon after we get back to Philadelphia, Isaac calls, wanting to talk to us. Apparently we aren't the only ones inspired to embark on a new journey after Wayne's death. Isaac has decided to join the Army. "Wayne's death got me thinking about how short life is and how quickly I am getting older. I'm not a kid anymore," he says. "The time has come for me to find my purpose in life and get some discipline. Simmy and I agree, and I hope you'll support me too."

We are surprised but pleased that more new growth is happening in our family in the wake of such a deep loss. Isaac spends the summer preparing to ship off to boot camp.

As always, summer gives way to fall, and soon the early signs of winter are upon us. Hector starts working a night shift in August at Project HOME, a program for homeless adults. This really changes the rhythm of our lives, but we're getting used to it.

Now, as the calendar turns to December, we have a difficult road trip ahead. We have to go to Vermont to testify for Fisher at a sentencing hearing. He's facing the possibility of the harshest sentence he's ever faced.

We spend the morning listening to all the testimony against Fisher. The judge orders a break for lunch, and we know we'll be called to the stand soon after.

"I felt sorrow, pain, and anger all at the same time as I was listening to all that," Hector reflects on the morning. "I don't know if our testimony will make any difference at all, but I hope at least when Fisher hears it, he'll know how much we love him. He's going to need to believe he has both our love and God's to sustain him in the years ahead."

"That judge showed no mercy," Hector says as we leave the courtroom. "Now all we can do is pray that God's grace and mercy will be with Fisher."

"I never thought our journey with him would come to this. My heart is breaking. I don't think anyone else would understand what I'm about to say, but I know you will." I'm trying to put my feelings into words. "As painful as it was to say good-bye to Adam, Dylan, and Wayne, in some ways today was more painful. We know those three are in a better place. But Fisher . . . I feel we've lost a son today in a much worse way than a death . . . "

"I do know what you mean. But as long as he's still alive, there is always hope. That's one lesson God has taught us over and over again. There is always hope."

Hope. That's the theme of my work, the theme of our lives, and the theme of Easter. It's hard to believe another Easter season is upon us. Soon we'll reach the one-year anniversary of Wayne's death.

"It's cousins day today, Sue. I'll have twelve kids for the afternoon."

"Enjoy," I say. "I've got some writing to do, but I'll come downstairs and join you for dinner."

"OK, kids, you have a couple of hours to play, ride your bikes, jump on the trampoline, or do some crafts inside. If you have any homework projects to work on, let me know if you need help," I hear Hector telling the kids as they tumble out of the car laughing and chattering to one another.

"What's for dinner, Poppa?" Jasmine asks.

"My famous Shepherd's Pie," he says.

"Yeah! I hope you make a big batch. I love your Shepherd's Pie and I'm hungry!" Angel shouts as she runs toward the backyard.

"Time to eat!" Hector calls, and I save my document so I can go downstairs to join them. How many times I have heard him call "time to eat!" to our kids over the years? And now it's the grand- and great-grandkids' turn to hear those words.

"Stop cutting, Chantelle. I was first," Esperanza cries out.

"Remember, the first shall be last and the last shall be first," Hector says.

"We know that, Poppa, you tell us that every week!" Esperanza says.

"Good. I'm glad you remember, so you won't mind going to the back of the line since you pushed your way to the front," he laughs. "You too, Chantelle."

"Titianna, since you are at the back of the line, you can be first today," I say, stepping into the kitchen.

"Ooops, that's OK, Laurie. We'll clean it up," Hector says as the juice cup tips over. . . .

"Now, if everyone is done eating," Hector says, "it's time for our reading. Who remembers what we talked about last time?"

"Jesus!" Ally says cheerfully. Hector and I both chuckle as we remember all the times our kids would offer up the "one-size-fits-all answer" when they were small.

"Yes, that's right. And what else do you remember? Who remembers what season it is?"

"Winter!" Tianna says confidently.

"Lent," Angel adds.

"And we learned there are 40 days in Lent just like Jesus was in the wilderness for 40 days," Esperanza says.

"And it rained for 40 days and 40 nights when Noah was on the ark," Jasmine adds.

This leads to a round of giggles as Esperanza, Chantelle,

Chloe, and Titianna all start singing the "Noah's Ark" song they learned in Sunday School.

"And what is Lent about?" Hector asks as the singing ends.

"Easter and going to church and the egg hunt and going out to eat!" Chloe says.

"You're right, Chloe. We do all of those things on Easter because it's a day to celebrate. But what are we celebrating?"

All the hands go up. Even Kaylen, Mackell, and Nicole are trying to get in on the action.

"He is risen indeed!" several kids shout at once.

"That's right," Hector says. "On Easter we celebrate Jesus rising to new life, so we can all have hope for new life. Lent is the time when we remember why he died, and we can be sorry that he paid the price for the times when we do something wrong or hurt someone. We take time during Lent to be sad that he had to die, and that makes us even more excited to celebrate that he is alive again on Easter morning."

"And that's why we wear pretty dresses!" Ally shouts.

"Indeed," Hector says. "Indeed."

"Next Saturday, let's use that gift certificate the Whites gave us and take Renee out to dinner for her birthday," I suggest to Hector after all the kids have gone home.

"Good idea," he says.

"Renee dozed off," I say as we pull into the restaurant parking lot a week later. I tap her on the shoulder and she stirs awake.

"Oh," she says, disoriented. "Are we there yet?"

Hector and I look at each other, smiling and replying at the same time: "No, we have miles to go . . . miles to go."

Afterword

"For where you go, I will go, and where you lodge, I will lodge. Your people shall be my people, and your God, my God."

Ruth 1:16

Background: Hector's Early Years

We were a good French Catholic family. We went to church every Sunday, said our Rosary every week, and went to confession at least twice a month. My mom read her Bible every day and was a great role model for us kids. She worked hard, caring for us every day, up at the crack of dawn washing clothes, making breakfast for my dad and lunches for each of us to bring to school. How I hated those tomato and mayonnaise sandwiches she would pack for me!

School at St Monica's went from 8:30 to 3:15. Most of the time, I enjoyed going to school. My older brothers would walk me to school until I was old enough to walk on my own, and then it was my turn to walk my younger brothers. I think it was my days going to St Monica's that the seeds of my faith in Christ were planted. I got a good grounding in the Word, but did not develop a strong relationship with God during those years. I always played "Let's make a deal" with God. The deal was always something like this: "Dear God, if you give me what I ask for, I'll go to church on Sunday." It only worked once in a while. I still ended up going to church because I'd get in trouble with my parents if I didn't.

So my days as a kid growing up in Barre, Vermont bring back mostly good memories. During the school years, my days started early with helping my brother, who had a morning newspaper to deliver, then getting to school early to meet up with my friends. We'd play baseball or football in the schoolyard. I had a couple of close friends that I hung with and we loved to tell jokes. I was popular for having lots of "good" (meaning off-color) jokes, which I got from my older brother Bernie!

I enjoyed most of my classes and developed a love for history as I got into high school. When the school day was over, I had a paper route to do and then I'd go home to the great smell of home-baked bread or donuts. My mom was a great cook. She did not have much to work with, but what she did have she knew how to use. We did get to watch some TV, but most of the time, I'd be outside playing a sport with my brothers and some other kids who lived in the neighborhood. It depended on the season—baseball in summer, football in fall, and, of course hockey in the winter.

Hockey was the family sport. All of us boys—10 altogether—played hockey and did well. We developed a reputation in our city and state for being the best hockey players around. Hockey was my life and I had some great coaches over the years. Mr. Otterman, my brother Bernie, and my high school coach, Paul Poirier. All three of them had an important and lasting impact on my life. Mr. Otterman was my PeeWee coach. He taught me the basics of the game. He was a kind person and I knew I could trust him. I loved riding in his car when we went to "away" games after I made it to the traveling team. It was fun staying at the hotels and going swimming during the winter. Mr. Otterman coached me until I reach the Bantam years, ages 13 to 15.

At that point, my brother Bernie coached me. He was a well-rounded hockey player. Bernie pushed me hard but was very encouraging. Bernie played for the high school team and understood strategy. He taught me a lot about being a two-way player— both offense and defense. He prepared me well for my high school years. During Pee Wee and Bantam, I was a good scorer; I seemed to have a natural talent for putting the puck in the net. I managed to get my name and picture in the newspaper often. I kept a scrapbook of all the newspaper clippings. It made me feel good to read and reread the articles.

There was always a lot of competition between the brothers in my family. To find out who was the best at anything—football, baseball, hockey, arm wrestling. You name it: my dad pitted us against each other, even boxing. I hated the boxing. I hated hitting my brothers and I hated getting hit. I think the forced boxing sessions were the root of years of problems between my brother Eddie and myself. Eddie is just a year younger than me, and my dad always compared him to me. In everything. Eddie had a rough relationship with my dad; he was named after him, and I guess he never lived up to the namesake in my dad's eyes. I often wondered if I had been given my dad's name how my life would have been different and how Eddie's would have been different. I think because Eddie did not live up to my dad's expectations he often bore the brunt of my dad's anger.

My dad was an alcoholic and often came home drunk on the weekends. He'd often be gone from Friday night to Sunday night. We never knew what kind of mood he'd be in when he came home. Would we get a beating or would we get a treat? He was unpredictable. If he was in a bad mood and anyone got out of line, we would all get it, and Eddie always got the worst of it. I'm not sure if I could have taken some of the beatings Eddie took. My dad used a strap, a horse whip, or the cord from his electric shaver. Boy did that hurt, and often left marks on our legs and backs. My mom often tried to stop him, but he just pushed her away. There was not much she could do but hold us after he was done.

Unfortunately, I do not have the fondest memories of my dad. I have heard from my older siblings that he was a nice guy, before I was born, in his younger years. I was not fortunate enough to see that side very often.

> I know he was old school, but I often thought, "How hard would it have been to say 'I love you' just once in a while?"

He did not always beat us and he did work during the week cutting stone in the local stone sheds. We had a home and food, but otherwise, he was not much of a father. I can never remember him saying to me, or any of us, that he loved us. I know he was old school, but I often thought, "How hard would it have been to say 'I love you' just once in a while?" Or even, "I'm proud of you, son." It just wasn't in him to do that.

Children have a natural love for their parents, but I always had mixed feelings about my dad. I do have some good memories, but the bad outweighs the good. He encouraged me to be good at sports and even came to a few games when I was a little kid, but this ended by the time I hit high school. I did like to go with him on Saturdays to do the groceries when he was sober. I would get a treat from the man at the grocery store. I can count all my good memories of my dad on my two hands. It seems to me there should have been more. It would have been nice to have had a full-time dad that I looked up to and I was proud of, but that was not to be.

All of these memories about my dad have had a huge impact on the choices I made and the type of father I tried to be for my kids.

It was during the high school years that I started to "find" myself. I continued to do well in hockey and other sports. I worked hard at it and wanted to be the best. After all, I had a family name to live up to. In the small town of Barre, Vermont, the Badeaus were the hockey family. My older brothers played and were pretty good at it. I can remember trying out for the varsity team as a freshman and being scared to death. I knew I had a good shot at making it, but still I worried. I did make it, and my high school career was off and skating.

I did well all four years and racked up a scoring title not only for my school but for the state—and as far as I know it has not been broken to this day. That got me lots of attention by fellow classmates and the media. Yet I had just a few friends. I was a bit of a loner. All I really needed was two or three friends I trusted.

It was through one of those friends that I met Sue. It was the fall of my junior year when I first noticed her from a distance. She was on the girls field hockey team and they were having practice. I determined in October 1973 to ask her out, but it took me until February 1974 to work up the courage to act on that conviction!

As we write this book, it has been 39 years since our first date, and looking back— what a journey it has been. Who would have thought we'd be where we are now? I believe it was divine intervention that brought us together and keeps us together. Sue was one of those special people you rarely get to meet. She was cute, smart, and very energetic. Her eyes were full of life. After our first date, I always wanted to be with her. We went to a school dance. Her dad dropped her off at the school and I met her at the door. I was so excited: my first real date. I had never really dated anyone before her. I had gone out a few times, but nothing that lasted. I walked her home after the dance and acted like a gentleman. Gave her a peck on the cheek and said I'd call her. At that moment I was the happiest boy in the world.

So the wheels were set in motion. God had set us on the path that has taken us to where we are today—and I am sure there are still some twists and turns in the road ahead.

Back then, God was someone you talked to on Sundays (or maybe Saturday night) and Christmas and Easter. He made you feel guilty about what you did during the week, so you tried to avoid him most of the time.

Sue opened my eyes to life and the possibility of bettering myself. I'm sure it's thanks to her that I ended up going to college. She saw potential in me and encouraged me to pursue it. Of course, I like to think it went the other way as well. It was through Sue that I became a Christian. She was going to some Bible studies at her dance teacher's house. I thought the lady was a little crazy, always reading her Bible and talking about God. Back then, God was someone you talked to on Sundays (or maybe Saturday night) and Christmas and Easter. He made you feel guilty about what you did during the week, so you tried to avoid him most of the time.

Sue eventually invited me to go to the Bible study with her, and I went. "Sure, why not, if it makes you happy," I remember saying. Little did I realize God was planting the seeds of faith that I would need later in my life. I guess He knew what I'd be up against for the next few decades!

It was during our college years that our relationship grew, but was also challenged, as one might expect. The college setting, for me, was an environment conducive to getting into trouble, and often my preferred activities were in direct conflict with my faith. It was very hard to maintain a relationship with God and stay true to my faith when I wanted to join in the constant partying with my friends. During my college years I got into a lot of drinking and carousing, and I must confess, at the time, I enjoyed it. I went to New England College, and my buddies and I renamed it "Not Exactly College" to suit our partying lifestyle. My college experience was a lot like the movie *Animal House* with fraternity and keg parties every weekend. I'd visit Sue at Smith and attend a black tie event and then come back to NEC and wear a toga for the next party.

Sue and I got engaged during her freshman year at Smith. We talked about marriage and we were very excited about our plans. I would quit school while she finished at Smith, and then I would go back to school and get my degree. It sounded great to us, but Sue's parents did not agree. They had higher hopes and dreams for their oldest child, and they quickly showed their fury. They had approved of Sue dating me during high school—I was the hockey star after all!—but when she went off to an Ivy League college, I think they hoped she would find a nice Amherst or Harvard man to marry and forget about her Frenchman from the wrong side of the tracks in Barre. Sue's family and their friends were several rungs up the social ladder above my working class family, and I often felt like a fish out of water when I went to her house.

I loved the Hoags; they always treated me well and made me

feel welcome. Sue's dad, Jim, especially filled in as a father figure for me during my high school years and beyond, and I deeply respected him for that. I learned many life lessons from him that I will never forget.

And I learned a few the night we met with Sue's parents to talk about our plans for marriage. In no uncertain terms they told us that they would not go along with our plans. They would have no part of it. If we proceeded with our idea, they would no longer contribute to Sue's education at Smith, and they would not contribute to a wedding either. We had a choice to make. Finish school, and then we could come back and talk about a wedding and our future plans. Or, go our own way without their support.

Of course we did not want to hear it, but we felt we had no choice but to listen. The next day, as we drove together back to college, we had plenty of time to be mad at them. "We can do what we want!" we exclaimed to one another. We were adults! We were smart! We would make it with or without them!

Fortunately, sanity prevailed. We calmed down over time and talked for hours. We finally came to our senses and agreed that they were right.

Fortunately, sanity prevailed. We calmed down over time and talked for hours. We finally came to our senses and agreed that they were right. We decided to finish school. I've come to the conclusion after all these years that God had to have had a hand in it because there is no way we would have made it being married so young. We both had a lot of growing up to do. God had other plans for us.

This event was a major turning point in our lives. We were not consciously thinking, *This is what God wants us to do*, but I do know after many years of following Christ that God does protect us from ourselves even when we don't realize it at the time.

We both had a lot of personal issues to work on. Sue will tell you about hers; my biggest issue was my addiction to alcohol. God worked with me on that for many years and, to some extent, even though I have not had a drink in several years, I have to say it is still a work in progress.

So, we waited. We finished college and then got married on July 14, 1979. The rest of our story begins on that day.

Background: Sue's Early Years

I was not only the first child born to my parents, but also the first grandchild on both sides. When I was born, I had four living grandparents, two living great-grandparents, aunts and great-aunts, uncles and great-uncles. On one side of the family were farmers and schoolteachers who had settled and lived in Vermont for generations; on the other side, recent immigrants from Spain and Italy.

My life began in the center of this rich constellation of family strength and pride.

Three years after my birth, my sister Nancy joined the family, and two years later, my sister Stephanie. I was fifteen by the time my only brother, David, was born. As the oldest, I got special privileges, like my own room and a double bed. Our mom was a dental hygienist, our dad an engineer who worked for the state highway department. My love affair with road trips probably started when my dad would take me with him to visit the job sites he worked on. We'd stay in his little trailer, and he'd let me wear his hard hat. I still have the hard hat on the wall above my desk, a daily reminder of the legacies of faith, family, and hard work I got from my parents.

Our family life had a predictable rhythm to it, often centered around food. Weekly visits to the butcher shop, where I was allowed to pluck a few horehound candies from the big barrel in the middle of the floor. Visits to Tia Dolly's farm for freshly churned butter or venison stew. Visits to Aunt Vera's farm for "sugar on snow" during sugaring season. Visits to Aunt Fran's farm to help milk the cows and ride the tractors. In the fall, my mom and other relatives made jars and jars of antipasto glistening with orange, green, and red vegetables and shiny black olives. For Thanksgiving, it was Aunt Nat's fudge we all looked forward to. In the winter, the puffy round loaves of homemade panetonne and tiny little boxes of imported torrone delighted us at Christmastime. Every year on Memorial Day we got to eat our breakfast outside on the picnic table for the first time of the season. And then came summer. Oh, in the summer—we went to Maine, and in Maine we ate lobster, bright red lobster, and buckets of steamers dipped in butter dripping luxuriously down our chins.

Besides the highway trips with my dad and the summer trips to Maine, we took other road trips. We went to Expo '67 in Canada, and to Washington, D.C. We went camping at Maidstone Lake in Vermont. My great-grandmother on my mother's side, "Abuelita," spent half of the year in Detroit with my great-aunt Josephine. Sometimes we took road trips to Detroit. The only goal was to get to Detroit in the shortest amount of time possible. The idea of intentionally taking a detour, or stopping to admire scenic vistas, was foreign, and so we barreled ahead, until we got to Detroit. Hot, sticky, sweaty—but safely.

My hometown of Barre, Vermont contained a rich stew of diverse cultural groups—mostly recent immigrants who hung onto their language, religion, and foods. We had neighbors and schoolmates who were Italians and Spaniards, French-Canadians and Irish, Syrians and Lebanese, Polish and Portugese. But it was not until we went to Detroit that I had the chance to play with black children for the first time.

My parents were deeply engaged in the civic life of the community. My mom was often the neighborhood captain for a variety of charities; my dad successfully ran for the school board. They'd have their friends over for election night parties and spirited discussions on the issues of the day. They were also active in the lives of their children as Brownie and Girl Scout troop leaders, Sunday school teachers, and little league coaches.

My father loved nearly all sports, but basketball and baseball were his favorites. He ran the Basketball Tournament Committee for many years and, as a teen, one of my first jobs was as his secretary, typing letters to school principals around the state. It was from these letters that I learned about his deep passion for sportsmanship. There weren't a lot of options for girls' sports, and as the father of three daughters, my dad sought to change that, paving the way for girls' field hockey to be introduced in our high school. It probably pained him to see what a terrible, uncoordinated player I was, but if it did, he never let on. He enthusiastically came to every game, home and away. He also took me and a carload of my girlfriends skiing nearly every weekend throughout the winter.

My mother loved cleanliness, order, and beauty and kept standards I've never been able to replicate but have always admired and valued. She loved shopping and turned the annual back-to-school preparations into fun outings as we went all the way to Burlington to go to Abernathy's and Magram's and Stride-Rite Shoes.

Education was probably the most important value stressed in our household, and we were surrounded by books. Fortunately for me, I loved books. I could get lost for hours with the Wilders on the Prairie, or in the Secret Garden, or investigating crimes with Nancy Drew. My love for reading spawned my passion for writing, and my parents were my biggest fans, even when poems I sent off to magazines were rejected. My first published writing was a poem written for Lincoln's birthday (back when we celebrated Mr. Lincoln and Mr. Washington on separate days). It began, "If Nancy Hanks came back to see what happened to Abe and she asked me . . . " and went on for three long stanzas. It was published in our local *Times-Argus* newspaper. Later, in high school, I got a job working for the other local paper, the *Washington World*.

Honesty and doing your best were also emphasized, and the only times I really remember getting into serious trouble as a child had to do with lies told or not trying hard enough. I got sent to bed without supper once for a bad report card—the message stuck with me, and I brought home mostly A's after that.

I was a chubby girl and not usually popular, although I hung around on the fringes of the popular crowd. I wanted to be skinny or at least waif-like, and yet whenever I felt bad, or happy, or discouraged, or proud, I ate a snack. I didn't like not being popular; I felt alone, on the outside looking in. I wrote about it. A lot. First in my diary, then in my poetry, and in high school, in my plays. One of my plays was chosen for the school one-act play competition. It was the first time I made the connection that it was OK not to be popular if it made me a better writer. The teachers who influenced me the most throughout school were those who nurtured and encouraged my writing, from my fourth-grade teacher, Mrs. Sullivan, who made us all recite poems every Friday, to my high school writing teachers, Mrs. Morris and Miss Watson, Mr. Comly, and Mr. Casey.

> I didn't like not being popular; I felt alone, on the outside looking in. I wrote about it. A lot. First in my diary, then in my poetry, and in high school, in my plays.

Not being popular meant I didn't have dates most Friday and Saturday nights when the popular girls had dates. I'd hear about the parties and dances on Monday morning in school and pretend it didn't matter. But it did. And then it happened. The star athlete of the entire school asked me out on a date. The hockey player in a hockey town. Number 9, the best player on the team. How did that happen? I don't know, but I wrote about it. I wrote a poem titled "Hockey Player" that captured how I felt as that fifteen-year-old girl being asked out by *the* Hector Badeau. I thought I got the prize. It never occurred to me that he felt the same way.

Who knew when we went to that first dance together that we'd still be dancing together 40 years later?

I grew up in a family of faith. It wasn't something spoken

of often; we didn't have family prayers or Bible studies. But we went to the Barre Congregational Church every week, and we understood that this was the foundation of our values. My great-aunt Ruth was the one who talked to me about God, gave me my first Bible, and taught me that faith is meant to be nurtured and grown. In high school, my ballet teacher, Ruth Vickery, and her friend Claudia Christmann turned me on to the idea that the Bible is a living Word, not a dusty relic of the past. In college my faith was further nourished by the Inter-Varsity Christian Fellowship, Logos Bookstore, and some young couples I met that became my lifelong friends and mentors, the Dissingers, Hulleys, and Wassmanns.

My parents first ignited a passion for and curiosity about politics and social justice issues, and some of my favorite memories are staying up late with my grandfather watching the Democratic and Republican conventions back when the conventions mattered. I carried this passion off to college with me and chose to live in the most integrated house on campus, the house where many of the black students and gay and lesbian students lived. I wanted to understand civil rights from the inside out.

Mostly, I became passionate about giving a voice to the voiceless and rooting for the underdog. Maybe some of this came from being a Red Sox fan in the years when they were always the underdog. Whether it's the "least of these" in Biblical parlance, or the "disenfranchised and oppressed" in sociology class, or the fat kid in second grade, I always wanted to speak up and stand up for the one(s) that no one else was speaking up and standing up for.

All of these influences . . . my Spanish and Italian and sturdy New England roots, my dad's love of sports, my mom's love of beauty, Barre's multicultural food heritage, English teachers, summer jobs, great-grandparents and great-aunts, little sisters and baby brother, Barre Congregational Church, Inter-varsity, Logos, and *Sojourners* magazine, a passion for justice and equality, the fat kid, the clutzy wannabe athlete, the ballet dancer, the camper, the skier, the aspiring poet, the girl with her daddy's hard hat, the high school sweetheart . . . these all conspired and contributed to making me the person I am today.

On July 14, 1979, I married that high school sweetheart, and the rest of our story begins on that day.

Are we there yet? Not a chance—we still have miles and miles and miles to go.

Badeau Family Children and Grandchildren (2013)— "Where Are They Now?"

James David (JD), age 44; fiancé, Tracy Chaperon, Highgate, VT
Married to Melissa Harper 1989–1999, 3 children:
    Kirsten (age 23), married to Denzell Washington,
    Philadelphia, PA
        Isaiah (age 4)
        Nalana (deceased)
        Daevonee (age 1)
    Whitney (age 22), Philadelphia, PA
        Kaylen (age 4)
    Erica (age 18) – Burlington, VT
Step-parent to children of Tracy Chaperon:
    Teagan
    Devin

Fisher Lee, 43, Beattyville, KY
Children with Jennifer Wyrocki:
    Alec (age 16), Middlebury, VT
    Emma (age 13), Middlebury, VT
    Other children of Jennifer Wyrocki:
    Jessica (age 22), Middlebury, VT
    Austin (age 18), Middlebury, VT
Child with Crystal Sweeney, Poultney, VT
    Jordan (age 12), Poultney, VT
Child with Shawna Bah, Brattleboro, VT
    Janessa (age 11), Brattleboro, VT

Lilly Mae, 42 and Larry Ashman, Barre, VT
    Ashley (age 21) and Santos DeJesus, Barre, VT
    Saphira (age 3)
    Lilo (6 months)

Renee Rachel, 41, Philadelphia, PA
    Daniel (age 16), Philadelphia, PA

Tricia Ann, 40 and Steven Bullis, Barre, VT
    Phillip (age 21) and Isabel Rodriguez, Barre, VT
        Laniah (3 months)
    Sean (age 16), Barre, VT
    Matthew (age 14), Barre, VT

David Lee, 38, Philadelphia, PA

Abel Rocky, 37, Philadelphia, PA
    Davon (age 10), Pittsburgh, PA

SueAnn Kim, 35, married to Roberto Vargas (2007), Philadelphia, PA
    Esperanza (age 12), Philadelphia, PA
    Angel (age 10), Philadelphia, PA
    Allegria (age 6), Philadelphia, PA
    Antonio (age 4), Philadelphia, PA
Birthmother to Milagro Kirpan (age 19), Montpelier, VT

Jose Carlos, 34, Zurich, Switzerland

George Christopher, 34, and Patrice Jones, Pittsburgh, PA
    Destin (age 11), Pittsburgh, PA

Chelsea Lynne, 33, married to Lashon Chris (2005), Philadelphia, PA
    Chloe (age 8), Philadelphia, PA
    Zara (age 2), Philadelphia, PA

Florinda Kim, 33, married to Larry Clark (2008), Philadelphia, PA
    Jasmine (age 13), Philadelphia, PA
    Chantelle (age 11), Philadelphia, PA
    Laurie (age 7), Philadelphia, PA
    Rosario (age 4), Philadelphia, PA

Isaac Stephen, 31, married to Simean Lib (2008), Ft. Gordon, GA

Raj Ashish, 30, Philadelphia, PA

Joelle Christina, 28, Philadelphia, PA
    Mackell Adam (age 5), Philadelphia, PA

Geeta Jenny, 29, Philadelphia, PA
    Titianna (age 8), Philadelphia, PA
    Tiana (age 6), Philadelphia. PA
    Nicole (age 3), Philadelphia, PA

Todd Michael, 27, Philadelphia, PA
    Nicoli (age 7), Philadelphia, PA

Dylan Ryan (1986-2010), deceased

Wayne Chan (1987-2012), deceased

Adam Joseph (1988-1999), deceased

Alysia Rochelle, 25, and Bernard Turner, Philadelphia, PA
    Ahmir (age 2), Philadelphia, PA
    Akeirah (age 1), Philadelphia, PA

Aaron Michael, age 23, Philadelphia, PA
    Aaron Jr. (age 3), Philadelphia, PA

Badeau Family Timeline

1973 – Hector and Sue begin dating

1979 – Hector and Sue graduate from college and are married in Fairlee, VT

1979-1983 – Badeaus own and operate Logos Bookstore in Northampton, MA. Church home is Mill River House Church, Northampton, MA

1980 – Daughter Chelsea Lynne is born

1981 – Son Jose Carlos, age 2.5, is adopted from El Salvador

1982 – Son Isaac Stephen is born

1983-1985 – Badeaus are Teaching Parents at a Boys' Town affiliated group home in Montpelier, VT. Church Home is Christ the Redeemer Lutheran Church, Berlin, VT

1983 – Son Raj Ashish is adopted from India as a 4-month-old infant (November)

1985-1988 – Badeaus are foster parents living in Cabot, VT and create an adoption agency, Rootwings Ministries, which then affiliates with the AASK America network founded by Bob and Dorothy DeBolt

1985 – Daughter Joelle is adopted as a 9-month-old infant from Florida (May)

1986 – Siblings Abel (10), SueAnn (9), George (8), and Florinda (6) are adopted from New Mexico (January)

1986 – Son Todd is adopted as a newborn infant in an open adoption from Bennington, VT (July)

1986 – Badeaus welcome their first international exchange student, Claudia, from Guatemala

1986-1989 – Badeaus operate a shipping and packaging company and begin an adoption bookstore

1987-1988 – Siblings JD (19), Fisher (18), Lilly (17), Renee (16), Trish (15), and David (13) are adopted from New Mexico, coming home at separate times over a five-month period (December 1987 – April 1988)

1989-1992 – Badeaus live in Barre, VT and continue to run Rootwings; both Hector and Sue also moonlight with other jobs; Church home is Barre Congregational Church in Barre, VT

1989 – Daughter Alysia is adopted as a 1-year-old from Austin, TX (May)

1989 – First of Badeau children graduate from high school (Fisher and Lilly), first son marries (JD), and first grandchild (Kirsten) is born

1990 – Son Dylan is adopted as a 4-year-old from Vermont (September)

1991 – Son Wayne is adopted as a 3-year-old from New York City (April)

1992 – Badeaus move from Vermont to Philadelphia, where they continue to live today. Hector is full-time parent and caregiver, Sue works in various positions in the child welfare field. Church home is Summit Presbyterian Church, Philadelphia, PA

1994 – Son Adam is adopted as a 6-year-old from Florida (November)

1995 – Son Aaron, sibling to Adam, is adopted as a 4-year-old from Florida (May)

1997 – Badeaus win "Adoption Excellence" award and are invited to the White House for signing of Adoption and Safe Families Act; they and most of family meet President and Mrs. Clinton

1998 – Daughter Geeta is adopted as a 14-year-old from Philadelphia (originally from India)

1999 – Sue is awarded a Joseph P. Kennedy Foundation Public Policy Fellowship and begins working for Senator John D. Rockefeller IV in

Washington, DC

1999–2001 – Badeaus serve as host family for international refugees from Kosovo and Sudan

1999 – Son Adam, with SanfilippoSyndrome, dies at home (December 30)

2005 – 2008 – Four Badeau children are married within a 3-year period

2008 – First great-grandchild, Isaiah, is born (July)

2010 – Son Dylan, with Shaken Baby Syndrome, dies at home (September 9)

2011 – Sue is awarded a Fellowship in the U.S. Department of Justice, Office of Juvenile Justice and Delinquency Prevention, through Casey Family Programs

2012 – Son Wayne, with Sanfilippo Syndrome, dies at home (April 17)

2012 – Hector joins the workforce as a support staff at Kairos House, of Philadelphia's Project HOME

Questions about foster care, adoption, juvenile justice, or parenting children with special needs? Visit the Badeaus' websites (www.badeaufamily.com and www.suebadeau.com) and watch for blog posts, replies to Frequently Asked Questions, and plans for their next book.

Questions about foster care, adoption, juvenile justice, or parenting children with special needs? Or interested in inviting Sue Badeau to speak at your next conference, training event, luncheon or retreat? Visit the Badeaus' websites (www. suebadeau.com and www.badeaufamily.com) for more information as well as for blog posts, replies to Frequently Asked Questions, and plans for their next book. You can also find them on Facebook and Twitter - @SueBadeau.